Enhancing Everyday
Communication for Children
with Disabilities

Enhancing Everyday Communication for Children with Disabilities

by

Jeff Sigafoos

Michael Arthur-Kelly

and

Nancy Butterfield

with contributions by
Phil Foreman
Vanessa A. Green
and
Mark O'Reilly

·P A U L·H·
BROOKES
PUBLISHING CO®

Baltimore • London • Sydney

Paul H. Brookes Publishing Co.
Post Office Box 10624
Baltimore, Maryland 21285-0624

www.brookespublishing.com

Typeset by Auburn Associates, Inc., Baltimore, Maryland.
Manufactured in the United States of America by
Versa Press, Inc., East Peoria, Illinois.

The case studies described in this book are composites based on the authors' actual
experiences. Individuals' names have been changed, and identifying details have
been altered to protect confidentiality.

Library of Congress Cataloging-in-Publication Data
Sigafoos, Jeff.
   Enhancing everyday communication for children with disabilities / by Jeff
Sigafoos, Michael Arthur-Kelly, and Nancy Butterfield ; with contributions by
Phil Foreman, Vanessa A. Green, Mark O'Reilly
      p.   cm.
   Includes bibliographical references and index.
   ISBN-13: 978-1-55766-716-8 (pbk.)
   ISBN-10: 1-55766-716-0 (pbk.)
   1. Developmentally disabled children—Means of communication.   2.
Developmentally disabled children—Rehabilitation.   I. Arthur-Kelly, Michael,
1959–   II. Butterfield, Nancy.   III. Title.
   HV891.S56 2006
   618.92′8588906—dc22   2005036549

British Library Cataloguing in Publication data are available from the British
Library.

Contents

Authors

Jeff Sigafoos, Ph.D., Professor, School of Education, University of Tasmania, Private Bag 66, Hobart, Tasmania 7001, Australia

Michael Arthur-Kelly, Ph.D., Senior Lecturer, Centre for Special Education and Disability Studies, The University of Newcastle, Callaghan, New South Wales 2308, Australia

Nancy Butterfield, M.Ed., Special Educator and Teacher Educator, Sydney, New South Wales, Australia

CONTRIBUTORS

Phil Foreman, Ph.D., Professor and Dean of Faculty of Arts and Education, The University of Newcastle, Callaghan, New South Wales 2308, Australia

Vanessa A. Green, Ph.D., Lecturer, School of Education, University of Tasmania, Private Bag 66, Hobart, Tasmania 7001, Australia

Mark O'Reilly, Ph.D., Professor, Department of Special Education, The University of Texas at Austin, 1 University Station, D5300, Austin, Texas 78712

Preface

In 1995, we wrote a short book titled *Partners in Everyday Communicative Exchanges: A Guide to Promoting Interaction Opportunities for People with Severe Intellectual Disability*. It was published in Australia by MacLennan & Petty and distributed in the United States by Paul H. Brookes Publishing Co. That concise book, which we affectionately referred to as *PIECE,* focused on the communication partners of individuals with multiple disabilities. These individuals often had severe to profound intellectual disabilities along with additional physical disabilities or sensory impairments. Today, the terms *developmental disabilities* and *physical disabilities* are used to describe individuals with these combinations of impairments. Our aim in writing *PIECE* was to describe evidence-based, yet practical, strategies for involving people with developmental and physical disabilities in meaningful and functional communicative exchanges. Our intended audience was parents, special education teachers, and speech-language pathologists.

Eleven years ago, there was relatively little information specifically aimed at supporting the communication partners of individuals with developmental and physical disabilities. Siegel-Causey and Guess (1989) had published an excellent book that highlighted the communicative potential of nonsymbolic or prelinguistic behaviors in students with developmental and physical disabilities. They also offered practical strategies for enhancing communicative interactions involving nonsymbolic behavior. Another source of inspiration was a massive textbook by Beukelman and Mirenda on augmentative and alternative communication (now in its third edition [2005]), which included a wealth of material on communicative intervention for individuals with various types of disabilities. Equally important as an early reference was the more specialized text by Reichle, York, and Sigafoos (1991) that described strategies for teaching augmentative and alternative communication systems to learners with severe disabilities and limited or no speech.

In all of these books, there did not seem to be much explicit information on practical strategies that partners could use to facilitate the transition to more advanced, symbolic, or conventional forms of communication among individuals with the most severe disabilities. *PIECE* was intended to fill this perceived gap.

Eleven years later, much has been learned about facilitating the transition from early and prelinguistic communication to more advanced and symbolic forms of communication. Indeed, entire volumes have been written on the topic (Reichle, Beukelman, & Light, 2002; Wetherby, Warren, & Reichle,

1998). Yet, there remains a gap between best practice as reflected in the accumulating knowledge base and the application of this information in everyday settings that include learners with the most severe developmental and physical disabilities. Hence, we decided to write this book to facilitate the transition from research to practice. Although *Enhancing Everyday Communication for Children with Disabilities* has a different title, it has the same focus and aim as *PIECE*. It reflects the many advances in research and practice that have occurred over the past decade.

Since 1995, we have continued our work that formed the basis for *PIECE*. Much has been learned from this work and from the findings of other researchers in the field, especially from the work of Joe Reichle. The accumulating evidence allows a more coherent and integrated approach to communication assessment and intervention than was possible 11 years ago. Accordingly, readers will notice that the content and organization of this book differ considerably from that of *PIECE*. And yet, while much is different, the book retains our original focus on promoting more effective and positive interactions between individuals with developmental and physical disabilities and their communicative partners.

We are grateful to the staff at Paul H. Brookes Publishing Co. for taking an interest in our work and for their thoroughly professional assistance in getting this book into print. We hope that you will find this book helpful in your work to enhance the everyday communication of children with developmental and physical disabilities.

REFERENCES

Beukelman, D.R., & Mirenda, P. (2005). *Augmentative and alternative communication: Supporting children and adults with complex communication needs* (3rd ed.). Baltimore: Paul H. Brookes Publishing Co.

Butterfield, N., Arthur, M., & Sigafoos, J. (1995). *Partners in everyday communicative exchanges: A guide to promoting interaction opportunities for people with severe intellectual disability*. Sydney, Australia: MacLennan & Petty.

Reichle, J., Beukelman, D.R., & Light, J.C. (Vol. Eds.), & Beukelman, D.R., & Reichle, J. (Series Eds.). (2002). *Augmentative and alternative communication series. Exemplary practices for beginning communicators: Implication for AAC*. Baltimore: Paul H. Brookes Publishing Co.

Reichle, J., York, J., & Sigafoos, J. (Vol. Eds.), & Beukelman, D.R., & Reichle, J. (Series Eds.). (1991). *Augmentative and alternative communication series. Implementing augmentative and alternative communication: Strategies for learners with severe disabilities*. Baltimore: Paul H. Brookes Publishing Co.

Siegel-Causey, E., & Guess, D. (1989). *Enhancing nonsymbolic communication interactions among learners with severe disabilities*. Baltimore: Paul H. Brookes Publishing Co.

Wetherby, A.M., Warren, S.F., & Reichle, J. (Vol. Eds.), & Warren, S.F., & Reichle, J. (Series Eds.). (1998). *Communication and language intervention series: Vol. 7. Transitions in prelinguistic communication*. Baltimore: Paul H. Brookes Publishing Co.

1

Key Concepts

JEFF SIGAFOOS, NANCY BUTTERFIELD,
AND MICHAEL ARTHUR-KELLY

INTRODUCTION

Communication intervention is a major priority for children with developmental and physical disabilities because these children typically lack speech
and language. Thus, in addition to their developmental and physical disabilities, they are also said to have severe communication impairments, which
makes them candidates for interventions to strengthen alternative modes of
communication (Beukelman & Mirenda, 2005). Parents, teachers, family, and
friends of children with developmental and physical disabilities must gain the
skills necessary to engage the individual in meaningful communicative exchanges involving various alternative forms of communication.

The failure to develop speech and language probably reflects a complex
interaction between etiology and environment. Whatever the cause, it is
clear that unlike typically developing children—who acquire speech and language without explicit or deliberate intervention—individuals with developmental and physical disabilities will more often than not fail to acquire any
appreciable amount of speech or language even with systematic instruction.
Instead, these individuals require explicit, deliberate, systematic, and often
highly structured intervention to develop their communicative potential in
ways that can compensate for the lack of speech and language.

Although they lack speech and language, most individuals with developmental and physical disabilities do attain at least a prelinguistic level of
communication development without explicit instruction. For example, they
might use informal behaviors such as reaching, leading another's hand, vocalizing, and making head movements; however, the communicative behaviors
they acquire in this way are often ineffective (vocalizing) or inappropriate

1

(leading others) and hence possibly stigmatizing. In nearly all cases, systematic and ongoing intervention implemented consistently by communication partners will be necessary to further develop the communication abilities of individuals with developmental and physical disabilities. *Intervention* in this context refers to the use of one or more instructional procedures to enhance communicative functioning. Although this task may seem daunting for parents, teachers, speech-language pathologists, and others who are communication partners for such individuals, effective intervention procedures are available. Indeed, researchers have produced a number of effective procedures for developing the communicative potential of learners with developmental and physical disabilities.

Less readily available are evidence-based guidelines for supporting the communication partners of individuals with developmental and physical disabilities. How can the parent, sibling, teacher, and peer engage the child in meaningful communicative exchanges and do so in ways that will not only enable the child to get his or her message across but also lead to further development of the child's communicative potential? These are the types of questions that this book addresses. Several key concepts relevant to these questions are reviewed in this chapter.

THE NEED TO UNDERSTAND BASIC PRINCIPLES AND KEY CONCEPTS

Although numerous assessment and intervention procedures exist for enhancing the communication skills of individuals with developmental and physical disabilities, effective intervention requires more than skillful implementation of these strategies. To be effective, communication partners must also understand the basic principles and key concepts that underlie the strategy. The reason is that the procedures must often be modified in light of individual circumstances, and, as Linscheid (1999) noted, modifying procedures to suit the individual requires an understanding of the basic respondent and operant learning principles that underlie the procedure. In addition to highlighting some of the basic learning principles that underlie effective intervention, this chapter reviews key concepts fundamental to the overall assessment and intervention process. We begin this review by considering quality of life.

QUALITY OF LIFE

It seems obvious that the absence of appropriate communication skills could negatively affect a child's overall quality of life. Indeed, communication is considered central to enhancing the overall quality of life of people with developmental disabilities (Ogletree & Oren, 2001). Quality of life can be viewed in terms of the extent to which the individual is able to participate in the full range of daily life activities (Schalock et al., 2002). It can also be viewed in terms of productivity and independence and gauged by the amount of choice and control that the person has over his or her life. For example, individuals who have more control over the activities they are involved in—and the people they interact with—might be considered to have a better quality of life than people who lack such control (Brown & Lehr, 1993; Ferguson, 1994; Kaiser & Goetz, 1993; Wilcox, 1992). Thus, at least some of the communication skills taught to the individual should enable the person to make choices and exert control over the environment.

Severe communication impairments might negatively affect the child's quality of life in at least two ways. First, the inability to speak limits the child's capacity to interact with parents, teachers, family, and friends. Second, lack of communication can also limit the child's participation across a range of home, school, vocational, and community-based activities. Quality of life will be enhanced when individuals with developmental and physical disabilities acquire effective communication skills that will enable them to achieve a variety of functional outcomes. Functional outcomes include the ability to 1) participate in meaningful communicative exchanges with others, 2) indicate wants and needs, 3) make choices, and 4) initiate and maintain social interactions.

It is probably not an overstatement to suggest that communication is essential for effective social interaction. Indeed, Ferguson (1994) went even further in suggesting that communication is perhaps the most important means by which individuals obtain membership in society. Whether it is the only means of obtaining membership is debatable, but communication certainly is a pervasive feature of nearly all social situations.

A fundamental principle underlying the approach presented in this book is that the aim of intervention should be to enhance quality of life by developing the individual's ability to participate and become a contributing member of society. Teaching functional communication skills is essential for enhancing participation and membership, but skill acquisition is only half the story. Equally important is the need to develop the skills of communication partners. Quality of life for children with developmental and physical disabilities will be enhanced when others in the environment learn to be more responsive communication partners (McLean & McLean, 1993; Meyer & Evans, 1993). To be more responsive, partners should first become familiar with the various ways that communication has been defined.

DEFINING COMMUNICATION

Operant behavior is influenced or controlled by its consequences. In *The Behavior of Organisms,* published in 1938, the psychologist Skinner demonstrated that consequences have powerful and predictable effects on behavior.

Communication is a special class of operant behavior that is effective only through the mediation of others. What makes communication special is the fact that such behavior produces reinforcing consequences only indirectly by first affecting the behavior of a partner or listener, who then provides (or mediates access to) reinforcement.

Another class of (noncommunicative) behaviors are those that are directly effective in producing reinforcing consequences and thus do not require the mediation of another person. A child with severe disabilities could gain access to a preferred toy either directly (by reaching for and grasping the toy) or indirectly by producing the manual sign TOY. Whether the manual sign worked, in the sense of enabling the child to get the toy, would depend on whether there was another person present who 1) saw that the child had made the sign, 2) could "read" the sign, and 3) was willing and able to retrieve the toy for the child. One can see how, unlike behaviors that are directly effective, the chance of being successful when communicating is less assured because of all the complicating factors that arise when one has to depend on first affecting the behavior of another person (Ferster, 1961).

Skinner (1957) referred to behaviors that are effective only indirectly, through the mediation of a communication partner or listener, as *verbal behavior*, and he described several types of verbal operants (see Table 1.1). It is impor-

Table 1.1.　Basic verbal operants

Operant	Definition and example
Mand	The mand is related to, or controlled by, a specific state of deprivation or aversive stimulation, such as a specific want or need. The function of the mand is to gain access to a reinforcer that matches the form of the response. The mand *water*, for example, would be controlled by thirst and reinforced by receiving a glass of water. Requesting and rejecting are subclasses of the mand.
Tact	The tact is controlled by a prior nonverbal stimulus, such as some object or event in the environment. The function of the tact is to direct the listener's attention to the object or event. The tact *phone*, for example, would be controlled by a ringing telephone and reinforced when the listener thanks the speaker and answers the telephone. Naming, labeling, and commenting can be considered synonymous with the tact.
Echoic	An echoic response is controlled by the partner's prior verbal behavior, with the form of the echoic response matching the form produced by the speaker. The teacher signs WATER, for example, and the child responds by producing the exact same sign. Imitating the verbal behavior of a partner is an echoic response.
Intraverbal	An intraverbal is also controlled by the partner's prior verbal behavior, but in this case the form of the response does not match the form produced by the speaker. Instead, the response is thematically related to the prior verbal stimulus. If the teacher asks what is needed for a camping trip, correct intraverbals would include *tent*, *sleeping bag*, and *backpack*. Intraverbal behavior involves classification and categorization and is essential for maintaining conversational exchanges.

tant to note that in Skinner's analysis, verbal behavior does not mean only speech. In fact, any behavior that provides an effective signal to a communication partner such that the partner is then able to mediate reinforcement meets Skinner's criteria for communication or verbal behavior. Hence, facial expressions, vocalizations, gestures, manual signs, or pointing to a picture on a communication board could all function as effective forms of verbal behavior.

Of course, for these communicative forms to be effective, there must be at least one partner who can interpret the form and provide the appropriate type of mediation. To mediate effectively, the partner must be responsive to the individual's various forms of communication and their functions. This task is not always easy because the person's communicative forms may be subtle, informal, and idiosyncratic, which can make them difficult to "read" or interpret. This complexity may partially explain why communication breakdowns are common for individuals with developmental and physical disabilities (Brady & Halle, 2002).

In addition to lacking conventional forms of communication, individuals may lack appropriate strategies for repairing communication breakdowns (Keen, 2003). For example, if a partner does not understand that a learner's vocalization means *I am in pain and need to be repositioned in my wheelchair,* the learner would benefit from having some other communicative behavior that the partner would be able to interpret. Perhaps the learner could operate a voice output communication aid (VOCA) with the recorded message "Please adjust my sitting position."

The definition of *communication* in terms of Skinner's analysis of verbal behavior is very different from other conceptualizations of communication. To better understand these differences, it may be instructive to consider other definitions of communication. The National Joint Committee for the Communicative Needs of Persons with Severe Disabilities, for instance, defined *communication* as

> Any act by which one person gives to or receives from another person information about that person's needs, desires, perceptions, knowledge or affective states. Communication may be intentional or unintentional, may involve conventional or unconventional signals, may take linguistic or nonlinguistic forms, and may occur through spoken or other modes. (1992, p. 2)

According to this definition, the function of communication is dependent on the extent to which there is shared meaning established between two or more people. Effective communication also requires that the partner understands the purpose of the interaction and can consider another's perspective. *Shared meaning* is when the speaker communicates with forms that the listener can read. *Perspective taking* means being able to interpret events from another person's perspective. For example, if it is clear that the partner has not understood, the learner must recognize the need to modify the form of communication so as to assist the partner in understanding. *Understanding*, in turn, might be viewed as the extent to which the partner correctly interprets the message as shown by making an appropriate response.

Consistent with Skinner's analysis, *communication* under this definition can also involve a variety of forms, such as vocalizations, body movements, facial expressions, and gestures. The nonspeech behaviors of individuals with developmental and physical disabilities often serve a communicative function or purpose. In order for the function or purpose to be realized, however, the listener or partner must be willing and able to mediate reinforcement for the speaker's behavior. That is, the partner must make an appropriate reply that will reinforce the learner's communication response.

Another view of communication is based on the work of Bruner (1975), who described three broad categories of communicative functions. First, the *social interaction function* refers to communicative behaviors that occur because in the past these acts have enabled the speaker to engage in social interaction with the partner. The function or purpose of the communicative behavior is to gain and maintain the attention of a partner, and the reinforcer mediated by the partner is simply the resulting social interaction. In many cases, it is assumed that conversational exchanges are initiated to achieve this social interaction function rather than for some more instrumental function, such as seeking information.

Second, the *declarative function* involves joint attention and tacting. Once joint attention is present, the speaker communicates in ways that in the past have been effective in directing the partner's attention to some aspect of the environment, which is a type of tact (see Table 1.1).

Third, *behavior regulation* refers to behaviors that have in the past enabled the individual to fulfill wants and needs through the actions of another person (Cress & Marvin, 2003; Snell, 2002). Mands, therefore, have a behavior regulation function.

Evidence suggests that individuals with developmental disabilities will often develop informal mands for behavior regulation, at the same time having few, if any, communicative behaviors related to more social and declarative functions, such as the tact (Cress, 2002; Ferster, 1961; Wetherby & Prizant, 1992). Thus, a logical beginning point for intervention is to strengthen the mand repertoire by targeting skills such as 1) requesting access to preferred objects or activities and 2) rejecting nonpreferred objects or activities (Schlosser & Sigafoos, 2002).

In fact, Drasgow, Halle, and Sigafoos (1999) suggested that an appropriate beginning point for communication intervention is to focus on replacing the person's existing prelinguistic mands with more conventional mand forms (e.g., manual signs, picture symbols, VOCAs). The goal in developing more conventional mand forms is to provide the individual with a more effective way of regulating the behavior of others. In addition to developing mands related to behavior regulation, it is important that children with developmental and physical disabilities are taught other communication skills that can be used for more social and declarative functions (Cress & Marvin, 2003). Because individuals with developmental and physical disabilities typically present with major impairments across the entire domain of communication, intervention will be required on each of several communication skills (see Table 1.2). This intervention is also necessary because generalization across skills is unlikely (Duker, Didden, & Sigafoos, 2004).

Table 1.2.   Examples of communication skills for intervention

Skill	Definition and examples
Request an object (mand)	Behaviors initiated by the individual that direct the partner to provide an object to the person (e.g., child looks at and points to a preferred toy that is out of reach). The function is to obtain the object.
Request an action (mand)	Behaviors initiated by the individual that direct the partner to cause an action to occur (e.g., child gives a soda can to the teacher so that the teacher will open it for him or her). Interest is on the action itself, not social interaction with the person that the individual is directing.
Get attention (mand or tact)	Behaviors used to call attention to the individual (e.g., child tugs at the teacher's clothes). The purpose may be to obtain attention (mand) or to gain attention so that the listener can then be directed to some aspect of the environment (tact).
Comment (tact)	Behaviors that direct the partner's attention to some observable referent, such as an action or movement, appearance, or disappearance of an object (e.g., child points to empty fruit bowl and signs ALL GONE).
Fulfill a social convention (intraverbal, tact, echoic)	Behaviors that occur in the context of a social routine or convention (e.g., child waves to visitor). Greetings, responding to one's name, and turn taking are included.
Reject (mand)	Behaviors that let the listener know that the child does not want something suggested or initiated by another, disapproves of something, or wishes to terminate an event that has already begun (e.g., child shakes head no when offered a nonpreferred toy).
Respond (intraverbal, mand, tact)	Behaviors produced in response to a question from another (e.g., child signs JUICE when the teacher holds up a cup and asks, "What kind of drink do you want?").
Request information (mand)	Behaviors that direct the receiver to provide information or clarification about an object, action, activity, or location (e.g., child points to a clock as if asking when lunch will be ready, and the teacher responds by saying it will be ready in 10 minutes).
Imitate (echoic)	Repeating the communication forms of another (e.g., the teacher signs WATER, and the child imitates the sign).

From Keen, D., Woodyatt, G., & Sigafoos, J. (2002). Verifying teacher perceptions of the potential communicative acts of children with autism. *Communication Disorders Quarterly, 23,* 137; adapted with permission.

INTENTIONALITY

Many definitions of *communication* refer to intentional and unintentional communication. *Intentional communication* is typically inferred if the individual shows one or more additional behaviors or characteristics when communicating. Some behavior characteristics that supposedly indicate intentionality include 1) alternating gaze between an object and a listener, 2) waiting for a response from the partner, and 3) persisting with the behavior until reinforcement is obtained (Stephenson & Linfoot, 1996). Whether an act would be defined as intentional, therefore, depends on the presence or absence of these types of behaviors; however, the intent of any given communicative act can be difficult to judge, especially for individuals with developmental and physical disabilities (Carter & Iacono, 2002). Still, the distinction between intentional and unintentional communication is often made in the literature and warrants further discussion.

The term *unintentional* (or *preintentional*) *communication* refers to situations when the partner assigns an intent, meaning, function, or purpose to the individual's behavior. For example, a child with developmental and physical disabilities might suddenly bounce up and down in his or her wheelchair when a new person enters the room. The teacher, sensing a connection, reacts ("Oh, I see you are greeting our visitor"), thereby attributing a social-communicative function to the child's behavior. Suppose, however, that the child's bouncing was not a greeting but rather the child's attempt to achieve a more comfortable seating position. In this case, the act of bouncing was not an intentional form of communication, despite the fact that the teacher reacted to it as if it were. It is also possible, however, that if the teacher consistently reacted to the child's bouncing as if it were a form of communication, then over time the child may in fact learn to bounce under conditions when the social interaction from the teacher would be a reinforcer. At that point, it would be reasonable to assume that the act has become an intentional form of communication.

TRANSITION STAGES

The shaping process outlined in the previous section may be an important mechanism in facilitating the transition from preintentional to intentional communication in typically developing infants. If this is true, then there is some reason to suspect that a similar, but perhaps more structured, process could also be useful in communication interventions for individuals with developmental and physical disabilities. That is, it may help to deliberately shape the individual's existing unintentional behaviors into intentional forms of communication by creating carefully structured social interactions that provide the necessary contingencies.

Among young children without disabilities, communication development is said to begin in the *perlocutionary* stage, which covers the period from birth to about 9 months of age (Bates, Camaioni, & Volterra, 1975; Halliday, 1975; Siegel-Causey & Bashinski, 1997). At this stage, many of the child's informal and idiosyncratic behaviors (e.g., vocalizations, facial expressions, body movements, gaze, informal gestures) are interpreted by parents as if the child were attempting to communicate. At the beginning, of course, this practice may involve a considerable amount of overinterpretation on the part of the parents (von Tetzchner, 1997). Instead, the child's earliest such behaviors may represent nothing more than involuntary movements or simple orienting responses to environmental stimuli.

Over time, and possibly as a result of the parents' frequent and contingent responses to these actions as if they were forms of communication, it is believed that these behaviors are in fact shaped into intentional forms of communication. This point marks the *illocutionary* stage, which typically emerges around 6–12 months of age. In the illocutionary stage, the various behaviors observed at the previous stage have now been established as intentional forms of communication. That is, the behaviors now occur because in the past they were followed by reinforcement mediated by the partner.

Beginning with the first words at around 12 months of age, the typically developing child then enters the third, or *locutionary,* stage of language development. This stage is associated with the acquisition of symbolic communicative acts (e.g., speech, formal gestures, use of pictorial representations; Bates, Benigni, Bretherton, Camaioni, & Volterra, 1979).

COMMUNICATIVE FORMS

The various conceptualizations of communication reviewed so far are consistent in recognizing that communicative behaviors can include a range of forms or modes, including speech, formal and informal gestures, and graphic-mode communication (e.g., pointing to pictures or line drawings). In the absence of intervention to build conventional and more symbolic forms of communication, individuals with developmental and physical disabilities may rely on body movements, vocalizations, and informal gestures. In some cases, they may even resort to problem behavior, such as aggression and self-injury, to communicate. Assessment strategies for identifying these forms and their possible communicative function are described in Chapter 2.

Communication is often multimodal, which means that it includes responses from different modes, such as combining gestures with vocalizations. Communicative exchanges frequently involve both informal and formal acts and aided and unaided modes. Intervention should include strategies to strengthen multimodal communication because each of these options can be used to achieve the range of communicative functions and skills listed in Tables 1.1 and 1.2.

Indeed, current best practice emphasizes the need for and value of multimodal communication because an individual may use a range of aided and unaided forms across contexts and partners to communicate (Siegel & Cress, 2002; Sigafoos & Drasgow, 2001). Although the use of more symbolic forms of communication is an important goal that will increase the individual's ability to communicate effectively across a range of community settings with a variety of partners, there may be situations when the individual is not able to gain access to a formal communication system, such as a communication board or VOCA. In these situations, the individual will need to be able to use other appropriate forms, such as gestures and vocalizations (Reichle, Halle, & Drasgow, 1998; Sigafoos & Drasgow, 2001).

The various definitions of *communication* and studies of early communication development—from perlocutionary, to illocutionary, to locutionary—suggest that many informal behaviors could be seen as potential communicative acts. Intervention for individuals who rely on informal or prelinguistic behaviors, therefore, is focused in part on 1) enhancing and strengthening any existing appropriate forms, 2) replacing inappropriate and ineffective forms, and 3) building new and more symbolic forms and modes of communication.

RECEPTIVE COMMUNICATION SKILLS

In addition to enhancing the individual's skills in producing effective communicative behaviors, intervention should also involve teaching the individual to function as a listener, or building receptive communication skills. This goal is necessary because participation in social-communicative interactions requires that the individual not only be able to produce communication but also be able to respond appropriately to the verbal behavior of others. Simply put, functional communication involves not only speaking but also listening (Sevcik & Romski, 2002).

A common training paradigm for teaching receptive communication to individuals with developmental and physical disabilities goes something like this: First, two or more objects (e.g., a cup and a spoon) are placed in front of the learner. Next, the teacher instructs the individual to "point to *cup*" or "point to *spoon*." The learner's task is to point to the item named by the teacher. When correct responses occur consistently across a number of objects, the learner is given credit for knowing or understanding the words. Receptive communication of this type can be easily taught by any teacher with basic competencies in fading, prompting, and differential reinforcement (Duker et al., 2004). The challenge, however, is to teach listener skills that are more functional. An example of a more functional listener skill would be to provide the right amount of money when the cashier says, "That will be $2.71."

Communication interventions for individuals with developmental and physical disabilities have rarely included this type of more functional receptive communication training (Sigafoos, 1997). Despite the relative lack of empirically validated instructional procedures for teaching functional listener skills, there is at least recognition that receptive skills should be an important component in any comprehensive intervention program for individuals with developmental and physical disabilities (Snell, 2002).

Impairments in receptive language may help to explain a number of the performance deficiencies common to individuals with developmental and physical disabilities. Consider the results of a longitudinal study into the relation between communication ability and problem behavior, which revealed a strong connection between impairments in receptive language and severity of problem behavior (Sigafoos, 2000). That is, individuals with greater impairments in receptive language had more severe problem behaviors. Findings of this type suggest that difficulties in understanding others may contribute to problem behavior. To counteract difficulties in understanding others, communication partners may need to incorporate a range of visual supports, such as the use of picture-based activity schedules (Dettmer, Simpson, Smith Myles, & Ganz, 2000).

PARTNER RESPONSIVITY

Bronfenbrenner (1995) highlighted the importance of caregiver responsiveness in influencing children's learning and development. Caregivers and other partners in communicative exchanges appear to play a critical role in facilitating communication development when they respond contingently to the individual's potential communicative acts. Being responsive also means providing structured opportunities for communication and using these opportunities to teach more symbolic forms of communication (Cress & Marvin, 2003; Snell, 2002).

To acquire new forms of communication, individuals with developmental and physical disabilities will typically require frequent and highly structured opportunities for learning. A responsive partner, therefore, is one who creates numerous structured opportunities for teaching communication. He or she also can recognize and capture opportunities that are learner initiated as evidenced by the appearance of an existing communicative form. Opportunities should be created and captured throughout the day and across many days, not just during designated training sessions.

Being a responsive partner is not easy. Indeed, even experienced teachers frequently fail to respond to learner-initiated communicative acts, especially when these acts involve informal behaviors, such as gaze, body movements, and undifferentiated vocalizations (Houghton, Bronicki, & Guess, 1987). Their lack of responsiveness can be explained by the fact that the communicative forms emitted by the learner are often too subtle and idiosyncratic; hence, their communicative potential goes unrecognized.

Keen, Sigafoos, and Woodyatt (2001) suggested a possible approach for training partners to be more responsive in such cases. The first step of their approach is to list all of the behaviors in the individual's repertoire that are potentially communicative. Next, assessments are conducted (see Chapter 2) to verify the communicative function, if any, of these potential communicative acts. Opportunities are created for the individual to express that function to determine if the presumed communicative behavior will occur. If it does, then there is some evidence that the behavior is in fact a form of communication. Finally, whenever the learner produces the form, the partner is taught to respond in ways that reinforce and strengthen appropriate and more symbolic forms. This brief description captures well the general approach to communication assessment and intervention that is delineated in more detail in the subsequent chapters of this book.

EVIDENCE-BASED PRACTICE

Numerous procedures have been proposed for teaching communication skills to individuals with developmental and physical disabilities. Within this range, there are procedures with varying degrees of empirical support. Some procedures, such as facilitated communication, have proven to be ineffective and, therefore, have no place in clinical practice (Mostert, 2001). Other procedures, although promising, need to be studied more carefully before their use can be justified (Heflin & Simpson, 1998). Fortunately, there are a large number of sensible strategies that have been subject to proper scientific study and that consistently produce positive outcomes. The procedures with the best track record share a common basis in that they are based on, and consistent with, respondent and operant learning principles (Duker et al., 2004).

Evidence-based practice dictates that only well-established or empirically validated procedures should be used. The logical implication is that communication intervention should be firmly grounded in operant and respondent learning principles. As noted by Sigafoos, Drasgow, and Schlosser (2003), however, evidence-based practice involves more than the use of empirically validated procedures. It also involves evaluating whether the procedure is in fact working for the individual. Partners will be more effective in enhancing the communication skills of individuals with developmental disabilities if they can modify proven interventions to suit the individual. This process requires ongoing evaluation and troubleshooting of intervention plans, as described in Chapter 6.

As mentioned previously, modifying the intervention to suit the individual requires a thorough understanding of the basic principles of learning that underlie the procedure (Linscheid, 1999). The remainder of this chapter reviews basic principles relevant to communication intervention for individuals with developmental and physical disabilities.

CREATING STRUCTURED OPPORTUNITIES FOR COMMUNICATION

One of the basic principles common to all effective interventions pertains to the provision of structured opportunities for communication. To enhance and strengthen communication abilities, individuals with developmental and physical disabilities must receive numerous and often highly structured opportunities for communication. Relying exclusively on incidental learning opportunities is unlikely to be effective for initial acquisition of new forms of symbolic communication, at least for individuals with severe and multiple disabilities.

A structured opportunity might begin with the partner simply offering a preferred object. Once this discriminative stimulus is presented, the individual is prompted to make the desired communication request; then, the listener provides access to the preferred item as reinforcement. Every structured opportunity should consist of at least the following three-term contingency: 1) discriminative stimulus, 2) response, and 3) reinforcing consequence. At the most basic level, the three-term contingency constitutes a single learning opportunity or discrete trial. In any given teaching session, however, the teacher may decide to implement 5, 10, or 20 such trials, thereby creating repeated and massed opportunities for learning within a single instructional event.

Assuming that discrete trial training requires an artificial context is a mistake. Discrete trials can and should be embedded into typical routines throughout the day. Requests for food should be taught at breakfast, lunch, snack times, and dinner. Requests for toys should be taught during all playtimes. An example of a discrete trial for teaching a child to request during a leisure activity is outlined in Figure 1.1.

Consistent implementation of discrete trials in combination with effective prompting, fading, and reinforcement (discussed next) can be an effective way of providing the structured learning opportunities that are often required to promote acquisition of new communication responses (Duker et

Figure 1.1. Example of a discrete trial involving a three-term contingency for teaching a student to request access to a preferred object using a manual sign.

al., 2004). In many cases, however, individuals with developmental and physical disabilities may fail to maintain and generalize communication skills unless opportunities are presented within typical routines.

Discrete trials or structured learning opportunities can and should be embedded into the numerous everyday routines in which communication is expected to occur (Cress & Marvin, 2003). For example, in the context of an afternoon tea break, the individual may be given an opportunity first to request which type of tea he or she wants (e.g., English Breakfast or Earl Grey) and then to request (or reject) milk and sugar. In this example, two discrete trials are embedded into the afternoon tea ritual.

Embedded instruction alone does not appear to be sufficiently powerful to ensure initial acquisition of communication skills among individuals with severe disabilities (Grisham-Brown, Schuster, Hemmeter, & Collins, 2000). Thus, there is often a need for more intensive teaching sessions during which a large number of instructional trials are presented, as this approach is generally more effective in promoting initial acquisition. When using embedded instruction, in contrast, it is often only possible to present a few learning trials during any given activity, although doing so can help to promote maintenance and generalization. We, therefore, recommend a combination of intensive discrete trial training and embedded instruction.

Given this recommendation, partners must learn how to provide structured opportunities during intensive training as well as across the range of typical activities that comprise the learner's routine (Butterfield & Arthur, 1995). When communication partners learn how to structure communication opportunities effectively and present discrete trials across a range of activities, the individual benefits by receiving increased opportunities for learning, communication, and social interaction.

PROMPTING AND FADING

Partners must ensure that every opportunity or trial ends with the learner making the correct response and being reinforced for that response. During the initial stages of training, however, the learner is unlikely to make the correct response, which means that the partner will have to use one or more prompts to ensure a correct response from the learner. Various prompts have been developed and shown to be effective for teaching communication skills to individuals with developmental and physical disabilities, including 1) spoken instructions (e.g., "Show me the sign for water"), 2) gestures (e.g., pointing to the correct line drawing on a communication board), 3) modeling or imitative prompts (e.g., demonstrating the correct manual sign while instructing the learner to "do this"), and 4) physical assistance (e.g., moving the learner's finger to touch the correct symbol on a VOCA) (Duker et al.,

2004). In addition, various prompting strategies or hierarchies have been empirically validated for teaching a variety of communicative forms and functions to individuals with developmental and physical disabilities, including most-to-least (i.e., physical, model, gesture, verbal) and least-to-most prompting (i.e., verbal, gesture, model, physical), graduated guidance (using the least amount of physical guidance necessary), and delayed prompting (e.g., waiting 5 or 10 seconds before prompting). The basic principle is that the partner must use a prompt or prompting strategy that will reliably evoke the correct response from the learner.

Once the learner is responding correctly and consistently with prompting, the partner must then begin the process of fading or eliminating the prompts so that the learner begins to respond independently. Again, there are numerous effective strategies for fading prompts, including 1) systematically moving from more- to less-intrusive prompts, 2) inserting a time delay between the discriminative stimulus and the delivery of the prompt, and 3) decreasing the amount or magnitude of prompting over successive trials (Duker et al., 2004). In most cases, prompts cannot be withdrawn suddenly but must be removed gradually, a process known as *prompt fading*. The basic principle is to gradually give less and less prompting as the learner becomes more and more independent.

REINFORCEMENT

Reinforcement of correct responses is critical for learning. Therefore, once the response occurs—whether prompted or not—the partner must deliver reinforcement as quickly as possible. There are at least two basic principles related to proper use of reinforcement. First, it is critical to ensure that the reinforcer delivered matches the function of the individual's communication response. If the learner requests a drink of water, for example, the appropriate reinforcement is for the partner to give the learner a glass of water to drink. In contrast, if the learner signs NO THANKS when offered a drink, then the appropriate reinforcement is for the partner to withdraw the offered beverage.

It is relatively easy to follow this rule when the individual produces a mand because the mand specifies its reinforcement. Difficulties can arise however, when teaching other verbal operants, such as a tact or an intraverbal, because the natural reinforcer is simply a relevant reply from the partner, rather than some more tangible outcome. The problem is that some individuals with developmental and physical disabilities appear to be unresponsive to such purely social consequences. It would, therefore, be difficult to teach them to tact, for example, without using some sort of contrived or artificial consequences as reinforcement during training. This situation is not necessarily a problem if the schedule of reinforcement can later be thinned so that it appears as if the learner is responding to the social consequences, rather than the occasional tangible reinforcer that is really maintaining the behavior.

Drasgow et al. (1999) suggested, however, that when partners use food as an artificial or contrived reinforcer for tacting objects, they may find that a child only tacts when hungry. After training, the motivation (e.g., hunger) to respond may be absent at times when it would be appropriate for the child to tact. The lack of motivation may explain why communication skills often fail to generalize.

A second critical aspect of using reinforcement effectively is to ensure that the learner is motivated to respond on each and every instructional opportunity. There is no sense in trying to teach a learner to request food and drink, for example, if the individual is not hungry or thirsty at the time. If the learner is not motivated when an opportunity is presented, then the partner does not have a reinforcer, and no learning will occur. In addition, if the partner persists at times when motivation is lacking, then the session may become aversive, and the learner may attempt to escape. Partners, therefore, must gain skills in recognizing when the learner is motivated to communicate. Because it may be difficult to capture a sufficient number of such opportunities, partners will also need to learn how to create motivation for communication (Sigafoos, 1999).

Sosne, Handleman, and Harris (1979) argued that creating the need for communication was the critical first step in teaching communication skills to individuals with developmental disabilities. They described various ways that partners can manipulate the environment to create the need for communication requesting, some of which are shown in Table 1.3.

INITIATION AND SPONTANEITY

One of the most frequently cited problems in communication intervention is ensuring spontaneous use of newly acquired communication skills (Halle, 1987). Spontaneity, or self-initiation, is seen as a critical aspect of communication. The ability to initiate communicative exchanges enhances an individual's control over the environment. Without this, individuals with developmental and physical disabilities may remain passive and unable to communicate unless prompted to do so by a partner. Obviously, such a state of prompt dependency is not ideal. Individuals are taught to communicate more effectively in part so that they are able to initiate social-communicative exchanges with others, meet their wants and needs, and exert control over the environment. Thus, their probability of communicating should not be completely dependent on partner prompts. Achieving spontaneity will depend to some extent on how well the partner can fade prompts.

Halle (1987) and others (e.g., Carter, 2002; Kaczmarek, 1990) suggested that spontaneity is best understood in terms of a continuum referenced to

Table 1.3. Creating the need for communication

Activity	Context	Creation of need*
Washing	Before eating	Soap and water
	After toileting	Soap and water
	When utensils and plates are dirty	Dish soap
	When tables and windows are dirty	Cleaner and window spray
Drying	After showering or bathing	Towel
	After washing hands	Towel
	When table, plates, and chair are wet	Towel and paper towel
Dressing	When waking	General clothing
	Before going outside	Coat and hat
	When it is raining	Raincoat, boots, and umbrella
	When it is cold or snowing	Boots, gloves, and hat
	Before bedtime	Pajamas
	Before swimming	Swimsuit, flippers, and mask
Mealtimes	At mealtimes	Utensils, napkin, and glass
	At all other times	Food item
Sleeping	At bedtime	Pillow, blanket
	At rest time	Cot, mat
Playtime	When swinging	Peer partner
	When using puzzles	Puzzle pieces
	When building with blocks	Blocks
	When coloring	Crayons
	When playing basketball	Basketball

*Items not available unless requested.

From Sosne, J.B., Handleman, J.S., & Harris, S.L. (1979). Teaching spontaneous-functional speech to autistic-type children. *Mental Retardation, 17,* 242; adapted by permission.

the obviousness of the antecedent that sets the occasion for the learner's communicative behavior (Figure 1.2). For example, if the manual sign WATER occurred when the person was thirsty, then it would be considered a more spontaneous mand or request than if the person had been shown a glass of water and told, "Show me the sign for *water*."

The extent to which the individual can be spontaneous may vary across environmental conditions, including the communication partner, the function of the communicative act, and the mode of communication being used

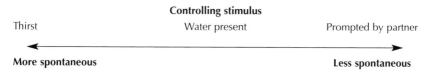

Controlling stimulus

| Thirst | Water present | Prompted by partner |

More spontaneous ← → **Less spontaneous**

Figure 1.2. A continuum of spontaneity for requesting a drink of water.

by the individual. Carter (2003a) reported that variations in spontaneity often depended on the partner's behavior and not just on the individual's communication skills. Partners who constantly anticipated the individual's communication needs, for example, tended to preempt the person from producing more spontaneous communication. In contrast, partners who waited for the individual to initiate tended to get more spontaneous (i.e., unprompted) communicative behavior from the person.

Carter (2003b) also noted that the probability of successful communication decreased with increasing spontaneity. Thus, if a self-initiated communication attempt is not immediately successful, it would be helpful for the individual to have a strategy for repairing the communicative breakdown. Unless partners teach an explicit and appropriate repair strategy, the learner may either give up or escalate to problem behavior (Brady & Halle, 2002; Keen, 2003). Chapter 4 reviews procedures for teaching communication repair strategies.

GENERALIZATION

"Generalization is the use of responses acquired during training in situations outside of the training environment, in other appropriate settings, with other people, and with other materials" (Duker et al., 2004, p. 147). For example, if the learner has been taught to initiate conversations with peers in the classroom, generalization occurs when the learner also can initiate conversations on different topics with siblings at home and with neighbors in the community. Duker et al. noted that the lack of generalization of newly acquired communication skills is a major problem in intervention programs for individuals with developmental and physical disabilities. Failure to show generalization may arise from problems with the training procedures or they may stem from lack of motivation (Drasgow et al., 1999). That is, newly acquired communication skills may not generalize because the individual was not taught to use the skill under novel conditions or because there is no motivation or need to respond when the generalization opportunity presented itself. In either case, a lack of generalized use will be evident, and, thus, partners need to know how to program for generalization. In addition to ensuring that motivation is present on generalization opportunities, there are a number of empirically validated strategies that can be used to promote the generalization of newly acquired communication skills (see Chapter 4).

BEHAVIORAL STATES

The assessment of behavioral states is an area of increasing importance in understanding the communicative potential of individuals with developmental and physical disabilities. A "behavior[al] state is a physiologic condition that reflects the maturity and organization of an individual's central nervous system" (Siegel-Causey & Bashinski, 1997, p. 109). It can be understood in terms of the degree of alertness and responsiveness that a person exhibits at any one time. For individuals with developmental and physical disabilities, the presence of certain behavioral states may influence social responsiveness, which in turn may influence partner responsiveness. Obviously, creating effective opportunities for communication is more difficult when the individual is asleep, drowsy, or engaged in highly agitated behavior. Of course, an unstimulating environment with few opportunities for communication may play a part in creating or maintaining the very same behavioral state that makes it difficult to provide effective learning opportunities (Arthur, 2003). The work of several researchers has highlighted the need to better understand the relation of internal and external factors to behavioral states and communicative responsiveness. As explained in Chapter 6, information of this type could prove to be important for tailoring interventions to better suit the individual's pattern of behavioral states (Arthur, 2004; Ault, Guy, Guess, Bashinski, & Roberts, 1995; Guess, Roberts, Siegel-Causey, & Rues, 1995).

PROBLEM BEHAVIOR

Problem behaviors such as aggression, self-injury, property destruction, and tantrums may serve a communicative function for some individuals (Carr, 1977). In such cases, acquisition of functionally equivalent communicative behaviors can be effective in reducing problem behavior (Reichle & Wacker, 1993). This treatment is known as *functional communication training*. Because a significant percentage of individuals with developmental disabilities have severe behavior problems, partners must know how to design and implement treatment programs involving functional communication training, which is the topic of Chapter 5. In some situations, the emergence of severe behavior problems could in fact be prevented or reduced with the early introduction of functional communication training (Mirenda, 1997; Sigafoos, Arthur, & O'Reilly, 2003). Partners should, therefore, consider the early introduction of communication intervention for the prevention of severe behavior problems in individuals with developmental and physical disabilities.

COLLABORATIVE TEAMING/INCLUSIVE EDUCATION

Communication is central to participation in society. Increasingly, individuals with developmental and physical disabilities are being educated within regular classroom and school settings. Inclusive practices require that communication assessment and intervention take place within the context of the general curriculum and regular school activities with both academic and social participation seen as the ultimate goals (Hunt, Soto, Maier, Muller, & Goetz, 2002). To achieve this end, various people, including parents, siblings, peers, teachers, classroom assistants, speech-language pathologists, and other therapists, may assist in the assessment and intervention process (Arthur & Foreman, 2002; DePaepe & Wood, 2001; Giangreco, 2000; Parette, Brotherson, & Huer, 2000; Snell, 2002; Warren, 2000).

The assessment and intervention strategies described in Chapters 2–5 are applicable for use by this range of people in inclusive settings. Although applicable across people and settings, specific assessment and intervention procedures will often need to be modified to suit the individual and context. This fact is another reason why an understanding of the basic principles that underlie the technique is so important.

Collaborative teaming requires regular team meetings, mutually defined goals, strong leadership, good interpersonal skills, and equity in participation of all team members. In addition, team members need to have a clear understanding of the roles and responsibilities of all of the participants as well as the ability to be flexible around role boundaries. To support the inclusion of individuals with developmental and physical disabilities through communication intervention, there may also be a need for specific training in recognizing individual behaviors as communicative and in the technical maintenance of aided communication systems (Soto, Muller, Hunt, & Goetz, 2001). By working together through collaborative teams, strategies to increase social participation and engagement can be built into the intervention program. All team members should be seen as important communication partners who share the responsibility to implement and monitor the intervention program.

SUMMARY AND CONCLUSIONS

This chapter has considered several concepts and basic principles that underlie communication assessment and intervention for individuals with developmental and physical disabilities. Subsequent chapters describe the application of these concepts and basic principles. Figure 1.3 outlines the general sequence of our approach to assessment and intervention that is developed in the remainder of this book.

Chapter 2 covers assessment strategies for 1) identifying existing communication forms, 2) verifying their communicative function, and 3) analyzing the communicative demands of the environment. It also describes the assessment of behavioral state and partner skills because this information may assist in developing more effective intervention plans. In Chapter 3, we consider how the resultant assessment information might be used to determine appropriate intervention pathways for individuals with varying com-

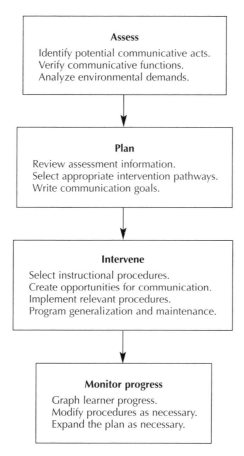

Figure 1.3. Outline of the assessment and intervention process.

municative skills and needs. Included in Chapter 3 are descriptions of several intervention pathways for making the transition from beginning communicator to more advanced and symbolic stages of development. Chapter 3 also considers factors for selecting appropriate communication modes (i.e., aided, unaided) and devices (e.g., VOCAs, picture symbols).

Chapter 4 reviews a number of empirically validated strategies for achieving the goals associated with each intervention pathway. Included in this review are procedures for facilitating the transition to more symbolic communication, as well as procedures for building spontaneity and promoting generalization and maintenance of newly acquired communication skills. Chapter 5 describes specialized assessment and instructional procedures for replacing problem behavior with appropriate forms of communication. Chapter 6 presents strategies for evaluating outcomes and making data-based decisions so that partners can modify procedures to better suit the individual. Finally, Chapter 7 consists of five case studies illustrating the approach to assessment and intervention application outlined in the previous chapters.

2

The Assessment Process

JEFF SIGAFOOS, MICHAEL ARTHUR-KELLY,
NANCY BUTTERFIELD, AND PHIL FOREMAN

INTRODUCTION

This chapter covers the assessment of communication skills and communication-related intervention needs of individuals with developmental and physical disabilities. Assessment strategies are described for achieving three outcomes: 1) identifying existing communicative forms, 2) verifying the communicative function of these forms, and 3) analyzing the communicative demands of the environment. In addition, we consider assessment of behavioral state and partner skills as such data may assist in developing more effective intervention plans. The information obtained through the assessment process is used for three purposes: 1) evaluating the communicative potential of existing behaviors within the individual's repertoire, 2) deciding on appropriate intervention pathways (see Chapter 3), and 3) prioritizing communication skills for instruction.

Because communicative behaviors are effective only indirectly, through the mediation of a listener, partner involvement is essential at each stage of the assessment process. Specifically, potential communicative acts within the individual's repertoire are first identified by soliciting information from partners via interviews or questionnaires. The communicative function, if any, of these potential communicative acts must then be verified, which requires direct observation during structured communicative interactions between the individual and one or more partners. Analysis of the environment to identify needed communication skills—which is useful in setting instructional priorities—also requires input from partners across a range of settings. The combination of assessment strategies described in this chapter will hopefully enable partners to integrate three aspects of communication, specifically the form and function of communicative behaviors and the context in which these behaviors occur or are expected to occur.

Although they lack speech, many individuals with developmental and physical disabilities engage in numerous behaviors that have or could have communicative potential. It stands to reason that a useful first step in the assessment process would be to identify the communicative potential of any responses that currently exist in the person's behavioral repertoire. The term *potential communicative act* refers to any existing behavior within the person's repertoire that might now, or could in the future, function as a form of communication. Partners must, therefore, understand the concept of the potential communicative act.

POTENTIAL COMMUNICATIVE ACTS

Recall from Chapter 1 that communication can be achieved through a variety of behaviors, not just through speech. Indeed, well before speech develops, children without disabilities produce a variety of behaviors—such as informal gestures, body movements, facial expressions, and vocalizations—that parents interpret as the child's way of communicating. Over time, and because of this overinterpretation, it is hypothesized that these various forms are shaped into intentional and more symbolic forms of communication. For most children, this process occurs incidentally without any explicit or deliberate instruction.

Individuals with developmental and physical disabilities who fail to develop speech often develop subtle, informal, and idiosyncratic communicative behaviors. In the absence of speech or some alternative mode of communication, these individuals may have little choice but to continue to rely on these various informal and idiosyncratic behaviors. Table 2.1 lists behaviors that have been identified as having a potential communicative function for individuals with developmental and physical disabilities.

Many of the behaviors listed in Table 2.1 are not obviously communicative, although the far right column lists a number of symbolic forms indicative of the locutionary stage of development. These symbolic forms do not develop without explicit and deliberate instruction of the type described in Chapter 4. The other columns list behaviors that often develop incidentally in the repertoires of individuals with developmental and physical disabilities. These behaviors may or may not function as forms of communication. Such behaviors are often referred to as unintentional or nonsymbolic acts, but we prefer the terms *prelinguistic* or *potential communicative acts* because they make no inferences about the communicative function or intentionality of the behaviors. It is important to avoid assigning a communicative function to such behaviors until verification assessments are completed.

Table 2.1. Examples of potential communicative acts

Vocalization	Body movement	Face/eye movement	Breathing	Problem behavior	Stereotypic movements	Symbolic forms
Make noises	Move closer	Purse lips	Rapid	Aggression	Flap arms	Speech
Yell/scream	Move away	Stare	Slow	Tantrum	Wring hands	Manual signs
Grunt	Tense/wiggle	Open eyes	Hold	Self-injury	Rock body	Gestures
Cry/whine	Reposition body	Close eyes	Swallow	Destroy items	Head weave	Head nod
Laugh	Reach/touch	Gaze away	Sigh			Pictures
	Push/pull/point	Gaze toward	Blow			

From Sigafoos, J., Woodyatt, G., Keen, D., Tait, K., Tucker, M., Roberts-Pennell, D., et al. (2000). Identifying potential communicative acts in children with developmental and physical disabilities. *Communication Disorders Quarterly, 21,* 79; reprinted by permission.

Whether these types of prelinguistic behaviors represent the perlocutionary (i.e., unintentional but potentially communicative) or the illocutionary (i.e., informal yet intentional) stage of communication development is often unclear. A verification assessment (described later) is thus necessary to determine whether any given act can be considered intentional; however, even when a behavior is determined to be lacking in communicative intent, it may still have communicative potential. That is, over time and by taking the appropriate intervention pathway (see Chapter 3), the behavior might be shaped into an effective and intentional form of communication.

The symbolic forms listed in the far right column of Table 2.1 include unaided (e.g., gestures, manual signs) and aided modes of communication (e.g., pictures). As mentioned previously, obtaining this level of communicative competence among individuals with developmental and physical disabilities will most likely require a carefully designed, highly structured, ongoing, and fairly intensive intervention effort.

The end goal of striving toward more symbolic forms is important because there are at least three potential problems with reliance on prelinguistic behaviors. First, some of these prelinguistic behaviors involve subtle or idiosyncratic responses (e.g., a flap of the hands, a subtle head movement toward an object) that may be difficult for partners to recognize as having communicative intent or potential. As a result, attempts to communicate using such behaviors may go unnoticed and hence fail to obtain reinforcement. Under this scenario, the behavior may eventually extinguish or—in an attempt to repair such communication breakdowns—the individual may escalate to more intense and problematic forms of behavior (e.g., screaming, tantrums). More symbolic forms, in contrast, are readily recognized as communicative across a range of partners and contexts.

Second, certain forms of prelinguistic behaviors are inappropriate and socially stigmatizing. Although they may be communicative, behaviors such as aggression, self-injury, and tantrums are clearly problematic and need to be replaced with more acceptable forms of communication (see Chapter 5). Other acts (e.g., whining, grabbing), although less problematic, do little to enhance social status and should also be targeted for replacement by teaching more symbolic forms that are functionally equivalent. *Functionally equivalent* means that the new symbolic form serves the same communicative purpose as the existing prelinguistic form.

A third problem with reliance on prelinguistic acts relates to quality-of-life issues that were considered in Chapter 1. There is little dignity in relying on prelinguistic forms of communication. Although these types of communication are acceptable in the short term and for young children, partners are obligated to assist the individual in developing more age-appropriate modes of communication. The long-term goal of communication intervention for individuals with developmental and physical disabilities should be to develop effective, multimodal forms of symbolic communication. Achieving this goal is essential if the individual is to become a full and actively participating member of society.

Despite these problems with reliance on prelinguistic behaviors for communication, there are also at least two reasons why partners must identify and make use of the existing and potential communicative acts in the person's repertoire. First, whether intentional or not, these types of prelinguistic behaviors have communicative potential. They, therefore, provide the raw material from which more symbolic communicative forms can be developed. The reactions of partners to these behaviors will largely determine the extent to which any given behavior becomes an effective communicative act.

Second, when prelinguistic behaviors are observed, they may signal that the motivation to communicate is present, which is the optimal time for partners to teach new forms of communication. Drasgow et al. (1999) referred to certain types of prelinguistic behaviors (e.g., reaching and leading) as *behavior indication*. That is, the appearance of the prelinguistic act within a communicative context (e.g., when a preferred object is in view but out of reach) indicates that the individual is attempting to communicate. When behavior indication is observed, one can, therefore, assume that the individual is in fact motivated to communicate. By capturing instances of behavior indication, the partner gains some assurance that the individual will be responsive to the systematic instruction provided at that time.

In addition, the instruction provided at the time can be tailored to the individual's existing motivational state. This adaptation, in turn, can help partners become more responsive because it is easier to ensure a match between partner response and the function or purpose of the individual's communication attempt. If the individual is indicating that he or she is finished with a task, for example, the partner can acknowledge the response ("Yes, I understand. You're telling me you've finished.") and provide the appropriate consequences (e.g., praising the individual for completing the task, removing the finished task materials, and assisting the person's transition to a preferred activity as reinforcement for completing the task).

Beginning the assessment process by first identifying the individual's potential communicative acts seems logical in order to enhance the efficacy of instruction. Once the communicative acts are identified, additional assessments can be conducted to verify the communicative function, if any, of these identified acts. Partners should aim to identify the full range of potential communicative acts in the person's repertoire. Accurate descriptions of existing and potential communicative behaviors—and gaps in the person's communication skills—constitute one type of assessment data that may assist the collaborative team in selecting relevant intervention goals and selecting appropriate intervention pathways (see Chapter 3).

INVENTORY OF
POTENTIAL COMMUNICATIVE ACTS

One promising approach for identifying potential communicative acts involves structured interviews or questionnaires with relevant communication partners (e.g., parents, teachers). This approach is consistent with the hypothesis that prelinguistic behaviors often develop into effective forms of communication when others consistently interpret and react to them as if they were in fact intentional forms of communication. Thus, to identify such potential communicative acts, it would seem to make sense to ask others to identify those behaviors in the person's repertoire that they consider to be communicative and then further specify what communicative function they believe the individual is attempting to express with each informal act. Several interview protocols and questionnaires have been developed for this purpose.

Schuler, Peck, Willard, and Theimer (1989), for example, described an interview protocol for identifying informal communication skills in individuals with severe communication impairments. Their protocol listed 23 behaviors (e.g., crying, aggression, passive gaze, vocalizations, facial expression, enactment, appropriate echolalia). During the interview, communication partners were asked to indicate whether the individual uses any of the forms to communicate one or more of the following functions: 1) request affection/interaction, 2) request adult action, 3) request object/food/thing, 4) protest, and 5) declaration/comment.

Schuler et al.'s (1989) work supports the value of beginning the assessment process by first conducting structured interviews to identify potential communicative acts. Others have also developed useful assessment protocols for identifying existing and potential communicative behaviors in the repertoires of individuals with developmental and physical disabilities (e.g., Donnellan, Mirenda, Mesaros, & Fassbender, 1984; Duker, 1999; Shaddock, Dowse, Richards, & Spinks, 1998; Siegel-Causey & Guess, 1989); however, many of these protocols are somewhat limited because they might sample only a few specific communicative functions. Developing a comprehensive inventory of potential communicative acts would seem to require an interview protocol that systematically samples the full range of communicative forms and functions.

Along these lines, Sigafoos, Woodyatt, Keen, et al. (2000) developed the Inventory of Potential Communicative Acts (IPCA). The IPCA is an empirically derived interview-based assessment protocol that focuses on the range of communicative forms and functions that have been observed in individuals with developmental and physical disabilities. A copy of the IPCA is included in Appendix A. Details about the IPCA and its development appear in Sigafoos, Woodyatt, Keen, et al. (2000). A checklist for assessing behavior indication has also been developed. (See Drasgow et al., 1999, for a discussion on the importance of assessing behavior indication.) This latter protocol is known as the Behavior Indication Assessment Scale (BIAS; see Appendix B). The BIAS is inspired by the Verbal Behavior Assessment Scale (VerBAS) developed by Duker (1999). This chapter describes how the IPCA might be used in clinical practice; the BIAS can be used in a similar manner.

The IPCA assessment begins by locating one or more partners to interview. Seeking partners who have known the individual for at least 6 months is best in order to ensure that the partners have had ample opportunity to become familiar with the individual and his or her communicative behaviors. Once a good informant is located, the purpose of the assessment–to identify any behaviors within the person's repertoire that might be used for communicating–is explained. Next, the term *potential communicative act* is defined, and examples of potential communicative acts are described to the partner. The behaviors in Table 2.1 are used as examples of potential communicative acts, but other behaviors unique to the individual could also be potential communicative acts. Then, the interview begins.

The interview covers 10 communicative functions derived from the work of Reichle, Halle, and Johnston (1993):

1. Social convention (e.g., greeting others, responding to one's name)

2. Attention to self (e.g., getting the attention of others, showing off)

3. Reject/protest (e.g., rejecting nonpreferred items, indicating *no*)

4. Request an object (e.g., requesting access to preferred objects or activities)

5. Request an action (e.g., requesting assistance with a task)

6. Request information (e.g., requesting the name of an object, requesting clarification)

7. Comment (e.g., alerting a communication partner to some relevant aspect of environment)

8. Choice making (e.g., choosing between two or more alternatives)

9. Answer (e.g., indicating yes or no to a question)

10. Imitation (e.g., imitating a head nod for yes or no)

Within each of these 10 categories, questions are asked about specific communication skills. To assess requesting an object, for example, partners are asked on the IPCA form to "describe how the individual lets you know if he or she wants 1) an object (e.g., toy or book), 2) something to eat, 3) more of something, 4) television or music, and 5) other." Figure 2.1 shows the general layout of the IPCA and sample questions for assessing behaviors related to social convention. It also illustrates the level of detail that is sought from the partners who are interviewed.

Social convention
Please describe how the individual . . .

Items	Behaviors	Examples
1. Greets you/others	_Smiles_ _Eye contact_ _Extends arms_	_When I walk up to Jenny in the morn-_ _ing and say hello, she always looks at_ _me, smiles, and reaches out her arms._
2. Indicates farewell to you/others		
3. Responds to his or her own name		
4. Other		

Figure 2.1. Sample answers for the social convention section of the Inventory of Potential Communicative Acts. (From Sigafoos, J., Woodyatt, G., Keen, D., Tait, K., Tucker, M., Roberts-Pennell, D., et al. [2000]. Identifying potential communicative acts in children with developmental and physical disabilities. *Communication Disorders Quarterly, 21,* 80; adapted by permission.)

Once the IPCA interview is completed, the information needs to be summarized for program planning. Initially, the partners' answers should be summarized for each section of the IPCA. This process will usually require some editing of the partners' verbatim answers.

Figure 2.2, a completed IPCA form, shows an example of the level of detail that is sought when summarizing partner interviews. The summary is based on an interview with Rita's teacher. As this form shows, Rita was said

Requesting an object

Please describe how the individual lets you know if he or she wants…

Items	Behaviors	Examples
1. An object (e.g., toy, book)	Reaches Moves closer Gazes toward	Occasionally, she will swipe at the windmill toy to make it go, if it is placed in front of her. She will look at, reach, or touch a choice of food/drink or will just touch her lunchbox.
2. Something to eat	Yells/bellows Gazes toward Moves closer Just picks it up and eats	If Rita sees the teacher's aide in the kitchen, she will go into the kitchen and hang around. She will wait for the teacher's aide to put milk in her bottle or will take food items if the teacher's aide is too slow in offering.
3. More of something	Moves away Spins around	On trampoline, if she wants "more," she will move to the middle of the mat, out of reach of us, or will spin away so that we can't remove her.
4. Television or music	Shakes head Stops movement Smiles	Sometimes, the school bus will be parked with the radio playing. Rita will stop, smile, and rock her head to the music.

Figure 2.2. Completed Inventory of Potential Communicative Acts for requesting an object for Rita, age 4;10. (From Sigafoos, J., Woodyatt, G., Keen, D., Tait, K., Tucker, M., Roberts-Pennell, D., et al. [2000]. Identifying potential communicative acts in children with developmental and physical disabilities. *Communication Disorders Quarterly, 21,* 77–86; reprinted by permission.)

to use a variety of behaviors to request an object, including reaching for an object, moving closer to an object, yelling, and shaking her head. The examples also provide useful information about the context in which these behaviors were said to occur.

They are very important for the next stage of assessment. Knowing the context in which the potential communicative act occurs is helpful because one can then recreate this context to observe whether the behavior does in fact occur consistently. If so, the act may in fact be a form of communication. Such observations, therefore, help to verify the communicative function of potential communicative acts that were identified via the interview process.

Before considering verification, however, it is useful to transfer the data from the summary portion of the IPCA onto the Scoring Grid (see Figure 2.3) for analysis. The Scoring Grid has columns for specific communicative functions and rows for listing behaviors. By transferring information to the Scoring Grid (i.e., darkening the corresponding squares), one can obtain a visual overview of the range of the individual's communicative forms and functions.

To fill out the Scoring Grid, enter the person's behaviors into the blank rows in the left-hand column of the grid. Then, follow each row across and darken the cells that correspond to the functions that have been identified by the IPCA for the specific behavior. Scanning the Scoring Grid from left to right indicates the range of communicative functions reported by the informant. Scanning from top to bottom indicates the range of specific behaviors that the partner interpreted as a form of communication. Each darkened square, therefore, can be viewed as a potential communicative act, and the overall pattern constitutes a profile of the person's communication repertoire.

The Scoring Grid shown in Figure 2.3 is based on information supplied by Tina's teacher. Tina is a 12-year-old girl with Rett syndrome. In this case, a visual inspection of Figure 2.3 suggests that Tina has a fairly restricted range of potential communicative acts. Her teacher noted 14 different behaviors in Tina's communication repertoire (i.e., 14 rows have black squares in them). Although Tina was said to have ways of indicating 8 of the 10 functions (i.e., does not *imitate* and does not *answer*), there are many empty columns related to specific communication skills (e.g., in the *attention to self* function, Tina does not *show off* or *join in*. Empty cells in the Scoring Grid represent gaps in the person's communication repertoire. Filling these gaps to expand the individual's communication repertoire represents a logical direction for intervention.

In summary, structured interviews using protocols such as the IPCA are intended as tools for systematically describing the individual's communication repertoire. The IPCA is specifically intended to provide a comprehensive inventory of potential communicative acts. The resulting data are also helpful in identifying gaps in the communication repertoire, which can then be addressed through intervention. This information is then used to determine appropriate intervention pathways (see Chapter 3).

Remember that the information obtained in the IPCA interview represents the perceptions of communication partners. Partners may overinterpret the individual's behaviors and assign communicative intent where none exists. In addition, partners' perceptions of the individual's communicative forms and functions might not be completely accurate because the communicative function of prelinguistic acts can be difficult to judge (Carter & Iacono, 2002; Sigafoos, Woodyatt, Keen, et al., 2000). Hence, there is a need to verify this preliminary assessment information through direct and repeated observation.

VERIFYING COMMUNICATIVE POTENTIAL

Verification is often necessary to determine if the potential communicative acts identified by partners are representative of the perlocutionary or illocutionary stage. This distinction is important because it directly influences the intervention pathways that would be pursued (see Chapter 3). Verification of communicative potential is akin to the process of functional analysis (Iwata, Dorsey, Slifer, Bauman, & Richman, 1982; Iwata et al., 1994), which is used to identify the function or purpose of problem behavior (see Chapter 5). A functional analysis of problem behavior seeks to identify the antecedents that set the occasion for problem behavior and the reinforcing consequences that maintain the behavior. When the controlling antecedents and consequences have been identified, the function or purpose of the behavior can often be isolated, which in turn "explains" the behavior.

The verification of potential communicative acts seeks to determine the function or purpose of prelinguistic behaviors. In particular, the aim is to determine if the behavior represents a form of communication and, if so, what function (e.g., mand, tact) the behavior serves. As in a functional analysis, evidence of communicative purpose or function is sought by exposing the individual to a number of assessment conditions (or verification trials) that are designed to evoke a specific communicative act.

For example, suppose that during the IPCA interview Jim's partner reported that he vocalized to gain attention. Verification trials could then be conducted to determine whether these vocalizations did in fact function as Jim's way of getting attention. The verification trials would involve recreating the relevant context or antecedent conditions (i.e., a partner is present but is not attending to Jim) and also providing the associated reinforcing consequences contingent on the behavior (i.e., if Jim vocalizes, then the partner gives him attention). If vocalizations occurred consistently under these conditions but not much at other times, then Jim's vocalizations would be confirmed as his way of getting attention.

Behaviors	Social convention				Attention to self					Reject/protest						Request object					dress
	greet	farewell	name	other	get attention	comfort	cuddle	shows off	other	routine	do	dislike	take	adult	other	object	food	more	TV or music	other	
lifts arms																					
body droop											■										
closes eyes												■									
cries																	■				
eye gaze	■													■		■					
eye point																		■			
holds hand																					
hyperactivity increases																					
increases eye gaze																					
kicks feet																					
knowing look		■																			
laughs																					
moves head toward																					
moves toward																					
negative facial						■											■				
positive facial																					
quizzical look																					
raises arm/rolls over					■																
refuses to swallow												■									
restless																					
shoulders up and back																					
smiles	■	■			■																
startles																					
tenses body																					
vocalizes																					
whines																					
won't look																					
yawns																					

Figure 2.3. Teacher responses to the Inventory of Potential Communicative Acts for Tina, a 12-year-old girl with Rett syndrome. (From Sigafoos, J., Woodyatt, G., Keen, D., Tait, K., Tucker, M., Roberts-Pennell, D., et al. [2000]. Identifying potential communicative acts in children with developmental and physical disabilities. *Communication Disorders Quarterly, 21*, 83; reprinted by permission.) (*Key:* CM, choice making.)

| Request action | | | | Request info | | | Comment | | | | | | | | | CM | | | | Answer | | | | Imitate | | | | | |
game	toilet	near	other	clarification	info	other	happy	sad	bored	funny	fright	pain	angry	tired	other	2 or more	wants	start	other	reacts	yes	no	other	speech	yes	no	shrug	point	other
									■																				
		■		■																									
																■													
							■																						
							■			■																			
				■																									
■																													
							■																						
											■																		

Although observations of students in natural settings and during structured tasks (Cirrin & Rowland, 1985) have provided evidence that students with developmental and physical disabilities may demonstrate a range of communicative functions, a structured verification assessment provides objective evidence on the probability with which a potential communicative act is likely to occur in any given context. This probability estimate (or verification rate) is useful in selecting appropriate intervention pathways.

Verification can be attempted using naturalistic and structured observations. Undertaking both naturalistic and structured observations is often helpful because there are advantages and disadvantages to each (Iacono, Waring, & Chan, 1996). Naturalistic observations are useful in helping to assess whether relevant stimuli that regularly occur in the natural environment (e.g., a broken toy or a missing, but needed object) actually set the occasion for a corresponding communicative act (e.g., request for help to fix the toy or request for the missing object). They can also reveal whether and how partners respond to the individual's communication initiations.

Some communicative functions, however, might not be observed during naturalistic observations because the opportunity for the communicative act might not arise. For example, there would be no chance of observing whether the child's repertoire included a communicative means for requesting help if there was no opportunity or need for the child to request help during the naturalistic observation. Similarly, the individual might in fact have several responses that function as tacts, but these might not be observed if there is nothing for the person to tact or comment on during the naturalistic observation.

Structured observations, therefore, may need to be designed in order to set the occasion for a range of communicative functions. A potential disadvantage of structured observations is the possible lack of ecological validity. That is, the conditions presented during the assessment might not correspond to the conditions present in the natural environment. Structured verification trials, however, can be designed and implemented in ways that are likely to enhance the ecological validity of the assessment process by making use of the examples provided by partners during the IPCA interview. By recreating the conditions described in these examples, the assessment incorporates the very same conditions (setting, materials, antecedents) that reportedly set the occasion for communication in the natural environment. For example, in Figure 2.2, the teacher provided a naturalistic example of how Rita indicated the communicative function of requesting more: "On the trampoline, if she wants 'more,' she will move to the middle of the mat, out of reach of us, or will spin away so that we can't remove her."

As mentioned previously, the aim of the structured verification trials is to create opportunities for communication that reflect the conditions that supposedly set the occasion for communication in the natural environment.

With Rita, for example, verification trials might be designed to assess the probability of Rita moving away and spinning around when given the opportunity to request more time on the trampoline. Specifically, a verification trial for this potential communicative act might consist of placing Rita on the trampoline and letting her bounce for 10 seconds. After this time, she would be interrupted from bouncing, and the partner would attempt to help her down from the trampoline. This action by the partner is designed to create the opportunity (or need) for Rita to indicate a request for more. At this point, the partner would look to see if Rita did in fact engage in behavior indication by moving to the middle of the trampoline and/or spinning away. If so, this action would provide some verification that Rita uses these behaviors to indicate a request for more.

As the example for Rita illustrates, structured verification trials can be individualized and based on the examples provided by the prior IPCA interview. Although the precise nature of the structured trials will be individualized, there are a number of basic principles to the verification procedure that apply across individuals and contexts.

Initially, the IPCA (see Figure 2.2) is reviewed to select examples for verification. Beginning with 3–4 examples that can be easily replicated in a structured assessment session is often helpful. Of course, a more comprehensive picture of the individual's communication repertoire will result if these 3–4 examples are selected from different sections of the IPCA in order to sample different communicative functions (e.g., attention-to-self, request an action, request an object, social convention).

For each example, it will be necessary to configure assessment trials and sessions that fit the example. This also demands an individualized approach. If the example focused on requesting a preferred food item, then it would make sense to conduct assessment trials during mealtimes, when the individual is likely to be hungry and hence motivated to request access to preferred foods. Although verification assessments will need to be individualized, many examples will lend themselves to a generic configuration that has been described by Sigafoos and his colleagues (e.g., Keen, Woodyatt, & Sigafoos, 2002; Tait, Sigafoos, Woodyatt, O'Reilly, & Lancioni, 2004).

A useful generic approach to configuring assessment involves the implementation of a series of 10-minute observation sessions. Usually, one session is conducted for each example. During the session, 10 discrete verification trials are implemented at approximately 1 trial per minute because each trial requires about 30–60 seconds to complete. These discrete verification trials are embedded into the natural flow of the activity that is referenced in the example.

To illustrate with Rita and the trampoline, 10 interruptions might be scheduled during the time when Rita would ordinarily be using the trampoline. A trial begins when she is interrupted, the partner waits 30 seconds for behavior indication from Rita, and then Rita is allowed to continue to bounce until the next interruption, which will occur 30–60 seconds later. The assessment session would continue until 10 such trials have been completed.

As Rita's trampoline example illustrates, a verification trial involves creating an opportunity for communication and then observing the individual's behavior for up to 30 seconds. During this 30-second interval, the partner watches the person and records what, if anything, the person does in response to the opportunity. Specifically, the partner looks to see if the person will engage in the corresponding potential communicative act identified during the IPCA interview. After 10 trials, the data are analyzed to determine the communicative potential of the act.

Consider the data presented in Figure 2.4, which shows the number of trials with occurrence of the potential communicative act. These data come from a verification assessment conducted with Jason, a 16-year-old boy with autism and severe communication impairments. The assessment was conducted to verify whether he would indicate a request for a preferred food item by reaching for that item. From the BIAS questionnaire, "reaches/touches/grabs" was identified as a potential communicative act for requesting access to preferred items (see Item III in Appendix B).

To verify this information from the BIAS, a 10-minute session was conducted during Jason's regular afternoon snack time. During the session, 10 verification trials were conducted. For each trial, preferred food items were placed on a tray. The tray was then placed in view but out of Jason's reach. To initiate each trial, the partner pointed to the tray and asked, "Let me know if you want something." After this, the partner waited 10 seconds to see if Jason would reach for an item. As the data in Figure 2.4 show, Jason did in fact reach during 9 of the 10 opportunities, which translates into a 90% verification rate.

These results support the hypothesis that reaching was a form of behavior indication for Jason. In this context, reaching could be interpreted as a communicative form that Jason used for requesting objects. The assessment process also revealed that the presence of preferred food items, which were visible but out of reach, was sufficient to evoke behavior indication from Jason. Information concerning the antecedent conditions that reliably evoke communication from the individual is helpful in deciding the type of procedure to use during intervention (see Chapter 4).

Given his consistency in reaching, an appropriate intervention pathway for Jason might be to shape the reach into a more symbolic and indirect form of requesting. Specifically, Jason might be taught to reach for and touch a graphic symbol corresponding to the item he wants. Chapter 3 explores this and other intervention pathways in more detail.

No hard and fast rules exist for interpreting the results of a verification assessment. Interpretation of the assessment data requires a considerable

Name: Jason _____ Date of assessment: March 12, 2004

Context: 10-minute session during afternoon snack time _____

Potential communicative act: Reaching for item _____

Directions:

Sit at the kitchen table with Jason. Place 3–4 preferred snack items on a tray. Make sure the tray is visible to Jason but out of his reach. Point to the tray and say, "*Let me know if you want something.*" At this point, wait 10 seconds. During this 10 seconds, record whether Jason reached toward the tray. At the end of 10 seconds, move the tray within reach and allow Jason to select one item from the tray. After he has made a selection and consumed the item, repeat the procedure until 10 trials have been conducted. Record a *yes* if Jason reached during the 10 seconds and a *no* if he did not reach during the 10-second interval.

Trial	Did Jason reach for an item within 10 seconds?		Describe any other behaviors that were observed
1	(YES)	NO	*After reaching, he then tapped his index finger on the table.*
2	YES	(NO)	*He pointed and vocalized but did not reach.*
3	(YES)	NO	
4	(YES)	NO	
5	(YES)	NO	
6	(YES)	NO	
7	(YES)	NO	*Jason first pointed to the tray and then reached for it. He also vocalized when reaching.*
8	(YES)	NO	
9	(YES)	NO	
10	(YES)	NO	

Figure 2.4. Sample data sheet showing results of the verification assessment for Jason.

amount of clinical judgment. With Jason (see Figure 2.4), the trend was clear, and the data were relatively easy to interpret. Because Jason consistently reached under conditions that were specifically designed to evoke requesting behavior, it seemed relatively safe to conclude that reaching was a form of behavior indication for requesting access to preferred objects.

The data obtained from a verification assessment are not always as clear as those obtained with Jason. Consider the results shown in Figure 2.5, which come from a study published by Keen et al. (2002). These data are a

---

Name: Rue_____ Date of assessment: May 3, 2005_____

Context: Classroom_____

Potential communicative act: Stopping and looking at the teacher_____

Directions:

Stand about 10 feet from Rue, and call his name. Make sure that he is not already looking at you when you call his name. After calling his name, wait 10 seconds to see if he looks at you. After 10 seconds, approach and interact with him.

Trial	Did Rue stop and look at the teacher?	Describe any other behaviors that were observed
1	YES (NO)	
2	YES (NO)	
3	(YES) NO	
4	YES (NO)	
5	(YES) NO	
6	(YES) NO	
7	YES (NO)	He stopped moving about but did not look.
8	YES (NO)	
9	(YES) NO	
10	(YES) NO	

Figure 2.5. Sample data sheet showing results of the verification assessment for Rue.

composite summary of more extensive results obtained during a verification assessment conducted with a young boy named Rue. Rue was 4 years, 11 months old. He had autism and was nonverbal. His teacher conducted the assessment in the classroom to verify whether Rue would respond to his name being called. From the IPCA interview, Rue was said to respond to such social greetings by stopping and looking at the teacher. This behavior pattern was thus considered a potential communicative act related to the Social Convention section of the IPCA (see Appendix A).

To verify this information from the IPCA, 10 opportunities for Rue to respond were presented. For each opportunity, the teacher called Rue's name and then waited 10 seconds for a response. During this 10-second interval, an observer recorded what Rue did, looking specifically to see whether Rue would "stop and look at the teacher."

As the data in Figure 2.5 show, Rue responded with the potential communicative act of stopping and looking during 5 of the 10 opportunities, which translates into a 50% verification rate. These results provide only partial verification. In this case, stopping and looking may or may not represent communicative acts related to social convention. In either case, the behaviors of stopping and looking occurred inconsistently when a relevant antecedent (i.e., someone calling Rue's name) was presented. Unlike data for Jason, Rue's data point to a different intervention pathway, one in which greater consistency in responding might be the initial goal.

As mentioned previously, the verification process is consistent with the logic of functional analysis (see Chapter 5). That is, verification assessment seeks to document—through direct and structured observations—whether the potential communicative act occurred under conditions indicative of a specific communicative function, such as requesting (mands) or commenting (tacts). In line with a behavioral-functional account of communication (Skinner, 1957), it is unlikely that this assessment goal would be reached by focusing on the individual's diagnostic label (e.g., autism, cerebral palsy) or by focusing on the form of the presumed communicative behavior (e.g., vocalizing, reaching, looking). Instead, the verification assessment seeks to identify the probability with which potential communicative acts are evoked by conditions that should set the occasion for communication. This information is used to make hypotheses related to the communicative function, if any, of the potential communicative act.

Varying results are likely to be obtained when verification assessments have been completed on 3–4 potential communicative acts. Table 2.2 presents a range of probable outcomes and some plausible interpretations and hypotheses associated with different verification rates.

Results of the verification assessment—and the subsequent interpretations and hypotheses regarding communicative potential and function—are used in planning the overall communication intervention program for the

Table 2.2.   Interpretations associated with different verification results

	Verification rate		
	0%–30%	40%–60%	70%–100%
Interpretation	The act occurs too inconsistently to be interpreted as communicative, although it may have some communicative potential.	This result provides partial verification. The act may or may not be a form of communication, but it has strong potential for communication.	The act is verified and can be interpreted as serving a specific communicative function for the individual.

individual. Specifically, these data are used in choosing appropriate intervention pathways (see Chapter 3). Once appropriate intervention pathways have been chosen, partners will need to select specific communication skills to target for instruction. These specific skills are then taught using the procedures described in Chapter 4. Examples of specific communication skills that might be targeted for instruction include 1) using the manual sign HELP to request assistance in operating a CD-player, 2) pointing to a WANT symbol to request access to preferred objects during mealtimes, and 3) looking at and waving to peers who enter the classroom.

Because individuals with developmental and physical disabilities need to be taught a large number of communication skills, establishing instructional priorities is critical. One way to set instructional priorities is to first target skills that enable the individual to meet the communicative demands of the environments in which he or she is expected to function. This information is gained from a systematic analysis of the communicative demands of the environment.

ANALYZING THE COMMUNICATIVE DEMANDS OF THE ENVIRONMENT

Needed communication skills often become evident when the communicative demands of the environment are analyzed. This analysis can be accomplished by conducting an ecological assessment. An ecological assessment examines activities that occur in typical environments and seeks to isolate the specific communication skills that will be needed if the person is to function effectively across those various environments and activities.

Another way of thinking about an ecological assessment is that it considers the context of communication. Context refers to all aspects of the environment, or the situations in which the student interacts, including personnel, setting, activity, time, and place. If priorities reflect skills in context, then it is more likely that selected goals will be functional for the person. Where attention is given only to assessing specific skills out of the context of daily activities, then partners run the risk of teaching skills that will not be functional. This, in turn, could limit spontaneous and generalized use of communication skills.

An ecological assessment or inventory (Brown et al., 1979) involves a number of steps as shown in Figure 2.6. The first step is to organize the assessment around the 1) domestic, 2) vocational or educational, 3) recreation–leisure, and 4) community living domains. In Steps 2 and 3, partners list the environments and subenvironments associated with each domain.

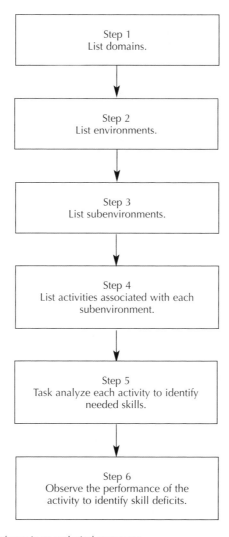

Figure 2.6. Outline of steps in an ecological assessment.

The domestic domain, for example, is typically associated with the home environment, which includes various subenvironments (e.g., living room, bedroom, bathroom, kitchen). Each of these subenvironments is associated with specific activities. Participating in these activities will require the person to acquire the corresponding skills, including relevant communication skills.

After activities are delineated in Step 4, the task is analyzed into its component steps (Duker et al., 2004). This task analysis (Step 5) will identify the specific responses and sequence of responses that are required in order for the person to complete the activity. In many cases, this analysis will highlight necessary communication skills. Once the task is analyzed, the person is presented with opportunities to perform the activity. The partner observes the individual's performance of the task to determine how many steps the person already completes independently (Step 6). It is best to repeat this baseline observation (Step 6) at least three times to obtain an adequate sample of the person's ability with respect to the activity. The skills of the task that the person does not currently perform, including any associated communication skills, can then be targeted for instruction.

Table 2.3 shows an ecological inventory for a local café environment. As shown in Table 2.3, numerous skills are required to successfully enter,

Table 2.3.   Ecological assessment of a café environment.

Subenvironments	Activities	Skills required
Front door area/entry	Enter the café, and walk to the counter.	Open the door. Enter the café. Locate and move to the counter.
Counter ordering area	Place your order.	Scan the menu. Decide what to order. Wait for the counterperson to appear and ask you for your order. Tell the counterperson what you want.* Pay for the order. Take your change.
Order pick-up area	Retrieve your order.	Move to the order pick-up area, and wait for the items. Take the correct items when they appear, and move to the condiment area.
Condiment area	Add honey or sugar, and fix the lid.	Add honey or sugar to your coffee. Stir the coffee. Place a lid on your coffee cup, and move to a table.
Table area	Drink your coffee, and socialize.	Find an unoccupied table. Drink your coffee. Converse with your partner.*
Restroom	Perform self-care.	Enter the restroom. Use the toilet. Wash and dry your hands.
Front door area/exit	Leave café.	Place your cup in the trash. Exit the café.

*Communication skills.

order, and enjoy coffee in a café. Some of the required skills involve the need for communicative forms that will be readily understood by typical members of the community. Results of an assessment with Robert, a 24-year-old man with severe intellectual disabilities, showed that although he had some informal ways of indicating when he wanted something to drink, these forms (e.g., reaching, leading) were neither effective nor appropriate for ordering coffee in a café. To promote greater participation and independence in this environment, priority goals for Robert might include teaching him more effective forms of communication for use in such environments.

Specifically, Robert would benefit from learning to order his preferred beverage using a VOCA. Additional procedures could be implemented to teach Robert to initiate conversational exchanges by selecting other line drawings on his VOCA. For example, Robert might be taught a few all-purpose tacts to evoke a reply from his partner (e.g., "Looks like rain." "Is that a new shirt?"). He would then need appropriate intraverbal responses (i.e., responses that are thematically related to the partner's prior speech) to keep the conversation flowing.

ASSESSING BEHAVIORAL STATE

When analyzing the communicative demands of the environment, it can be helpful to also gather information about the individual's levels of alertness or behavioral state. It may also help to know what, if any, contextual factors might be influencing the person's behavioral states or levels of alertness. There is some evidence that a person's behavioral state influences the extent to which the person will be responsive to social interaction and communication intervention (Woodyatt, Marinac, Darnell, Sigafoos, & Halle, 2004). Information of this type can often be gained by conducting a behavioral state assessment as described in numerous studies (Arthur, 2003; Ault et al., 1995; Guess et al., 1995).

A behavioral state assessment seeks information about levels of alertness and the person's involvement or engagement with communication partners and the environment. The data-gathering process involved in behavioral state assessment may be helpful when the goal is to analyze the extent to which the person attempts to communicate and is responsive to communication initiations by others. As noted in Chapter 1, individuals with developmental and physical disabilities often engage in subtle, informal, and idiosyncratic behaviors that could represent attempts to communicate. By observing and coding the person's behavioral state (e.g., awake-active, drowsy, crying), partners may be able to enhance their intervention efforts. For example, this type of information may indicate that during certain activities the individual's typical behavioral state (e.g., drowsy) is less than conducive to instruction. Hence, part of the intervention plan might be to manipulate certain variables (e.g., time of day, pace of instruction) in an effort to increase the person's level of alertness and, therefore, increase the person's responsiveness to instruction.

Observing and coding behavioral states can be difficult (Woodyatt et al., 2004). One approach that might be more practical for partners to use in applied settings is shown in Table 2.4. Included in Table 2.4 are sample data from an observation of Sophie, a 6-year-old girl with developmental and physical disabilities. Sophie's observed behavioral states, communicative interactions, and communication partners were sampled for 15 minutes per day for several days. The data in Table 2.4 come from one of those 15-minute sessions.

Inspection of Table 2.4 reveals several important patterns. First, Sophie was observed to be more alert and engaged during times when communicative events involving her were occurring. This was true whether the communicative interaction included peers or the teacher. Second, as Sophie shifted into states of drowsiness, communication opportunities diminished. These data suggest that the provision of social interaction may be one way to increase the amount of time that Sophie is alert. Instruction to develop her communicative potential could then be incorporated into these episodes of social interaction. During these times, Sophie is most likely to be alert and perhaps more responsive to instruction.

Table 2.4.   Data from an observation of Sophie, a 6-year-old with developmental and physical disabilities

Interval	Behavioral state	Interaction	Partner
1	AWAA	CI	P
2	AWAA	CI	P
3	AWAA	CI	P
4	AWIA	PC	P
5	DR	PC	P
6	DR	NC	NP
7	DR	NC	NP
8	DA	PC	T
9	DA	PC	T
10	AWIA	CI	T
11	AWIA	CI	T
12	AWAA	CI	P
13	AWAA	CI	P
14	CR	CI	T
15	CR	CI	T

Key: AWAA, awake–active–alert; AWIA, awake–inactive–alert; CI, communicative interaction; CR, crying; DA, daze; DR, drowsy; NC, no communication; NP, no partner; P, peer; PC, partner communicative cue: no student response; T, teacher.

ASSESSING PARTNER SKILLS

Partners obviously play an integral role in facilitating communicative inter-action with individuals who have developmental and physical disabilities. Assessing partner skills and making use of these assessment data in planning interventions is, therefore, important. Knowledge of partner skills will assist in selecting the types of procedures that might be necessary to enhance the individual's communication skills and increase the individual's involvement in social interaction across a range of partners. Specifically, determining whether partners are responsive to the potential communicative acts of indi-viduals with developmental and physical disabilities is useful. Some of the questions an assessment of partner skills might seek to answer include:

1. Do partners acknowledge the person's prelinguistic behaviors?

2. Do partners interpret these behaviors as communicative?

3. Do partners respond to the potential communicative act in ways that correspond to the presumed function or purpose of the act?

Responsivity can be considered greater when these questions can be answered in the affirmative. Without this level of responsivity, communica-tion breakdowns may occur, and the individual's communication develop-ment may be hindered (Wilcox, Kouri, & Caswell, 1990). Table 2.5 lists some additional partner skills that are useful to consider during assessment. Assessment data related to the skills listed in Table 2.5 can only be obtained

Table 2.5. Assessment of partner skills

Partner skill	Description
Creates opportunities	The partner provides numerous structured opportunities by creating a need for the individual to use communication (see Table 1.3).
Waits for a response	After creating the need, the partner waits at least 10 sec-onds to allow the individual sufficient time to respond.
Gives an expectant look	The partner looks expectantly at the individual while wait-ing for a communication response.
Acknowledges potential communicative acts	When the individual engages in a potential communicative act, the partner acknowledges that the act has been observed (e.g., "Oh, I see you are reaching for the toy.").
Prompts transition to symbolic forms	The partner prompts alternative forms of communication when a behavior indication is observed (e.g., as the child reaches for the toy, the partner prompts the child to sign WANT).
Delivers reinforcement	The partner provides immediate consequences that match the function of the individual's communicative act (e.g., after the child prompts the manual sign WANT, the partner gives the child the requested toy).

by direct observation of the partner as he or she interacts with the individual across a range of typical activities. As a general guideline, at least 60 minutes of observations consisting of 10-minute sessions across at least six different time periods and activities should be completed. During the observations, data are recorded about such things as the number of opportunities created, whether and how long the partner waited for a response from the individual, and whether and how the partner responded to potential communicative acts produced by the individual.

Useful information can be obtained by watching how the partner interacts with the individual. This information can be used in at least two ways. First, if the results of the observation suggest that partners are not very responsive to the individual, then it may be necessary to teach partners how to be more responsive. Second, this information might also help one decide which intervention procedures might best match the partner's interactive style.

SUMMARY AND CONCLUSIONS

The assessment tactics described in this chapter provide a significant amount of information from which to build a profile of the individual's communication repertoire. Once obtained, this information must be interpreted and reviewed in light of the communicative demands of typical environments. Doing so will hopefully point to appropriate intervention pathways as well as to priority communication goals to target for instruction within the selected pathways. The next chapter (Chapter 3) describes three intervention pathways that can be pursued depending on the communicative potential of responses within the individual's repertoire. Of course, considering behavioral state and partner skills as part of the assessment process is important. This information can assist in selecting appropriate intervention procedures.

Although assessment is an ongoing process, the data generated from an initial interview with partners—and from analyses of the environment, behavioral state, and partner skills—provide the foundation from which to begin the intervention process. The first step of the intervention process, as explored in Chapter 3, is to select appropriate intervention pathways.

3

Intervention Pathways

JEFF SIGAFOOS, VANESSA A. GREEN,
NANCY BUTTERFIELD, AND MICHAEL ARTHUR-KELLY

INTRODUCTION

This chapter describes intervention pathways for developing an individual's communicative potential. Recall from Chapters 1 and 2 that the overall aim of intervention is to develop symbolic forms of communication. The intervention track or pathway, therefore, should seek to teach communication skills that the person will need to participate across a range of environments, activities, and partners.

We use the term *pathway* in a metaphorical sense. It captures the essence of the main goal of intervention, which is to help move the individual from less to more symbolic stages of communication. An intervention pathway can be thought of as the process of teaching the individual more symbolic forms of communication. Pathways can be conceptualized in terms of a developmental progression, which is intended to facilitate the transition from beginning (perlocutionary, illocutionary) to more advanced (locutionary) stages of communication.

For individuals with developmental and physical disabilities, systematic instruction within a carefully organized intervention pathway is often necessary to promote the transition from beginning to more advanced stages of communication. This progression is unlikely to occur incidentally but rather requires a carefully designed intervention plan that makes use of empirically validated instructional procedures. Pathways can also be viewed as one way of organizing the intervention plan. Acquisition of appropriate and symbolic communication is more likely when partners incorporate empirically validated instructional procedures into an intervention pathway that considers

1) the communicative potential of existing behaviors, 2) the context in which communication is expected to occur, and 3) partner expectations and skills.

This chapter describes three intervention pathways: 1) the Interpretive Pathway, 2) the Enhancement Pathway, and 3) the Replacement Pathway. Figure 3.1 shows the route taken in each pathway and the connections among the three pathways. Although Figure 3.1 shows that these three pathways are connected at some points and that each leads to the same end goal of symbolic communication, the three pathways have distinct starting or entry points.

The appropriate starting or entry point depends on results from assessments described in Chapter 2, particularly results from the verification trials. Different entry points are indicated for prelinguistic behaviors with varying communicative potential, which is, in turn, based on results of the prior verification assessment. Behaviors with more communicative potential enter pathways (i.e., the Enhancement or Replacement Pathway) that begin closer to the end goal. Behaviors interpreted as having less communicative potential require a different starting point for intervention and, therefore, enter earlier pathways (i.e., the Interpretive or Enhancement Pathway). Because individuals are likely to present with a range of prelinguistic acts, each assessed with varying communicative potential, it is typically the case that the

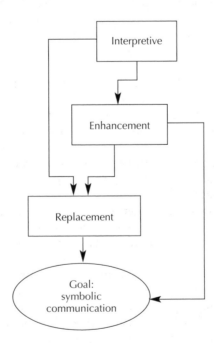

Figure 3.1.　Diagram showing the relationship among the three intervention pathways.

individual will be concurrently exposed to more than one intervention pathway. That is, because each individual is likely to have behaviors representing different stages of communication development, it is likely that each individual could benefit from multiple intervention pathways.

INTERPRETIVE PATHWAY

The Interpretive Pathway is so named because it emphasizes consistent interpretation of existing behaviors as forms of communication. To illustrate, consider a situation in which partners report that a specific response (e.g., looking at an item) is the individual's way of requesting that item. In this scenario, the Interpretive Pathway would emphasize the need for all partners to interpret and respond to each and every instance of that act as if it were in fact a request. The act may then begin to occur more consistently and thereby become a more effective form of communication for the individual.

Recall from Chapter 2 that some behaviors identified as communicative by partners might not be verified as such. These are acts with verification rates in the 0%–30% range. Although such acts might represent the perlocutionary or illocutionary stage of communication development, this inconsistency limits their potential to serve as effective forms of communication for the individual. Thus, the aim of the Interpretive Pathway is to seek greater consistency in the use of potential communicative acts. The pathway is designed for acts that were identified as communicative by partners but were inconsistently observed during the verification assessment. These acts may have some communicative potential if they can be made to occur more consistently.

Associated with this aim are two more specific objectives. The first is to increase the overall frequency of a potential communicative act. The second is to bring the act under stimulus control. That is, the intent of the Interpretive Pathway is to not only make the behavior more likely to occur or more consistent but also to make it more likely to occur under the right conditions. The right conditions are simply those during which a particular communicative function would be appropriate or expected to occur. Mealtime, for example, is one condition during which requests for food and drink are appropriate and often expected to occur. Similarly, a difficult work task is one condition under which requests for assistance might be both appropriate and necessary.

To achieve these specific objectives, consider possible reasons for inconsistency in the first place. First, inconsistency may suggest that the behavior is not in fact a form of communication. For example, a young girl with Rett syndrome might "stop and look" when her name is called, but this reaction could reflect a mere startle or orienting response.

When partners consistently respond to the behavior in a communicatively relevant manner, then the behavior should, over time, acquire a social-communicative function. Specifically, if every time the child stopped and looked she received a positive response from a partner, then eventually a new communicative function might be established for what was originally a noncommunicative act. What was once a reflex or startle response may become a type of greeting or the child's way of recruiting social interaction. As noted in Chapter 1, ensuring consistent partner responses to the individual's existing prelinguistic acts is crucial in shaping these acts into intentional forms of communication (Warren & Yoder, 1998).

Second, inconsistency in a response may reflect lack of motivation. For example, if the behavior is a mand or request, then it may only occur when the relevant motivational conditions are present. It might, thus, be the level of motivation that is inconsistent, rather than the behavior. This scenario would indicate the need for partners to enhance motivation by arranging the environment to create the need for communication (see Table 1.3) and by providing opportunities for communication at times when it is clear that the motivation to communicate is strong. Within the Interpretive Pathway, partners would wait for signs of possible behavior indication, consistently interpret these as an indication of motivation, and respond accordingly.

For example, when a child moves toward an activity, partners may agree to consistently interpret this as an indication that the child wants to participate. Partners would then acknowledge ("Oh, I bet you want a turn.") and enable the child to participate in the activity. If the child approaches more often, then one may conclude that the partners' response was reinforcing. Over time, the act of approaching others might come to be used by the child as a communication request for indicating "I want a turn."

Third, inconsistency may result when opportunities to communicate arise at times when the individual is in a behavioral state (e.g., drowsy, seizure) that is less than conducive for responding to such opportunities. A failure to obtain responses during certain behavioral states should not be taken as an indication that the individual lacks responses with communicative potential. Nor do such observations necessarily indicate that the individual lacks any motivation to communicate. Instead, partners should be aware that the prevailing behavioral state almost certainly influences the probability of obtaining a response—communicative or otherwise—from the individual.

Partners should aim to create opportunities for communication when the individual is in a behavioral state associated with greater responsiveness (e.g., awake, alert). It might, however, also be the case that by interacting with the person—by creating an opportunity for communication—partners may in fact be able to shift the person into a behavioral state that is more conducive to instruction. For example, a drowsy person may become more alert when partners initiate social interaction.

Finally, inconsistency may be related to stage of development. Emerging behaviors may occur more inconsistently than well-established acts. The

Interpretive Pathway is well suited to situations involving emerging communicative potential, but it may also be an appropriate entry point when the observed inconsistency stems from some of the other reasons mentioned previously. When inconsistency arises because the behavior is newly emerging, the Interpretive Pathway emphasizes the need for partners to respond consistently to the emerging acts in order to strengthen the acts and facilitate the transition from the perlocutionary stage to more obvious representatives of the illocutionary stage of communication development.

Basic principles of developmental and operant psychology underlie the Interpretive Pathway. From the developmental perspective, the basic principles relate to partner overinterpretation and responsivity. Many early prelinguistic behaviors (e.g., vocalizations, body movements, facial expressions) are viewed as having communicative potential. For that potential to be realized, however, partners must interpret the acts as if they did indeed have a specific communicative function (e.g., request an object, request assistance). In addition to providing a consistent interpretation, partners must respond to the acts in ways that are appropriate to the interpretation. For example, an act interpreted as a request for an object would require the partner to respond by providing the requested object.

From operant psychology, the basic principle associated with the Interpretive Pathway is *contingent reinforcement*. That is, if partners respond consistently to the act and the act becomes more frequent and consistent, then one can conclude that the partners' responses did in fact function as reinforcement. If the act did not increase even when partners were consistent in their responses to it, then the partners' responses did not function as reinforcement.

The function of the individual's behavior may have been misinterpreted. For example, suppose partners suspect that a child's act of looking intently at an object is his or her way of indicating that he or she wants that object. Partners, therefore, decide to respond to this behavior by giving the child whatever it is that he or she happens to be looking at. If the receipt of objects looked at is at least occasionally reinforcing, then the act of *looking at objects* should increase, at least under certain conditions; however, if *looking at objects* does not increase, then the receipt of the object was not a reinforcer, and the act of looking was most likely not the child's way of indicating his or her desire for objects. Instead, it is possible that the child looked at items for other noncommunicative reasons, such as a visual orienting response.

The Interpretive Pathway is the entry point for behaviors that occur inconsistently during verification trials but are viewed as having some communicative potential. As suggested in Chapter 2, this situation would be indicated by a 30% or less verification rate. An act is considered to have communicative potential when it is within the physical capabilities of the individual and occurs—or can be prompted to occur—during social interactions with partners; however, before entering a potential communicative act into the Interpretive Pathway, the act must meet the additional prerequisite of social acceptability. That is, the form or topography of the act must be appropriate or allowable.

This detail is important because the initial aim of the pathway is to increase the frequency and consistency of the behavior. If the form of the behavior is not socially acceptable, then this aim is obviously contraindicated. Screaming, tantrums, and other problem behaviors—even when they have a clear communicative basis—would not be appropriate for the Interpretive Pathway. Instead, any behavior with communicative potential that is inappropriate and unacceptable would enter the Replacement Pathway described later in this chapter.

When an appropriate act with communicative potential enters the Interpretive Pathway, one or more empirically validated instructional procedures (see Chapter 4) are implemented to increase the frequency and promote more consistent use of the act during relevant communicative interactions with partners. Once a reliable and clinically significant increase has been obtained (see Chapter 6), the act is typically shifted to the Enhancement Pathway, although in some cases the Interpretive Pathway may represent the end point for some acts. That is, intervention may be considered successful when the act has been made to occur more frequently and consistently.

In still other cases, partners may decide to bypass the Enhancement Pathway and direct the next stage of intervention to replacement. The decision to follow with an enhancement or replacement approach depends on several factors, including 1) the form of the behavior that was increased in the Interpretive Pathway, 2) the demands of the environment, and 3) the overall aim of intervention for the individual. These factors are further explored when considering the Enhancement and Replacement Pathways, respectively.

For now, it is important to note that the Interpretive Pathway is the starting point for interventions focused on facilitating the transition from perlocutionary to illocutionary stages of communication development; however, not all individuals and not all acts with communicative potential will need to start at this beginning stage. The summary in Table 3.1 will assist partners in deciding when the Interpretive Pathway would be the appropriate starting point for intervention.

Although the Interpretive Pathway may be an appropriate starting point for some individuals and some potential communicative acts, so far there has been little research to validate this recommendation. The Interpretive Pathway has been derived more from basic theoretical principles than from empirical evidence; however, emerging literature (see Harwood, Warren, & Yoder, 2002, for a review) is starting to provide some support for the potential benefits of this intervention pathway. Specifically, evidence from studies of typically developing children suggests that language development is accel-

Table 3.1. Main features of the Interpretive Pathway

Feature	Summary description
Emphasis	This pathway emphasizes consistent interpretation and partner responses to existing or emerging behaviors as if the behaviors serve specific communicative functions.
Aims/objectives	This pathway aims to make the behavior occur more frequently and consistently under appropriate communicative conditions.
Rationale	When partners provide a consistent interpretation and response, the act may begin to occur more frequently and consistently under appropriate communicative conditions and thereby become a more effective form of communication for the individual.
Basic principles	Consistent partner responses may facilitate the transition from the perlocutionary to the illocutionary stage of communication development. The partner's response may also function as reinforcement for potential communicative acts, thereby increasing their frequency and bringing the acts under stimulus control.
Entry point	This entry point is indicated when the goal is to strengthen existing behaviors that are considered to have some communicative potential but have low verification rates (0%–30%).
Prerequisites	The acts must be socially acceptable in at least some contexts and easily within the physical capabilities of the individual.
Direction	When acts occur consistently under appropriate conditions, they are shifted to either the Enhancement or the Replacement Pathway. This decision will depend on the form of the behavior, environmental demands, and the overall aim of the intervention program.

erated when parents are more responsive to their children's early emerging communicative behaviors (Harwood et al., 2002). The opportunity to be responsive would obviously depend on the frequency with which the individual initiates and whether the acts used can be readily interpreted by partners. As noted in Chapter 2, however, individuals with developmental and physical disabilities may initiate less frequently and rely on informal, subtle, and idiosyncratic acts that may be difficult for partners to interpret (Sigafoos, Woodyatt, Keen, et al., 2000).

Prior to intervention, many individuals with developmental and physical disabilities may have only a limited number of responses in their repertoires that may or may not have much communicative potential. Even when existing acts have some communicative potential, it is often difficult to determine exactly what the individual is attempting to communicate with the act. For example, it may be difficult to determine if the act of wiggling in the presence of an object is an attempt to request, reject, or merely comment on the object.

All of these factors make it more difficult for partners to recognize and interpret attempts by the individual to communicate. The individual, in turn, fails to obtain the types of consistent responses from partners that would help to establish potential acts as more effective forms of communication. Logically, it would seem to make sense to identify potential communicative acts (see Chapter 2), and then ensure that partners learn to recognize and respond to these acts in a consistent manner, which is, of course, the logic underlying the Interpretive Pathway.

When a potential communicative act occurs consistently, it is important to ensure that the response is effective, or can be readily interpreted by a range of partners without the need for special partner training. When the act occurs in a given context, what the person is attempting to communicate should be obvious to partners even if they do not know the individual very well. Any consistently occurring act can be shaped into a more effective communication signal by either enhancing the form of the act or by replacing it with another communicatively equivalent behavior. In the next section, we describe the intervention pathway for enhancing the communicative effectiveness of existing and consistently occurring behaviors.

ENHANCEMENT PATHWAY

The Enhancement Pathway focuses on developing additional forms that can be used in conjunction with existing behaviors. In this way, the pathway seeks to enhance or complement the existing acts to make them more recognizable, and hence more effective, communication signals. To illustrate, consider a situation in which partners report that a specific response (e.g., positive vocalization) is the individual's way of greeting family and friends. In this scenario, the Enhancement Pathway would focus on building an additional behavior to compliment the vocalization. The individual might be taught to wave and vocalize when greeting others. By doing so, the new, combined act may provide a more effective signal to partners, and even partners unfamiliar with the individual would readily understand that the child's act of waving and vocalizing is a type of greeting. As a result, it is more likely that partners will respond consistently to the act, thereby strengthening the act as an effective form of communication for the individual.

In many cases, a verification assessment will provide evidence to support the interpretation of some existing act, such as an undifferentiated vocalization or a particular body movement, as a form of communication for the individual. Although some of these prelinguistic forms may be readily interpreted by partners familiar with the individual, it is also the case that others who are unfamiliar with the person may find the acts difficult, if not impossible, to interpret. Hence, there is often a need to enhance existing acts by pairing them with more conventional and readily interpreted forms. Thus, the aim of the Enhancement Pathway is to make existing acts more effective signals for a range of communication partners by adding a new and more recognizable form to the existing act.

The Enhancement Pathway is designed for acts that were identified as communicative by partners and that occurred fairly consistently during direct structured observations, as evidenced by verification rates of 40% or greater (see Table 2.2). These acts are interpreted as having clear communicative potential. Indeed, acts with high verification rates (e.g., 70%–100%) are assumed to represent the illocutionary stage of communication development and are assumed to serve specific identifiable communicative functions for the individual (e.g., request an object, greeting, reject/protest, comment). Although their communicative potential may be clear, their effectiveness as communication signals may be limited to a small number of partners who are familiar with the individual. The individual's ability to communicate with a range of partners is likely to be enhanced if the act can be expanded so that it becomes easier for all partners to interpret.

The basic principles of the Enhancement Pathway are related to the concepts of behavior indication, reinforcement, and response synthesis. Specifically, if the existing acts entering the Enhancement Pathway are in fact well-established forms of communication, then as Drasgow et al. (1999) noted, their occurrence should indicate that the individual is motivated to communicate. For example, if the act of vocalizing when a partner appears is correctly interpreted as a social greeting, then its occurrence indicates that the individual is motivated to greet the partner. The individual would likely be reinforced by a reciprocal response from the partner.

Because the individual is motivated, intervention can focus on prompting an additional response, such as a wave, at that moment. Once the new response is prompted, the partner would respond accordingly, thereby reinforcing the combined act of vocalizing and waving. Over time, given a consistent history of reinforcement for the combined acts, the two once-separate responses might emerge as a single response unit. This end result of the two acts fusing into a single, albeit multicomponent, response unit could be viewed as a type of response integration or synthesis.

To maintain this synthesis, it will be important for partners to insist that both responses must occur together before they respond. That is, they should respond to the act only when both components occur in close temporal order. Initially, this may require the need to prompt the new response as soon as the individual initiates the existing form. Over time, as the prompts are faded, the two forms should begin to occur closely together in time and independently.

Other interesting combinations and temporal orderings of the two responses might be observed. For example, it is possible that the new form may come to occur by itself. This is not necessarily a problem because the new form by itself should provide an effective communication signal. More problematic are situations where the old form occurs without the new form or the new form occur long after the old form. These problems might occur if partners reinforce the old form alone or if they wait too long after the old form occurs before prompting the new form. These potential problems indicate the need for partners to monitor the individual's response patterns to detect and correct any such problems (see Chapter 6).

As mentioned previously, the Enhancement Pathway is the entry point for behaviors that occur fairly consistently during verification trials and are thus viewed as having clear communicative potential. When an appropriate act that occurs consistently and has clear communicative potential enters the Enhancement Pathway, one or more empirically validated instructional procedures (see Chapter 4) may be indicated for combining the old and new forms into a single communicative act. Once the combined responses occur reliably together, it might be appropriate to move to the Replacement Pathway, although in some cases the Enhancement Pathway may represent the end point.

This decision will depend on how effective the new form has been in making the now-combined act an effective signal for partners. If the enhanced act is readily interpreted by a range of partners, then there is no reason why the individual cannot continue to use it; however, if the enhanced act is still less than optimal as a signal for some partners or in some contexts, then it may be necessary to further enhance the act or replace it with a conventional symbolic form. For example, the quality of the act might be further enhanced with speech output.

In addition, the appropriateness of the enhanced act may diminish over time as the individual ages and begins to more independently gain access to additional environments, such as community and work settings. These settings may demand more symbolic and age-appropriate forms of communication, which would indicate the need to enter the Replacement Pathway. Table 3.2 describes essential features of the Enhancement Pathway. This summary is meant to help partners decide when the Enhancement Pathway would be the appropriate starting point for intervention.

Tait and her colleagues (2004) described an intervention consistent with the logic of the Enhancement Pathway. This description appeared within a larger study on training parents to be more responsive to the potential communicative acts of children with cerebral palsy. Based on an initial IPCA interview, one of the participants (Mary) would reportedly "look at objects" as a means of requesting access to preferred objects. Verification assessments confirmed that the act of looking was consistently observed when Mary was offered a preferred toy. The act was, therefore, interpreted as Mary's way of requesting access to preferred objects; however, it was also decided that this act might be unlikely to evoke a response from partners because it did not include establishing joint attention with the partner (McArthur & Adamson, 1996; Mundy & Willoughby, 1998). Indeed, partners might interpret Mary's act of looking as merely a blank stare indicative of a dazed behavioral state.

Table 3.2. Main features of the Enhancement Pathway

Feature	Summary description
Emphasis	This pathway focuses on developing additional forms that can be used in conjunction with existing behaviors.
Aims/objectives	This pathway aims to create an enhanced or combined act that provides a more effective communication signal to partners.
Rationale	Although some existing acts may be appropriate and have clear communicative potential, they might be readable by only a limited set of familiar partners. Enhancing the act by adding an additional and more recognizable form should make the new combined act easier for unfamiliar partners to interpret.
Basic principles	Three basic principles underlie the Enhancement Pathway: 1) behavior indication, 2) reinforcement, and 3) response synthesis. Occurrence of the existing act indicates that the person is motivated to communicate. At this time, the partner can acknowledge the existing act, prompt the new act, and then reinforce the new enhanced act. This process should lead to response synthesis in which the two once-separate responses fuse into a single and more effective communicative act.
Entry point	This pathway is the entry point for subtle or idiosyncratic behaviors that are socially acceptable and have clear communicative potential. Generally, it is indicated by verification rates higher than 40%.
Prerequisites	The existing act must be socially acceptable and readable by at least some partners. It is helpful if the act can occur simultaneously with the new form that is being added to enhance the act.
Direction	When the new enhanced act occurs consistently under appropriate conditions, the individual may continue to use the act for communication. Alternatively, intervention might shift to the Replacement Pathway to develop forms that are appropriate for the individual's age and current and future environments.

Thus, to enhance the act, Mary was taught to establish joint attention by alternating her gaze from the toy, to the partner, then back again to the toy. During a structured one-to-one playtime, teaching opportunities were created by offering preferred toys. When Mary looked at the toy, she was then prompted to look at the partner and then to look back to the toy. The new enhanced act increased because Mary was consistently given her toy only after she alternated her gaze from the toy, to her partner, then back to the toy.

Sigafoos et al. (2004) described a slightly different application of the logic of enhancement. The study involved two students with developmental disabilities who consistently used behavior indication (e.g., reaching, leading) to gain access to preferred snack foods. The communicative potential of behavior indication was demonstrated during an initial baseline phase during which the partner was highly responsive to the occurrence of behavior indication.

One could envision situations under which partners might not be as responsive to the students' acts of behavior indication. For example, if the partner was distracted, then any such acts might go unnoticed. A communication breakdown would ensue. It would, therefore, make sense to teach individuals how to repair communication breakdowns by engaging in an enhanced communication response.

The approach used by Sigafoos et al. (2004) was to improve the existing acts of behavior indication by teaching the students to use a VOCA as a communication repair strategy. When behavior indication did not work, the students were taught to repair the communication breakdown by pointing to a WANT symbol on the VOCA. Pressing the WANT symbol generated the recorded message ("I want more."), which was considered a more effective communication signal for a distracted partner. As VOCA use was acquired, the students often emitted both responses (i.e., VOCA and behavior indication) simultaneously, illustrating the enhancement principle. Thus, another way to enhance the individual's existing repertoire of potential communicative acts is to teach enhanced forms that can be used as repair strategies.

In summary, the Enhancement Pathway is intended to make existing forms more effective communication signals for partners by adding a new form to the existing act. In some cases, the existing act may be ineffective because of a communication breakdown. For these situations, enhancement can be achieved by teaching additional communicative acts that would function as effective repair strategies.

REPLACEMENT PATHWAY

The Replacement Pathway is so named because it focuses on replacing existing forms with new and more symbolic forms. New forms are taught that will serve the same communicative function or purpose as the existing forms. Said another way, this pathway seeks to teach functionally equivalent alternatives to existing communicative forms.

To illustrate, consider a situation in which partners reported that a specific response (e.g., wiggling) was the individual's way of indicating when he was finished with an activity. The response is interpreted as meaning "I'm done and want to stop." In this scenario, the Replacement Pathway would focus on building a new behavior to replace wiggling. The new behavior would involve a more symbolic form that would evoke the same interpretation and response from partners. Potential replacement behaviors might include the manual sign FINISHED or pointing to the printed word *finished* on a VOCA to produce the recorded message "I am finished now and would like to stop."

The Replacement Pathway is intended for existing acts that occur consistently and are verified as serving a specific communicative function. Although these features might also indicate entry into the Enhancement Pathway, there are at least two reasons why one might opt to pursue a replacement approach rather than enter the Enhancement Pathway. First, contextual factors may make replacement more desirable than enhancement.

Although wiggling might occur consistently and is easily interpreted by familiar partners, it may be completely ineffective with unfamiliar partners. In addition, the form or topography of the response (i.e., wiggling arms and legs) may be stigmatizing for the individual. In some contexts, such as in the community or as the person ages into adolescence, wiggling might be viewed as immature and serve to identify the person as different or as having a disability. Therefore, as the person gets older and enters environments that include more unfamiliar partners (e.g., community and vocational settings) it often will be far better to replace existing idiosyncratic acts with more symbolic forms rather than to allow these acts to continue, even in an enhanced state.

Second, some acts may be unacceptable even though they occur consistently and are easy for partners to interpret. A person might have a tantrum to request objects. Although the tantrum might be easy to read as a form of communicative requesting, it will still need to be replaced with acceptable forms of requesting. Indeed, many individuals with developmental and physical disabilities appear to acquire problematic forms of communicative behavior (Sigafoos, Arthur, et al., 2003). A major intervention priority is to replace these forms by teaching functionally equivalent alternatives. The best alternatives involve symbolic forms of communication that are not only acceptable and easily interpreted by a range of partners but also serve the same communicative function or purpose for the individual. Because there are several unique issues that bear on the use of communication training to replace problem behaviors, Chapter 5 covers this topic in more detail.

Consider a situation in which a verification assessment provides evidence to support the interpretation of some existing act as a form of communication. At this point, partners will need to decide whether this act should enter the Replacement or the Enhancement Pathway. Partners should ask themselves whether the existing act is socially acceptable and whether it will remain acceptable and effective over time. If the answer is no, then the Replacement Pathway would be indicated.

The basic principles underlying the logic of the Replacement Pathway are related to the concepts of functional equivalence (Carr et al., 1994) and response efficiency (Horner & Day, 1991). Functional equivalence refers to the connection between the existing act and the new, more symbolic form that is selected to replace it. These two behaviors must be functionally equivalent in the sense of having the same communicative function or purpose. For example, if the existing act represented the child's way of gaining access to preferred objects, then the development of a more symbolic requesting response would represent a functionally equivalent alternative. In contrast, if the existing act targeted for replacement was the child's way of avoiding non-preferred objects, then a more symbolic rejecting response would represent a functionally equivalent alternative.

Verification assessments are often sufficient to reveal the function of existing behaviors. When partners obtain high verification rates, it is often possible to accurately infer the function or purpose of the act. For instance, if the individual consistently looks at preferred items when offered, then it would seem reasonable to interpret looking as the person's way of indicating a request. Similarly, if the person consistently wiggles after completing a task, then it may be reasonable to interpret this act as an indication that the person has finished, equivalent to saying, "I'm done and want to stop."

It may be necessary in other cases, however, to undertake a more thorough functional assessment of the act to identify its communicative function or purpose. Function or purpose in this sense refers to the antecedent conditions that set the occasion for the behavior and the consequences that maintain the behavior. When the controlling antecedents and consequences have been isolated, the behavior has been explained and its function identified. Currently, best practice indicates the need to undertake a thorough functional assessment to identify the function of problem behaviors (Sigafoos, Arthur, et al., 2003), but the same procedures could be used with potential communicative acts that are not necessarily problematic. Chapter 5 describes functional assessment methodologies in more detail.

The second basic principle underlying the logic of the Replacement Pathway is the concept of response efficiency. Evidence from basic (Herrnstein, 1970) and applied research (Horner & Day, 1991), suggests that in order to replace an old behavior with a new, functionally equivalent alternative, the new behavior must be made more efficient than the old act. Efficiency in this sense means that the new behavior requires less effort and leads to more consistent and immediate reinforcement than the existing act. In addition to selecting an alternative response that is more efficient, it is also important to reduce the efficiency of the old act.

This means that partners must select a new response form that is within the person's physical abilities and easy for the person to produce. In some cases, meeting this requirement will necessitate consideration of the cognitive demands of the alternative response (Sigafoos & Mirenda, 2002). Pointing to a symbol on a communication board may appear to require little physical effort, but if the board contains 20–30 different symbols, then it may in fact be quite cognitively demanding for the individual, especially at the beginning stages of intervention. In addition, partners must be diligent in responding consistently and immediately to the new behavior. They should acknowledge and reinforce the new form and ignore or extinguish the old form.

When an existing act is targeted for replacement, one or more empirically validated instructional procedures (see Chapters 4 and 5) may be indicated for replacing the old form with a new and more symbolic one. The intervention is considered successful when the new form occurs consistently and when the old form no longer or rarely occurs. Table 3.3 summarizes the essential features of the Replacement Pathway.

Keen et al. (2001) described an intervention consistent with the logic of the Replacement Pathway. The study involved four children with autism. Existing prelinguistic behaviors were identified using the IPCA and verified as serving a clear communicative function using procedures described in Chapter 2. For example, it was verified that some children would consistently use behavior indication (e.g., reaching) to request access to preferred objects. Initially, three existing communicative acts (e.g., reaching to request a preferred object, making a choice, approaching the teacher to request a turn) were selected for each child.

Replacement forms that were considered more recognizable and symbolic were defined to achieve the same communicative functions as these existing acts. For example, instead of reaching to request a turn using an item, one child (Beth) was taught to select a photograph of the desired item. The Replacement Pathway was pursued rather than the Interpretive or Enhancement Pathway because the existing prelinguistic acts were already

Table 3.3. Main features of the Replacement Pathway

Feature	Summary description
Emphasis	This pathway focuses on replacing existing acts with more symbolic and appropriate forms of communication.
Aims/objectives	This pathway aims to teach new forms that will serve the same function or purpose as existing acts and will, therefore, take the place of existing acts and be used instead of the existing acts.
Rationale	Some existing forms that serve a clear communicative function may be inappropriate, unacceptable, or limiting. These acts can be reduced if the person acquires alternative forms that will serve the same communicative function.
Basic principles	The new replacement form must be functionally equivalent to, and more efficient than, the old form.
Entry point	This entry point is indicated when the goal is to replace existing behaviors that have a clear communicative basis with new and more symbolic forms.
Prerequisites	Existing acts must occur consistently and have a clear communicative function but otherwise be considered inappropriate, unacceptable, or limiting. The new replacement behavior must be functionally equivalent and more efficient than the old form.
Direction	Intervention is considered successful and complete when the new replacement form occurs consistently and under appropriate conditions and when the old form does not occur or only rarely occurs.

occurring consistently and the forms of the existing acts were considered less than optimal for effective and acceptable communication, especially as the children got older.

Once in the Replacement Pathway, the teacher created opportunities for teaching the replacement behaviors. Opportunities for Beth to request were created by presenting a preferred snack item out of reach and at the same time placing the photographic symbol in front of her. As Beth reached for the food item, the teacher prompted her to point to the corresponding photograph, then reinforced this response by giving Beth access to the requested snack item. Reaching, therefore, indicated that Beth was motivated to request, but it was no longer reinforced as a requesting response. Instead, the new response of touching the photograph was prompted as Beth began to reach. Prompting involved using the least amount of physical guidance necessary. Once prompted, verbal feedback was provided ("Good! You touched the photograph to ask for a snack."), and the new response was reinforced by giving Beth the requested object.

Similar procedures were used with the other children to replace their existing forms with new and more symbolic replacement forms. With continued intervention the children came to use the new forms independently, and the old existing forms showed a collateral decrease. These trends suggested that the new forms had replaced the old forms, thus leaving the children with more symbolic and effective forms to serve communicative functions that were already in their repertoires.

SUMMARY AND CONCLUSIONS

The three intervention pathways described in this chapter (i.e., Interpretive, Enhancement, and Replacement) are intended to provide some direction to partners in their quest to facilitate the individual's transition to more effective and symbolic communication. Each pathway represents the entry point for acts of differing communicative potential as determined by the assessments described in Chapter 2. The decision to pursue one pathway rather than another also depends on whether existing acts are judged to be socially acceptable and are likely to be effective in the long term across a range of partners and communicative contexts.

Because communicative contexts are likely to change in relation to the environment and as the individual ages, there will often be a need to move an act from one pathway to another over time. In addition, it is important to remember that the act—not the individual—enters a particular pathway. In many cases, the individual will be receiving intervention within each pathway at the same time. Although one act may be targeted for enhancement, other existing and potentially communicative acts might be better suited to the Interpretive Pathway, and still others might be the focus of a replacement-based intervention.

The conceptualization of intervention foci in terms of pathways is novel. As is often the case with anything novel and unique, the ultimate utility of a pathway orientation has yet to be fully determined. The three pathways described in this chapter are derived from empirically validated principles of behavior, and communicative acts are behavioral acts as noted in Chapter 1. In addition, each pathway has a compelling logic, appears promising, and has at least some evidential support from applied intervention studies involving individuals with developmental and physical disabilities. Partners must implement empirically validated procedures to achieve the aim of the pathway and facilitate the transition across pathways toward the ultimate goal of more symbolic, effective, and socially appropriate forms of communication.

4

Instructional Procedures

Jeff Sigafoos, Michael Arthur-Kelly,
and Nancy Butterfield

INTRODUCTION

This chapter aims to facilitate the implementation of an evidence-based approach to communication intervention (Schlosser, 2003). To facilitate partner use of evidence-based practice, this chapter describes a number of empirically validated instructional procedures for strengthening, enhancing, and replacing the potential communicative behaviors of individuals with developmental and physical disabilities. The use of empirically validated procedures—firmly grounded in the basic principles of learning and development and implemented within an appropriate intervention pathway—constitutes an evidence-based approach to communication intervention.

As briefly indicated in Chapter 1, numerous instructional procedures have been developed and shown to be effective for increasing the communicative behaviors of individuals with developmental and physical disabilities (Reichle, Beukelman, & Light, 2002; Schlosser, 2003). This chapter extends that brief discussion by providing a more detailed description of specific instructional procedures that can be used by partners to enhance the communicative functioning of individuals with developmental and physical disabilities. Instead of presenting a large number of strategies, we concentrate on describing a smaller number of instructional procedures and attempt to illustrate the basic principles that underlie each procedure. The content of this chapter is, therefore, selective rather than comprehensive because, ultimately, knowledge of the basic principles is more important than knowing about any specific technique. Furthermore, the selected procedures are those that have been validated through applied intervention research involving children, adolescents, or adults with developmental and physical disabilities.

Each description includes a consideration of the purposes of the procedure, a step-by-step process for implementing the procedure, and an accompanying example to illustrate how partners might use the procedure.

In line with the intervention pathways outlined in Chapter 3, partners must be able to select the procedure that is best suited to the aims of the intervention, whether that goal be to strengthen, enhance, or replace existing and potential communicative acts. We have, therefore, organized procedures in terms of three intervention goals: 1) procedures for *strengthening* potential communicative acts, 2) procedures for *enhancing* communicative acts, and 3) procedures for *replacing* communicative acts. Although this organization corresponds to the Interpretive, Enhancement, and Replacement Pathways described in Chapter 3, it is important to note that there is no one-to-one correspondence between procedures and pathways. Some procedures may be effective within, and appropriate for, more than one pathway. Nonetheless, this organizational framework should enable partners to select intervention procedures that are best suited to the goals of the intervention, which, of course, vary depending on the communicative act and the intervention pathway into which the act is entered.

In addition to selecting procedures that match the goals of the intervention pathway, partners will often need to modify specific procedures to suit the individual and the context in which intervention occurs. As noted in Chapter 1, modifying procedures to suit the individual requires an understanding of the basic principles that underlie the procedures. Thus, our description of each class of procedures includes consideration of the underlying basic principles.

In addition to procedures for strengthening, enhancing, and replacing communicative acts, this chapter also describes empirically validated strategies for promoting maintenance and generalization of communicative behaviors. Consideration is also given to strategies that partners can use to create opportunities for communicative interaction and instruction. Effective use of empirically validated instructional procedures requires partners who are skilled at both implementing the procedure and creating effective opportunities for communication.

PROCEDURES FOR STRENGTHENING POTENTIAL COMMUNICATIVE ACTS

The aim of intervention within the Interpretive Pathway is to strengthen existing behaviors that appear to have some communicative potential. Procedures for achieving this aim derive from a common logic and are grounded in the basic principles of reinforcement and partner responsivity. To strengthen the communicative potential of existing acts, logic would dictate the need for partners to consistently respond to the act as if it had a specific communicative function. Instructional procedures in the class, therefore, focus on getting partners to interpret and respond to existing acts as if these were forms of communication. Consistent interpretation and reinforcing responses from partners may facilitate the transition of an individual's potential communicative acts from the perlocutionary to the illocutionary stage of communication development.

Much has been written on the importance of the transition from perlocutionary to illocutionary stages of communication (Bates et al., 1979; Bates et al., 1975). Supporting individuals with developmental and physical disabilities in making this transition is often difficult (McCathren, 2000). Problems with this transition may inhibit the development of functional symbolic communication. Consequently, it is important to ensure that effective procedures for facilitating this transition are incorporated into the Interpretive Pathway.

Several researchers (e.g., McCathren, 2000; Warren & Yoder, 1998) have described procedures that can be used to strengthen potential communicative acts in individuals who respond inconsistently or at very low rates. The basic principles or approaches that underlie these interventions include 1) following the person's lead (i.e., looking for instances of potential communicative acts), 2) using prompts to ensure the potential communicative act occurs, 3) arranging the environment to create the opportunity and need for the person to communicate, and 4) developing turn-taking routines. These basic principles are often packaged into a general milieu teaching approach (Hancock & Kaiser, 2002; Kaiser, Hancock, & Nietfeld, 2000; Kaiser, Yoder, & Keetz, 1992). Underlying this general approach is the need for teaching partners to be highly responsive to the individual's potential communicative acts (Yoder & Warren, 1998). Empirically validated procedures for strengthening existing acts with the Interpretive Pathway, include 1) contingent responding, 2) referencing, and 3) wait and signal.

Contingent Responding

Contingent responding refers to a procedure in which partners provide consistent feedback to an individual when he or she engages in an act that is judged to have some communicative potential. The logic of this procedure is consistent with that of the Interpretive Pathway in that contingent responses by partners are needed to increase the rate—and hence the communicative potential—of existing behaviors within the individual's repertoire (Cress & Marvin, 2003; Pecyna-Rhyner, Lehr, & Pudlas, 1990). In some cases, partners may be responding contingently to behaviors that are not communicative. For example, the individual may produce a facial expression, body movement, or gesture that does not serve a communicative function, even though the act occurred during a structured interaction with a partner. In this example, the behavior might be interpreted by partners as if it were an illocutionary act when it may in fact be a perlocutionary one. Still, the partner might nonetheless decide to respond as if the act were an intentional form of communication.

The strategy is one of deliberate overinterpretation. Over time, if partners provide a consistent and reinforcing consequence to the individual when the act occurs, the individual may learn that the act is an effective way of engaging and interacting with partners so as to obtain reinforcing consequences from the partner. In this scenario, contingent responding is consistent with the logic of structured overinterpretation (von Tetzchner, 1997) as discussed in Chapter 1. Table 4.1 delineates the steps of the contingent responding procedure.

When using contingent responding, it is important to consider the specific nature of the partner's response to the individual's potential communicative acts (Cress, 2002; McCathren, 2000; Yoder, McCathren, Warren, & Watson, 2001; Yoder & Warren, 1998). A partner might respond to an individual's potential communicative act by following the individual's focus of attention, such as by looking at the object that a child has initiated a gaze toward. This action is known as a *nonlinguistic contingent response*.

Another type of partner response involves verbally commenting on or acknowledging an individual's behavior. For example, when seeing the child

Table 4.1. Implementation steps and example for contingent responding

1. When interacting with an individual, a partner should observe carefully for occurrences of the identified potential communicative acts that are to be strengthened. For example, during an interactive play routine of tickle and hide with a young child, a partner observes for occurrences of body movements, which were previously identified as the child's way of indicating he or she wants more of the activity.

2. When the act is observed, the partner should use the context to decide the most relevant communicative function to assign to the act. For example, the young child's partner may decide that in the play context, the act should be interpreted as indicating a desire for more play.

3. When the act is observed, the partner should verbally acknowledge the occurrence of the act and its presumed function. For example, the young child's partner might say, "Oh, I see you are moving your arms. This means you want more."

4. In addition to verbal acknowledgment, the partner provides a consequence that is relevant to the presumed function of the act. For example, the young child's partner would then reengage the child in the play activity.

look at a toy, the partner might acknowledge this as a request by saying, "Oh, I see you are looking at the toy, and I understand that you want the toy." This type of contingent response from a partner is known as *verbal acknowledgment* or a *linguistic contingent response* (Tait et al., 2004). The idea is that a partner can respond quickly and contingently to an individual's potential communicative act by verbally acknowledging what the individual might be trying to communicate. This process is referred to as *linguistic mapping*.

In some cases, these types of linguistic and nonlinguistic responses may not be sufficient to reinforce, and hence strengthen, an individual's potential communicative act. In addition, the partner must make sure to provide the individual with a reinforcing consequence that matches the presumed communicative intent of the potential communicative act. Immediate reinforcement by the partner is perhaps the most critical step in using contingent responding.

Referencing

Referencing is a procedure that can be used by communication partners to direct an individual's attention to an object and an attending partner (McLean & Snyder-McLean, 1987), or establish joint attention. Mundy and Vaughan (2002) defined *joint attention* as the ability to coordinate or direct a partner's attention to a particular referent as part of a social-communicative interaction. Many individuals with developmental and physical disabilities have impairments in establishing joint attention; therefore, specific instructional procedures to develop joint attention skills are often indicated as part of the overall communication intervention.

Joint attention skills can make existing communicative acts more explicit and, therefore, more effective communication signals for partners. Referencing is, therefore, indicated when it is difficult to determine from context alone just what the individual is attempting to communicate. For example, during an academic activity, a student might begin to wiggle and squirm in his or her wheelchair. Partners observing this action may conclude that the child is attempting to communicate unhappiness about something, but they may be unable to determine exactly what the child is unhappy about. Through referencing, partners attempt to teach the individual to direct potential communicative acts to specific referents. If the child learns to shift his or her gaze from some glue that has spilled on his or her shirt, to the partner, then back to the spilled glue, the partner may be better able to determine that the child is attempting to communicate that he or she is upset because glue has spilled on his or her clothing.

The individual must learn that an effective signal is one in which the object of interest is made known to the partner during the communicative interaction. He or she must develop the ability to direct the partner's attention to the object of interest prior to or while communicating about that object. Table 4.2 delineates the steps of the referencing procedure. A potential byproduct of using referencing is that the individual and partner may develop a flow to their exchanges that includes greater social interaction or communicative turn taking.

Wait and Signal

Through the wait and signal strategy, a partner systematically pauses within the context of a familiar interactive routine and signals expectantly that a communication response is needed from an individual (Harrison, Lombardino, & Stapell, 1987). The underling principle of this procedure is consistent with another strategy known as expectant delay (Kozleski, 1991). With both wait and signal and expectant delay, the partner pauses in order to create the opportunity and need for communication. While waiting, the partner looks expectantly at the individual by arching his or her eyebrows, tilting his or her head, and opening his or her mouth slightly. This expectant look on the part of the partner is assumed to be a critical aspect of the pro-

Table 4.2.   Implementation steps and example for referencing

1. When interacting with an individual, a partner should observe carefully for occurrences of any identified potential communicative acts, even though these acts might not be directed toward the partner or a specific object. For example, at snack time, a child prefers to drink milk rather than juice. The child reaches for the beverages but does not look at a partner or direct the reach precisely to the preferred beverage.

2. The partner attempts to make eye contact with the individual and then verbally acknowledges the act. The individual may need to be prompted to look at the partner. For example, when the child reaches toward the beverages, the partner could establish eye contact and say, "Look at me. Okay, I see you are telling me you want a drink."

3. After looking at the partner, the individual may need to be prompted to look at and reach for the specific item that is desired (e.g., milk) and then look back to the partner. For example, the partner would look at the child again and acknowledge the joint attention. "Yes, I see that you are telling me you want the milk."

4. In addition to verbal acknowledgment, the partner provides a consequence that is relevant to the presumed function of the act but only after the individual has established joint attention. For example, the partner should give the child the milk after the child has shifted his or her gaze back to the partner.

cedure and is intended to provide a clear signal or discriminative stimulus for a communication response on the part of the individual.

By waiting, the partner is attempting to create the opportunity and need for communication. Therefore, partners must wait a sufficient amount of time so that the individual becomes motivated to communicate. Generally, a partner should be prepared to wait at least 5 seconds. In many cases, however, it may be more effective to wait longer. A 10- or 30-second wait may be necessary to build motivation for some learners. In addition, some individuals may need this extra time to initiate and complete a communicative act.

As with referencing, the wait and signal procedure might also be an effective way of developing turn taking within predictable routines, such as play and leisure routines, self-care and daily living routines, and vocational and community access routines. By waiting and indicating that a response is expected, a partner also provides opportunities for an individual to take a turn. Wait and signal may thus be one way to begin to develop natural conversational exchanges between the individual and his or her partners. Table 4.3 outlines the steps of the wait and signal procedure.

PROCEDURES FOR ENHANCING POTENTIAL COMMUNICATIVE ACTS

The aim of intervention within the Enhancement Pathway is to complement existing behaviors with new forms in order to make the new combined communicative act a more effective communication signal. Within this pathway, it is assumed that the existing behaviors are intentional forms of communication that serve clear communicative functions, such as requesting an object, rejecting a nonpreferred activity, or directing a partner's attention to some aspect of the environment. Hence, the Enhancement Pathway is intended for acts that have made the transition from the perlocutionary to the illocutionary stage of communication development but remain less than optimal in terms of representing effective forms of communication.

Existing forms that are entered into the Enhancement Pathway are often informal or idiosyncratic and thus difficult for some partners to interpret. When the topography of the existing forms (e.g., body movements, vocalizations, facial expressions) is difficult for some partners to interpret, one logical solution is to enhance these existing forms by complementing them with additional and more symbolic forms. By complementing existing forms with more conventional forms, the new combined or enhanced act should prove more effective across a range of partners.

Although the logic of the Enhancement Pathway may seem compelling, surprisingly little intervention research has been conducted on enhancing existing forms of prelinguistic behaviors by developing complementary forms. Instead, more effort has been directed at replacing these types of informal or

Table 4.3. Implementation steps and example for wait and signal

1. Wait and signal is best suited to a predictable routine that involves repeating some action, such as eating from a spoon, operating a toy, bouncing on a trampoline, or washing dishes. A partner begins the activity as usual and completes about 3–4 turns with the individual. These activities can be selected from the Inventory of Potential Communicative Acts. The partner should select activities that the individual knows well and will attempt to continue when they stop. For example, the partner may select a wind-up toy and present 3–4 turns with the toy.

2. On the fourth or fifth turn, the partner pauses the activity, looks expectantly at the individual, and waits. During this time, the partner looks for the individual to engage in any potential communicative act that was identified as the person's way of indicating a desire to continue an activity. For example, after the toy has wound down four times, the partner would wait 10 seconds before winding it up again for the fifth turn. While waiting, the partner would look expectantly at the child.

3. When the potential communicative act is observed, the partner verbally acknowledges the response (e.g., "I see you are reaching for the toy. This means you want another turn.").

4. In addition to verbal acknowledgment, the partner provides a consequence that is relevant to the presumed function of the act. For example, the partner should wind up the toy and let it run again.

5. If the individual does not engage in the potential communicative act while the partner is waiting, then the partner should do one of two things. First, the partner may decide to wait longer as a way of increasing the individual's need and motivation to communicate. This action would be taken if the partner has reason to suspect that the response will occur if the wait time is increased. Second, the partner may decide to prompt the potential communicative act when the wait interval expires and then reinforce the prompted response. For example, if the child did not reach for the toy within 30 seconds, the partner may decide to physically assist the child to reach out for the toy using the least amount of physical guidance that is necessary. Although the response is being prompted, the partner would verbally acknowledge and then reinstate play by winding up the toy again.

prelinguistic communicative acts with more conventional and symbolic forms. Although this goal of intervention also is legitimate, to retain existing acts may be useful in some cases, especially if these acts will be effective for the individual with at least some of his or her regular communication partners.

For example, a person may engage in undifferentiated vocalizations to communicate when he or she is unhappy. Some partners may be quick to interpret the meaning of the person's vocalizations and respond to them in ways that function as reinforcement for the individual. The "correct" partner response may be something as simple as removing a nonpreferred stimulus that is irritating the individual. There is no reason why this individual should not be encouraged to use such vocalizations to communicate.

Other partners, however, might find it difficult to interpret the person's vocalizations. For example, a child's mother may be more accustomed to the child's vocalizations than the school's speech-language pathologist. It would be easier for partners to be highly responsive if the individual's vocalizations were complemented with additional and more conventional forms that would make the meaning of the person's communicative act easier to interpret. The individual, in turn, would benefit because his or her partners would be better able to understand what he or she is attempting to communicate and, thus, the person's communicative acts are more likely to lead to reinforcement. Along these lines, procedures based on the more basic operant principles of response chaining and shaping may be indicated.

Response Chaining

Duker et al. (2004) considered the concept of response chaining in teaching individuals with developmental and physical disabilities. A *response chain* is typically defined as an orderly and integrated sequence of responses. To make toast, for example, requires a person to complete a sequence of responses in a predetermined order (e.g., put bread slices in toaster, depress lever to lower bread, remove bread from toaster when finished).

In communicative intervention, the concept of response chaining can be used to enhance existing prelinguistic acts. The focus of response chaining in this context is to teach an individual to produce the existing act and then to produce a second response that consists of a new and more symbolic form that will complement the current response. To make sure that the second response will in fact complement the old form, the old form and the new form should occur simultaneously or very closely together in time. With response chaining, therefore, partners wait for the existing response to occur but withhold reinforcement until the new response occurs.

Initially during intervention, the new form is prompted immediately after a partner observes the existing act. Over time, as the prompt is faded, the individual should learn to produce both forms simultaneously or in rapid succession, rather than only producing the old prelinguistic form in isolation. Table 4.4 shows the steps of this procedure.

Shaping

Shaping, also called the *method of successive approximation,* is an interactive process involving both differential reinforcement and extinction (Skinner, 1953). Specifically, during the shaping process, some preselected variations

Table 4.4. Implementation steps and example for response chaining

1. Response chaining is best suited to a context in which some prelinguistic act (e.g., body movement, vocalization, or facial expression) occurs consistently as a form of communication. For example, the Inventory of Potential Communicative Acts and verification assessments might have revealed that a person consistently greets others by making an undifferentiated vocalization. Partners may, therefore, decide to use the response chaining procedure at times when there will be opportunities to greet others, such as when the person enters the vocational setting or the classroom each morning, and when the person returns home from work or school each evening.

2. Because the selected context is one in which the prelinguistic act is likely to occur, partners should be ready to prompt the new complementary form as soon as the existing act occurs. For example, when the person enters the classroom in the morning and vocalizes, the partner should immediately prompt the person to wave. The prompt might consist of using the least amount of physical guidance necessary to assist the person with waving. Waving, in this example, is meant to serve as a complementary and more symbolic form. It should enhance the effectiveness of the previous existing act of greeting, which consisted only of vocalizing.

3. While prompting the new form, the partner can acknowledge and reinforce the communicative act. For example, while prompting the person to wave, the partner can acknowledge the greeting (e.g., "Hello, John, it is nice to see you today.") and respond in kind by waving back to the person.

4. Over successive opportunities, the prompt is faded by waiting longer before prompting. For example, after prompting the person to wave immediately after a vocalization occurs, the partner should start to wait 3, 5, and then 10 seconds before prompting the wave. This delay will create the opportunity for the person to independently chain the new waving response to the existing vocal greeting.

of the existing act are reinforced while other variations of the existing act are ignored or placed on extinction. Shaping can be applied to various dimensions of the existing potential communicative act, including the form or topography, intensity, and timing or fluency of the act.

With speech, for instance, partners often shape more precise vocalizations by demanding forms that sound more and more like the correct word. In teaching a child to tact or name a ball, for example, partners may initially accept and reinforce any vocalization. Over time, however, partners may only come to accept vocalizations that include the *ba* sound and, still later, only vocalizations that are fully formed (e.g., *ball*).

Although the previous example focused on shaping the topography of the act, in other cases partners may use shaping to increase the intensity of the behavior. Some individuals, for example, might vocalize too softly to be heard. In such case, partners may apply the concept of shaping by reinforcing only louder and louder vocalization until the person is vocalizing with sufficient intensity to be heard by partners. This approach might also be used to shape up more noticeable gestures. For example, a child might wiggle in his or her wheelchair to indicate to partners that he or she would like his or her seating position readjusted. If the wiggling is of too low intensity, however, partners might not notice the act. Shaping might, therefore, be used to select more intense and noticeable acts.

Shaping can also be used to increase fluency by making reinforcement contingent on more fluent performances and extinguishing or withholding responses that do not meet the increasingly stringent fluency criteria. This use of shaping might be critical when a person is supposed to produce a response chain consisting of the old form, then the new form. Unless the old and new form occur at roughly the same time, the existing act is unlikely to be enhanced by the inclusion of a new complementary form.

Therefore, partners may initially reinforce only those chains in which the old and new forms occur within 10 seconds of each other. Next, reinforcement occurs only for those instances in which the old and new forms occur within 5 seconds of each other, and then within 2–3 seconds of each other. In this way, the response chain can be shaped into an integrated unit in which both responses in the chain occur simultaneously or in close temporal sequence.

Shaping might also be applied for the purpose of developing idiosyncratic forms of communication into more conventional responses (Harrison et al., 1987). With shaping, partners assist a person to develop more conventionality in communicative forms. An idiosyncratic greeting gesture, for example, might be shaped into an easily recognized form, such as waving, thereby enabling the person to communicate more effectively with unfamiliar partners. Shaping, therefore, can help develop transitional forms that may be better suited to a range of partners and settings. Table 4.5 shows the implementation steps and provides an example related to the use of shaping to facilitate the transition from idiosyncratic to more conventional forms of communication.

Although shaping is presented here as an enhancement strategy, it may also be indicated when the goal is to replace existing forms with more appropriate forms. Drash, High, and Tudor (1999), for example, described a shaping procedure for replacing inappropriate vocalizations. In this study involving young children with autism, the children's negative vocalizations were shaped into more acceptable vocal mands or requests.

Table 4.5.   Implementation steps and example for shaping

1. Shaping is suited to several situations in which an existing act occurs consistently. The aim is to enhance the topography, intensity, or fluency of the act in order to make it a more effective communication signal. For example, the Inventory of Potential Communicative Acts and verification assessments might have revealed that a child consistently makes a vocal sound (*da*) to request preferred beverages. Although the vocal response is easily interpreted by some familiar partners, it is too idiosyncratic to be effective in inclusive settings with unfamiliar partners. Partners, therefore, may decide to attempt to enhance the act by shaping the response into something that sounds more like the spoken word *drink*.

2. Opportunities are created that reliably evoke the existing act. For example, at snack time, the partner can offer a drink, which should reliably evoke the vocal response *da*. Because the selected context is one in which the prelinguistic act is likely to occur, partners should wait for any variation in the existing form that represents a closer approximation of the final desired form. For example, if the person makes any sound that seems more like the word *drink*, then the partner would reinforce this and extinguish the old form.

3. When a more approximate variation occurs, the partner acknowledges the form and reinforces the communicative act. For example, if the person makes the sound *dra*, the partner would say, "Oh, you want a drink," and also give the person something to drink.

4. Over successive opportunities, the partner would wait for response forms that more closely approximate the final desired form by reinforcing minor variations that represent closer and closer approximations.

PROCEDURES FOR
REPLACING COMMUNICATIVE ACTS

In many cases, the goal of intervention is to replace existing prelinguistic behaviors with more symbolic forms of communication. This goal is consistent with the logic of the Replacement Pathway described in Chapter 3. Instead of reaching or grabbing to request objects, for example, a person might be taught to produce manual signs, select line drawings from a communication board, or use a VOCA to indicate wants and needs. Similarly, instead of making a negative vocalization or tensing one's body to reject, a person might be taught more conventional ways of rejecting, such as using a headshake gesture for no. As a third example, if a person currently engages in some idiosyncratic gesture to initiate social interactions with others, then it would be logical and less limiting to teach the person to use a VOCA to initiate conversations. The person might, for example, have symbols that when touched produce conversation starters (e.g., "Nice weather today." "Did you see the game last night?" "What did you do over the weekend?").

In the long term, the development of a more symbolic system of communication is the goal. Symbolic forms enable the person to communicate more effectively with a range of partners in inclusive environments. In addition, symbolic forms are less stigmatizing than the informal or idiosyncratic forms of communicative behaviors often seen in the repertoires of individuals with developmental and physical disabilities. Furthermore, as individuals mature, the development of symbolic forms to replace existing prelinguistic forms is age appropriate.

Functional communication training (Carr et al., 1994; Durand, 2001; Wacker, Berg, & Harding, 2002) is the principal approach to intervention within the Replacement Pathway. From a developmental perspective, functional communication training is used to facilitate the transition from the illocutionary to the locutionary stage of communication development. The basic operant principles underlying this approach are related to the concepts of functional equivalence and response efficiency.

Functional equivalence in this context refers to teaching symbolic forms that serve the same communicative function as the existing prelinguistic acts. For example, if bouncing up and down and vocalizing is a person's current way of initiating social interactions, then the goal of intervention might be to replace these prelinguistic acts with a symbolic form that can also be used to initiate social interaction. The replacement form might consist of using a gesture (e.g., waving) or operating a VOCA with the recorded message "Hi, I want to talk to you."

Similarly, if a person stands by a door and jumps up and down to indicate the desire to exit, then the goal of intervention might be to replace this prelinguistic act with a symbolic form that can also be used to indicate a desire to leave or exit. The replacement form might consist of using a gesture (e.g., using the manual signs I WANT TO LEAVE) or operating a VOCA with the recorded message "Can I leave now?" It is important for partners to realize that the symbolic form must be functionally equivalent to the existing prelinguistic act.

Response efficiency refers to the relative ease and effectiveness of the replacement behavior that is targeted for instruction in comparison to the existing prelinguistic forms (Horner & Day, 1991). Generally, in order for a new symbolic form to replace an existing prelinguistic form, the symbolic form must be more efficient than the existing form. *Efficient* in this context means that the symbolic form is easy for a person to do and leads to more immediate and consistent reinforcement from partners.

If the new symbolic form is too complicated or requires too much effort, then the person will continue to use the existing prelinguistic form.

Thus, it is best for partners to select symbolic forms that are easily within the person's physical and cognitive capabilities. In addition, when teaching the replacement form, partners should be careful not to reinforce the old form. That is, only the symbolic form is reinforced while the existing prelinguistic form is placed on extinction.

Functional communication training has been used primarily in the treatment of problem behavior. When problem behaviors have a communicative function, the treatment involves replacing the existing problem behavior by teaching more appropriate forms (e.g., use of manual signs, use of a picture communication board) that serve the same communicative functions as a person's existing problem behaviors. For example, Durand (2001) described the use of functional communication training with an 11-year-old boy with autism and severe intellectual disabilities. The boy engaged in frequent self-injury, which appeared to function as a communicative reject or protesting response. Specifically, self-injury occurred when task demands were presented and appeared to be the child's way of escaping from the task.

Durand hypothesized that the child was attempting to escape from the task because it was too difficult. Consequently, the child was taught a communication alternative, which consisted of using a VOCA to request help with the task. As the child learned to request help, self-injury decreased. Because of the importance of functional communication training to the treatment of problem behaviors in individuals with developmental and physical disabilities, Chapter 5 covers this topic in more detail.

Following the logic of the Replacement Pathway, functional communication training has also been used recently to replace potential communicative acts that were not necessarily problematic. In one relevant study, Keen and her colleagues (2001) taught teachers to use functional communication training to replace prelinguistic behaviors in four children with autism. Initially, three existing communicative functions (e.g., requesting, rejecting, social greeting) were selected for each child. Next, the IPCA was used to identify the existing prelinguistic behaviors that the children used to achieve these functions. The third step of the intervention process was to select more symbolic replacement forms that the children could use to achieve these same three communicative functions.

After a baseline phase, the teachers in this study received an in-service training program that included ongoing consultation and feedback. As part of the training, the teachers were taught how to encourage, acknowledge, and react to the replacement forms. As a result of this intervention with the teachers, the children learned the replacement forms, and as they did, the prelinguistic behaviors decreased. These results suggest that the teacher-implemented intervention was effective in replacing prelinguistic behaviors with alternative and more advanced forms of functional communication.

Tait et al. (2004) replicated this intervention approach with young children with cerebral palsy. This intervention was conducted in the home, and the researchers taught the parents how to use functional communication training to replace existing prelinguistic forms. In most cases, when the parents began implementing functional communication training, the replacement forms increased, and existing prelinguistic forms generally decreased.

Wacker et al. (2002) delineated the steps involved in implementing functional communication training. Table 4.6 describes each step and includes an illustrative example. Briefly, an initial verification assessment is conducted to identify the function or purpose of existing behaviors at the illocutionary stage of development. Next, a symbolic form of communicative behavior is identified that serves the same function as the existing illocutionary act. Third, the symbolic replacement behavior is prompted to occur under the same conditions that set the occasion for existing prelinguistic behavior. If the symbolic replacement behavior is prompted and reinforced so that it is more efficient than the prelinguistic form, then acquisition of the symbolic replacement behavior should occur. Of course, it is important to fade the prompts so that the symbolic replacement behavior occurs independently.

INSTRUCTIONAL PROCEDURES FOR PROMOTING MAINTENANCE AND GENERALIZATION

Lack of maintenance and generalization are frequently cited problems in communication intervention programs for individuals with developmental and physical disabilities (Duker et al., 2004). In this context, *maintenance* refers to the continued use of the newly strengthened or enhanced communicative act after the instructional procedure has been withdrawn. For example, after using contingent responding or the wait and signal procedure to increase the consistency of a potential communicative act, partners want that act to maintain at a consistently high level. Similarly, after using response chaining to enhance a given act, it is important that the two responses—which represent the now-combined act—continue to occur consistently together. Within the Replacement Pathway, *maintenance* refers to continued use of the new symbolic form instead of the old prelinguistic form after the intervention procedures (e.g., creating opportunities, response prompting, reinforcement of the symbolic form, extinction of prelinguistic form) associated with functional communication training have been withdrawn.

Maintenance can be thought of as a type of generalization across time. More specific types of generalization are also often sought during communication intervention programs for individuals with developmental and physical disabilities. In this context, generalization refers to the extent to which newly

Table 4.6. Implementation steps and example for functional communication training

1. Functional communication training is used when existing, clearly communicative acts are either inappropriate, stigmatizing, age-inappropriate, or otherwise limiting. The person would, therefore, benefit from learning a more symbolic replacement behavior. For example, the Inventory of Potential Communicative Acts and verification assessments might have revealed that an adolescent consistently wiggles in his wheelchair as a way of indicating when he wants more of a particular activity. Although familiar partners might easily interpret the meaning of the existing response, it is too idiosyncratic to be effective in inclusive settings with unfamiliar partners. In addition, the existing act might need to be replaced because it is not age appropriate and could be stigmatizing. Partners, therefore, may decide to replace the act by teaching the person to use a voice-output communication aid that includes a symbol for requesting MORE (e.g., "I want more.")

2. Opportunities are created that reliably evoke the existing prelinguistic act. For example, during a preferred activity that the individual is clearly enjoying, the partner might temporarily interrupt the activity to create the need and motivation to communicate. Initially, of course, this interruption is likely to set the occasion for the prelinguistic form (e.g., wiggling). The partner must, therefore, be prepared to immediately prompt the new form, before the individual has a chance to use the existing prelinguistic form.

3. As soon as the new form occurs, even if it had to be prompted, the partner should acknowledge and reinforce the new form. For example, if the person presses the correct panel on the VOCA, the partner would say, "Oh, you want more," then reinstate the preferred activity. If the old form occurs, it should be ignored, and the activity should not be reinstated until the new form occurs.

4. Over successive opportunities, the partner would wait longer and longer before prompting the new symbolic form so as to promote independence. In addition, the partner should use the least amount of prompting necessary to ensure that the new symbolic form occurs. In some cases, it may be necessary to prevent the individual from producing the old form or interrupt the old form if it begins to occur.

developed communicative behaviors occur across other relevant partners, settings, and materials that were not specifically present during instruction.

For example, having strengthened a prelinguistic act at school with teachers and peers, the individual should generalize the act to the home setting with parents and siblings. Similarly, having enhanced a particular form of prelinguistic behavior by pairing it with a conventional gesture, the individual should use the gesture to request a range of preferred items and activities. When a prelinguistic form that was used to reject a variety of nonpreferred activities has been replaced with a symbolic form of communication, such as manual signs, it would be useful for the manual signs to generalize to the entire range of nonpreferred activities that previously evoked the prelinguistic form of rejecting.

Although problems with maintenance and generalization are common, there are a number of empirically validated procedures that can be implemented by partners to promote maintenance and generalization. Table 4.7 describes five well-established procedures for promoting maintenance and generalization of newly developed communication skills among individuals with developmental and physical disabilities. These procedures can be used

Table 4.7. Instructional procedures for promoting maintenance and generalization

Strategy	Description
Introduce natural reinforcement contingencies.	Teach responses that will lead to reinforcement in the natural environment. For example, a manual sign may not work for ordering a meal at a restaurant unless the waitperson is familiar with sign language. Instead, teaching the individual to use a voice-output communication aid may be indicated (Rotholz, Berkowitz, & Burberry, 1989).
Train sufficient exemplars.	Make use of a number and variety of stimuli during training. For example, if the individual is being taught to request preferred leisure materials, then training should include several different types of leisure materials.
Use common stimuli.	Use training materials that would also be found across a range of settings. For example, the use of commercially available line drawings that are likely to be found in many settings may be one way to ensure that symbolic (graphic-mode) communication skills are maintained and will generalize across settings.
Use loose training.	Vary the discriminative stimuli and prompts used during training so that the individual does not learn to respond to only one specific type of discriminative stimulus or prompt.
Provide intermittent reinforcement.	After acquisition, shift to a more intermittent schedule of reinforcement. Instead of reinforcing every response, for example, reinforce only every third or fourth response on average. This will make the newly developed response more resistant to extinction in the natural environment, where reinforcement is unlikely for each and every response.

Source: Duker et al. (2004).

during or after the initial instructional phase to strengthen, enhance, or replace potential communication.

CREATING OPPORTUNITIES FOR COMMUNICATION

As mentioned in Chapter 1, an important component of being an effective partner to individuals with developmental and physical disabilities is the need to provide extensive opportunities for communication. Partners must, therefore, learn how to provide opportunities for communication across the range of environments and activities during which communication is expected. Sigafoos (1999) described a number of procedures that partners can use to create the opportunity and need for communication. These opportunities can be created and used as the context for strengthening, enhancing, or replacing communicative acts. In addition, they can be created as a way of maintaining and promoting the generalization of communicative acts that have already been strengthened, enhanced, or replaced.

Table 4.8 describes several empirically validated strategies that partners can use to create opportunities for communication. Research has shown that when partners implement effective opportunities using these types of strategies, individuals with developmental and physical disabilities will often show a significant increase in their communication responses (Downing, 2005; Grunsell & Carter, 2002; Kaiser & Goetz, 1993; Sigafoos, Kerr, Roberts, & Couzens, 1994).

SUMMARY AND CONCLUSIONS

The instructional procedures summarized in this chapter should enable partners to be more successful in strengthening and enhancing potential communicative acts, as well as replacing prelinguistic acts with more formal and symbolic forms of communication. Three classes of instructional procedures were described that correspond loosely to the three intervention pathways discussed in Chapter 3; however, some of the procedures are clearly relevant to more than a single intervention pathway. Partners should match the procedure to the specific goal of intervention. In addition, they should understand the basic principles that underlie these instructional procedures so that they will be able to modify the procedure to suit the unique characteristics of the individual, the potential communicative act, and the context in which that act occurs. Instruction is best undertaken in the same contexts in which the individual currently communicates or is expected to communicate.

When implementing one or more of these procedures to strengthen, enhance, or replace potential communicative acts, it is important to consider

Table 4.8. Procedures for creating opportunities for communication

Procedure	Description
Missing item format	This procedure involves withholding one or more items necessary for the activity. An individual is required to request the missing item when it is needed. If a request does not occur, a partner prompts a correct response, then delivers the missing item.
Blocked response, or interruption strategy	This procedure involves blocking or interrupting a person from completing or continuing an activity. To continue the activity, the individual is required to produce a relevant communication request. If a request does not occur, then a partner would prompt the correct request before enabling the person to continue the activity.
Incomplete presentation	An individual is given some, but not all, of the materials needed for an activity, which creates the need for the person to make additional requests for more. Additional requests are prompted by a partner before giving more of the materials. Over time, the prompts are faded so that the individual makes independent requests for more.
Delayed assistance	An individual is presented with a task that requires the assistance of a partner (e.g., opening a package), which creates opportunities for teaching the person to request help. The partner waits until the individual indicates a request for help before providing the needed assistance.
Wrong item format	After an individual has indicated a request, a partner provides the wrong item. For example, if the person asks for juice, the partner might mistakenly provide a glass of water, which creates opportunities for teaching the individual to reject the wrong item and request the correct item.

Source: Sigafoos (1999).

issues of maintenance and generalization. Maintenance and generalization can be addressed during the initial stages of instruction or following a period of implementation in which the potential communicative acts have been successfully strengthened, enhanced, or replaced. In either case, additional procedures of the type presented in Table 4.7 may need to be used by partners to ensure maintenance and generalization. One should not automatically expect that newly developed communication skills—whether strengthened, enhanced, or replaced—would maintain and generalize unless additional procedures are implemented to specifically promote maintenance and generalization.

All of the instructional procedures described in this chapter depend to some extent on the partner's ability to create effective opportunities for communication. Partners need to create opportunities that will reliably evoke the potential communicative act so that those acts can be either strengthened, enhanced, or replaced. Although partners can and should make use of naturally arising opportunities, many opportunities will need to be created in order to provide sufficient learning experiences for individuals with developmental and physical disabilities. Once the goals of the pathway have been achieved, partners must continue to create opportunities for communication as these opportunities can then be used to promote maintenance and generalization.

5

Replacing Problem Behavior

JEFF SIGAFOOS AND MARK O'REILLY

INTRODUCTION

Those who have spent a fair amount of time among people with developmental and physical disabilities will no doubt have come across some individuals who exhibit problem behavior. Of course, nearly everyone has engaged in actions that others consider to be inappropriate or problematic at one time or another. For most of us, the occasional instance of problem behavior causes little concern because the frequency and severity of such outbursts are within acceptable limits. Unfortunately, for many people with developmental and physical disabilities, certain types of problem behavior may occur with sufficient frequency and severity to cause serious injury and damage.

In such cases, parents, educators, and therapists are obliged to provide some type of intervention to reduce the troublesome acts and increase the person's participation in meaningful activities. As a parent, educator, or therapist who might be expected to provide such intervention, it will be important for you to understand why problem behaviors occur and what can be done about them. This chapter addresses these two issues, focusing primarily on entering problem behaviors into the Replacement Pathway, in which the aim will be to replace the problematic forms with more appropriate and symbolic forms of communication.

Problem behaviors can take many and varied forms, but those that tend to cause the most concern include acts of aggression, self-injury, and property destruction (Sigafoos, Arthur, et al., 2003; Tutton, Wynne-Willson, & Piachaud, 1990). This chapter focuses on assessment and intervention strategies for these types of problem behaviors. Specifically, it

- Considers some of the reasons why problem behaviors occur
- Discusses some possible communicative functions of problem behavior
- Describes strategies for assessing the communicative function of problem behavior
- Illustrates procedures for teaching communication alternatives to replace problem behaviors

The emphasis is on the replacement of problem behavior by teaching communication alternatives, which is consistent with the major theme of this book and reflects the finding that problem behaviors often appear to be correlated with communication impairments (Chamberlain, Chung, & Jenner, 1993; Schroeder, Schroeder, Smith, & Dalldorf, 1978; Sigafoos, Elkins, Kerr, & Attwood, 1994; Talkington, Hall, & Altman, 1971). Among individuals with developmental and physical disabilities, those with fewer communication skills are more likely to display aggressive or self-injurious behavior (Sigafoos, Arthur, et al., 2003). Evidence of a relation between communication impairments and problem behavior has lead to the hypothesis that some problem behaviors may actually represent prelinguistic, yet intentional, forms of communication, at least for some individuals with developmental and physical disabilities (Durand, 1990).

Because of the demonstrated effectiveness of replacement-based and communication-based interventions for the treatment of problem behavior (Didden, Duker, & Korzilius, 1997)—an intervention approach that is consistent with the logic of replacement outlined in Chapter 3—some further aims of this chapter are to

- Explain how the interpretation of problem behavior as communication may lead to an effective replacement-based intervention
- Review strategies to assess the communicative function of problem behavior
- Describe strategies to replace and possibly prevent problem behavior

In particular, strategies to teach alternative communication skills to replace problem behaviors will be discussed; however, readers are urged to consult Carr et al. (1994) and Wacker et al. (2002) for a more complete description of this approach.

Of course, it is important to point out that interventions based on teaching alternative and replacement communication skills are not the only available methods for reducing problem behavior among individuals with developmental and physical disabilities. Readers are urged to consult other sources (e.g., Fleming & Kroese, 1993; Kiernan, 1994; Repp & Singh, 1990; Sigafoos, Arthur, et al., 2003) to obtain information on other strategies, such as behavioral momentum, differential reinforcement of incompatible behavior, and arranging the environment to prevent problem behavior.

In addition, the approach presented in this chapter is based on fundamental principles of learning and development. Specifically, it involves the use of functional communication training to replace problem behavior (Carr et al., 1994; Wacker et al., 2002). This method is based in part on the premise that some problem behaviors may represent learned behaviors that are often maintained by reinforcing consequences, such as attention, access to preferred objects or activities, and escape from nonpreferred tasks (Carr, 1977).

An underlying theme of this chapter is that understanding why problem behavior occurs is extremely important so that appropriate intervention strategies can be designed and implemented. To begin, it will help to develop an understanding of some of the reasons why problem behavior occurs. Initially, this discussion will diverge from the main emphasis, which is the analysis of the possible communicative function of problem behavior; however, such a diversion is necessary to gain an appreciation for the varied factors that may influence problem behavior among individuals with developmental and physical disabilities.

FACTORS THAT INFLUENCE PROBLEM BEHAVIOR

A distinction can be made between the form and the function of communicative behavior. The same distinction applies to problem behavior. With respect to assessment and intervention, what the student does (e.g., aggression, self-injury) is often less important than why. This section considers some of the reasons why problem behavior occurs.

Biological Factors

There is evidence that certain biological conditions are associated with problem behavior (Carr & Smith, 1995; Cataldo & Harris, 1982). One example is Lesch-Nyhan syndrome, a sex-linked metabolic disorder that affects only boys (Lesch & Nyhan, 1964). The syndrome is associated with extreme forms of self-injury, characterized by biting of the lips, tongue, and fingers. Another example is Rett syndrome. Children with Rett syndrome display stereotypic hand wringing and sometimes self-injurious hand biting (Olsson & Rett, 1985).

Children with Lesch-Nyhan or Rett syndrome may seem unlikely to respond to educational overtures; however, the problem behaviors associated with these two syndromes often vary in relation to the presence of adults or task demands (Anderson, Herrmann, Alpert, & Dancis, 1975; Oliver, Murphy, Crayton, & Corbett, 1993), which suggests that educational and behavioral interventions are of potential benefit even when the problem behavior has an organic basis (Anderson, Dancis, & Alpert, 1978; Duker, 1975; Paisey, Whitney, & Wainczak, 1993).

Psychological Factors

Some people with developmental and physical disabilities may develop psychiatric disorders, which may exacerbate problem behavior (Matson & Mayville, 2001; Singh, Sood, Sonenklar, & Ellis, 1991). A probable interaction between manic depression and problem behavior, for example, was shown in two case studies reported by Lowry and Sovner (1992). A display of problem behavior does not in itself imply psychiatric disturbance. Instead, the frequency or intensity of the problem behavior may vary in relation to other observable indices of the suspected disorder, such as dramatic changes in sleeping or eating habits (O'Reilly, 1995, 1997).

It also might help to think of psychiatric disorders as a type of contextual variable or setting event that influences the behavior indirectly rather than as a direct cause of problem behavior—that is, as an event that predisposes the person to respond with aggression or self-injury. One of the people described by Lowry and Sovner (1992), for example, became self-abusive if asked to get out of bed but only during his depressed phase. Depression appeared to be a setting event for self-injury related to escape from staff demands.

Medical Factors

Medical conditions can exacerbate problem behavior (Bosch, Van Dyke, Milligan Smith, & Poulton, 1997; Gunsett, Mulick, Fernald, & Martin, 1989). Gedye (1989), for example, found evidence to suggest that in certain cases frontal lobe seizures may produce aggressive outbursts. An acute injury or infection, however, might act more like a setting event for problem behavior. For example, personal observations by the first author of this chapter (Sigafoos) suggested that one young man referred for behavioral intervention showed increased aggression and self-injury as a result of an abscessed tooth. When this dental problem was corrected, his problem behaviors were greatly reduced. Another young man showed a noticeable increase in previously low levels of head banging that appeared to be associated with an ear infection. After medical treatment, head banging once again returned to its more typical low level. These examples confirm the need for routine medical examination.

Environmental Factors

A classic study by Horner (1980) demonstrated that problem behavior can be exacerbated by an impoverished environment. Horner went into a large institution to observe the adaptive and maladaptive behavior of five children with profound intellectual disabilities. First, these children were observed in their dayroom, which contained little more than a black-and-white television and a few pieces of furniture. Next, the children were observed when the environment had been physically enriched by introducing a number of toys into the setting. Finally, the environment was enriched socially as well as physically by having adults provide social praise to the children when they were engaged in appropriate toy play.

The first setting generated the most problem behavior. Physical enrichment reversed this trend, and the addition of social enrichment produced further reductions in problem behavior. The decrease in problem behavior was associated with increased toy play, suggesting that toy play had replaced or displaced problem behavior.

The message for communication partners is clear. Efforts to manage problem behavior should be part of a more comprehensive plan to improve an individual's lifestyle (Sprague & Horner, 1991). This broader approach has come to be known as *positive behavior support* (Carr et al., 2002). Positive behavior support plans should entail providing varied and meaningful activities (i.e., an enriched environment).

Providing a meaningful lifestyle for individuals with developmental and physical disabilities is important in its own right; however, this factor alone may not be sufficient to reduce problem behavior in every instance (Mulick & Kedesdy, 1988). More focused interventions may be required for some individuals. It is not uncommon to observe aggression and self-injury among children born and raised in typical family situations with ample opportunities for meaningful and varied experiences. After ruling out biological, psychological, and medical factors, one is left with the very real possibility that some children learn to display problem behavior because such acts have been reinforced by others in the past and because the children lack alternative behaviors (Carr, 1977).

Learning Factors

A variety of learning processes may been implicated in the emergence and maintenance of problem behavior in individuals with developmental and physical disabilities (Sigafoos et al., 2004). These processes appear to account for a large percentage of cases of problem behavior in individuals with developmental and physical disabilities (Iwata et al., 1994). Three main categories of learning processes that have been implicated are positive reinforcement, negative reinforcement, and automatic reinforcement.

Positive Reinforcement   Some problem behaviors are maintained by positive reinforcement in the form of attention from adults or access to preferred objects (see Mace, Lalli, & Pinter-Lalli, 1991, for a review). When adults are nearby but not providing attention, for example, some individuals are likely to display aggression or self-injury, probably because in the past such behaviors were followed by attention. Similarly, when a favorite toy is taken away, some individuals will have a tantrum because they often will get the toy back. Problem behavior in the first instance is said to be *attention motivated*, whereas in the second instance, it might be called *object motivated*.

Negative Reinforcement In addition to positive reinforcement, some problem behaviors are maintained by negative reinforcement in the form of escape or avoidance (Carr, Newsom, & Binkoff, 1980; Iwata, Pace, Kalsher, Cowdery, & Cataldo, 1990). Individuals may learn to display aggression when presented with a difficult task, for example, because this has enabled them to escape from or avoid the task in the past. Similarly, toddlers often have tantrums when asked to go to bed. When a child's parents "give in" and allow him or her to stay up, the child's tantrum is reinforced. In these cases, the problem behaviors can be called *escape motivated*. Other individuals may exhibit problem behavior in the presence of others to avoid social interaction (Taylor & Carr, 1992). Problem behavior in this case also could be viewed in terms of escape and avoidance.

Automatic Reinforcement Some have speculated that problem behaviors that occur in unstimulating environments or at times when the learner is otherwise unengaged may generate a form of sensory stimulation, or *automatic reinforcement* (Iwata, Vollmer, & Zarcone, 1990; Lovaas, Newsom, & Hickman, 1987). In these cases, the problem behavior directly produces consequences that may serve as reinforcement. Because the behavior produces reinforcing consequences directly, rather than through the mediation of a communication partner, the behavior is said to be maintained by automatic reinforcement.

COMMUNICATION
ALTERNATIVES TO PROBLEM BEHAVIOR

After considering some of the reasons why problem behaviors occur, it is probably clear how some such behaviors could be viewed in terms of the communicative functions outlined in Chapter 1. Self-injury maintained by attention, for example, might be viewed as a rather unconventional but nonetheless effective mand or more specifically as a way of recruiting attention. When the self-injury is displayed by a person who has no other effective means of recruiting attention, a communicative basis for the problem behavior seems plausible. Similarly, problem behavior that is object motivated could be interpreted as a simple mand or request (e.g., "I want") or as the person's way of indicating a preference or making a choice. Again, if the person has no better alternative means of making such requests, it is not unreasonable to suggest that problem behaviors could have developed to "fill the communication void."

When dealing with problem behaviors that are attention motivated, some logical communication alternatives should be apparent. In this case, it would make sense to focus on teaching communication skills that would enable the person to gain attention and maintain a social interaction with the communication partner. Skills of this type would enable the person to gain the attention of others, thereby serving the same function as the problem behavior. When the person is able to gain attention more consistently and reliably by exhibiting an alternative communication response (e.g., vocalizing, gesturing, using a VOCA), attention-motivated problem behavior should become unnecessary.

Similarly, object-motivated aggression or self-injury might be replaced by teaching the person a better way to request objects, make choices, or indicate preferences. The same logic can be applied when selecting communication alternatives for escape-motivated behavior problems. In such cases, the use of vocalizations, gestures, or communication devices to reject, request assistance, or protest may represent functionally equivalent, yet socially acceptable, alternatives (Carr, 1988; Wacker et al., 2002). When confronted with a difficult task, an acceptable alternative might be for the child to request assistance ("Help"), rather than engage in aggression or self-injury. Again, the rationale for this approach is that the communication alternative may eventually come to replace problem behaviors maintained by negative reinforcement.

What about problem behaviors related to medical conditions, impoverished environments, or psychiatric disorders? Clearly, these issues must be addressed. Medical professionals with the relevant expertise should treat any related medical or psychiatric conditions. Social workers must assure that the person's environment meets quality standards. Not all problem behavior is necessarily best viewed as a form of communication or best managed through communication intervention (see Sigafoos, Reichle, & Light-Shriner, 1994, for an extended discussion of this issue). It would be hard to interpret problem behavior related to mania or depression, for example, in terms of functional communication. Nonetheless, communication intervention is indicated for any individual with severe communication impairments.

Consider a child who displays self-injury when alone or otherwise unoccupied. The child may not be communicating any particular message intentionally, but there would probably be no harm in interpreting these acts as if the child were communicating a message such as "I'm bored" (Donnellan et al., 1984). If the interpretation were correct, then one would expect the self-injury to decrease as the child learns to request preferred objects or activities (toys, games) under these same antecedent conditions (i.e., when alone or otherwise unoccupied).

Similarly, problem behavior that occurs in response to some acute medical condition does not necessarily involve intentional communication. Nonetheless, the child might be taught to seek assistance when so distressed by communicating, "I'm sick." Again, teaching this alternative may reduce the problem behavior.

To select an appropriate communication alternative, one must first determine the function of the problem behavior. It would probably be less effective to teach a child to request objects if his or her problem behavior is attention motivated. Similarly, it would make little sense to have the child recruit attention if his or her problem behaviors are related to task or social avoidance (Carr & Durand, 1985). It is critical to ensure a close match between the function of the problem behavior and the function of the communication alternative. A thorough assessment of problem behavior is recommended as the basis for selecting appropriate communication alternatives.

FUNCTIONAL ASSESSMENT OF PROBLEM BEHAVIOR

The purpose of a functional assessment of problem behavior is to identify the antecedent and consequent conditions that respectively evoke and maintain the problem behaviors of any given individual. This information may enable one to develop a hypothesis as to why these problem behaviors occur. A clear hypothesis provides the basis for selecting an appropriate communication alternative to replace the problem behavior. Several procedures that can be used to conduct a functional assessment of problem behavior are reviewed next, but for a more detailed discussion see Durand and Crimmins (1991), Sigafoos, Arthur, et al. (2003), and Wacker et al. (2002).

Interviews and Questionnaires

Perhaps the easiest way to try to discover why a problem behavior occurs is to ask those familiar with the individual. Parents, teachers, or therapists are often able to provide very precise and accurate answers to questions such as "Why does Robert hit himself?" or "Why do you think Julie hits and kicks other people?" In some instances, however, it may be difficult to answer such questions because the controlling variables are not always obvious. For such cases, it may help to ask a series of more indirect questions such as (O'Neill et al., 1997; Van Houten et al., 1988)

• Are there any conditions under which this behavior always occurs?

• Are there any conditions under which this behavior never occurs?

- What usually happens immediately before the behavior is exhibited?
- What usually happens immediately after the behavior?

The answers to such questions might provide clues as to the antecedents and consequences that evoke and maintain the problem behavior. In addition to interviews, standardized questionnaires might be used to collect assessment information. Durand and Crimmins's (1988) Motivation Assessment Scale is one example. It consists of 16 items designed to determine if the problem behavior is attention, escape, object, or sensory motivated. The Questions About Behavioral Function (QABF; Paclawskyi, Matson, Rush, Smalls, & Vollmer, 2000) is another questionnaire/checklist for assessing the communicative function of problem behavior.

A potential problem with interviews and questionnaires is that both depend on third-party informants who, due to differing perceptions, may not always provide reliable or valid information (Newton & Sturmey, 1991; Sigafoos, Kerr, et al., 1994; Zarcone, Rodgers, Iwata, Rourke, & Dorsey, 1991). If you ask two people the same question, for example, you may get two completely different answers; however, data indicate that the QABF does appear to have good psychometric properties, including adequate interrater and test–retest reliability (Paclawskyi et al., 2000). Still, information obtained via interviews or questionnaires should be verified before it is used to select an intervention strategy. Naturalistic observations and structured functional assessment can be used to verify information obtained from interviews, questionnaires, and checklists.

Naturalistic Observation

One way to verify interview or questionnaire data is through *naturalistic observation*. The process is similar to that described in Chapter 2 for any type of potential communicative act. Suppose, for example, that an interview, such as the IPCA, suggested that a particular form of problem behavior was the individual's way of gaining attention. In the natural environment, during verification assessment, one might expect to observe higher rates of the problem behavior when others are present but not actually attending to the individual. In addition, problem behavior should be rare when that person is receiving attention. Finally, if it was also observed that the person at least occasionally received attention immediately after engaging in the problem behavior, then there would appear to be some confirmation of the initial hypothesis.

Similarly, if the questionnaire results implicated escape or avoidance as the controlling variables, then one would expect high rates of problem behavior when demands were made of the individual and low rates when those demands were removed. Naturalistic observations typically involve keeping a record of the circumstances that surround incidents of problem behavior (e.g., time of day, setting, antecedents, consequences); however, this approach to naturalistic observation can be cumbersome. It depends on detecting patterns from the data, which often requires the observation of a great many incidents. In the natural environment, this process may take some time because the events that normally evoke problem behavior may themselves be rare.

When working with a child who hits and kicks others to escape from certain activities, for example, parents and teachers may simply avoid those tasks with that child. An observer in that particular situation might never see the relationship between task demands and aggressive behavior because potentially evocative task demands are never presented to the child. This situation can make it difficult to verify the function of the problem behavior.

Scatter Plots

A potentially useful tool that may make naturalistic observations less cumbersome is the scatter plot technique described by Touchette, MacDonald, and Langer (1985). With this procedure, the entire day or a selected period of the day (e.g., 10 A.M. to 2 P.M.) is divided into intervals of 30 minutes. During each interval, an observer keeps track of how many problem behaviors occur. Observations might continue for a period of 5–7 days or until some pattern is revealed on the scatter plot (Lalli & Goh, 1993). The resulting data may give an indication of when problem behavior is likely to occur as well as times when problem behavior is unlikely to occur. By relating this information back to the activities that were occurring during each 30-minute interval, it may be possible to generate some hypotheses as to the controlling variables.

For example, suppose the pattern indicated frequent problem behavior between 11:30 A.M. and noon (i.e., right before lunch) and very little problem behavior during (12:00–12:30 P.M.) or immediately after lunch (12:30–1:00 P.M.). Such a pattern might suggest a relationship between problem behavior and the scheduling of meals. Alternatively, it could indicate a problem with that particular prelunch activity. In either case, it may be possible to reduce problem behavior by making a simple change to the learner's schedule. That is, provide lunch at 11:30 A.M., and wait until after lunch to implement the activity that was previously implemented at that time.

It would appear that the scatter plot technique may be most useful for problem behavior that occurs in relation to certain times of the day or specific activities that occur at regular times, rather than behaviors that occur in relation to antecedents, such as the withdrawal of attention or the presentation of demands, which may be more evenly distributed throughout the day. It would also appear that the use of scatter plots would be most efficient in situations when there is a consistent daily routine.

Structured Observations

When the initial hypothesis concerning the function of a problem behavior proves difficult to verify through naturalistic observations, even with the scatter plot, it may help to implement a more structured assessment or *functional analysis* of the problem behavior (Iwata et al., 1982). This approach is similar to the verification assessment described in Chapter 2. Even if good information is obtained from the naturalistic assessment, structured observations provide further verification and a context that may be used during the initial phase of intervention, as discussed later. There has been a considerable amount of research on the use of functional analysis procedures for the assessment of problem behavior (Wacker et al., 2002).

Typically, in a functional analysis, the rate of problem behavior is observed under a number of highly structured "analog" conditions. Conducting a proper functional analysis often requires a fair degree of time, control, and resources that may be difficult to provide in applied settings. In response to these potential difficulties, Sigafoos and Meikle (1996) described a modified approach to assess the problem behaviors of two boys with autism. The approach was based on the logic of the verification assessment procedures described in Chapter 2.

Specifically, for this assessment, a teacher conducted 20 brief (1- to 2-minute) trials over 5 days for each of four conditions (i.e., attention, escape, object, sensory). During attention trials, the teacher remained near the child but ignored him for up to 1 minute (antecedent). If at any time during this minute the child displayed problem behavior, the teacher gave the child her undivided attention for the next minute (consequence). A high percentage of problem behavior in the first minute of attention trials, combined with little or no problem behavior in the second minute, suggested that the behavior was indeed *attention motivated*.

During escape trials, the teacher presented an academic task and prompted the child to participate every 10 seconds for up to 1 minute. If at any time during this minute the child displayed problem behavior, the teacher removed the task materials and demands but continued to observe the child's behavior for the next minute. A high percentage of problem behavior in the first part of escape trials, combined with little or no problem behavior in the second part, suggested an escape or avoidance hypothesis.

For the object trials, preferred items, such as toys, drinks, and snacks, were withdrawn during the first minute or until the child displayed problem behavior. At this point, the child was allowed access to the items for the next minute. Again, high rates of problem behavior in the first minute and low rates during the second minute suggested that the problem behaviors were maintained by positive reinforcement in the form of access to preferred objects.

Finally, during sensory trials, the child was simply observed for a period of 2 minutes when he was alone and unoccupied. Any behavior here was assumed to be related to sensory feedback or automatic reinforcement. The overall results suggested that both boys' problem behaviors were attention motivated and object motivated and demonstrated that functional analysis procedures can be modified for use in the classroom.

SELECTING THE REPLACEMENT RESPONSE

When assessment results allow some confidence as to the probable factors maintaining the person's problem behavior, selection of a functionally equivalent communication alternative is often quite obvious. Even when the controlling variables are clear, however, there may be several equally appropriate communication alternatives. Table 5.1 lists some possible communication replacements for attention-, escape-, object-, and sensory-motivated problem behavior.

At present, there is little information concerning which of these possible options might represent the "best" alternative for each type of problem behavior. Perhaps the best alternative can be defined only after reviewing the unique characteristics of the individual and his or her particular situation. Consider the individual who displays problem behavior to avoid tasks. When the task is relatively unimportant, the person might be taught to reject that task or request some alternative; however, if the task must be completed

Table 5.1. Communication replacements for problem behavior

Operant function	Possible communication replacement
Gain or maintain attention/social interaction	Recruit attention (e.g., "Come here.")
	Request affection (e.g., "Hug, please.")
	Solicit praise (e.g., "How am I doing?")
	Initiate greetings (e.g., "Hello.")
Escape or avoid an object or activity	Reject/protest (e.g., "No, thanks.")
	Request assistance (e.g., "Help, please.")
	Request alternative (e.g., "Any others?")
	Request a break (e.g., "Can I have a break?")
Gain access to an object or activity	Request objects (e.g., "I want a drink.")
	Request activity (e.g., "I want to go for a walk.")
	Indicate preferences (e.g., "I prefer Irish Breakfast tea.")
	Make choices (e.g., "I want that one.")
Obtain direct sensory consequences	Request stimulating objects/activities (e.g., "Can I watch a movie?")
	Request attention/social interaction (e.g., "Let's talk.")
	Indicate boredom (e.g., "I'm bored. Let's do something.")

(e.g., job duties), then it would make more sense to teach the person to request "help" when needed or to request occasional short breaks.

The results from a verification assessment or functional assessment may not always yield a clear picture of the controlling variables for the person's problem behaviors, which makes it more difficult to identify a logically related intervention strategy. Alternatively, the assessment results may suggest multiple reasons for the problem behavior. For example, the aggression and self-injury exhibited by the two boys in the Sigafoos and Meikle (1996) study appeared be maintained by attention *and* by access to preferred objects. The results from the functional assessment suggested the need to teach two types of communication alternatives–requests for attention and requests for preferred objects–in order to replace the boys' problem behaviors.

SELECTING REPLACEMENT MODES AND VOCABULARY

In addition to selecting appropriate communicative functions to replace problem behavior, the exact form of the communication alternative will need to be defined before beginning intervention to teach the replacement behavior. Specifically, it should be determined whether the communication alternative will be taught in the vocal, gesture, or graphic mode. A child could be taught to request a drink, for example, by asking for it by name (vocal mode), by using a manual sign (gesture mode), or by pointing to the picture of a cup on a VOCA (graphic mode). To recruit attention, a child might be taught to vocalize an approximation of "come here," wave his or her hand in the air for others to see, or operate a VOCA with the message "Come here, please" (Sigafoos, Pennell, & Versluis, 1996). When problem behavior occurs to escape or avoid, the communication alternative may involve teaching the child to reject nonpreferred objects or activities (Sigafoos, O'Reilly, Drasgow, & Reichle, 2002). Developing appropriate rejecting skills, in turn, might consist of teaching the child to say "no" (vocal mode), shake his or her head to indicate no (gesture mode), or point to a symbol that represents "No thanks," "Stop that," "Help," or "Break time."

In addition to defining the modes of communication, the exact vocabulary, gestures, or symbols that will be taught also should be determined. The reinforcers that maintain object-motivated aggression, for example, may be many and varied (e.g., food, beverages, toys) or fairly specific (i.e., the individual has a tantrum only to request access to a preferred DVD movie). In the first instance, a generalized request ("Want") might be the most economical response to target for instruction, but in the latter case, it may be best to teach the individual a rather more explicit request ("I want to watch Shrek 2").

Several words or gestures conceivably could be taught to replace attention-motivated problem behavior. Some teachers and parents accept any vocalization the child makes as a legitimate request for attention or, depending on the child's existing skills, may respond only to the phrase *come here*. Similarly, in the gesture mode, a request for attention could involve simply waving the arm or, depending on the person's dexterity, the fairly natural gesture of flexing one's index finger.

The exact form of the communication alternative for escape-motivated behavior may depend on whether avoidance of the task is acceptable. If so, the individual may be taught the simple rejecting response *no*. If not, the learner will be reinforced for participating in the task but also might be taught to ask for help or to request a break using some appropriate word, gesture, or symbol.

CRITERIA FOR SELECTING A REPLACEMENT RESPONSE

When selecting an alternative form of communication to replace problem behavior, several factors may influence whether the alternative will come to replace the problem behavior. First, it is critical to ensure that the communication alternative actually serves the same communicative function as the problem behavior. In addition to this, however, it may help for the communication alternative to meet the following criteria:

1. The communication alternative is socially acceptable.

2. The communication alternative is easy to perform.

3. Partners are able to interpret the meaning of the new behavior.

4. Partners are able and willing to reinforce the act immediately and consistently.

Any communication response that is taught to replace the problem behavior should be socially acceptable. If partners do not favor the form of the proposed alternative, the social validity of the entire intervention program may be jeopardized. Second, the alternative communicative behavior should be easy for the individual to do. According to the law of least effort, the behavior that requires the least effort to produce is the one that is most likely to occur (Wacker et al., 2002). Thus, unless the communication alternative is easier than head banging, for example, the problem behavior may continue, especially if it continues to be reinforced. In other words, do not make the communication alternative too difficult or sophisticated, at least not initially.

During the initial stages of communication intervention to replace the problem behavior, the communication alternative should be reinforced consistently, each and every time it occurs, so that it becomes fluent for the individual to produce. At the same time, it will be necessary to make sure that problem behavior is no longer reinforced; otherwise, it may continue to occur because, from the learner's perspective, it still works. After the communication alternative occurs reliably and with little or no problem behavior, it should then be possible to encourage its use in the presence of more incidental and naturally occurring reinforcement.

Finally, the communication alternative should be readily interpreted by others. If other partners readily understand the alternative communication, they are perhaps more likely to reinforce it, which should, in turn, facilitate generalization and maintenance. In short, the communication alternative must be more efficient and effective in procuring reinforcement across settings, partners, and time if it is to replace the problem behavior (Horner & Day, 1991).

PROCEDURES FOR TEACHING THE COMMUNICATION REPLACEMENT BEHAVIOR

How does one actually go about teaching communication alternatives to replace problem behavior? Consider, for example, a child who engages in self-injury as a way of recruiting attention. Intervention in this case might consist of teaching the child to initiate social interactions by gesturing for others to come. But how does one actually teach the child to produce this new attention-getting gesture instead of resorting to self-injury?

Or how about a child who has tantrums to communicate requests for access to preferred objects? A possible communication alternative may be to teach the child to request preferred objects by pointing to pictures of those same items, rather than by throwing a tantrum. But, again, exactly how does one teach the child to request preferred objects by pointing to pictures?

As a third example, you may encounter individuals who hit, kick, and bite to escape from difficult tasks. So, in an effort to reduce the difficulty of the task and thereby hopefully eliminate the conditions that evoke aggression, it is reasoned that the person should be taught to sign HELP when difficulty is encountered. What would you actually do to teach this person to sign HELP as an alternative to hitting, kicking, or biting?

The task of teaching communication alternatives to replace problem behavior may at first seem daunting; however, it is important to keep in mind that teaching communication alternatives to replace problem behavior is in many respects identical to the task of replacing any existing potential communicative act with a more symbolic alternative. The logic is consistent with the Replacement Pathway described in Chapter 3. As such, the same basic principles considered within the Replacement Pathway and some of the same instructional procedures described in Chapter 4 can be applied. There are, however, a few issues that make intervention to replace problem behavior somewhat different from instruction designed solely to establish a new communication skill.

Considering the Context of Instruction

One such issue is the context of instruction. That is, where and under what conditions should the instructional procedures be implemented? When the goal of instruction is to replace problem behavior by teaching a functionally equivalent alternative, at least some instruction probably needs to occur under the same conditions that evoke the problem behavior.

It may be possible to start teaching the alternative response under conditions different from those that evoke and maintain the problem behavior. Once established, procedures might then be implemented to promote generalization of the communication response to the conditions that currently evoke problem behavior. Even in this sequence, however, instruction in the presence of those variables that actually control the problem behavior probably needs to be arranged at some point to ensure that replacement has occurred.

For example, if self-injury typically occurs when adults are present but not attending to the child, then this same situation might be arranged several times a day so that the child can be prompted to use the alternative gesture for "come here." Or, with the youngster who has tantrums to get toys and candy, teachers and parents might arrange for such items to be visible but just out of the child's reach. Such conditions are ripe for a tantrum, but instead, the parent or teacher would be quick to prompt and reinforce an alternative request (i.e., pointing to a picture of the desired item), thereby starting to establish this request as an alternative to tantrums.

For the third example, the child who hits others to escape from difficult tasks, a functional assessment might be used to determine if certain steps in the task evoke problem behavior. If so, intervention might involve prompting the child to sign HELP immediately prior to encountering one of these difficult steps. After requesting HELP, the teacher or parent provides the needed assistance, which should function to reinforce the communication alternative and eliminate the need for aggression.

As these three examples illustrate, instruction to teach the communication alternative will often occur under those same conditions which currently evoke and maintain problem behavior.

Managing Problem Behavior During Instruction

A second issue that makes intervention to replace problem behavior somewhat unique is the possibility that problem behavior may occur during instruction to teach the replacement behavior. When intervention begins, the individual is unlikely to produce the communication alternative independently and may, therefore, continue to display problem behavior, particularly if instruction occurs under the same conditions that typically evoke the problem behavior. Therefore, instruction must not only include procedures for teaching the desired alternative but also require additional strategies for responding to problem behavior if and when it occurs. Alternatively, instructional opportunities might be designed in order to prevent or minimize problem behavior (see Duker et al., 2004, for an extended discussion of this issue).

Relevant to this issue, several studies have demonstrated that problem behaviors can be reduced by teaching functionally equivalent communication skills (Bird, Dores, Moniz, & Robinson, 1989; Carr & Durand, 1985; Durand & Carr, 1991; Fisher et al., 1993; Wacker et al., 2002; Wacker et al., 1990). In these studies, procedures to teach the communication alternative have generally involved the use of verbal or gestural cues and modeling or physical prompting. After the communication alternative has been prompted, it is immediately reinforced. Over time, the amount of prompting is faded as the learner begins to respond independently.

Although such procedures may promote the acquisition of alternative communication skills, problem behaviors are still often observed, especially during the early stages of intervention. As a result, procedures to teach the communication alternative are typically combined with additional strategies such as extinction, response interruption, or brief response restriction to manage instances of problem behavior. Even with consistent use of such additional strategies, however, some individuals may emit a substantial number of problem behaviors during the early stages of instruction to teach the replacement behavior. If problem behaviors occur frequently during the early stages of instruction, then they may persist even as the individual begins to produce the communication alternative independently. In some cases, it may be desirable to adopt procedures to prevent or minimize problem behavior.

Along these lines, Sigafoos and Meikle (1996) described an errorless approach for teaching communication alternatives to problem behavior that flowed from their functional analysis described previously. The intent of this approach was to prevent the occurrence of problem behavior during the early stages of intervention. Initially, the two participating boys were prompted to produce the communication alternative immediately after exposure to the conditions that typically evoked problem behavior. This brief exposure was designed to preempt problem behavior. Instead, the children were immediately prompted to use the communication alternative before any problem behavior could occur. After prompting, reinforcement identical to that which maintained their problem behaviors was provided.

As the children became more independent in using their new communication skills, the amount of time they were exposed to the initial "provoking" conditions was increased from 1 second to 3 seconds. With this shift, both children started to use their newly acquired communication skills independently. In addition, problem behaviors, which previously occurred at nearly every opportunity, were virtually eliminated.

Table 5.2 provides an outline of how this approach was used to replace attention-motivated aggression and self-injury with the natural gesture of tapping the teacher on the shoulder. Similar steps were followed to replace object-motivated problem behavior with requests for preferred items. Using this approach, both children were taught alternative communication skills that effectively replaced their problem behaviors. In addition, very few instances of problem behavior were observed during intervention, so additional strategies to manage such instances were largely unnecessary.

COMMUNICATION INTERVENTION FOR PREVENTING PROBLEM BEHAVIOR

Given that functional communication training of the type outlined in Table 5.2 is an effective approach for replacing problem behaviors (Wacker et al., 2002) and considering the possibility that some problem behaviors may emerge when conventional language skills are slow to develop, communication intervention also might hold promise for the prevention of problem behavior in young children with developmental and physical disabilities and limited speech skills by providing them with communication intervention from an early age. Although there are few guidelines for designing curricula

Table 5.2. Procedures to replace attention-motivated problem behavior

Step	Implementation of procedure
1. Create the need.	A partner sits next to an individual but withholds attention for a few seconds. This step represents the antecedent condition that typically evokes the problem behavior if the partner ignores the person long enough.
2. Prompt the response.	Before the person has a chance to display the problem behavior, the partner turns to him or her and says, "If you want me, do this." At the same time, the partner prompts the individual to tap him or her on the shoulder, which is the communication alternative.
3. Provide reinforcement.	After the individual has been prompted to request attention, the partner provides praise ("Good, you asked for me.") and also gives the person undivided attention for the next 1–2 minutes.
4. Fade the prompt.	Steps 1–3 are then repeated several times a day to provide a sufficient number of opportunities for the individual to learn the new communication skill; however, on each successive opportunity the partner fades the amount of prompting (using time delay) and increases the amount of time attention is withheld to promote independence.

to prevent problem behavior, a possible approach might involve the early introduction of one or more communication modes (speech, gesture, graphic). In addition, communication partners would need to recognize and respond consistently to an individual's other acceptable forms of potential communicative acts in an effort to strengthen and shape these into more functional forms of expression (Siegel-Causey & Guess, 1989). All of these tactics are designed to provide the child with a variety of acceptable communication alternatives to problem behavior.

In addition to having multiple modes of communication, a number of communicative functions covered in Chapter 1 should be taught to provide the individual with a comprehensive communication repertoire. To prevent the possible emergence of attention-motivated problem behavior, for example, early intervention might include teaching the child to gain attention, initiate interactions, and maintain social interactions. To prevent object-motivated problem behavior, one might help the child better indicate preferences, make choices, and request preferred objects and activities. In addition, it would make sense to teach a variety of assistance-seeking and rejecting skills to prevent escape-motivated problem behaviors from developing. Some children seek to avoid social interactions, so any such problem behaviors might be prevented by teaching the child how to terminate social interactions in an acceptable fashion from an early age.

Although not all children are likely to develop each of these different types of problem behavior, it is probably not uncommon for a given problem behavior (e.g., self-injury) to serve multiple functions (e.g., gain attention, access preferred objects, and escape from task demands). Early intervention to teach numerous communicative functions may lessen the chance that problem behaviors would emerge to fill a particular void. Of course, in addition to teaching a number of fairly specific communication skills, much problem behavior could no doubt be prevented by simply creating better interactions between the individual and his or her communication partners, as well as enriching their environments and developing more meaningful lifestyles.

SUMMARY AND CONCLUSIONS

This chapter reviews some of the reasons why problem behavior occurs and considers some of the factors that influence problem behaviors in individuals with developmental and physical disabilities. Evidence suggests that some problem behaviors might be interpreted as a form of communication. It is possible that some problem behaviors emerge because individuals with developmental and physical disabilities have difficulty learning more conventional ways to communicate.

As noted in Chapter 1, communication can take a variety of forms. Some of these forms may be conventional (e.g., speech, sign language), but others may be informal and idiosyncratic, such as a child who tugs at a partner's sleeve for attention. It is important for parents, teachers, and therapists to recognize that sometimes informal and idiosyncratic communications may even take the form of aggression, self-injury, property destruction, or other problem behavior.

Considerable evidence also suggests that problem behaviors can often be treated effectively by teaching a functionally equivalent alternative. This alternative might consist of some more acceptable form of communication. Communication intervention may form a useful part of any plan to support people with developmental and physical disabilities who engage in severe problem behaviors. It is an educative approach to treatment that seeks to replace problem behaviors with functionally equivalent communication alternatives.

Based on the premise that some problem behaviors may actually represent rather unconventional forms of communication, this approach to treatment also may hold promise for the prevention of serious problem behaviors among individuals with developmental disabilities; however, supporting people with problem behavior may often require more than just communication intervention. Instead, success could depend on the ability to provide a range of educational, social, therapeutic, and medical services as part of a comprehensive positive behavior support plan.

6

Monitoring Progress

MICHAEL ARTHUR-KELLY AND NANCY BUTTERFIELD

INTRODUCTION

This chapter describes strategies for evaluating intervention plans and monitoring the progress of individuals as they participate in one or more of the intervention pathways described in Chapter 3. Without a dynamic approach to program tracking and review, it is possible to waste teaching time or to frustrate the individual. An effective communication intervention program will be one in which student and partner skills and needs are carefully identified, the process of learning to communicate is considered, and strategies are introduced and monitored in a way that naturally enhances functional communication throughout the day. Accordingly, adapting or combining a number of the techniques and principles outlined in this chapter may be appropriate.

Monitoring the various aspects of the intervention process is necessary. For example, the specific goals and objectives of intervention will often need to be modified in light of data collected during the implementation of instructional procedures. A particular instructional procedure may be started and then continued, extended, modified, or dropped–depending on the individual's response to the instructional procedure. The whole intervention process should be systematic and responsive to the individual's performance.

MONITORING PARTNER SKILLS

In addition to monitoring the progress of the individual receiving intervention, it is also important to monitor the partners' skills. Perhaps the simplest way to evaluate the degree to which partners' skills have been attained is to observe partners during communicative interactions with the individual with developmental and physical disabilities. The observer can make notes on the partners' interaction styles or collect more specific data, such as whether a partner provides effective opportunities, is responsive, acknowledges communicative acts, uses prompts effectively, and provides appropriate consequences. Feedback should be provided to partners on the skills observed. Alternatively, a partner might collect data on his or her own performance using a self-monitoring approach. For example, partners might collect data on the average amount of time they wait before prompting a response.

MEASURING CHANGE

How and what are measured in terms of the communication skills of the individual is dependent to some extent on the objectives that have been set and the types of instructional procedures being implemented. For one individual, detailed anecdotal records may provide a rich source of information. In another case, however, more precise records of responses on a trial-by-trial basis may be needed. The quality and usefulness of the data collected (rather than the technical complexity of data collection and analysis) is the point to be emphasized. In essence, how the data are used is what counts.

Daily reviews of progress, for example, may help to ensure that partners set new objectives when appropriate. Alternatively, data are needed to assist partners in deciding whether the instruction being given to the individual needs to be refined, extended, maintained, or modified, as mentioned previously. Collecting and evaluating data are critical to ensure that progress is monitored effectively. It is extremely important to make use of performance data to evaluate progress on a regular basis.

The dimensions of change in performance often depend on the content of the communication objectives that have been established. Partners must consider the wider influences on the individual's communication repertoire, including the influence of partner skills. An individual might be learning to communicate a particular function or respond to natural cues; however, partner progress in communication responsiveness will also play a part in improving the individual's communicative competence. Because communication is a shared process, it is important to recognize the overlap of these two processes of change.

Discriminative Stimuli or Cues

An increasing emphasis on functional and contextually relevant communication processes has underlined the importance of the individual being able to recognize the discriminative stimuli or natural cues that set the occasion for specific types of communicative acts. The following questions can be used as a guide in monitoring this aspect of communication:

1. What are the discriminative stimuli or natural cues for this particular communicative function in each environment?

2. Are these cues currently sufficient to evoke an appropriate response from the individual? If not, partners may need to make use of instructional prompts to evoke the response.

3. Are the details of any artificial communicative cues or prompts that should be used clearly described as part of the instructional procedure?

4. Is the delivery of cues and prompts consistent across partners?

5. Is there a provision for the fading of instructional prompts and cues? If so, is information on the effectiveness of this fading process being collected and evaluated?

Instructional Prompts

The use of prompts in teaching can be highly productive; however, it is important that their use be monitored so that individuals do not become prompt dependent. Although prompts may be necessary during the initial stages of instruction, fading these as quickly as possible is important to ensure acquisition of more independent communication skills. The following questions may be useful in monitoring and evaluating progress:

1. How did partners come to select the prompts?

2. Are response prompts clearly specified in the instructional procedures?

3. Are these prompts consistently delivered by partners?

4. Is there a plan for fading prompts, and is this plan being implemented effectively?

5. Do objectives reflect increasing opportunities for functional and meaningful communication?

6. If not, how can instruction be altered to encourage this process?

Reinforcement

It is also important to monitor and evaluate the effectiveness of reinforcement procedures. Some individuals might become dependent on contrived reinforcement. The following questions can be considered when monitoring the effectiveness of reinforcement:

1. Was a preference assessment conducted to identify appropriate types of reinforcement?

2. Is the type and quantity of reinforcement specified, and is reinforcement delivered consistently?

3. Are these factors being reviewed actively?

4. Are artificial reinforcers being decreased quickly and effectively?

MONITORING IN NATURAL CONTEXTS

Undertaking systematic monitoring of the individual's progress when providing instruction during typical activities is sometimes difficult. The best way of tackling this problem will vary from person to person and setting to setting. To assist partners in monitoring progress during instruction, the following points should be considered.

First, it is important to consider the attitudes of partners. The partners' attitudes toward and expectations of an individual in a communicative exchange may influence the individual's performance. Given the interactive and interpersonal bases of communication, techniques designed to enhance skills may be affected by the presumptions of the people who are implementing the procedures (Butterfield & Arthur, 1995). Partners who have high yet realistic expectations may help enhance the communicative performance of the individual. For example, in considering the use of a delay in providing a desired object as a natural cue for requesting, the partner who is in touch with the individual's tendency to be impatient will do well to find another way to occasion a communicative interaction instead of just waiting longer.

Second, the notion that generalization is enhanced when teaching occurs across a variety of settings, partners, activities, and materials is now generally accepted (Snell & Brown, 2000; Westling & Floyd, 1990). Generalization can, therefore, be programmed by including a variety of settings, partners, activities, and materials during instruction. This statement does not infer the abandonment of structure but rather the integration of manageable ways of monitoring progress into the very activities and transactions in which one wishes to promote continuing skill use.

Third, monitoring should not interfere with effective teaching. If a partner is too busy collecting data, he or she might miss many valuable opportunities for interaction simply because of a failure to attend to the exchange and to the individual's performance. To increase manageability of data collection, limiting data collection initially to certain probe sessions, rather than trying to collect data during every session, may be helpful. A useful way to begin with an individual is to set aside one particular activity for the collection of data while maintaining an interactive perspective throughout the day and across all activities. Partners should identify objectives that are attainable, can be monitored in ways that are practicable, and do not interrupt the flow of the activity or interaction.

Fourth, having a clearly defined plan for fading prompts and contrived reinforcers may be helpful in order to encourage independent performance and attention to naturally occurring supports for communication. Fading prompts involves decreasing reliance on extra information, assistance, or encouragement while drawing attention to the natural features of the communication environment that facilitate interaction. This practice may, for example, involve a manipulation of time, stimulus materials, reinforcement types and schedules, qualitative changes in assistance levels, or, commonly, a combination of such procedures. Typically, the process of fading is achieved by pairing artificial features of the stimulus, behavior, or consequence with those the individual can expect to experience independently. Table 6.1 identifies some common progress points in communication interventions and suggests ways to modify aspects of the program.

OUTCOME CONSIDERATIONS

The process of evaluation is complex and multifaceted. We are interested in measurement and evaluation in terms of two dimensions: the communication process and communication outcomes (Arthur-Kelly, 2005; Brown & Snell, 1993; Haring & Breen, 1989). To this point, we have discussed the process of assessing, programming, teaching, and evaluating progress made in communication interventions. The focus has been on the students and their immediate communication partners.

In this section, we consider the effectiveness of the communication intervention as related to the wider linkages that influence an individual's quality of life. Both the process and the outcomes of the intervention are of concern in this context. The process of learning can be evaluated in terms of how well the intervention improved the functional skills of the individual. Outcome

Table 6.1. Progress points and suggested actions

What to do when	Action
An individual does not have existing forms and/or functions	Review assessment information.
An individual has lower-than-expected progress	Review assessment information, intervention pathways, and teaching strategies.
An individual has no independent use of skills	Check fading procedures.
An individual has few opportunities for communication	Increase the number of opportunities provided.
Short-term objective(s) are achieved	Set new objective(s) in light of assessment information and long-term objectives.
Long-term objectives(s) are achieved	Provide follow-up assessment.
Partner goals are achieved	Identify follow-up goals.

measures are designed to indicate the effect of these skills on the broader experience of the individual by considering indexes such as participation, autonomy, and control. Brown and Snell noted that "outcome measures offer information regarding the general effect of a program on a person's quality of life" (1993, p. 152). Brown, Gothelf, Guess, and Lehr (1998) indicated that it is vital to ensure that these outcomes are meaningful and empowering.

An ecological framework, which incorporates the immediate and wider social context, is crucial in the design of communication intervention programs. For example, the characteristics of individuals and their instructional settings constantly interplay with the input of communication partners and the broader inclusion of people with developmental and physical disabilities in the community. In terms of defining best practice, then, this approach means that there is little point, for example, in improving individual communication abilities if generalized improvements in interactive opportunities and experiences do not also form part of this process of development (Jackson, 1993).

When reviewing the overall outcomes and processes in operation for an individual, the following questions may provide a starting point for analysis:

1. Has the communication intervention been effective in building on the person's strengths and identified needs by increasing independence, choices, and control for the individual?

2. Have all of the relevant immediate social contexts supported the progress made by the individual?

3. What changes have occurred in the wider social contexts of the individual, and how have such changes influenced communicative activity and inclusion?

4. Are there strong linkages between individual needs and learning processes, and immediate social contexts and wider social contexts?

5. How can such linkages be enhanced?

SUMMARY AND CONCLUSIONS

This chapter introduces some strategies and considerations designed to assist in the effective monitoring and evaluation of a communication intervention. Monitoring includes reviewing progress made by the individual during intervention, evaluating the effects of specific procedures, and monitoring partner skills. Various approaches can be taken in monitoring, including anecdotal notes, direct observations, and self-evaluation by partners.

The important point is to select a monitoring procedure that is suited to the intervention pathway, the goal of intervention, the individual, and the context in which instruction occurs. The information collected is used to monitor progress and to determine if and when procedures need to be modified. Along these lines, partners should monitor the cues, prompts, and reinforcers used during instruction. Communication intervention should lead to improved quality of life for individuals with developmental disabilities. Systematic monitoring is often necessary to determine the extent to which the outcomes from communication intervention are meaningful and empowering.

7

Case Studies

NANCY BUTTERFIELD, MICHAEL ARTHUR-KELLY,
AND JEFF SIGAFOOS

INTRODUCTION

This chapter illustrates the concepts and procedures considered in Chapters 1–6 through a series of five case studies. Each case study was selected to illustrate the different intervention needs that partners are likely to encounter among individuals with developmental and physical disabilities. For each case study, we describe the assessment, intervention pathways, and instructional procedures that were used.

CASE STUDY 1: STRENGTHENING POTENTIAL COMMUNICATIVE ACTS

Liana was an 8-year-old girl who attended a school that included students with severe and multiple disabilities. Due to her very limited motor control and lack of formal expressive language skills, Liana was dependent on those around her for help with her daily needs. Liana's apparently passive role in just about every interaction meant that others believed that she had virtually no influence over her environment or the activities and routines that she experienced both at school and in the home where she lived.

Assessment

School staff were concerned that it would be difficult to find ways to involve Liana in decisions about her daily life, in order to maximize her active participation in the various events that make up a typical day. A few ideas were tested. First, a number of staff members watched routines, such as mealtime, and wrote notes about the communicative interactions occurring between Liana and her partners. These naturalistic observations lasted about 10 minutes and were conducted across a range of daily activities. After taking notes for several days, all of the partners involved with Liana got together and discussed the patterns they could see in the notes.

Based on their knowledge of Liana and these naturalistic observations, the communication partners were able to identify a number of potential communicative acts. For example, a number of partners noted that Liana sometimes made a faint smiling expression. This potential communicative act was interpreted by partners as Liana's way of indicating that she wanted more of an object or activity. These types of acts were considered appropriate forms of communication; however, it was unclear if these potential acts were in fact representative of the perlocutionary or illocutionary stage of communication development.

Intervention Pathway

The decision was, therefore, made to enter these types of acts into the Interpretive Pathway, with the goal of increasing the consistency and frequency with which they occurred during communicative interactions with partners. For example, one goal was to increase Liana's use of the smiling expression as a way of requesting more of a preferred object or activity.

Instructional Procedures

The partners created opportunities for Liana to request more within typically classroom activities by withholding a preferred item or interrupting an activity. Staff verbally acknowledged Liana when she smiled during these opportunities, and they consistently reinforced the response as a request by giving Liana more of the relevant object or activity.

Modifying the Program

Informal notes on progress were made and circulated among staff members to encourage consistency in using the instructional procedures. Liana's communication partners soon found that time was a major consideration in this procedure. Specifically, they got better results by waiting for 25–30 seconds after an opportunity to request more arose.

Outcomes

Eventually, a faint smile became a consistent way for Liana to achieve this particular communicative function, which opened the way for Liana to develop more control of her environment and play a more active part in communication processes. This increased power changed many of the expectations previously held by her partners. The partners now began to expect a response from Liana in situations in which they had never attempted to include her input.

Summary

This case study underlines the importance of careful observation and partner skills in changing the communicative lives of individuals with developmental and physical disabilities. By recognizing the influence of factors such as partner wait times and consistency and by systematically using information collected in natural learning environments, Liana's partners helped her develop her potential communicative act into a reliable form of communication.

CASE STUDY 2: INCREASING SOCIAL INTERACTION

Bill was a 7-year-old boy with a severe intellectual disability and cerebral palsy. He attended the neighborhood school and lived at home with his parents and two siblings. He was not able to walk or stand, but he could sit independently. The extent of his visual ability was unknown.

Assessment

Informal interviews with partners revealed that Bill mainly used prelinguistic forms of communication. For example, he appeared to seek continuation of a social interaction by reaching out and touching the adult with whom he was interacting. In addition, at mealtimes, he often kept his eyes shut. Because Bill was able to interact with people at other times (e.g., social games, routines), it was decided that he also needed to interact more with the person assisting him at lunchtime.

Intervention Pathway

Partners agreed that more time needed to be taken to include interactions during mealtimes. The communication objective was that Bill would open his eyes and look at the person assisting him at mealtimes in response to the cue, "Bill, look at me. Do you want some lunch?" In addition, his communication partners agreed that they needed to recognize that mealtime was an appropriate, natural context for promoting social interaction. They, therefore, had to respond consistently to Bill so as to increase potential communicative acts that occurred during mealtimes.

Instructional Procedures

Referencing was the selected strategy with the request for Bill to look, followed by directing him to the person assisting him with his meal and his food.

Outcomes

Bill initially opened his eyes and looked to the side as he moved his head about. He gradually focused his attention toward the person interacting with him so that finally he stopped moving his head and looked directly at the person talking to him and assisting him with his meal.

Bill also became more responsive when others outside the classroom interacted with him. If spoken to, he would lift his head and look at the person interacting with him. As a result, more people began to take the time to talk with Bill.

He was also observed to pay more visual attention to things happening in the classroom. For example, he would follow someone moving across the room. The behavior of looking to the person interacting with him transferred to other activities throughout the day.

Summary

This case study illustrates how the partners attempted to use the referencing procedure to increase Bill's social interaction during mealtimes. The establishment of a social connection with the person assisting him with his meal appeared to have a significant impact on Bill's overall quality of life.

CASE STUDY 3: ENHANCING POTENTIAL COMMUNICATIVE ACTS

Sue was a 13-year-old girl who attended a school that included students with moderate or severe intellectual disabilities. She was independently mobile, had good vision and fine motor control, did not speak, and had no recognized symbolic communication system, despite the fact that many years had been put into teaching Sue to point to line drawings in response to requests such as "Show me the cup."

Assessment

Informal observations indicated that Sue appeared to show several forms of potential communicative acts. For example, during a favorite activity, such as looking at a magazine with a partner, she would often vocalize, take the partner's hand, single out the pointer finger, and physically assist that person to point to a picture in the magazine. This act was interpreted as a tact or her way of commenting on the picture. In addition, she appeared to engage in mands such as picking up her lunch bag to indicate that she wanted to eat. Similarly, she would often stand outside the classroom door looking toward the restrooms as if indicating the need to use the toilet.

Intervention Pathway

Given that these existing behaviors were informal and idiosyncratic, it was decided that these potential communicative acts should be enhanced by developing additional and more symbolic forms of communication.

Instructional Procedures

The activity selected for the initial phase of instruction was a snack time routine in the classroom. The communication goals were to get Sue to 1) point to the picture card for *drink* and look to the communication partner following the mand "Tell me you want a drink," and 2) point to the picture card for *biscuit* and look to the communication partner following the mand "Tell me you want a biscuit." Instruction occurred after Sue reached for either the juice or the biscuit. Thus, a response chaining procedure was also implemented.

During the initial phase of instruction, Sue was offered a drink and a biscuit. The pictures for each were also present when Sue used behavior indication; the communication partner acknowledged her response, then asked her to request using the pictures (e.g., "Oh, I see you're thirsty. Tell me you want a drink."). At this point, the behavior of pointing to the card was modeled, and Sue was physically assisted to point to the card. She was then given the requested item.

Outcomes

With this procedure, Sue learned to point to the picture card to request a drink and a biscuit and to look to the communication partner.

Summary

The response chaining procedures appeared to be an effective way of beginning a symbolic, picture-based communication system for Sue. The plan was that Sue could also continue to use behavior indication to request other items that she did not have symbols for until these additional vocabulary symbols were taught. In this way, her informal prelinguistic forms of behavior indication were enhanced with picture symbols.

CASE STUDY 4: DEVELOPING SYMBOLIC FORMS OF COMMUNICATION

Robert was a 10-year-old boy with autism and severe cognitive impairments. He attended a classroom at his local school. Robert had no speech but did have a number of gestures in his repertoire that had clear communicative functions. Because he was getting older, Robert needed to use age-appropriate forms of communication. Thus, it was important to ensure that he developed more symbolic forms of communication to replace his informal gestures.

Assessment

Detailed interviews with partners revealed that Robert's main forms of communication involved the use of informal gestures that were directed at objects and symbols (e.g., inconsistent pointing at preferred items). In addition, to obtain things he wanted, Robert usually did so in a rather informal manner (e.g., standing near the refrigerator to request food). Robert appeared capable of producing a number of communicative functions using these informal gestures, although most of these gestures functioned as mands for access to preferred objects ("I want.") or to escape nonpreferred activities ("Let me out of here."). When denied access to a preferred object after making a gesture, Robert often became aggressive, suggesting that escalation to aggression was a type of communication repair strategy.

Intervention Pathway

Robert's existing gestures were considered appropriate but limiting forms of communication, especially as he was likely to have to communicate with a range of partners in community settings as he got older. Thus, it was decided to enter these acts into the Replacement Pathway with the priority to teach Robert more socially appropriate, consistent, and effective ways of getting his message across.

Instructional Procedures

Initially, Robert was taught to use a VOCA to request access to preferred objects. Six preferred items were introduced, all of which were highly preferred by Robert. Six corresponding line drawings (e.g., chips, puzzle) were affixed to the communication device, and an appropriate message (e.g., "I want some chips." "I want to work on a puzzle.") was produced when a drawing was pressed. Robert was taught to point to the corresponding picture on the communication device to request an object. Specifically, he was taught to scan the array of pictures on the device and then select the picture that corresponded to the item he wanted. As soon as he selected a picture, the partner gave him the requested item.

Outcomes

Progress was slow but consistent, with the data indicating that Robert was increasingly displaying positive communicative behaviors using the more symbolic voice-output devices. As he made progress, opportunities were expanded across settings, and the array of picture symbols was increased. A key to the whole program was the training of partners across settings to expect and reinforce Robert's use of the VOCA to request preferred objects. Partners provided opportunities for Robert to request preferred objects throughout the day.

Summary

This case study illustrates a replacement-based intervention. Informal gestures that could be read by only a few familiar partners were replaced by teaching Robert to use a VOCA. The VOCA was likely to be more effective across a range of partners and settings.

CASE STUDY 5: REPLACING CHALLENGING BEHAVIOR

Christopher was a 3-year-old boy with severe intellectual disabilities and some motor control impairments. He also was said to engage in "autistic-like behaviors." He did not speak and appeared to have no existing acts that had good communicative potential.

Assessment

Christopher was observed in an early intervention classroom. When first seen, he was sitting on the floor, his legs stretched out in front of him. Maintaining this position was apparently difficult for him because of his motor control problems. After 15 seconds or so, the strain became too much, and his head plopped forward, striking the floor with a thump. There was then a slight pause, followed by a most distressing bout of crying. His teacher rushed to his side to provide comfort and attention. With Christopher calm once again, the teacher placed him in the exact same sitting position and walked away.

Technically, Christopher had engaged in head banging, which was quickly followed by teacher attention. At this point, however, it would be quite incorrect to assume that head banging occurred to obtain teacher attention. Instead, the "cause" of this particular instance of head banging was, no doubt, quite accidental. Christopher fell over and banged his head simply because he lacked sufficient trunk control to maintain an upright sitting position.

Despite the fortuitous nature of this incident, the observations ended with a fear of what could happen if similar sequences of events were repeated often enough. Another visit 2 months later confirmed this lingering fear. Christopher now had a great welt on his forehead from repeated contact with the floor. During this second brief visit, no less than five separate incidents of forceful head banging were observed.

Each incident followed the same course. Christopher was again seated on the floor but seemed to have less trouble maintaining an upright position—

his trunk control may have improved somewhat during the 2-month lapse. He then looked at his teacher, who stood in view across the room, and in a seemingly deliberate fashion threw his head forward, striking the floor with a sharp crack. The teacher came immediately. She lifted Christopher from the floor, said a few comforting words, checked the wound, and eventually returned Christopher to an upright sitting position, leaving him once again unattended until the next incident.

This case study clearly shows how head banging initially resulting from poor posture control was relatively quickly shaped into an effective means of communication for obtaining attention. It also illustrates how challenging behavior might emerge through the interaction of developmental and environmental factors, that is, as a result of Christopher's poor posture control, limited communication development (e.g., inability to recruit attention by speaking), and the reaction of others (e.g., attention from the teacher contingent on self-injury).

Intervention Pathway

Given that Christopher's head banging now seemed well established as a means of requesting attention, an effective intervention plan might involve teaching him a more appropriate way of gaining the teacher's attention.

Instructional Procedures

The instructional procedure used with Christopher was functional communication training. Specifically, he was taught to use a VOCA to gain attention, using procedures described in Chapter 5 (see Table 5.2). The procedure was implemented in his classroom. The teacher interacted with Christopher, then told him, "I have to go." The teacher then walked away while a second partner prompted Christopher to press the switch on the VOCA to generate the recorded message "Come here, please." When the teacher heard the message, she came back and reinforced Christopher with attention. Over teaching sessions, prompting was faded using a time-delay procedure.

Outcomes

Christopher quickly learned to use the VOCA to request attention. As he learned to use the device, his self-injury decreased, suggesting that the use of the VOCA had replaced his self-injury.

Summary

Christopher's self-injury appeared to develop into a form of communication because it was often followed by attention from partners. The act would thus be interpreted as a form of communication that was used to gain attention.

Because self-injury was not acceptable, it was entered into the Replacement Pathway. Self-injury was replaced by teaching Christopher to recruit attention with a more appropriate form of communication, which involved using a VOCA.

SUMMARY AND CONCLUSIONS

These five case studies illustrate the use of the Interpretive, Enhancement, and Replacement Pathways in combination with a range of instructional procedures. The procedures used in these case studies were derived from empirically validated principles of learning and development; however, as noted in some of the cases, the procedures often needed to be modified in light of the unique circumstances of the individual. The communication needs, and hence the types of communication goals and indicated procedures, will vary greatly among individuals with developmental and physical disabilities because each individual is unique. In considering the individual case, partners will be more successful if they can adopt a systematic approach.

The systematic approach outlined in this book and illustrated in these five case studies involves a number of integrated steps:

1. Identifying and verifying the communicative function of existing responses within the person's repertoire

2. Entering the existing acts into one or more appropriate intervention pathways

3. Implementing one or more appropriate instructional procedures to achieve the goal of the selected pathway

4. Monitoring progress to determine if and how the procedures may need to be modified.

We believe that these four steps constitute one potentially effective approach to communication intervention, and we hope that this approach will assist partners as they work toward improving the quality of life of individuals with developmental and physical disabilities.

References

Anderson, L., Dancis, J., & Alpert, M. (1978). Behavioral contingencies and self-mutilation in Lesch-Nyhan disease. *Journal of Consulting and Clinical Psychology, 46,* 529–536.

Anderson, L.T., Herrmann, L., Alpert, M., & Dancis, J. (1975). Elimination of self-mutilation in Lesch-Nyhan disease. *Pediatric Research, 9,* 257.

Arthur, M. (2003). Socio-communicative variables and behavior states in students with profound and multiple disabilities: Descriptive data from school settings. *Education and Training in Developmental Disabilities, 38,* 200–219.

Arthur, M. (2004). Patterns amongst behavior states, socio-communicative, and activity variables in educational programs for students with profound and multiple disabilities. *Journal of Developmental and Physical Disabilities, 16*(2), 125–149.

Arthur, M., & Foreman, P. (2002). Educational programming for students with high support needs: Report data from teachers, paraprofessionals and other professionals working in Australian schools. *Developmental Disabilities Bulletin, 30,* 115–139.

Arthur-Kelly, M. (2005). Planning effective teaching strategies. In P. Foreman (Ed.), *Inclusion in action* (3rd ed., pp. 174–208). Melbourne, Australia: Thomson Learning.

Ault, M.M., Guy, B., Guess, D., Bashinski, S., & Roberts, S. (1995). Analyzing behavior state and learning environments: Application in instructional settings. *Mental Retardation, 33,* 304–316.

Bates, E., Benigni, L., Bretherton, I., Camaioni, L., & Volterra, V. (1979). *The emergence of symbols: Cognition and communication in infancy.* San Diego: Academic Press.

Bates, E., Camaioni, L., & Volterra, V. (1975). The acquisition of performatives prior to speech. *Merrill-Palmer Quarterly, 21,* 205–226.

Beukelman, D.R., & Mirenda, P. (2005). *Augmentative and alternative communication: Supporting children and adults with complex communication needs* (3rd ed.). Baltimore: Paul H. Brookes Publishing Co.

Bird, F., Dores, P.A., Moniz, D., & Robinson, J. (1989). Reducing severe aggressive and self-injurious behaviors with functional communication training. *American Journal on Mental Retardation, 94,* 37–48.

Bosch, J., Van Dyke, D.C., Milligan Smith, S., & Poulton, S. (1997). Role of medical conditions in the exacerbation of self-injurious behavior: An exploratory study. *Mental Retardation, 35,* 124–130.

Brady, N.C., & Halle, J.W. (2002). Breakdowns and repairs in conversations between beginning AAC users and their partners. In D.R. Beukelman & J. Reichle (Series Eds.) & J. Reichle, D.R. Beukelman, & J.C. Light (Vol. Eds.), *Augmentative and alternative communication series: Exemplary practices for beginning communicators: Implications for AAC* (pp. 323–351). Baltimore: Paul H. Brookes Publishing Co.

Bronfenbrenner, U. (1995). Developmental ecology through space and time: A future perspective. In P. Moen, G.H. Elder, Jr., & K. Luscher (Eds.), *Examining lives in context: Perspectives on the ecology of human development* (pp. 619–647). Washington, DC: American Psychological Association.

Brown, F., Gothelf, C.R., Guess, D., & Lehr, D.H. (1998). Self-determination for individuals with the most severe disabilities. *Journal of The Association for Persons with Severe Handicaps, 23,* 17–26.

Brown, F., & Lehr, D.H. (1993). Making activities meaningful for students with severe multiple disabilities. *Teaching Exceptional Children, 25*(4), 12–16.

Brown, F., & Snell, M.E. (1993). Measurement, analysis, and evaluation. In M.E. Snell (Ed.), *Instruction of students with severe disabilities* (4th ed., pp. 152–183). New York: Macmillan/Merrill.

Brown, L., Branston-McLean, M.B., Baumgart, D., Vincent, L., Falvey, M., & Schroeder, J. (1979). Using the characteristics of current and subsequent least restrictive environments as factors in the development of curricular content for severely handicapped students. *AAESPH Review, 4,* 407–424.

Bruner, J.S. (1975). The ontogenesis of speech acts. *Journal of Child Language, 2,* 1–19.

Butterfield, N., & Arthur, M. (1995). Shifting the focus: Emerging priorities in communication programming for students with severe intellectual disability. *Education and Training in Mental Retardation and Developmental Disabilities, 30,* 41–50.

Carr, E.G. (1977). The motivation of self-injurious behavior: A review of some hypotheses. *Psychological Bulletin, 84,* 800–816.

Carr, E.G. (1988). Functional equivalence as a mechanism of response generation. In R.H. Horner, G. Dunlap, & R. Koegel (Eds.), *Generalization and maintenance: Life-style changes in applied settings* (pp. 221–241). Baltimore: Paul H. Brookes Publishing Co.

Carr, E.G., Dunlap, G., Horner, R.H., Koegel, R.L., Turnbull, A.P., Sailor, W., et al. (2002). Positive behavior support: Evolution of an applied science. *Journal of Positive Behavior Interventions, 4,* 4–16.

Carr, E.G., & Durand, V.M. (1985). Reducing behavior problems through functional communication training. *Journal of Applied Behavior Analysis, 18,* 111–126.

Carr, E.G., Levin, L., McConnachie, G., Carlson, J.I., Kemp, D.C., & Smith, C.E. (1994). *Communication-based intervention for problem behavior: A user's guide for producing positive change.* Baltimore: Paul H. Brookes Publishing Co.

Carr, E.G., Newsom, C.D., & Binkoff, J.A. (1980). Escape as a factor in the aggressive behavior of two retarded children. *Journal of Applied Behavior Analysis, 13,* 101–117.

Carr, E.G., & Smith, C.E. (1995). Biological setting events for self-injury. *Mental Retardation and Developmental Disabilities Research Reviews, 12,* 94–98.

Carter, M. (2002). Communicative spontaneity in individuals with high support needs: An exploratory consideration of causation. *International Journal of Disability, Development, and Education, 49*(3), 225–242.

Carter, M. (2003a). Communicative spontaneity of children with high support needs who use augmentative and alternative communication systems: I. Classroom spontaneity, mode, and function. *Augmentative and Alternative Communication, 19*(3), 141–154.

Carter, M. (2003b). Communicative spontaneity of children with high support needs who use augmentative and alternative communication systems: II. Antecedents and effectiveness of communication. *Augmentative and Alternative Communication, 19*(3), 155–169

Carter, M., & Iacono, T. (2002). Professional judgments of the intentionality of communicative acts. *Augmentative and Alternative Communication, 18*, 177–191.

Cataldo, M.F., & Harris, J. (1982). The biological basis for self-injury in the mentally retarded. *Analysis and Intervention in Developmental Disabilities, 2*, 21–39.

Chamberlain, L., Chung, M.C., & Jenner, L. (1993). Preliminary findings on communication and challenging behaviour in learning difficulty. *British Journal of Developmental Disabilities, 39*, 118–125.

Cirrin, F.M., & Rowland, C.M. (1985). Communication assessment of nonverbal youths with severe/profound mental retardation. *Mental Retardation, 23*, 52–62.

Cress, C.J. (2002). Expanding children's early augmented behaviors to support symbolic development. In D.R. Beukelman & J. Reichle (Series Eds.) & J. Reichle, D.R., Beukelman, & J.C. Light (Vol. Eds.), *Augmentative and alternative communication series: Exemplary practices for beginning communicators: Implications for AAC* (pp. 219–273). Baltimore: Paul H. Brookes Publishing Co.

Cress, C.J., & Marvin, C.A. (2003). Common questions about AAC services in early intervention. *Augmentative and Alternative Communication, 19*(4), 254–272.

DePaepe, P.A., & Wood, L.A. (2001). Collaborative practices related to augmentative and alternative communication: Current personnel preparation programs. *Communication Disorders Quarterly, 2*, 77.

Dettmer, S., Simpson, R.L., Smith Myles, B., & Ganz, J.B. (2000). The use of visual supports to facilitate transitions of students with autism. *Focus on Autism and Other Developmental Disabilities, 15*(3), 163–169.

Didden, R., Duker, P., & Korzilius, H. (1997). Meta-analytic study of treatment effectiveness for problem behaviors with individuals who have mental retardation. *American Journal on Mental Retardation, 101*, 387–399.

Donnellan, A.M., Mirenda, P.L., Mesaros, R.A., & Fassbender, L.L. (1984). Analyzing the communicative functions of aberrant behavior. *Journal of The Association for Persons with Severe Handicaps, 9*, 201–212.

Downing, J.E. (2005). *Teaching communication skills to students with severe disabilities* (2nd ed.). Baltimore: Paul H. Brookes Publishing Co.

Drasgow, E., Halle, J., & Sigafoos, J. (1999). Teaching communication to learners with severe disabilities: Motivation, response competition and generalization. *Australasian Journal of Special Education, 23*(1), 47–63.

Drash, P.W., High, R.L., & Tudor, R.M. (1999). Using mand training to establish an echoic repertoire in young children with autism. *Analysis of Verbal Behavior, 16*, 29–44.

Duker, P. (1975). Behaviour control of self-biting in a Lesch-Nyhan patient. *Journal of Mental Deficiency Research, 19,* 11–19.

Duker, P.C. (1999). The Verbal Behavior Assessment Scale (VerBAS): Construct validity, reliability, and internal consistency. *Research in Developmental Disabilities, 20,* 347–353.

Duker, P.C., Didden, R., & Sigafoos, J. (2004). *One-to-one training: Instructional procedures for learners with developmental disabilities.* Austin, TX: PRO-ED.

Durand, V.M. (1990). *Severe behavior problems: A functional communication training approach.* New York: Guilford Press.

Durand, V.M. (2001). Functional communication training: A contemporary behavior analytic intervention for problem behavior. *Focus on Autism and Other Developmental Disorders, 16,* 110–119.

Durand, V.M., & Carr, E.G. (1991). Functional communication training to reduce challenging behavior: Maintenance and application in new settings. *Journal of Applied Behavior Analysis, 24,* 251–264

Durand, V.M., & Crimmins, D.B. (1988). Identifying the variables maintaining self-injurious behavior. *Journal of Autism & Developmental Disorders, 18,* 99–117.

Durand, V.M., & Crimmins, D.B. (1991). Teaching functionally equivalent responses as an intervention for challenging behavior. In B. Remington (Ed.), *The challenge of severe mental handicap: A behavior analytic approach* (pp. 71–95). Chichester, England: John Wiley & Sons.

Ferguson, D.L. (1994). Is communication really the point? Some thoughts on interventions and membership. *Mental Retardation, 32,* 7–18.

Ferster, C.B. (1961). Positive reinforcement and behavioral deficits of autistic children. *Child Development, 32,* 437–456.

Fisher, W.W., Piazza, C.C., Cataldo, M.F., Harrell, R., et al. (1993). Functional communication training with and without extinction and punishment. *Journal of Applied Behavior Analysis, 26,* 23–36.

Fleming, I., & Kroese, B.S. (1993). *People with learning disability and severe challenging behaviour: New directions in services and therapy.* Manchester, UK: Manchester University Press.

Gedye, A. (1989). Episodic rage and aggression attributed to frontal lobe seizures. *Journal of Mental Deficiency Research, 33,* 369–379.

Giangreco, M.F. (2000). Related services research for students with low-incidence disabilities: Implications for speech-language pathologists in inclusive classrooms. *Language, Speech, and Hearing Services in School, 31,* 230–239.

Grisham-Brown, J., Schuster, J.W., Hemmeter, M.L., & Collins, B.C. (2000). Using an embedded strategy to teach preschoolers with significant disabilities. *Journal of Behavioral Education, 10,* 139–162.

Grunsell, J., & Carter, M. (2002). The behavior chain interruption strategy: Generalisation to out-of-routine contexts. *Education and Training in Mental Retardation and Developmental Disabilities, 37*(4), 378–390.

Guess, D., Roberts, S., Siegel-Causey, E., & Rues, J. (1995). Replication and extended analysis of behavior state, environmental events, and related variables among individuals with profound disabilities. *American Journal on Mental Retardation, 100*(1), 36–50.

Gunsett, R.P., Mulick, J.A., Fernald, W.B., & Martin, J.L. (1989). Indications for medical screening prior to behavioral programming for severely and profoundly mentally retarded clients. *Journal of Autism and Developmental Disorders, 19,* 167–172.

Halle, J. (1987). Teaching language in the natural environment: An analysis of spontaneity. *Journal of The Association for Persons with Severe Handicaps, 12,* 28–37.

Halliday, M. (1975). Learning how to mean. In E. Lenneberg & E. Lenneberg (Eds.), *Foundations of language development: A multi-disciplinary approach* (Vol. 1, pp. 239–265). San Diego: Academic Press.

Hancock, T.B., & Kaiser, A.P. (2002). The effects of trainer-implemented enhanced milieu teaching on the social communication of children with autism. *Topics in Early Childhood Special Education, 22*(1), 39–54.

Haring, T.G., & Breen, C. (1989). Units of analysis of social interaction outcomes in supported education. *Journal of The Association for Persons with Severe Handicaps, 14,* 255–262.

Harrison, J., Lombardino, L.J., & Stapell, J.B. (1987). The development of early communication: Using developmental literature for selecting communication goals. *Journal of Special Education, 20,* 463–473.

Harwood, K., Warren, S., & Yoder, P. (2002). The importance of responsivity in developing contingent exchanges with beginning communicators. In D.R. Beukelman & J. Reichle (Series Eds.) & J. Reichle, D.R. Beukelman, & J.C. Light (Vol. Eds.), *Augmentative and alternative communication series: Exemplary practices for beginning communicators: Implications for AAC* (pp. 59–95). Baltimore: Paul H. Brookes Publishing Co.

Heflin, L.J., & Simpson, R.L. (1998). Interventions for children and youth with autism: Prudent choices in a world of exaggerated claims and empty promises: Part I. Intervention and treatment option review. *Focus on Autism and Other Developmental Disabilities, 13,* 194–211.

Herrnstein, R.J. (1970). On the law of effect. *Journal of the Experimental Analysis of Behavior, 13,* 243–266.

Horner, R.D. (1980). The effects of an environmental enrichment program on the behavior of institutionalized profoundly retarded children. *Journal of Applied Behavior Analysis, 13*(3), 473–491.

Horner, R.H., & Day, H.M. (1991). The effects of response efficiency on functionally equivalent competing behaviors. *Journal of Applied Behavior Analysis, 24,* 719–732.

Houghton, J., Bronicki, G.J., & Guess, D. (1987). Opportunities to express preferences and make choices among students with severe disabilities in classrooms. *Journal of The Association for Persons with Severe Handicaps, 12,* 18–27.

Hunt, P., Soto, G., Maier, J., Muller, E., & Goetz, L. (2002). Collaborative teaming to support students with augmentative and alternative communication needs in general education classrooms. *Augmentative and Alternative Communication, 18,* 20–35.

Iacono, T., Waring, R., & Chan, J. (1996). Sampling communicative behaviours in children with intellectual disability in structured and unstructured situations. *European Journal of Disorders of Communication, 31,* 106–120.

Iwata, B.A., Dorsey, M.F., Slifer, K.J., Bauman, K.E., & Richman, G.S. (1982). Toward a functional analysis of self-injury. *Analysis and Intervention in Developmental Disabilities, 2,* 3–20. Reprinted in *Journal of Applied Behavior Analysis (1994), 27,* 197–209.

Iwata, B., Pace, G., Dorsey, M., Zarcone, J., Vollmer, T., Smith, R., et al. (1994). The functions of self-injurious behavior: An experimental-epidemiological analysis. *Journal of Applied Behavior Analysis, 27,* 215–240.

Iwata, B.A., Pace, G.M., Kalsher, M.J., Cowdery, G.E., & Cataldo, M.F. (1990). Experimental analysis and extinction of self-injurious escape behavior. *Journal of Applied Behavior Analysis, 23,* 11–27.

Iwata, B.A., Vollmer, T.R., & Zarcone, J. (1990). The experimental (functional) analysis of behavior disorders: Methodology, applications, and limitations. In A. Repp & N.N. Singh (Eds.), *Perspectives on the use of nonaversive and aversive interventions for persons with developmental disabilities* (pp. 301–330). Sycamore, IL: Sycamore Publishing.

Jackson, L. (1993). Elements of a theoretical structure that will support best practices in communication facilitation. *Journal of The Association for Persons with Severe Handicaps, 18,* 143–160.

Kaczmarek, L.A. (1990). Teaching spontaneous language to individuals with severe handicaps: A matrix model. *Journal of The Association for Persons with Severe Handicaps, 15,* 160–169.

Kaiser, A.P., & Goetz, L. (1993). Enhancing communication with persons labeled severely disabled. *Journal of The Association for Persons with Severe Handicaps, 18,* 137–142.

Kaiser, A.P., Hancock, T.B., & Nietfeld, J.P. (2000). The effects of parent-implemented enhanced milieu teaching on the social communication of children who have autism. *Early Education and Development, 11,* 423–446.

Kaiser, A.P., Yoder, P.J., & Keetz, A. (1992). Evaluating milieu teaching. In S.F. Warren & J.E. Reichle (Series & Vol. Eds.), *Communication and language intervention series: Vol. 1. Causes and effects in communication and language intervention* (pp. 9–47). Baltimore: Paul H. Brookes Publishing Co.

Keen, D. (2003). Communicative repair strategies and problem behaviours of children with autism. *International Journal of Disability, Development, and Education, 50,* 53–64.

Keen, D., Sigafoos, J., & Woodyatt, G. (2001). Replacing prelinguistic behaviors with functional communication. *Journal of Autism and Developmental Disorders, 31,* 385–398.

Keen, D., Woodyatt, G., & Sigafoos, J. (2002). Verifying teacher perceptions of the potential communicative acts of children with autism. *Communication Disorders Quarterly, 23*(3), 133–143.

Kiernan, C. (1994). *Early intervention and challenging behaviour.* Manchester: University of Manchester, Hester Adrian Research Centre.

Kozleski, E.B. (1991). Expectant delay procedure for teaching requests. *Augmentative and Alternative Communication, 7,* 11–19.

Lalli, J.S., & Goh, H. (1993). Naturalistic observations in community settings. In S.F. Warren & J. Reichle (Series Eds.) & J. Reichle & D.P. Wacker (Vol. Eds.), *Communication and language intervention series: Vol. 3. Communicative alternatives to challenging behavior: Integrating functional assessment and intervention strategies* (pp. 11–39). Baltimore: Paul H. Brookes Publishing Co.

Lesch, M., & Nyhan, W.I. (1964). A familial disorder of uric acid metabolism and central nervous system function. *American Journal of Medicine, 36,* 561.

Linscheid, T.R. (1999). Commentary: Response to empirically supported treatments for feeding problems. *Journal of Pediatric Psychology, 24,* 215–216.

Lovaas, O.I., Newsom, C., & Hickman, C. (1987). Self-stimulatory behavior and perceptual reinforcement. *Journal of Applied Behavior Analysis, 20,* 45–68.

Lowry, M.A., & Sovner, R. (1992). Severe behaviour problems associated with rapid cycling bipolar disorder in two adults with profound mental retardation. *Journal of Intellectual Disability Research, 36,* 269–281.

Mace, F.C., Lalli, J.S., & Pinter-Lalli, E. (1991). Functional analysis and treatment of aberrant behavior. *Research in Developmental Disabilities, 12,* 155–180.

Matson, J.L., & Mayville, E.A. (2001). The relationship of functional variables and psychopathology to aggressive behavior in persons with severe and profound mental retardation. *Journal of Psychopathology & Behavioral Assessment, 23,* 3–9.

McArthur, D., & Adamson, L. (1996). Joint attention in preverbal children: Autism and developmental language disorder. *Journal of Autism and Developmental Disorders, 26,* 481–496.

McCathren, R.B. (2000). Teacher-implemented prelinguistic communication intervention. *Focus on Autism and Other Developmental Disabilities, 15*(1), 21–29.

McLean, J., & Snyder-McLean, L. (1987). Form and function of communicative behaviour among persons with severe developmental disabilities. *Australia & New Zealand Journal of Developmental Disabilities, 13,* 83–98.

McLean, L.K., & McLean, J.E. (1993). Communication intervention for adults with severe mental retardation. *Topics in Language Disorders, 13,* 47–60.

Meyer, L.H., & Evans, I.M. (1993). Science and practice in behavioral intervention: Meaningful outcomes, research validity, and usable knowledge. *Journal of The Association for Persons with Severe Handicaps, 18,* 137–142.

Mirenda, P. (1997). Supporting individuals with challenging behavior through functional communication training and AAC: Research review. *Augmentative and Alternative Communication, 13,* 207–225.

Mostert, M.P. (2001). Facilitated communication since 1995: A review of published studies. *Journal of Autism and Developmental Disorders, 31,* 287–313.

Mulick, J.A., & Kedesdy, J.H. (1988). Self-injurious behavior, its treatment, and normalization. *Mental Retardation, 26,* 223–229.

Mundy, P., & Vaughan, A. (2002). Joint attention and its role in the diagnostic assessment of children with autism. *Assessment for Effective Intervention, 27,* 57–60.

Mundy, P., & Willoughby, J. (1998). Nonverbal communication, affect, and social-emotional development. In S.F. Warren & J. Reichle (Series Eds.) & A.M. Wetherby, S.F. Warren, & J. Reichle (Vol. Eds.), *Communication and language intervention series: Vol. 7. Transitions in prelinguistic communication* (pp. 111–133). Baltimore: Paul H. Brookes Publishing Co.

National Joint Committee for the Communicative Needs of Persons with Severe Disabilities. (1992, March). Guidelines for meeting the communication needs of persons with severe disabilities. *Asha, 34,* 1–8.

Newton, J.T., & Sturmey, P. (1991). The Motivation Assessment Scale: Inter-rater reliability and internal consistency in a British sample. *Journal of Mental Deficiency Research, 35,* 472–474.

Ogletree, B.T., & Oren, T. (2001). Application of ABA principles to general communication instruction. *Focus on Autism and Other Developmental Disabilities, 16*(2), 102–109.

Oliver, C., Murphy, G.H., Crayton, L., & Corbett, J.A. (1993). Self-injurious behavior in Rett syndrome: Interactions between features of Rett syndrome and operant conditioning. *Journal of Autism & Developmental Disorders, 23,* 91–109.

Olsson, B., & Rett, A. (1985). Behavioral observations concerning differential diagnosis between the Rett syndrome and autism. *Brain and Development, 7,* 281–289.

O'Neill, R.E., Horner, R.H., Albin, R.W., Sprague, J.R., Storey, K., & Newton, J.S. (1997). *Functional assessment and program development for problem behavior: A practical handbook* (2nd ed.). Pacific Grove, CA: Brooks/Cole Publishing.

O'Reilly, M.F. (1995). Functional analysis and treatment of escape-maintained aggression correlated with sleep deprivation. *Journal of Applied Behavior Analysis, 28,* 225–226.

O'Reilly, M.F. (1997). Functional analysis of episodic self-injury correlated with recurrent otitis media. *Journal of Applied Behavior Analysis, 30,* 165–167.

Paclawskyi, T.R., Matson, J.L., Rush, K.S., Smalls, Y., & Vollmer, T.R. (2000). Questions About Behavioral Function (QABF): A behavioral checklist for functional assessment of aberrant behavior. *Research in Developmental Disabilities, 21,* 223–229.

Paisey, T.J., Whitney, R.B., & Wainczak, S.M. (1993). Noninvasive behavioral treatment of self-injurious hand stereotypy in a child with Rett syndrome. *Behavioral Residential Treatment, 8,* 133–145.

Parette Jr., H.P., Brotherson, M.J., & Huer, M.B. (2000). Giving families a voice in augmentative and alternative communication decision-making. *Education and Training in Mental Retardation and Developmental Disabilities, 35*(2), 177–190.

Pecyna-Rhyner, P., Lehr, D.H., & Pudlas, K.A. (1990). An analysis of teacher responsiveness to communicative initiations of preschool children with handicaps. *Language, Speech, & Hearing Services in Schools, 21,* 91–97.

Reichle, J., Beukelman, D.R., & Light, J.C. (Vol. Eds.) & Beukelman, D.R., & Reichle, J. (Series Eds.). (2002). *Augmentative and alternative communication series: Exemplary practices for beginning communicators: Implications for AAC.* Baltimore: Paul H. Brookes Publishing Co.

Reichle, J., Halle, J.W., & Drasgow, E. (1998). Implementing augmentative communication systems. In S.F. Warren & J. Reichle (Series Eds.) & A.M. Wetherby, S.F. Warren, & J. Reichle (Vol. Eds.), *Communication and language intervention series: Vol. 7. Transitions in prelinguistic communication* (pp. 417–436). Baltimore: Paul H. Brookes Publishing Co.

Reichle, J., Halle, J., & Johnston, S. (1993). Developing an initial communicative repertoire. In S.F. Warren & J. Reichle (Series Eds.) & A.P. Kaiser & D.B. Gray (Vol. Eds.), *Communication and language intervention series: Vol. 2. Enhancing children's communication: Research foundations for intervention* (pp. 105–136). Baltimore: Paul H. Brookes Publishing Co.

Reichle, J., & Wacker, D. (Vol. Eds.). & Warren, S.F., & Reichle, J. (Series Eds.). (1993). *Communication and language intervention series: Vol. 3. Communicative alternative to challenging behavior: Integrating functional assessment and intervention strategies.* Baltimore: Paul H. Brookes Publishing Co.

Repp, A. & Singh, N.N. (Eds.). (1990). *Perspectives on the use of nonaversive and aversive interventions for persons with developmental disabilities.* Sycamore, IL: Sycamore Publishing.

Rotholz, D., Berkowitz, S., & Burberry, J. (1989). Functionality of two modes of communication in the community by students with developmental disabilities: A comparison of signing and communication books. *Journal of The Association for Persons with Severe Handicaps, 14,* 227–233.

Schalock, R.L., Brown, I., Brown, R., Cummins, R.A., Felce, D., Matikka, L., et al. (2002). Conceptualization, measurement, and application of quality of life for persons with intellectual disabilities: Report of an international panel of experts. *Mental Retardation, 40,* 457–470.

Schlosser, R.W. (Ed.). (2003). *The efficacy of augmentative and alternative communication: Toward evidence-based practice.* San Diego: Academic Press.

Schlosser, R.W., & Sigafoos, J. (2002). Selecting graphic symbols for an initial request lexicon: Integrative review. *Augmentative and Alternative Communication, 18,* 102–123.

Schroeder, S.R., Schroeder, C.S., Smith, B., & Dalldorf, J. (1978). Prevalence of self-injurious behaviors in a large state facility for the retarded: A three-year follow-up study. *Journal of Autism and Childhood Schizophrenia, 8,* 261–269.

Schuler, A.L., Peck, C.A., Willard, C., & Theimer, K. (1989). Assessment of communicative means and functions through interview: Assessing the communicative capabilities of individuals with limited language. *Seminars in Speech and Language, 10,* 51–62.

Sevcik, R., & Romski, M.A. (2002). The role of language comprehension in establishing early augmented conversations. In D.R. Beukelman & J. Reichle (Series Eds.) & J. Reichle, D.R. Beukelman, & J.C. Light (Vol. Eds.), *Augmentative and alternative communication series: Exemplary practices for beginning communicators: Implications for AAC* (pp. 453–474). Baltimore: Paul H. Brookes Publishing Co.

Shaddock, A.J., Dowse, I., Richards, H., & Spinks, A.T. (1998). Communicating with people with an intellectual disability in guardianship board hearings: An exploratory study. *Journal of Intellectual & Developmental Disability, 23,* 279–294.

Siegel, E.B., & Cress, C.J. (2002). Overview of the emergence of early AAC behaviors. In D.R. Beukelman & J. Reichle (Series Eds.) & J. Reichle, D.R. Beukelman, & J.C. Light (Eds.), *Augmentative and alternative communication series: Exemplary practices for beginning communicators: Implications for AAC* (pp. 25–58). Baltimore: Paul H. Brookes Publishing Co.

Siegel-Causey, E., & Bashinski, S.M. (1997). Enhancing initial communication and responsiveness of learners with multiple disabilities: A tri-focus framework for partners. *Focus on Autism and Other Developmental Disabilities, 12*(2), 105–120.

Siegel-Causey, E., & Guess, D. (1989). *Enhancing nonsymbolic communication interactions among learners with severe disabilities.* Baltimore: Paul H. Brookes Publishing Co.

Sigafoos, J. (1997). A review of communication intervention programs for people with developmental disabilities. *Behaviour Change, 14,* 125–138.

Sigafoos, J. (1999). Creating opportunities for augmentative and alternative communication: Strategies for involving people with developmental disabilities. *Augmentative and Alternative Communication, 15,* 183–190.

Sigafoos, J. (2000). Communication development and aberrant behavior in children with developmental disabilities. *Education and Training in Mental Retardation and Developmental Disabilities, 35*(2), 168–176.

Sigafoos, J., Arthur, M., & O'Reilly, M. (2003). *Challenging behavior and developmental disability.* London: Whurr.

Sigafoos, J., & Drasgow, E. (2001). Conditional use of aided and unaided AAC: A review and clinical case demonstration. *Focus on Autism and Other Developmental Disabilities, 16*(3), 152–161.

Sigafoos, J., Drasgow, E., Halle, J.W., O'Reilly, M., Seely-York, S., Edrisinha, C., et al. (2004). Teaching VOCA use as a communicative repair strategy. *Journal of Autism and Developmental Disorders, 34,* 411–422.

Sigafoos, J., Drasgow, E., & Schlosser, R.W. (2003). Strategies for beginning communicators. In R.W. Schlosser (Ed.), *The efficacy of augmentative and alternative communication: Toward evidence-based practice* (pp. 324–346). San Diego: Academic Press.

Sigafoos, J., Elkins, J., Kerr, M., & Attwood, T. (1994). A survey of aggressive behaviour among a population of persons with intellectual disability in Queensland. *Journal of Intellectual Disability Research, 38,* 369–381.

Sigafoos, J., Kerr, M., Roberts, D., & Couzens, D. (1994). Increasing opportunities for requesting in classrooms serving children with developmental disabilities. *Journal of Autism and Developmental Disorders, 24,* 631–645.

Sigafoos, J., & Meikle, B. (1996). Functional communication training for the treatment of multiply determined challenging behavior in two boys with autism. *Behavior Modification, 20,* 60–84.

Sigafoos, J., & Mirenda, P. (2002). Strengthening communicative behaviors for gaining access to desired items and activities. In D.R. Beukelman & J. Reichle (Series Eds.) & J. Reichle, D.R. Beukelman, & J.C. Light (Vol. Eds.), *Augmentative and alternative communication series: Exemplary practices for beginning communicators: Implications for AAC* (pp. 123–156). Baltimore: Paul H. Brookes Publishing Co.

Sigafoos, J., O'Reilly, M., Drasgow, E., & Reichle, J. (2002). Strategies to achieve socially acceptable escape and avoidance. In D.R. Beukelman & J. Reichle (Series Eds.) & J. Reichle, D. Beukelman, & J. Light (Vol. Eds.), *Augmentative and alternative communication series: Exemplary practices for beginning communicators: Implications for AAC* (pp. 157–186). Baltimore: Paul H. Brookes Publishing Co.

Sigafoos, J., Pennell, D., & Versluis, J. (1996). Naturalistic assessment leading to effective treatment of self-injury in a young boy with multiple disabilities. *Education & Treatment of Children, 19,* 101–123.

Sigafoos, J., Reichle, J., & Light-Shriner, C. (1994). Distinguishing between socially and nonsocially motivated challenging behavior: Implications for the selection of intervention strategies. In M.F. Hayden & B.H. Abery (Eds.), *Challenges for a service system in transition: Ensuring quality community experiences for persons with developmental disabilities* (pp. 147–169). Baltimore: Paul H. Brookes Publishing Co.

Sigafoos, J., Woodyatt, G., Keen, D., Tait, K., Tucker, M., Roberts-Pennell, D., & Pittendreigh, N. (2000). Identifying potential communicative acts in children with developmental and physical disabilities. *Communication Disorders Quarterly, 21,* 77–86.

Sigafoos, J., Woodyatt, G., Tucker, M., Roberts-Pennell, D., & Pittendreigh, N. (2000). Assessment of potential communicative acts in three individuals with Rett syndrome. *Journal of Developmental and Physical Disabilities, 12,* 203–216.

Singh, N.N., Sood, A., Sonenklar, N., & Ellis, C.R. (1991). Assessment and diagnosis of mental illness in persons with mental retardation: Methods and measures. *Behavior Modification, 15,* 419–443.

Skinner, B.F. (1938). *The behavior of organisms.* New York: Appleton-Century-Crofts.

Skinner, B.F. (1953). *Science and human behavior.* New York: Macmillian.

Skinner, B.F. (1957). *Verbal behavior.* Mahwah, NJ: Prentice-Hall.

Snell, M.E. (2002). Using dynamic assessment with learners who communicate nonsymbolically. *Augmentative and Alternative Communication, 18,* 163–176.

Snell, M.E., & Brown, F. (Eds.). (2000). *Instruction for students with severe disabilities* (5th ed.). Upper Saddle River, NJ: Merrill/Prentice Hall.

Sosne, J.B., Handleman, J.S., & Harris, S.L. (1979). Teaching spontaneous-functional speech to autistic-type children. *Mental Retardation, 17,* 241–244.

Soto, G., Muller, E., Hunt, P., & Goetz, L. (2001). Critical issues in the inclusion of students who use augmentative and alternative communication: An educational team perspective. *Augmentative and Alternative Communication, 17,* 62–72.

Sprague, J.R., & Horner, R.H. (1991). Determining the acceptability of behavior support plans. In M. Wang & M.C. Reynolds (Eds.), *Handbook of special education: Research and practice: Vol. 4. Emerging programs: Advances in education* (pp. 125–142). Elmsford, NY: Pergamon Press.

Stephenson, J., & Linfoot, K. (1996). Intentional communication and graphic symbol use by students with severe intellectual disability. *International Journal of Disability, Development, and Education, 43,* 147–165.

Tait, K., Sigafoos, J., Woodyatt, G., O'Reilly, M.F., & Lancioni, G.E. (2004). Evaluating parent use of functional communication training to replace and enhance prelinguistic behaviours in six children with developmental and physical disabilities. *Disability & Rehabilitation, 26,* 1241–1254.

Talkington, L.W., Hall, S., & Altman, R. (1971). Communication deficits and aggression in the mentally retarded. *American Journal of Mental Deficiency, 76,* 235–237.

Taylor, J.C., & Carr, E.G. (1992). Severe problem behaviors related to social interaction: I. Attention seeking and social avoidance. *Behavior Modification, 16,* 305–335.

Touchette, P.E., MacDonald, R.F., & Langer, S.N. (1985). A scatter plot for identifying stimulus control of problem behavior. *Journal of Applied Behavior Analysis, 18,* 343–351.

Tutton, C., Wynne-Willson, S., & Piachaud, J. (1990). Rating management difficulty: A study into the prevalence and severity of difficult behaviour displayed by residents in a large residential hospital for the mentally handicapped. *Journal of Mental Deficiency Research, 34,* 325–339.

Van Houten, R., Axelrod, S., Bailey, J.S., Favell, J.E., Foxx, R.M., Iwata, B.A., et al. (1988). The right to effective behavioral treatment. *The Behavior Analyst, 11,* 111–114.

von Tetzchner, S. (1997). Communication skills among females with Rett syndrome. *European Child and Adolescent Psychiatry, 6,* 33–37.

Wacker, D.P., Berg, W.K., & Harding, J.W. (2002). Replacing socially unacceptable behavior with acceptable communication responses. In D.R. Beukelman & J. Reichle (Series Eds.) & J. Reichle, D.R. Beukelman, & J.C. Light (Vol. Eds.), *Augmentative and alternative communication series: Exemplary practices for beginning communicators: Implications for AAC* (pp. 97–121). Baltimore: Paul H. Brookes Publishing Co.

Wacker, D.P., Steege, M.W., Northup, J., Sasso, G., Berg, W., Reimers, T., et al. (1990). A component analysis of functional communication training across three topographies of severe behavior problems. *Journal of Applied Behavior Analysis, 23,* 417–429.

Warren, S. (2000). The future of early communication and language intervention. *Topics in Early Childhood Special Education, 20*(1), 33–37.

Warren, S.F., & Yoder, P.J. (1998). Facilitating the transition from preintentional to intentional communication. In S.F. Warren & J. Reichle (Series Eds.) & A.M. Wetherby, S.F. Warren, & J. Reichle (Vol. Eds.), *Communication and language interven-*

tion series: Vol. 7. Transitions in prelinguistic communication (pp. 365–384). Baltimore: Paul H. Brookes Publishing Co.

Westling, D.L., & Floyd, J. (1990). Generalization of community skills: How much training is necessary? Journal of Special Education, 23, 386–406.

Wetherby, A.M., & Prizant, B. (1992). Profiling young children's communicative competence. In S. Warren & J. Reichle (Vol. & Series Eds.), Communication and language intervention series: Vol. 1. Causes and effects in communication and language intervention (pp. 217–253). Baltimore: Paul H. Brookes Publishing Co.

Wilcox, M.J. (1992). Enhancing initial communication skills in young children with developmental disabilities through partner programming. Seminars in Speech and Language, 13, 194–212.

Wilcox, M.J., Kouri, T.A., & Caswell, S. (1990). Partner sensitivity to communication behavior of young children with developmental disabilities. Journal of Speech & Hearing Disorders, 55, 679–693.

Woodyatt, G., Marinac, J., Darnell, R., Sigafoos, J., & Halle, J. (2004, December). Behaviour state analysis in Rett syndrome: Continuous data reliability measurement. International Journal of Disability, Development and Education, 51(4), 383–400.

Yoder, P.J., McCathren, R.B., Warren, S.F., & Watson, A.L. (2001). Important distinctions in measuring maternal responses to communication in prelinguistic children with disabilities. Communication Disorders Quarterly, 22, 135–147.

Yoder, P.J., & Warren, S.F. (1998). Maternal responsivity predicts the prelinguistic communication intervention that facilitates generalized intentional communication. Journal of Speech, Language, & Hearing Research, 41, 1207–1219.

Zarcone, J.R., Rodgers, T.A., Iwata, B.A., Rourke, D.A., & Dorsey, M.F. (1991). Reliability analysis of the Motivation Assessment Scale: A failure to replicate. Research in Developmental Disabilities, 12, 349–360.

A

Inventory of Potential Communicative Acts

BACKGROUND

The Inventory of Potential Communicative Acts (IPCA) is based on 3 years of research funded by The University of Queensland and the Australian Research Council. It was developed by Jeff Sigafoos from The University of Tasmania and by Gail Woodyatt, Deb Keen, Kathleen Tait, Madonna Tucker, and Donna Roberts-Pennell from The University of Queensland. To date, the research and field testing have involved more than 30 children with developmental disabilities and severe communication impairments. Current research is examining the validity of the IPCA for intervention purposes. At the present time, the instrument can be used for gathering descriptive information on communicative behaviors.

The IPCA is designed to be completed by educators, therapists, family members, or other people who know the individual well enough to serve as useful informants. As a general rule of thumb, anyone who has known and cared for the individual for at least 6 months could complete the IPCA. The IPCA seeks to identify any potential communicative acts that might be used by an individual for any of 10 different communicative functions.

A *potential communicative act* is defined as any behavior that you think the individual uses for communicative purposes. These behaviors might include vocalizations, body movements, facial expressions, breathing patterns, challenging behaviors, or stereotyped movements. They might also include more symbolic forms of communication, such as speaking some single words, producing a few manual signs, or using a picture-based communication board. To help you in identifying these types of behaviors, Table 2.1 lists a number of behaviors that are used by some individuals with developmental disabilities and severe communication impairments to communicate with others.

This list is not exhaustive. In completing the IPCA, you are encouraged to identify any behaviors that you have observed the person using while communicating with others.

With the IPCA, the specific meaning that a person is attempting to communicate with a particular behavior is referred to as the *communicative function*. The IPCA seeks information on 10 distinct functions. Under each of these 10 functional categories, a number of more specific communicative functions are included. Again, this list of specific communicative functions is not exhaustive, and you are encouraged to include other specific messages or purposes that the person has been observed to express. Space is provided for you to record examples of other specific functions.

DIRECTIONS

The IPCA consists of a series of questions that are designed to identify the behaviors that a person uses to communicate. In completing the device, you are asked to list behaviors that you have observed the person using for a number of specific communicative functions. The IPCA also asks you to provide a concrete example of the circumstances under which the person has been observed using the behavior to communicate. These examples should be as detailed as possible. In writing your examples, please provide information about *when, where,* and *how* the behavior occurs.

If the person does not seem to express one of the specific functions, then you should write *Does not do this* in that section. For example, the first question asks you to *Describe how the person greets you/others.* For this question, you may have noticed that the person greets you by making eye contact, smiling, and extending his or her arms outward. Your specific example might be something such as *When I first see her in the morning and say "Hello," she always looks at me, smiles, and reaches out her arms.*

SCORING GRID

A Scoring Grid is included at the end of this inventory. The Scoring Grid is designed to provide a visual summary of the information documented on the IPCA form. First of all, you would enter the person's behaviors into the blank spaces in the first column of the grid. Completing the Scoring Grid involves shading in those cells corresponding to the behaviors and functions that have been identified in the IPCA. For example, if the IPCA reveals that a person uses the behaviors of Reaching to make a Choice, then the cell that corresponds to the intersection of this behavior and this function would be shaded in. If an individual does not exhibit a particular behavior/function combination, then that cell would be left blank.

Once all of the identified behavior/function cells have been filled in, the Scoring Grid can be used to give an indication of the extent of a person's communicative repertoire. Scanning the completed Scoring Grid from top to bottom, for example, will provide a overview of the different behaviors that the person uses to communicate, whereas scanning from left to right will indicate the range of communicative functions exhibited by the individual. A more detailed summary of the information from the IPCA will come from examining individual cells as they indicate exactly what behavior(s) an individual uses to communicate a specific function.

A summary of the information from the IPCA can be shared among educators, therapists, family members, peers, and other relevant individuals to ensure that all communication partners are aware of the behaviors that the individual uses to communicate and what these behaviors mean when they occur in a particular context. When all communication partners are aware of the information collected in the IPCA, there is a much better chance that the person's communication attempts will be encouraged, acknowledged, and reacted to appropriately.

Inventory of Potential Communicative Acts

Date: _____

Name of the individual: _____

Name of the informant: _____

Informant's relationship with the individual:

   ❏ Teacher   ❏ Parent   ❏ Other _____ (Specify)

How long have you known this individual? _____ years _____ months

Individual's date of birth: _____

Diagnoses: _____

Social convention
Please describe how the individual...

Items	Behaviors	Examples
1. Greets you/others	_____ _____ _____	_____ _____ _____
2. Indicates farewell to you/others	_____ _____ _____	_____ _____ _____
3. Responds to his or her own name	_____ _____ _____	_____ _____ _____
4. Other	_____ _____ _____	_____ _____ _____

Attention to self
Please describe how the individual...

Items	Behaviors	Examples
1. Gets your attention	_____ _____ _____	_____ _____ _____
2. Seeks comfort	_____ _____ _____	_____ _____ _____
3. Requests a cuddle/tickle	_____ _____ _____	_____ _____ _____
4. Shows off	_____ _____ _____	_____ _____ _____
5. Other	_____ _____ _____	_____ _____ _____

Reject/protest
What does the individual do if...

Items	Behaviors	Examples
1. His or her routine is disrupted	_____ _____ _____	_____ _____ _____
2. He or she is required to do something that he or she doesn't want to do	_____ _____ _____	_____ _____ _____
3. He or she doesn't like something	_____ _____ _____	_____ _____ _____
4. A favorite toy/food is taken away	_____ _____ _____	_____ _____ _____
5. An adult stops interacting with him or her (e.g., stops playing)	_____ _____ _____	_____ _____ _____
6. Other	_____ _____ _____	_____ _____ _____

Requesting an object
Please describe how the individual lets you know if he or she wants…

Items	Behaviors	Examples
1. An object (e.g., toy, book)	_____ _____ _____	_____ _____ _____
2. Something to eat	_____ _____ _____	_____ _____ _____
3. More of something	_____ _____ _____	_____ _____ _____
4. Television or music	_____ _____ _____	_____ _____ _____
5. Other	_____ _____ _____	_____ _____ _____

Requesting an action
Please describe how the individual lets you know if he or she wants or needs...

Items	Behaviors	Examples
1. Help with dressing	_____ _____ _____	_____ _____ _____
2. Help with a game	_____ _____ _____	_____ _____ _____
3. To go to the bathroom	_____ _____ _____	_____ _____ _____
4. Someone to come/be near	_____ _____ _____	_____ _____ _____
5. Other	_____ _____ _____	_____ _____ _____

Requesting information
Please describe how the individual lets you know he or she wants...

Items	Behaviors	Examples
1. Clarification (e.g., if he or she doesn't understand something you said)	_____ _____ _____	_____ _____ _____
2. Information about something (e.g., the name of something)	_____ _____ _____	_____ _____ _____
3. Other	_____ _____ _____	_____ _____ _____

Inventory of Potential Communicative Acts (IPCA). From *Enhancing Everyday Communication for Children with Disabilities* by Jeff Sigafoos, Michael Arthur-Kelly, and Nancy Butterfield. Copyright © 2006 Paul H. Brookes Publishing Co., Inc. All rights reserved.

Comment

Please describe how the individual lets you know he or she...

Items	Behaviors	Examples
1. Is happy, pleased, enjoying something, or excited	_____	_____
	_____	_____
	_____	_____
2. Is unhappy, sad, or anxious	_____	_____
	_____	_____
	_____	_____
3. Is bored or disinterested	_____	_____
	_____	_____
	_____	_____
4. Finds something funny	_____	_____
	_____	_____
	_____	_____
5. Is frightened or surprised	_____	_____
	_____	_____
	_____	_____
6. Is in pain or feels sick	_____	_____
	_____	_____
	_____	_____

(continued)

7. Is angry or feels frustrated	_____ _____ _____	_____ _____ _____
8. Is tired	_____ _____ _____	_____ _____ _____
9. Other	_____ _____ _____	_____ _____ _____

Choice making (CM)
Please describe how the individual...

Items	Behaviors	Examples
1. Makes a choice between two or more objects (e.g., foods, drinks, toys)	_____ _____ _____	_____ _____ _____
2. Chooses what he or she wants to do	_____ _____ _____	_____ _____ _____
3. Chooses when to start or stop an activity	_____ _____ _____	_____ _____ _____
4. Other	_____ _____ _____	_____ _____ _____

Answer
Please describe how the individual...

Items	Behaviors	Examples
1. Reacts when someone talks to him or her	_____ _____ _____	_____ _____ _____
2. Tells you yes in response to a question	_____ _____ _____	_____ _____ _____
3. Tells you no in response to a question	_____ _____ _____	_____ _____ _____
4. Other	_____ _____ _____	_____ _____ _____

Imitation

Please describe how the person imitates or attempts to imitate the following communicative actions of others...

Items	Behaviors	Examples
1. Another's speech (e.g., sentences, single words, vocalizations)	_____ _____ _____	_____ _____ _____
2. Head nod "Yes"	_____ _____ _____	_____ _____ _____
3. Head nod "No"	_____ _____ _____	_____ _____ _____
4. Shrugging shoulders	_____ _____ _____	_____ _____ _____
5. Pointing	_____ _____ _____	_____ _____ _____
6. Other	_____ _____ _____	_____ _____ _____

Behaviors	Social convention				Attention to self					Reject/ protest						Request object					
	greet	farewell	name	other	get attention	comfort	cuddle	shows off	other	routine	do	dislike	take	adult	other	object	food	more	TV or music	other	dress

Request action				Request info			Comment									CM				Answer				Imitate					
game	toilet	near	other	clarification	info	other	happy	sad	bored	funny	fright	pain	angry	tired	other	2 or more	wants	start	other	reacts	yes	no	other	speech	yes	no	shrug	point	other

Inventory of Potential Communicative Acts (IPCA). From *Enhancing Everyday Communication for Children with Disabilities* by Jeff Sigafoos, Michael Arthur-Kelly, and Nancy Butterfield. Copyright © 2006 Paul H. Brookes Publishing Co., Inc. All rights reserved.

B

Behavior Indication Assessment Scale

BACKGROUND

The Behavior Indication Assessment Scale (BIAS) was inspired by the Verbal Behavior Assessment Scale (Duker, 1999). It is based on the Inventory of Potential Communicative Acts (IPCA) and is intended to be used as a brief supplement to the IPCA when there is a need to conduct a more in-depth assessment of communicative forms related to requesting and rejecting. The BIAS focuses on identifying communicative forms related to the major subclasses of the mand (i.e., gaining attention, requesting, and protesting/rejecting). Assessment of these subclasses of the mand is seen as a major priority in communication intervention for children with developmental and physical disabilities because this class of verbal behavior is usually one of the first to develop and these skills are highly functional for children. As with the IPCA, the BIAS is intended to be used by parents, teachers, and others who know the individual well enough to provide accurate information about the person's existing mand forms.

DIRECTIONS

The purpose of the BIAS is to identify specific behaviors that the person uses to communicate basic wants and needs. There are 12 questions. For each question, please indicate how often (never, sometimes, often, or always) each of the listed behaviors occurs. If the individual uses some *other* behavior, please briefly describe what the person does to communicate.

The BIAS is primarily a descriptive tool to help partners create an objective profile of the person's communicative forms and functions. The numerical rating scale may be useful in aiming to quantify the person's communication profile. This quantitative summary may assist in program planning and monitoring of the intervention plan.

For example, suppose the results of the BIAS indicate that the person often uses problem behavior in an attempt to gain attention. That is, this particular item in the BIAS is given a numerical rating of 2. In contrast, the person only sometimes uses sign language or conventional gestures in an attempt to gain attention. That is, this item is given a rating of 1.

These ratings suggest a logical intervention direction. Specifically, partners may decide to intervene in an attempt to increase the person's use of sign language or gestures for gaining attention. By doing so, partners would also be looking for a collateral decrease in the use of problem behaviors for gaining attention. Over time, if the intervention plan is effective, then the rating for the use of sign language or gestures to gain attention should increase to 3, whereas the rating for the use of problem behavior for gaining attention should decrease to 1 or 0.

The BIAS might, therefore, be used as a quick way of attempting to monitor progress. It should be noted, however, that the BIAS provides only an indirect assessment of the person's communication profile and only an indirect measure of progress. Information obtained from the BIAS should be supplemented and validated with direct observation.

Behavior Indication Assessment Scale

Part A: Gaining and Maintaining Attention and Social Interaction

I.   How does the person attempt to get your attention?

		Never	Sometimes	Often	Always
1.	Uses problem behaviors (tantrums, aggression, self-injury)	0	1	2	3
2.	Makes sounds/noises	0	1	2	3
3.	Uses his or her eyes (e.g., looks at you intently)	0	1	2	3
4.	Makes a distinctive facial expression (e.g., arched eyebrows)	0	1	2	3
5.	Moves body (e.g., arches back, moves head)	0	1	2	3
6.	Reaches/touches/grabs	0	1	2	3
7.	Guides another person's hand/leads the person somewhere	0	1	2	3
8.	Points with isolated index finger	0	1	2	3
9.	Uses sign language or conventional gestures	0	1	2	3
10.	Uses pictures/symbols/communication board	0	1	2	3
11.	Uses an electronic communication device	0	1	2	3
12.	Speaks in words or sentences	0	1	2	3
13.	Other (please describe): _____	0	1	2	3

II. How does the person let you know when he or she wants to continue to have your attention or continue to interact with you?

		Never	Sometimes	Often	Always
1.	Uses problem behaviors (tantrums, aggression, self-injury)	0	1	2	3
2.	Makes sounds/noises	0	1	2	3
3.	Uses his or her eyes (e.g., looks at you intently)	0	1	2	3
4.	Makes a distinctive facial expression (e.g., arched eyebrows)	0	1	2	3
5.	Moves body (e.g., arches back, moves head)	0	1	2	3
6.	Reaches/touches/grabs	0	1	2	3

	Never	Sometimes	Often	Always
7. Guides another person's hand/leads the person somewhere	0	1	2	3
8. Points with isolated index finger	0	1	2	3
9. Uses sign language or conventional gestures	0	1	2	3
10. Uses pictures/symbols/communication board	0	1	2	3
11. Uses an electronic communication device	0	1	2	3
12. Speaks in words or sentences	0	1	2	3
13. Other (please describe): _____	0	1	2	3

Part B: Requesting Objects and Activities

III. How does the person let you know when he or she wants a preferred object, such as food, drink, or toy?

	Never	Sometimes	Often	Always
1. Uses problem behaviors (tantrums, aggression, self-injury)	0	1	2	3
2. Makes sounds/noises	0	1	2	3
3. Uses his or her eyes (e.g., looks at you intently)	0	1	2	3
4. Makes a distinctive facial expression (e.g., arched eyebrows)	0	1	2	3
5. Moves body (e.g., arches back, moves head)	0	1	2	3
6. Reaches/touches/grabs	0	1	2	3
7. Guides another person's hand/leads the person somewhere	0	1	2	3
8. Points with isolated index finger	0	1	2	3
9. Uses sign language or conventional gestures	0	1	2	3
10. Uses pictures/symbols/communication board	0	1	2	3
11. Uses an electronic communication device	0	1	2	3
12. Speaks in words or sentences	0	1	2	3
13. Other (please describe): _____	0	1	2	3

IV. How does the person let you know when he or she wants to do something, such as go outside to play?

	Never	Sometimes	Often	Always
1. Uses problem behaviors (tantrums, aggression, self-injury)	0	1	2	3

		Never	Sometimes	Often	Always
2.	Makes sounds/noises	0	1	2	3
3.	Uses his or her eyes (e.g., looks at you intently)	0	1	2	3
4.	Makes a distinctive facial expression (e.g., arched eyebrows)	0	1	2	3
5.	Moves body (e.g., arches back, moves head)	0	1	2	3
6.	Reaches/touches/grabs	0	1	2	3
7.	Guides another person's hand/leads the person somewhere	0	1	2	3
8.	Points with isolated index finger	0	1	2	3
9.	Uses sign language or conventional gestures	0	1	2	3
10.	Uses pictures/symbols/communication board	0	1	2	3
11.	Uses an electronic communication device	0	1	2	3
12.	Speaks in words or sentences	0	1	2	3
13.	Other (please describe): _____	0	1	2	3

V. How does the person let you know when he or she wants *more* of a preferred object, such as more food or drink?

		Never	Sometimes	Often	Always
1.	Uses problem behaviors (tantrums, aggression, self-injury)	0	1	2	3
2.	Makes sounds/noises	0	1	2	3
3.	Uses his or her eyes (e.g., looks at you intently)	0	1	2	3
4.	Makes a distinctive facial expression (e.g., arched eyebrows)	0	1	2	3
5.	Moves body (e.g., arches back, moves head)	0	1	2	3
6.	Reaches/touches/grabs	0	1	2	3
7.	Guides another person's hand/leads the person somewhere	0	1	2	3
8.	Points with isolated index finger	0	1	2	3
9.	Uses sign language or conventional gestures	0	1	2	3
10.	Uses pictures/symbols/communication board	0	1	2	3
11.	Uses an electronic communication device	0	1	2	3
12.	Speaks in words or sentences	0	1	2	3
13.	Other (please describe): _____	0	1	2	3

VI. How does the person let you know when he or she wants to continue a preferred activity, such as playing a game?

		Never	Sometimes	Often	Always
1.	Uses problem behaviors (tantrums, aggression, self-injury)	0	1	2	3
2.	Makes sounds/noises	0	1	2	3
3.	Uses his or her eyes (e.g., looks at you intently)	0	1	2	3
4.	Makes a distinctive facial expression (e.g., arched eyebrows)	0	1	2	3
5.	Moves body (e.g., arches back, moves head)	0	1	2	3
6.	Reaches/touches/grabs	0	1	2	3
7.	Guides another person's hand/leads the person somewhere	0	1	2	3
8.	Points with isolated index finger	0	1	2	3
9.	Uses sign language or conventional gestures	0	1	2	3
10.	Uses pictures/symbols/communication board	0	1	2	3
11.	Uses an electronic communication device	0	1	2	3
12.	Speaks in words or sentences	0	1	2	3
13.	Other (please describe): _____	0	1	2	3

_____

Part C: Protesting and Rejecting

VII. How does the person let you know that he or she does NOT want a particular item?

		Never	Sometimes	Often	Always
1.	Uses problem behaviors (tantrums, aggression, self-injury)	0	1	2	3
2.	Makes sounds/noises	0	1	2	3
3.	Uses his or her eyes (e.g., looks at you intently)	0	1	2	3
4.	Makes a distinctive facial expression (e.g., arched eyebrows)	0	1	2	3
5.	Moves body (e.g., arches back, moves head)	0	1	2	3
6.	Reaches/touches/grabs	0	1	2	3
7.	Guides another person's hand/leads the person somewhere	0	1	2	3

	Never	Sometimes	Often	Always
8. Points with isolated index finger	0	1	2	3
9. Uses sign language or conventional gestures	0	1	2	3
10. Uses pictures/symbols/communication board	0	1	2	3
11. Uses an electronic communication device	0	1	2	3
12. Speaks in words or sentences	0	1	2	3
13. Other (please describe): _____	0	1	2	3

VIII. How does the person let you know when he or she does NOT want to begin to participate in an activity that has just started?

	Never	Sometimes	Often	Always
1. Uses problem behaviors (tantrums, aggression, self-injury)	0	1	2	3
2. Makes sounds/noises	0	1	2	3
3. Uses his or her eyes (e.g., looks at you intently)	0	1	2	3
4. Makes a distinctive facial expression (e.g., arched eyebrows)	0	1	2	3
5. Moves body (e.g., arches back, moves head)	0	1	2	3
6. Reaches/touches/grabs	0	1	2	3
7. Guides another person's hand/leads the person somewhere	0	1	2	3
8. Points with isolated index finger	0	1	2	3
9. Uses sign language or conventional gestures	0	1	2	3
10. Uses pictures/symbols/communication board	0	1	2	3
11. Uses an electronic communication device	0	1	2	3
12. Speaks in words or sentences	0	1	2	3
13. Other (please describe): _____	0	1	2	3

IX. How does the person let you know when he or she is finished with or that he or she has had enough of a particular object or activity, such as indicating that he or she has had enough to eat or drink?

	Never	Sometimes	Often	Always
1. Uses problem behaviors (tantrums, aggression, self-injury)	0	1	2	3
2. Makes sounds/noises	0	1	2	3

	Never	Sometimes	Often	Always
3. Uses his or her eyes (e.g., looks at you intently)	0	1	2	3
4. Makes a distinctive facial expression (e.g., arched eyebrows)	0	1	2	3
5. Moves body (e.g., arches back, moves head)	0	1	2	3
6. Reaches/touches/grabs	0	1	2	3
7. Guides another person's hand/leads the person somewhere	0	1	2	3
8. Points with isolated index finger	0	1	2	3
9. Uses sign language or conventional gestures	0	1	2	3
10. Uses pictures/symbols/communication board	0	1	2	3
11. Uses an electronic communication device	0	1	2	3
12. Speaks in words or sentences	0	1	2	3
13. Other (please describe): _____	0	1	2	3

X. How does the person let you know that he or she does NOT want your attention or that he or she does NOT want to interact with you?

	Never	Sometimes	Often	Always
1. Uses problem behaviors (tantrums, aggression, self-injury)	0	1	2	3
2. Makes sounds/noises	0	1	2	3
3. Uses his or her eyes (e.g., looks at you intently)	0	1	2	3
4. Makes a distinctive facial expression (e.g., arched eyebrows)	0	1	2	3
5. Moves body (e.g., arches back, moves head)	0	1	2	3
6. Reaches/touches/grabs	0	1	2	3
7. Guides another person's hand/leads the person somewhere	0	1	2	3
8. Points with isolated index finger	0	1	2	3
9. Uses sign language or conventional gestures	0	1	2	3
10. Uses pictures/symbols/communication board	0	1	2	3
11. Uses an electronic communication device	0	1	2	3
12. Speaks in words or sentences	0	1	2	3
13. Other (please describe): _____	0	1	2	3

Index

Page numbers followed by *f* indicate figures; those followed by *t* indicate tables.

THE HIDDEN DIMENSIONS OF ANNUAL REPORTS

Sixty Years of Social Conflict at General Motors

MARILYN KLEINBERG NEIMARK

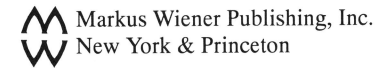

Markus Wiener Publishing, Inc.
New York & Princeton

For information write to:
Markus Wiener Publishing, Inc.
225 West 34th Street, New York, NY 10001

Distributed exclusively in the United Kingdom and Continental Europe by:
Paul Chaoman Publishing, Ltd.
144 Liverpool Road, London N1 1LA
Tel: 071-609-5315   Fax: 071-700-1057

Library of Congress Cataloging-in-Publication Data

Neimark, Marilyn Kleinberg
       The hidden dimensions of annual reports: sixty years of social conflict at
General Motors/Marilyn Kleinberg Neimark. (Critical accounting theories)
       Includes bibliographical references.
       ISBN 1-55876-054-7
       1. General Motors Corporation—Accounting—History. 2. Automobile
industry and trade—United States—History. 3. Social accounting—United
States—History. 4. Social respodnsibility in vusiness—United States—History.
I. Title. II. Series.
HD9710.U54G4752   92-19221
338.7'6292'0973—dc20   CIP

British Library Cataloguing-in-Publication Data

Neimark, Marilyn
       Hidden Dimensions of Annual Reports:
       Sixty Years of Social Conflict at General Motors
       I. Title.
       ISBN 1-85396-220-1

Printed in the United States of America on acid-free paper.

CONTENTS

INTRODUCTION

As I write this introduction President George Bush is in Japan, accompanied by the Chairmen of the Big Three of the American-owned automobile industry, hats in hand. The President is seeking Japan's help in bolstering both a sinking U.S. economy and his sinking, for the moment at least, political prospects. The auto-industry heads are seeking relief for their ailing enterprises. (Note the hyphenated "American-owned." America's Big Three — General Motors (GM), Ford, and Chrysler are no longer the Big Three in terms of market share in U.S. car sales. In 1991, for the first time, Chrysler, with 8.5% of the U.S. car market, was removed from the number three position by not one, but two, Japanese auto-makers: Honda, with 9.8%, and Toyota, with 9.0%.)[1] Bush's trip illustrates starkly the link between the fortunes of the U.S. automobile industry — and Corporate America in general — and that of the U.S. economy.

Fifteen years ago, when Charles Lindblom published his book, *Politics and Markets: The World's Political-Economic Systems,* some reviewers challenged his claim that "Businessmen generally and corporate executives in particular take on a privileged role in government that is, it seems reasonable to say, unmatched by any leadership group other than government officials themselves."[2] Yet one cannot imagine George Bush taking any other group of leaders with him to Japan. Trade union officials? Religious leaders? Educators? Politicians? Doctors? Lawyers? Artists? Feminists? African-American community leaders? Other government officials? No other group of Americans plays a role comparable to business in determining "jobs, prices, production, growth, the standard of living and the economic security of everyone" — even, as George Bush knows only too well, the survival of the government itself.[3]

In the U.S., as in other private enterprise economies, major decisions are delegated to the corporate sector. It is through these discretionary decisions, and the enormous impact they have on the well-being of everyone, that business derives its privilege. Lindblom identifies a number of discretionary decisions made everyday by businessmen in private enterprise economies, decisions that are subject to little if any popular control

1

yet that decide the very structure and nature of an economy. Among these decisions are the following:

- what kinds of products to develop and when to bring them to the marketplace
- whether workers should be displaced by automation
- the nature and timing of technological innovations
- the organization of the workforce
- plant location
- how air, water, and earth are to be polluted
- product prices
- whether to make and how to finance new investments
- the magnitude and character of public information (otherwise known as advertising and public relations)
- who will be appointed to top management positions
- how much of corporate funds to assign to education, research, the arts and other public programs; and what kinds of programs to support

These "private" business decisions are motivated by private interests — the quest for enterprise profitability and growth — yet they have profound social and economic impacts. Business decisions determine in large part what life in a nation will be like, from products to values to the quality of the environment. There is, then, a tension between the need for corporate accountability for the social consequences of their activities and, in the absence of a command economy, the need to provide businesses with sufficient inducements to continue to perform the important economic and social tasks that have been delegated to them. Government is located at the intersection of these dual needs, sometimes leaning in the direction of assuring accountability, but more often leaning in the direction of providing inducements to business to make decisions that it is hoped will provide jobs, incomes, and overall well-being (as we've seen in the deregulation momentum of the Reagan and Bush administrations).

The public accounting profession is part of the overall regulatory apparatus in the U.S. and other industrialized nations, although using the term "public" in talking about the public accounting profession is somewhat misleading. Public accounting firms are privately held, profit-making enterprises, which operate in a highly competitive marketplace (albeit one dominated by six international firms). As a self-regulating industry, the public accounting profession in the U.S. is largely free to set its own rules and evaluate its own and its clients' performances (subject to the ultimate oversight of Congress and the SEC). Moreover, public accounting firms are hired, fired, and compensated by the very enterprises they are charged with overseeing. Like the government, the public accounting profession is located at the intersection of the dual needs of public accountability and private interests. And like the government, the public accounting profession more often inclines towards the latter than towards the former.

Contrary to the claims of accounting textbooks and the accounting profession's official literature, accounting standards and techniques are not socially neutral and Certified Public Accountants are not independent professionals who work in the public interest. Like the business decisions referred to above, accounting decisions have important social consequences. Too often, in making these decisions, the public accounting profession plays a partisan role by aligning itself with management and a subset of shareholders.[4]

Decisions about how to account for post-retirement benefits such as pensions and health care, for example, can determine workers' benefits. The Generally Accepted Accounting Principles (GAAP) governing pensions have allowed some companies to appropriate millions of dollars in arguably "excess" pension fund assets. Other companies have used the Financial Accounting Standards Board's (FASB) recent ruling on recording post-retirement health benefits to justify the termination of such plans (even though the requirement to account for these previous commitments has no cash flow effect).

Many critics of the accounting profession claim that it contributed to the severity of the current banking crisis by overlooking unsound financial reporting practices and dubious banks loans. The savings and loan industry's problems, for example, were masked for years by a variety of creative accounting measures, authorized by federal regulators, and accepted and implemented by the accounting profession. For years, auditors stood by silently while banks kept loans to developing countries on their books at full value, even as identical loans were being traded in financial markets at deep discounts. Nor did the accountants speak out when banks made additional loans, whose primary purpose was to provide cash for paying interest on earlier debt; or when the banks failed to record an economic loss on restructured loans, whose present value was less than that of the loans they replaced.

Accounting information is used to justify decisions to close plants and to gain concessions from labor (often as the price for keeping plants open). Confronted by the abstract statistics produced by accountants and the authority of GAAP, union and local governments seldom succeed in challenging such actions. In health care, the introduction of financial controls in hospitals is transforming the nature of health care decisions and the quality of the relationships between patients, nurses, and doctors. In the public sector, accounting information is used to justify cuts in social services and the privatization of state activities that do not provide "value for money." As more and more state activities are brought under the discipline of accounting, our ability to assess the need for and quality of social programs is being diminished.

These cases are but a few examples of the ways accounting becomes embroiled in contemporary conflicts, influences decisions and determines the distribution of income and wealth among various interests. But accounting's social significance does not rest on its distributional consequences alone. Accounting is also important because of what, by its very existence, it precludes. The energy that goes into sustaining the conventional accounting model prevents the emergence of an activist accounting that has other allegiances and outcomes. It is the possibility of such an alternative accounting that forms the basis of "critical accounting."

The term critical accounting refers to the work of a heterogenous group of accounting scholars who view the public accounting profession's claims to neutrality and independence with skepticism.[5] They are critical of the public accounting profession's response to the growing social impact of modern transnational corporations and the challenges they present. For many of these scholars, the most important questions facing accounting today are threefold: How should we manage these institutions? How should we assess their social productivity and worth? How are they to be made accountable and to whom?[6]

If one is going to take the issue of accountability seriously one must imagine, not only a radically different role for accountants and a radically different kind of accounting, but a vehicle for communication that differs from today's financial statements and the annual reports in which they appear. As a vehicle for ensuring corporate accountability, these financial statements and annual reports are woefully inadequate. Consider, for example, the conflicts of interest that divide the two groups that the FASB claims are the primary users of financial statements: investors and creditors. Have certified financial statements really been meeting the information needs of all investors and creditors (not to mention employees, suppliers, customers, and communities) in situations involving "greenmailing," leveraged buyouts, the sale of insurance company loss reserves, in-substance defeasance, insider trading, junk bonds, or any of the numerous scandals that have rocked the American economy? To what extent can we claim that today's financial statements are meeting the information needs of employees concerned with the adequacy of the provisions being made for their pensions or the identity of toxic substances they are exposed to at work? Or the needs of citizens of developing countries who are being sold products that violate health and safety regulations in their countries of origin? How well met are the information needs of communities concerned with the level of pollutants being discharged into their air, water, and earth, or with the consequences of plant closures? The list of those to whom corporations must be accountable and who need better information about business activities in order to hold their own in struggles over economic resources and the quality of life goes on and on.

One way to imagine a different future is to begin by understanding and reassessing the past. That is one of the tasks I've set for myself in writing this book. I want to look at corporate annual reports in a new way for an accountant. I want to examine, not the certified financial statements, but the text and photos that accompany them. (For convenience I will use the term "annual report" to refer to these nonfinancial components of annual reports.) I want to understand the ways their contents change over time and relate to the concerns of the various constituencies whose lives and livelihoods are shaped by the issuing enterprise. It is these relationships that constitute the "hidden dimensions" of the book's title.

When I decided to focus my study of annual reports on General Motors (GM), my choice was to some degree opportunistic. The Ross Institute at New York University had a collection of GM's annual reports, from the company's inception in 1913 through the 1960s. Eugene H. Flegm, General Director of the Controller's Staff at GM, willingly sent the more recent reports and even filled in a few of the ones I was missing. I could not have picked a more appropriate industry or company for this study. For over a decade, GM and the U.S. auto-industry have engaged in a massive restructuring that is changing where, how, and by whom motor vehicles are manufactured. This restructuring is being duplicated throughout America's manufacturing and service industries, with equally profound consequences. Although the lives of all of us in the U.S. and elsewhere will never be the same as a result, the restructuring is taking place in the virtual absence of any popular control, without any true corporate accountability.

To understand the current restructuring and the problems of accountability that it presents, however, we need to understand its origins. These origins go back to the last depression and the institutional and ideological framework carved out by industrial giants, such as GM, the newly emergent industrial unions, such as the United Auto Workers (UAW), and the U.S. government. This framework, while it lasted, promised something to everyone. For the corporations that dominated the mass production sector, and for government, it promised labor peace and a new level of social consumption to help absorb a productive capacity that had doubled during the war. For those workers who were covered by the collective bargaining agreements, it promised a trade-off that provided increasing wages and benefits in exchange for the right to power and decision making, both on the job and in the public policy arena. But the continued viability of this framework had several preconditions. The participating corporations had to maintain their oligopolistic control over domestic markets and their worldwide productivity superiority, and the economy had to continue expanding. The industrial unions had to maintain their capacity to organize and mobilize the working class. And the state required sufficient revenues to fund the consequences of the corporate sector's tendency to generate surplus industrial capacity, surplus labor, environmental damage, and the threats to social harmony and political stability these consequences pose. These preconditions began to unravel in the 1970s, and the sources of this disintegration lay in the terms of the framework itself and in the ideologies that both reinforced and destabilized it.

This book examines the current restructuring of capital, its historical origins, and the issues of accountability it raises, through the experiences of GM. GM's annual reports provide a unifying thread for the narrative and a way of entering the network of interrelationships between GM and its work force, the state, domestic and international competitors, customers, suppliers, dealers, women, minorities, and the communities in which the company's products are produced and sold. Although GM's annual reports cannot be taken at face value, they also cannot be dismissed easily. They form part of the symbolic universe of language, signs, meanings, norms, beliefs, perceptions, and values through which the company defines itself and its relationships with others as it strives to create and maintain the conditions for its continued profitability and growth. The question for those of us concerned with accountability is whether these annual reports are too important to be left in the hands of corporate managers and public relations experts.

*   *   *

In a nation that exalts property rights to the level of natural rights, it is all too easy to forget that one's ideas are seldom, if ever, uniquely one's own, even when the conventions of footnoting do not require attribution, and even when the lineage of any single idea has faded into the mists of one's past. And so I want to publicly acknowledge my indebtedness to my colleague, Tony Tinker, and to my partner, Alisa Solomon, for ideas, both remembered and forgotten; for their advice and continuing encouragement; and for their patience with me over the many years it took for this book to be written.

CHAPTER *I*

THAT WAS THEN, THIS IS NOW

Whether it is described as the globalization of capital, the deindustrialization of America, the second industrial revolution, or the advent of the hollow corporation, the restructuring of American industry, that began in the mid-1970s and accelerated through the next decade, has fundamentally changed virtually every aspect of America's economic life — including the products and services we consume and where, how and by whom they are produced — as well as our beliefs about America's place in the world. Nowhere has this transformation been more visible than in the world's largest manufacturing activity, the motor vehicle industry.

Do you remember the controversy when Charles Wilson, President Eisenhower's Secretary of Defense and former President of General Motors asserted, "What's good for GM is good for America"? What Wilson actually said was:

> For years, I thought what was good for our country was good for General Motors and vice versa.[1]

But the confusion is understandable. In the living memory of most Americans, the fortunes of General Motors and those of the U.S. have seemed virtually inseparable. If the auto industry sneezed, it usually meant that the U.S. economy was catching a cold, which should not be surprising for an industry that, in 1987, accounted for nearly 30% of quarterly changes in overall economic activity.[2]

For anyone over 40, today's motor vehicle industry is nothing like the behemoth of our childhoods, when the Big Three (GM, Ford and Chrysler), and their products, shaped our fantasies and our lives; when the car you drove said all there was to say about who you were in the social pecking order; when the struggles between Big Business and Big Labor seemed to be between evenly matched adversaries; and when the future success of the

7

American automobile industry and of the U.S. and its economy seemed both assured and as one.

Once virtually the exclusive preserve of the U.S. carmakers, and dominated by GM since 1930, the auto industry today is a complex of European, Japanese and American firms. GM's market share – in 1965 around 50% in North America and 30% worldwide – has fallen to just over 35% and 16% respectively; and in the U.S., Honda may soon displace Chrysler in the Big Three.[3] Without mandatory quotas that restrict Japanese exports to European Community countries and "voluntary" quotas that restrict these imports to the U.S., GM's market share (as well as that of the other Big Three and the European manufacturers) would be even less. Chrysler's Lee Iacocca recently backed a United Auto Workers (UAW) plan to cap Japanese companies' share of the U.S. car market at a level well below the 32% they captured last year (a statistic that includes Japanese made cars sold by Chrysler, Ford and GM).[4] Not surprisingly, it is Japanese engineering, Japanese styling, Japanese quality, Japanese production methods and labor-management relations, and Japanese competition that dominate every discussion of the industry and its future.

Yet even as these discussions take place, they are being overtaken by events on the ground. A proliferation of equity investments, acquisitions, joint ventures, co-production arrangements, research and development co-operation, intercompany sourcing of parts and components, and transplants (foreign-owned manufacturing facilities) are transforming not only our notions of what constitutes "the enterprise" and how we measure industrial concentration and market share, but also such distinctions as what we mean when we say a vehicle is domestic or foreign, is the product of a particular manufacturer, or even that a particular production method is Japanese or American. No one has been more central to, and more deeply affected by, these changes than American workers. "Will America soon be asked to celebrate Labor Day without a labor movement?"

The Nation asked this question in September, 1984, noting that:

> Trade unions are in worse shape than at any time since the New Deal. The unionized percentage of the workforce is at its lowest level since 1940 and dropping fast. And even as it gambles on Walter Mondale's long-shot Presidential bid, organized labor seems on the verge of disappearing as a major force in national politics.[5]

Indeed, in the period since their 1984 and 1988 Presidential election debacles, the leaders of the Democratic Party have been virtually tripping over each other in the rush to distance themselves from organized labor, whose membership is at its lowest level in at least fifty years. Excluding government employees, a mere 12% of the labor force belongs to labor unions (among government workers the percentage is an anemic 16%).[6] The picture for the UAW is no brighter. Today's UAW has more than one-third fewer members than it did at its peak in 1979. At GM the decline has been over 40%, from 502,000 active UAW workers in 1979 to under 300,000 in the fall of 1990, and GM is said to want to shed a further 100,000 workers by the end of the decade.[7] Between 1978 and 1988, the number of UAW jobs in supplier plants in the U.S. dropped from 151,000 to 79,000.[8] Nor are the UAW's blue-collar workers the only employees affected by the industry's restructuring. In the past decade, the Big Three have slashed white collar employment from 30% to 50% and further cuts are expected. Adding insult to injury, in 1986 GM scrapped the annual cost of living adjustment for white collar workers in North America (a benefit that had been seen as virtually sacrosant since it was introduced in 1948); and in 1987 the company switched to a *merit* system for determining annual raises for salaried white collar employees. From now on 10% of them will be designated top performers, 80% as mid-range, and 10% substandard, and compensation determined accordingly.[9]

The decline in automotive employment in the U.S. is not simply the result of a declining market. Although the rate of growth in the domestic (U.S. and Canada) market has been slowing since the middle of the 1960s, the number of cars and light trucks sold continues, on average, to grow.[10] Rather than market weakness, the drop in employment primarily reflects decisions by automotive manufacturers about where, by whom, and how automobiles will be built, and the changing balance of power between the manufacturers and the UAW.

The Changing Locus of Production

"There is no such thing as a West German, Japanese, or U.S. economy," writes *The Wall Street Journal.* "There is instead a world economy, intricately interlinked, with annual international trade flows of $1.8 trillion and capital movements many times that."[11] And in no industry, perhaps, is this more evident than in the manufacture, distribution and sale of automobiles. Not only are individual firms increasingly engaged in production and distribution on a global scale — overall, the U.S. is both the largest importer of foreign-produced vehicles and parts and the largest exporter of capital for the production of automotive vehicles and parts abroad[12] — but a growing number of inter-firm transactions are linking enterprises throughout the world in a variety of ways including equity arrangements, joint ventures, deals to supply parts or components, marketing or distribution arrangements, technology agreements and manufacturing tieups. One of the consequences of these myriad connections is that many old distinctions — between domestic and foreign cars, for one — are gradually disappearing. The Opel Kadett, designed by GM's German subsidiary, for example, may be manufactured in South Korea by Daewoo (50% owned by GM), or by GM subsidiaries in Europe or Brazil. It may then be sold in the U.S. as a Pontiac LeMans, or in Canada as the Optima. The Ford Probe was designed and engineered by Japan-based Mazda Motor Company (25% owned by Ford), under a joint venture agreement, and manufactured in Flat Rock, Michigan. The Chevy Nova was designed by Toyota and is built in California by NUMMI, a joint venture between Toyota and GM. A car in GM's Geo line may be built in Japan, South Korea or California by Suzuki Motors (5.3% owned by GM), Isuzu Motors (40.2% owned by GM), Daewoo, or at NUMMI. Your GM or Chrysler may have a transmission built by New Venture Gear, Inc., a joint venture owned by Chrysler (64%) and GM (36%). Industrie Pinninfarina SpA, in Italy, designs and supplies the body for GM's Cadillac, Allante. The car is then shipped to the U.S. where it is joined with its chasis and power train in final assembly.[13] The connections between automakers have become so numerous that Ward's Automotive International publishes a 27-page booklet and accompanying map each year, explaining in detail the affiliations among the world's automotive enterprises.[14]

Automotive manufacturers search the world both for markets and for the best sites and partners for supplying their global needs for research and development, design and engineering, parts and components, and assembly facilities. The criteria vary but usually include the following:

- the nature of the available labor force (low wages and workers who are willing to cooperate with management are considered strong points and, depending upon the work to be done, so are relatively high education levels and technical skills);
- how friendly the local government is to business (are environmental and worker safety regulations weak? are wage levels controlled and trade union activities prohibited or restricted? do tax and tariff policies favor business? are subsidies, loans or loan guarantees available?);
- the relative strength of the local currency (the weaker the currency the less costly the investment); and
- the importance of the local consumer market.

When GM decided to build an assembly plant in Zaragoza, Spain — a politically conservative region where plant closures had created a desperate job crisis, in a country with a national unemployment rate of 21% —

they were attracted by the region's low wages and its hungry labor force. Some 80,000 workers applied for 6,200 jobs and were put through a barrage of interviews and psychological and hands-on tests.[15] Similar labor-cost and management concerns were behind GM's decision to move many labor-intensive operations, such as cutting and sewing car seats and assembling electrical wire harnesses, to 17 factories in Mexico.[16] In contrast, the availability of skilled workers and advanced technology were among the factors that prompted GM to acquire Lotus in England and Hughes Electronics and EDS in the U.S. Japanese investments in manufacturing facilities in the U.S. and their purchases of parts and components from U.S. firms reflect different concerns: the relative weakness of the dollar against the yen and the need to placate the government of its most important foreign market.[17] The recent rush to negotiate various equity, co-production and joint venture arrangements with formerly state-owned enterprises in Eastern Europe reflects a combination of these concerns — cheap labor, favorable government policies and lax regulations, accessibility to current and potential markets.[18] Today, Ford's and GM's worldwide facilities are so extensive that they export virtually none of their North American production and import a substantial part of their small car production.

At the same time that U.S. car-makers are transferring the production of parts and components, as well as entire automobiles, to company-owned sites and/or partners outside the U.S., foreign manufacturers, most notably the Japanese, are increasingly replacing their exports to the U.S. with U.S.-based production facilities, sometimes in partnership with one of the Big Three. In 1981 the Japanese manufactured no automobiles in the U.S.; by 1990 they were manufacturing 1.78 million. There are now ten transplants in the U.S. and four in Canada. Four of the U.S. and one of the Canadian transplants are joint ventures between one of the Big Three and a Japanese partner; these are the only transplants that are unionized.[19]

Following on the heels of the transplants are as many as 300 Japanese suppliers of auto-parts who operate either independently (one-half of the Japanese transplants are wholly owned) or through joint ventures or licensing arrangements with domestic companies.[20] Like the OEMs (Original Equipment Manufacturers, in this case, the car companies) the supplier transplants were motivated by a variety of concerns: encouragement from the OEMs themselves, who prefer the quality, cost structure and familiarity of known suppliers, with whom they are often linked in Japan; sensitivity to U.S. government and public concerns regarding the local content levels of cars assembled in the U.S.; and the dollar's weakness against the yen, which makes U.S. investments relatively inexpensive.

The entry of transplants into the supplier market has triggered changes that reflect those taking place among vehicle manufacturers: changes in the composition of the industry, its production and distribution methods, and its relations with the OEMs. Until the mid-1980s each of the Big Three purchased parts and components from thousands of companies so that there would always be a back-up in case a parts-maker failed.[21] Now that has changed as U.S. manufacturers struggle to catch up with the Japanese in both cost and quality by cutting back on the number of supplier firms,[22] forging more intimate and long-term relations with the survivors, and demanding both lower costs and higher quality. One result is that the number of supplier firms today is one-half that of the 1980s, and in many of the surviving firms, profits are lower at best.[23] To the consternation of the UAW, Ford recently bailed out one of its troubled and notoriously anti-union suppliers, Magna International, with loans and a 49% partnership.[24] But auto-makers are keeping up the pressure: in January, 1991, for example, GM began sending letters to suppliers asking for further price cuts.[25] Some suppliers are claiming that they incur expenses for engineering and development work, and then either lose the jobs to lower bidders, or face constant demands for further price reductions.[26]

In an editorial in *Wards Auto World*, Edward Miller writes that: "As their imports keep falling and U.S. production picks up Honda, Nissan and Toyota are *becoming* the American auto industry or at least a very big part of it. They are weaving themselves right into the fabric. It's not us versus them; they are becoming us."[27] According to *Wards*, the initial transplants had no real commitment to the U.S. beyond exploiting the market.[28] The most skilled and best-paying jobs were kept back in Japan, while the vast majority of jobs in the U.S. were semi-skilled. When Toyota announced its initial investment in Georgetown, Kentucky, in 1985, the company's head actually admitted to a reporter that the planned assembly plant would provide more direct jobs in Japan than in the U.S. Because such a large part of the initial transplant vehicles were assembled from parts shipped from Japan, these early transplants had little effect on the U.S.-Japan trade deficit in autos. But, says *Wards*, "that was then."

In 1990, Honda sold more cars in the U.S. from its transplants (54.3%) than it imported (45.7%), a feat helped along by the recession-weakened U.S. market, which is growing more slowly than transplant output. Honda's goal, *Wards* reports, a goal also shared by Toyota and Nissan, is to produce totally U.S.-designed, -engineered and -built cars and trucks. To achieve this, the "Other Big Three" are beginning to hire American engineers, designers and managers for their studios and offices, and to develop and expand U.S.-based design and engineering facilities.[29]

In large part because of the increasing presence of supplier transplants and joint ventures with U.S. firms, the domestic content of transplant fleets has increased in recent years and, at least according to manufacturers' reports, now ranges from 65% to 75%.[30] Despite this increase, *Wards* reported in July 1990 that the auto parts industry accounted for $10 billion of the $49 billion trade deficit the U.S. had with Japan. (The total auto deficit, cars and parts, accounted for two-thirds of the total deficit.) Indeed, the deficit is so high that the Japanese transplants would have to double their capacity to 4 million cars per year and export *every one of them* to erase the auto portion[31.] UAW head Owen Bieber, among others, questions these domestic content figures. In one case, for example, a U.S. supplier with an order from a Japanese firm was told to purchase Japanese steel. But because the supplier is a U.S. firm, the product was listed as having 100% domestic content.[32] Bieber asserts that the domestic content figures are also overstated because they reflect the impact of the dollar's weakness against the yen, and because they include services such as advertising. "I think if you look at legitimate apples-to-apples," he says, "you are talking in the high 40% range for U.S. content."[33]

Bieber's skepticism about the domestic content figures reflects his concern with declining UAW employment in both OEM and supplier firms in the U.S. The automobiles, parts and components, purchased from overseas by U.S.-based manufacturers (whether Big Three or transplants) represent jobs that are not being done by UAW workers in the U.S. But increasingly the production of automobiles, parts and components, in the U.S. itself, does not necessarily mean UAW jobs either.

With the exception of those transplants that are joint ventures with one of the Big Three, the OEM and supplier transplants in the U.S. are not unionized, and the UAW's organizing efforts to date have not been successful. (The UAW lost an organizing election at Nissan's Smyrna plant in 1989, and has not felt confident enough to push for votes at Honda's, Toyota's or Subaru-Isuzu's independent plants.) Union organizing efforts have not been helped by the fact that more than 80% of all workers under age 35 in the U.S. have no union members in their households,[34] nor by the decision by car-makers to locate their new North American plants in traditionally non-unionized regions.

Even where the new plants include the UAW (for example, at the Big Three transplants as well as at newly constructed factories such as GM's Saturn plant in Spring Hill, Kentucky), the union has agreed to pre-production agreements that give management increased flexibility in running the plants, so that they can reduce the number of labor hours required to produce an automobile. Union jobs are also being lost through plant closings as the Big Three bring their productive capacity into line with the reality of the marketplace. During the past 10 years, for example, GM has closed all or part of 31 assembly and component plants. In October, 1990, the company announced that it planned to close up to nine more assembly plants (four of which had already been "idled indefinitely"), as well as related parts plants. Despite these cuts, GM continued to have excess capacity and faced losses of $6 billion to $8 billion in North America, its largest ever. In December, 1991, chairman and chief executive, Robert C. Stempel, announced plans to close a further 21 plants (6 assembly plants, 4 powertrain plans and 11 component plants) by the mid-1990s.[35]

In addition to changing where and by whom cars are made — from North America to overseas sites in Europe, Asia, Mexico and South America and, within North America, from traditonally unionized Big Three plants to transplants and new, "leaner" factories — the restructuring of the motor vehicle industry is also changing how cars are made.

The New Technology and Social Organization of the Workplace

"More than ever," the headline in *Business Week* reads, "industry is pinning its hopes on factory automation."[36] "High technology," the article promises, "is reinventing the factory. . . . These plants, which can build a high variety of flawless products and switch from one product to another on cue from a central computer, herald a new age in manufacturing." Throughout the 1980s, the auto industry, and no company more so than GM, bet heavily on technology to improve both productivity and quality. Beginning with the formation of GMF Robotics, a 50/50 joint venture with the Japanese robot producer, Fanuc, Ltd., in 1982, GM made a series of high-profile, high-tech investments. In 1984 GM spent $2.5 billion to purchase EDS, an expert in computer design, programming and management; and in 1985 GM spent $2.7 billion to acquire Hughes Electronics.[37] GM also acquired a minority position in Teknowledge, Inc., an artificial intelligence company specializing in expert systems development, and five other small high tech companies involved in developing artificial vision systems and computerized navigation systems for drivers.[38]

One of the major problems faced by manufacturers using high tech systems from different suppliers is that the variety of electronic brains, robots, and machine tools that will make up the so-called "factory of the future" cannot communicate with each other. Hence, a second step in GM's strategic commitment to deploying high technology in its factories was to develop a standardized communication system, the manufacturing automation protocal (MAP).[39] GM announced that it would not buy machines for its factories that cannot observe MAP. Leading an insurrection of major manufacturers in 1985, GM forced some one hundred suppliers of factory automation equipment (from small Silicon Valley firms to giants such as AT&T, IBM, Hewlett-Packard, and Digital Equipment) to endorse MAP.

Advanced technology translates into reduced labor costs both directly, by reducing the number of labor hours required to produce a vehicle, and indirectly, through its impact on quality and the locus at which decision making occurs. As quality improves (computers do not have hangovers or make mistakes), and as testing is automated and built into the production process itself, fewer inspectors and rework operators will be needed. Just-in-time inventory systems, impossible without supporting computer systems, rely on suppliers to deliver inventories close to the work site and reduce, not only inventory investment, but also the number of persons involved in material handling and inventory control. The new technology, along with an associated reorganization of the labor process (to which I will return below), is relocating decision making, either upwards to central management, or downwards to the shop floor, where decisions can now be made by less trained, lower salaried workers with the help of "expert systems." No longer needed are the cadres of middle managers, executive assistants, financial analysts, production controllers and so on, who previously collected, organized and analyzed data before decisions could be made, either by them or by higher level managers. Personnel savings are also realized as computerized design systems, with multi-dimensional design capabilities, reduce both the number of designers, drafters and engineers and the need to construct physical models. Although software innovations such as these reduce busywork and increase the challenge of some jobs, fewer employees will be needed overall.

To realize these labor savings, however, the new technology must be effectively implemented. Within the next decade, said Roger Smith, GM's chairman and chief executive officer, in 1985: "Every single device and function in our plants from machine handling to machining, assembly, inspection and maintenance will be under computer control."[40] But implementation has turned out to be more difficult than expected. Productivity at GM's low technology joint venture with Toyota in Fremont, California, regularly outstrips that at most of GM's new plants, such as Buick City and Hamtramck. Although many of the initial problems at GM's new plants were technological — the high tech equipment needed fine tuning and the various systems needed to be better integrated — the source of other problems seems to have been managerial. Many of the robots, initially heralded as the "silver bullet that would kill the werewolf responsible for quality and production problems," fell short, not because of any inherent technical problems, but because "they were being improperly installed, maintained or programmed."[41] According to auto-expert, David Cole, the industry's strategy should have been to first improve the management of its existing technology (through work rule changes, better personnel screening, training and participative management programs, and more efficient inventory management), and only then to shift to advanced technology.[42] Before they began to introduce robotics, the Japanese already had disciplined production floors and standardized work procedures.[43]

What critics, like Cole and *Wards'* Drew Winter, miss, however, is the part played by the new technology in persuading workers to accept the very shop floor changes they advocate. In 1982, then UAW President, Douglas Fraser promised to be "more responsive to innovative job assignments."[44] But while this "unprecedented pledge" may have opened the way for GM's management to seek work rule changes in its U.S. facilities, the changes could not be forced on locals by Fraser. They had to be individually negotiated. The loss of jobs to high technology was part of the arsenal used by auto-makers to induce workers to accept fundamental changes in the social organization of the workplace.

GM's experience with Saturn exemplifies the company's high-tech dreams as well as the problems encountered in realizing them. GM started out by trying to design a facility so automated that much of it would run without human workers.[45] Automated guided vehicles were to carry car chassis from robot to robot. Instead of the traditional assembly line, where each car frame moves along miles of conveyers at a predetermined speed and passes through each station, whether it needs to or not, the idea was for cars to be carried only to the stations they needed. Moreover cars were to stay at each station for as long as necessary for the work to be completed and tested. In the process of shrinking Saturn down — from a $5 billion investment, that would employ 6,000 workers and produce 500,000 subcompacts selling for $6,000 and getting gas mileage of 45MPG City/60 Highway, to a $2–3.5 billion investment, employing 3,000 workers, and producing 240,000 compacts selling for $10–12,000 and gas mileage of 25MPG City/35 Highway — some of these high tech dreams also fell by the wayside.

Saturn is a highly integrated facility that combines paint shop, body and assembly plant, power-train factory (that casts, machines and assembles the cars' engines and transmissions), a plastic molding plant and a shop for assembling the instrument panel and dash into a single unit. The materials and parts flow smoothly and directly from one location to the next — in sharp contrast with the traditional GM assembly plant which gets its key components from factories hundreds of miles away — and parts that must be delivered come, not to a central loading dock, but directly to where they are needed. But there still is an assembly line, the first one made of wood, which makes it easier on workers' feet.

Saturn's assembly line consists of a series of wood pads, called skillets. Each skillet carries a pallet that holds the car body. As the car body moves down the line it raises or lowers to make it more accessible to workers. Unlike regular assembly lines, where workers walk (or run) to keep up with the car, Saturn workers ride with the car on the skillet and then walk back to the next one. As cars leave the plant, Saturn's computers automatically authorize payment to suppliers (part of Saturn's all-electronic financial system, although the system is still not the paperless wonder originally envisioned).

But in the end, Saturn's technology turns out not to be very different from that used at many modern auto plants: a snafu in processing front fenders led to an embarrassing delay in the car's launch date; other plant problems have limited Saturn to 50% of its planned output; the car itself, while garnering praise for its design and handling, is not the promised revolutionary advance over the Japanese and is entering an already crowded field; and the current plant capacity is half that needed for the facility to break even. A *Wall Street Journal* article points out that: "For roughly what GM spent at Spring Hill, Honda got not one but two assembly plants with total annual capacity of 510,000 cars — more than double Saturn's. Honda also got a factory capable of building almost all the engines, transmissions and related components needed by its auto-assembly operations and its Ohio motorcycle plant. . . . Does GM need an expensive new operation to do what Honda does as a matter of course — build top quality cars at competitive prices in the U.S.?" they ask. Indeed, when GM talks about Saturn today, technology takes a clear back seat to labor-management issues.

In 1985, Saturn employees accepted a union agreement without job classifications or work rules and waived all UAW seniority rights to return to their old plants. They also agreed to accept at least 20% less in pay than UAW and salaried workers at other GM facilities; the balance is contingent on meeting productivity and other targets.[46] In return, Saturn employees are heavily involved in all of the enterprise's operations. In addition to helping to develop many factory processes (something workers do at many plants today), they also participate in teams that help select suppliers, dealers, the advertising agency and even the paving material for the parking lots, and they interview and hire their co-workers. Workers receive from 100–750 hours of training including a five-day awareness training workshop, designed to teach them how to work in teams and build consensus.

The reorganization of the work process on the shop floor, exemplified for GM by its Saturn facility, is an integral part of the restructuring taking place in the automobile industry, a restructuring that in some ways reflects a major change in automotive management attitudes. In 1975, GM's Vice Presidents of Industrial Relations and Personnel Administration, George B. Morris and Stephen Fuller, respectively, when asked about the team approach then being used by Swedish auto companies, made it clear that the company saw only a limited future for such innovations.[47] According to Morris, workers prefer the assembly line:

> In the typical assembly operation, the man has a fairly simple job assignment. He doesn't have a multiplicity of things to do. He can develop a style, a method and rhythm which permits him to do the job in his own way and at his own pace. In a typical group system the individual has a lot of things to do. The whole psychology of the job has been changed for him. He has a much greater responsibility than before and he finds it quite frustrating because instead of three elements to his operation he now has 20 or 30. . . . The people told us they didn't like this extra responsibility.

In addition, Morris continued: "You just couldn't build a plant big enough to handle that volume of production on a team basis." There just isn't enough space to store all the materials and parts one would need. Today, the team concept, largely borrowed from Japanese, not Swedish, methods, and honed at GM's joint venture with Toyota (NUMMI, in Fremont, California), forms the keystone of GM's new system of production management. Along with the team concept, the new management system includes:

- just-in-time inventory management (a system that relies on suppliers to deliver inventories close to the work site in sufficient quantities to meet only immediate needs);
- "pay for knowledge" (the more jobs workers learn, the higher their pay);
- drastic reductions in job classifications and work rules; and
- "jointness" (increased cooperation between the UAW and management).

By March, 1988, the team concept was installed or planned for at least 17 General Motors assembly plants, as well as in some parts plants, in 6 Chrysler plants, in Ford's Rouge Steel and Romeo engine facilities, and in all of the wholly or partly Japanese-owned plants.[48] At GM's Delco Remy parts plant near Albany, N.Y., for example, the assembly line workers, called "quality operators," are organized in teams where they are lumped into one job classification, instead of the seventy-five or more found in a typical parts plant.[49] Through the "pay for knowledge" system, workers are expected to know all the jobs in their teams, and assignments are changed hourly to maintain efficiency and reduce monotony. The teams are responsible for monitoring their own scrap and materials costs, and meet every morning with management to discuss production schedules and problems. The new work rules began paying off for GM very quickly: volume increased without additional hours, costs fell, and *the salaried workforce was cut 15%*.

For its proponents — who include automotive executives, members of the business press, business school professors, and the UAW's international leadership — the new production management system and the spirit of cooperation between the UAW and automotive management that it reflects is both necessary and desirable. From automotive executive:

> A real spirit of cooperation between management and labor is taking hold in the auto industry. (Roger Smith, GM Chairman, in GM's 1983 annual report, a year after GM experienced its first loss year since the 1920s and the UAW accepted its first concessionary contract.)

to UAW executive:

> Owen [UAW President, Owen Bieber] has shown his ability to realize the times are changing, and we can't stay at arms length from management. We have to develop a cooperative relationship. (Ernest Lofton, Detroit area member of the UAW's Executive Board, in the *Wall Street Journal*, October 16, 1984.)

to university professors:

> It is . . . a landmark pact that shows labor and management in a new cooperative arrangement. . . . Management and labor have committed themselves to a partnership. . . . GM has acknowledged that a partnership with the union is a necessary ingredient of its business strategy. . . . The union, for its part, has not cut into GM's flexibility in conducting its business. (Harvard Business School Professor, Quinn Mills, regarding the 1984 UAW-GM agreement, in the *New York Times*, October 7, 1984.)

> The union is recognizing finally that the well-being of workers is intrinsically tied to the well-being of the company. They are not trying to pretend these are two different things any more. (MIT Economics Professor and Labor Relations scholar, Martin Weitzman, regarding the 1985 Saturn contract, in *Fortune*, November 11, 1985.)

to government official:

> Tremendous economies have been realized because of this cooperation through work teams, fewer job classifications and work task

flexibility. . . . I can't recall ever being in a plant where I heard the word 'fun' being used so much. (U.S. Secretary of Labor, William E. Brock, announcing the selection of NUMMI as a model of labor-management cooperation by the International Labor Organization, in *Wards Auto World,* June 1986.)

the sentiments are much the same. No one paid much attention to Pete Kelly, a dissident leader of the UAW local in Warren, Michigan, when he later pulled out a letter from GM management to its employees in October, 1934, which expressed remarkably similar sentiments: "It is only by real teamwork that we can maintain the quality of our products and satisfy the buyers upon whom all of us depend for a living."[50]

For its critics, the new production system is called "management by stress" and its ultimate goal is to reduce employment. When GM's Van Nuys plant manager, Ernest Schaefer, returned from a trip to Japan, he told the workers: "'The Japanese work smarter, not harder. . . . If we are to compete with the Japanese then we must do it on an equal footing, utilizing the team concept to optimize our jobs.' He then added that the Japanese produce the same number of cars as the United States with only 25% of the workforce."[51] But according to its critics, harder work is exactly what the new production system means. According to the Transnationals Information Exchange's *General Motors Counter Annual Report, 1987:* "The system, including its human elements, operates in a state of permanent stress. Workers are expected to continually *kaizen,* or seek improvement in their jobs, i.e., to speed themselves up. No replacement workers are on the payroll — the existing workforce has to make up for absences," the report continues. And "accompanying the team concept has been an emphasis on more management control over the way workers do their jobs. At the most 'advanced' team concept plants, such as NUMMI, every motion is strictly specified and workers are not allowed to deviate from the specifications. The 'worker autonomy' which is supposed to be part of the team concept turns out to be a myth. The only 'autonomy' involved in the team concept is that sometimes team members get to decide among themselves how to distribute extra work which is assigned to the team." Writing about NUMMI, the star in GM's new production management crown, the *New York Times* reports that: "Fear, not just Japanese style management, drives NUMMI workers to perform so well."[52] But the team concept does not depend on fear alone; it also constructs a rhetoric that on the one hand appeals to workers' genuine feelings of alienation and on the other hand manipulates these feelings to instill "team consciousness." One critic writes that: "Workers are encouraged to be on the lookout for so-called malingerers or slackers, who hamper production."[53] At NUMMI, teams have separate "team rooms," so that workers don't even share a common area during their breaks.

According to some critics, the team concept also dismantles for good the traditional mode of shop floor organization in which workers are represented by the union steward and management by the foreman, and grievances are resolved by an elaborate adjudication system.[54] At NUMMI, for example, the Team Leader is a union member appointed by management (at other places, such as the joint Ford-Mazda plant at Flat Rock, Michigan, the Team Leader is chosen by the Team itself). Team Leaders have management authority and function as assistant supervisors, for example by taking attendance, administering overtime scheduling, and so on. Above them are Group Leaders who are formally management. Team Leaders and Group Leaders collaborate and grievances are supposed to be collectively worked out by the Team. Under the new production management system, unions become outsiders, "little more than the dispenser of various forms of private social insurance."

But just as important as the new production system itself, is the way it has been installed by GM. At new plants, it's been easy: with the acquiescence of the UAW, GM has simply put it in place unilaterally. But at existing plants, it has required the threat of losing work or seeing the plants shut down to persuade local unions to accept the new production management system as well as work rule concessions and reduced labor costs.

Whipsawing and the New Balance of Power

Whipsawing is what companies like GM do when they pit workers in different plants against each other. Indeed, many local union officers and members now refer to union members in other plants as "the competition."[55] To get GM to reverse plans to close two Fisher Body "hardware" plants, for example, GM persuaded the UAW to increase hourly worker output by 20%.[56] The company then demanded and got matching gains from four other hardware plants by threatening to close at least one of them. At Fisher Body's Chicago stamping plant, workers agreed to givebacks after GM stripped the plant of at least two major jobs, laid off close to 200 workers, and transferred work to plants that had already agreed to concessions. When GM decided to add to the production of the J-body sub-compact, the company announced a competition for the first new work to the most cooperative and quality-conscious of the three plants that built the car. The first winners were workers at GM's Lordstown plant. They won by agreeing to speed up the assembly line, to make other jobs throughout the plant more strenuous, and to settle hundreds of outstanding job grievances. When the UAW in Canada went on strike in 1984, GM Chairman Roger Smith warned that a prolonged strike might discourage further GM investments: "Things like this [strike] will be a factor in our long term planning," he said.[57]

Whipsawing is not only used to get concessions from workers. GM, for example, pitted states against each other in choosing the site for its Saturn plant.[58] The winner, Tennessee, granted enormous tax breaks to GM and agreed to spend $72 million for roads, worker training and education. GM will pay no property taxes on the site, to which it has full rights, although the land is owned formally by the county industrial board, a public body that issued bonds to help finance construction. Instead of taxes, GM will reimburse the county through installment payments over a 40 year period. For the first ten years, GM will make flat payments amounting to at least $70 million less than it would have owed in taxes; then it will be taxed on only 25% of the factory's assessed value (less depreciation and any losses). More recently, GM's new Chairman, Robert Stempell, was asked whether GM was considering producing its planned electric car at the Van Nuys plant, for which no production is currently planned after 1992. He replied: "You saw the initiatives out there. You saw what they're asking us to do on things like clean air and so forth. It's very difficult environmentally to do business out there, so that's a negative."[59]

The UAW has not tried to stop whipsawing. Instead it institutionalized it in the 1987 national agreement which committed the local unions to explore, with local managements, ways to make their plants more efficient; the contract listed both team concept and local deviations from the national agreement as possible ways to do this. In exchange, the UAW claimed that the new national agreement would provide job security for its members. GM promised, for example, not to lay off any workers during the life of the contract except — and these proved to be big exceptions — if sales dropped to a level that made it uneconomical to continue producing vehicles; except for the 16 plants GM had already announced it would close; and except for plants shut because of "consolidations." Officially, GM did not close any additional plants during the life of the contract. But they indefinitely idled facilities in Pontiac, Michigan, Leeds, Missouri, Framingham, Massachusetts, and Lakeville, Georgia. (The UAW did contest these closings, but lost an arbitrator's ruling.)

In its latest agreement with the UAW, GM has agreed to substantially guarantee the incomes of workers now on the job for *the next three years,* or until the $3.5 billion fund for laid-off workers runs out, whichever comes first. According to UAW head, Bieber, this provision means that

"UAW members now have total income security."[60] Workers on layoff will receive extra layoff benefits. Both groups of workers will receive extra incentives for early retirement. The trade-off for this income protection is that GM will continue to rapidly shrink its workforce. By agreeing to this formulation, Bieber seems to be equating income security with job security. A contract that provides wages and benefits to laid-off workers for a limited time period (the life of the latest contract or for however long the unemployment fund remains liquid, whichever is shorter), and at the same time allows overall employment to fall, is not job security. It is a strategy which leaves the door open for the Big Three to match their manpower levels to their smaller market share. If this happens, the automobile industry may be reduced to a small, secure, core workforce, a cadre of laid-off workers living on the dole, and a limited number of union jobs for new workers. If this sounds familiar, it should: we saw it last in the longshoremen's and newspaper pressmen's unions. The difference here, labor analyst Jane Slaughter notes, is that the auto industry isn't dramatically downsizing per se; it is the number of union jobs that is being reduced.[61]

Also built into the 1990 contract is a continuation of the practices of speedup, whipsawing and outsourcing (the practice of securing parts and components, previously made by the automobile manufacturer, from independent suppliers) Local labor management job security and operational effectiveness committees are empowered by the contract to address what are euphemistically called "work standards on operations that fully utilize employees and alternative work schedules."[62] The former translates into moving closer to the goal of 60 seconds assigned time out of every minute; the latter refers to GM's goals of a ten-hour day, four-day week at straight time, and a three shift operation—both of which will allow GM to use its assembly lines closer to 24 hours a day and thereby combine production into fewer plants. GM already uses three shift production at three of its European plants and has plans for others. It has brought UAW officials from its Lordstown and Saturn plants to study the scheduling at its Antwerp plant.[63] Outsourcing is encouraged by the contract's acceptance of the principle that work that can be done more cheaply must be. Hence, the contract provides that if a local can prove that it can do certain work competitively, GM is supposed to bring the work in-house. But this pits unionized U.S. workers against non-union workers in the U.S. and in low wage third world countries. (UAW President Bieber has said that he will not allow jobs to be taken away from UAW parts plants, however.)[64]

Despite the critics, and the active dissident movement within the UAW, New Directions, the 1990 contract passed with overwhelming support. And as the UAW scrambles to make concessions that it hopes will enable

U.S. manufacturers to catch up with the Japanese, the target keeps moving. A recent Massachusetts Institute of Technology (MIT) study finds that on the average, Japanese companies take less than 17 hours to make a car, compared to 25 hours for U.S. companies, and 36 hours for the Europeans.[65] The Japanese also develop new models in 46 months, while the Americans and the Europeans need closer to 60 months. Nor are the Japanese about to stay where they are. Honda, for one, says its goal is to be able to develop new models in 24 months; Toyota says it hopes to produce different models to order on the same line. Today the Japanese rely far less on automation than do the Americans: at Toyota only 8% of the functions on its final assembly line are automated. Robots are used only in operations which are dangerous or dirty, such as pressing and painting. According to Shoichiro Irimajiri, an Executive Vice President at Honda, "the human being is the most flexible robot. The more automation you add, the more rigid your production line becomes." He might have added, and the more vulnerable to labor action.

What are we to make of the restructuring that is taking place in the motor vehicle industry? How can one explain the surprisingly passive response of the rank and file and union leadership as the Big Three say goodbye to thousands of high-paying blue collar jobs — particularly when contrasted with the activism of the last major crisis for the industry, the Depression in the 1930s? What does the restructuring suggest for the future of General Motors, the automobile industry, the U.S. workforce and the U.S. economy? Is what's good for GM still good for America? Was it ever?

In the following chapters I will show that the framework within which the present restructuring is taking place has its origins in the last transformation of capital-state-labor relations which followed the economic crisis of the 1930s. Today's crisis, and the capacities of participants to deal with it, are linked to an institutional and ideological edifice inherited from earlier eras. It is only by understanding the construction of this edifice, the ways it helped to resolve the crisis of the 1930s for each of the protagonists, and its inherent contradictions, that we can come to an appreciation of the current situation and what it suggests for the future. To do this, we need an historical perspective that will enable us to view the present as part of a continuum that connects the past with the future. In the next chapter I will begin introducing this perspective by critically examining the conceptual framework that currently dominates the study of business history and organizational change in the U.S.: the Transaction Cost approach.

CHAPTER II

THE TRANSACTION COST APPROACH TO ORGANIZATIONAL CHANGE

For close to two decades, the transaction cost approach has dominated the way the history of the modern corporation has been taught in business schools. Most closely associated with Oliver Oliver Williamson, who introduced it in his book, *Markets and Hierarchies,* published in 1975, its intellectual roots lie in 19th century social Darwinism, and more recently, as well as more directly, in the writings of Ronald H. Coase and Alfred D. Chandler, Jr.[1]

According to Coase, business firms and markets are alternative forms of economic organization.[2] Which alternative is preferable depends upon the relative costs of organizing transactions. To transact through markets, for example, individual commodity producers must identify the relevant prices, discover with whom to deal, inform them that they wish to deal and on what terms, negotiate and conclude numerous contracts, and devise monitoring mechanisms to ensure that contract terms are being observed. In place of this complicated and costly structure of individual bargains between various cooperating factors of production, the business firm substitutes an administrative authority (the entrepreneur-co-ordinator) to direct production and allocate resources. But bureaucracies also impose costs, and Coase argues that the costs of organizing increase as firms grow and the types of transactions to be organized differ in kind and place. Hence there are diminishing returns to organizing transactions within firms rather than within markets. Inventions which tend to reduce the spatial distribution of transactions (such as the telephone) or improve managerial efficiency (such as the computer) tend to reduce the costs of administering transactions within firms and hence increase optimal firm size.

Chandler's *Strategy and Structure* was also an important source for Williamson.[3] Chandler claims that a combination of exogenous technological and market changes lead to new business strategies (such as large scale production of standardized products, national and international distribution, vertical integration and diversification) which, in turn, result in new organizational structures that economize and improve upon administrative coordination, the modern divisionalized corporation. He attributes the growth and development of the modern corporation to the competitive cost advantages gained from the search for ever greater administrative efficiencies in the face of changing markets and technologies.

The Transaction Cost Explanation of the Modern Corporation

Williamson builds upon these earlier ideas to explain the historical development of the modern multinational corporation. He argues, in an article with William Ouchi, that the driving force for the main institutional changes that have occurred since, as well as prior to, the industrial revolution — including the formation and development of the corporation — has been transaction cost economizing.[4]

Several elements form the core of Williamson's transaction cost theory. The basic unit of analysis is the transaction. A transaction occurs "when a good or service is transferred across a technologically separable interface."[5] The critical dimensions for describing a transaction are its frequency, uncertainty, and the amount of transaction-specific investments in physical or human capital (such as specialized language, training, learning-by-doing). Transaction costs are the costs associated with facilitating such transfers. They include the costs of executing the transactions as well as the costs of removing the frictions that impede the formation of markets or the functioning of bureaucratic organizations. Human agents are a source of transaction costs because of their limited cognitive capacity in the face of environmental uncertainty and complexity (bounded rationality) and their opportunism (self-interest seeking with guile). These behavioral assumptions are so important to Williamson and Ouchi that they actually argue that the problem of economic organization reduces to a single issue: "Organize transactions in such a way as to economize on bounded rationality while simultaneously safeguarding those transactions against the hazards of opportunism."[6]

The goal of organizing transactions is to minimize transaction costs, thereby maximizing profits. This is achieved by appropriately matching the governance structure through which transactions are mediated with the nature of the transactions (their uncertainty, frequency, and the extent of transaction specific investment) and the limits imposed by human beings' bounded rationality and opportunism. Williamson identifies a range of governance mechanisms that may be appropriate in a transaction cost economizing sense.[7] At one extreme are the occasional or recurring exchanges that require no transaction-specific investment (for example, when homogenous goods and/or services are exchanged, when the specific identity of the trading partners is unimportant, when each transaction is a discrete event) and for which markets are the cost-economizing structure. At the other extreme are the recurring exchanges that require highly specialized transaction-specific investments, for which the cost-economizing structure is one that internalizes the exchanges within a unified framework, the organization. In between these extremes a variety of alternative governance structures may be appropriate, such as joint ventures or formally relying on third-party arbitration (as in some employer-union relationships). The modern corporation, according to Williamson, is an efficient (that is, transaction cost minimizing) governance structure that administers and monitors a network of contracts that link factor and product market participants (such as customers, employees, and suppliers of goods, services and capital). In a series of articles Williamson explains and justifies various developments in the history of the corporation over the past 150 years, as transaction cost reducing (and hence efficiency enhancing) improvements over their predecessors.

For example, in his article, "The Organization of Work," Williamson challenges researchers who attribute the historical emergence of factory production and subsequent organizational innovations, including the hierarchical division of labor, primarily to capitalists' efforts to secure control over the production process and thereby acquire a greater share of the economic pie.[8] In contrast, Williamson argues that the transitions from the putting-out system to the factory, and from inside-contracting within the factory to capitalist authority relations, were principally motivated by efficiency considerations. Although the rewards for such innovations were initially captured by their initiators, the new methods were then widely imitated, rates of return were reduced to competitive levels, and the benefits were diffused throughout society. Because of these innovations, the economic pie grew larger and all participants shared in it.

In making his argument, Williamson cites the inefficiencies associated with both the putting-out system and inside contracting. Williamson draws on Harry Braverman, whose work is highly regarded by labor theorists on the left (although not uncritically so), when he notes that the putting-out system was "plagued by problems of irregularity of production, loss of materials in transit and through embezzlement, slowness of manufacture, lack of uniformity and uncertainty of the quality of the product."[9] Most important, says Williamson, the entrepreneur was unable to make changes in the production process because it was in the hands of dispersed, autonomous producers. Williamson uses Katherine Van Wezel Stone's study of the transformation of the steel industry in the late 19th century to illustrate the problems associated with inside contracting. The skilled workers, who belonged to the Amalgamated Association of Iron, Steel and Tin Workers, had authority over every aspect of steel production. There was constant haggling over the details of work, output per worker was restricted, production procedures were proscribed and innovations were supressed. In 1892, Henry Frick and Andrew Carnegie, with the assistace of both state and federal governments, challenged the union's hegemony at the Homestead mill. After a serious of violent confrontations, the company prevailed, and by 1910 the steel industry was non-union. The Homestead defeat was followed by the introduction of "unprecedented developments in steel making."[10] For Williamson, these institutional changes and subsequent technological innovations were geared to achieving efficiency. For Bowles and Gintus, Marglin, and Stone, among others, they are part of a continuing struggle between capital and labor over control of the production process and the fruits of labor.

Williamson uses his transaction cost economizing/ efficiency enhancing framework to explain other structural changes in the corporation.[11] In the second half of the 19th century a number of organizational innovations made it possible for businesses to exploit the economies of scale inherent in the technological developments of the period. These organizational changes — which included the administrative organization of the firm by functional responsibility, the separation of line and staff activities, and lateral, forward, and backward integration — made it possible to efficiently manage large enterprises. But the growth of large, unitary, functionally organized firms also resulted in increased operating costs. Williamson and Ouchi attribute these increased costs to the overhead required to achieve coordination among what were not recognized as effectively decomposable parts; to the congestion and spill-over costs associated with forced interdependencies; and to the difficulties of detecting and controlling opportunistic subgoal pursuits.

Divisionalization reduced these transaction costs by assigning semi-autonomous standing to subunits within the firm. A central office carries out strategic planning (which was previously confused with operations), assigns investment resources to high yield uses, and audits and assesses the performance of the semi-autonomous operating divisions. The multi-divisional firm, writes Williamson, "takes on many of the properties of (and is usefully regarded as) a miniature capital market."[12] Conglomerates and the multinational corporations take divisionalization a step further by extending these transaction cost economies to less closely related and previously autonomous entities.

The conglomerate replaces the market interface between previously independent divisions and stockholders with an administrative interface. Williamson suggests that we view the general office of the conglomerate as "an agent of the stockholders whose purpose is to monitor the operations of the constituent parts."[13] The general office yields a variety of transaction cost economies. Monitoring benefits accrue because the general office has access to information that was not previously available to outside investors. And because the general office can more easily remove or reassign managers based on their performance, it also possesses staffing advantages over labor markets. Resource allocation becomes more efficient because cash flows all revert to the general office regardless of where they originate. There they can be reallocated among competing alternatives in accordance with prospective yields. An unanticipated benefit of the conglomerate form derives from the ever-present possibility of a take-over that it poses for all firms; a potentiality that increases the efficiency of the market for corporate control.

According to Williamson, the multinational corporation extends the asset management advantages of the conglomerate from a domestic base to include foreign operations. It makes it possible for the enterprise to develop a global strategy and a worldwide perspective. Most importantly, it offers the benefits of technology transfer which would otherwise be discouraged by the difficulties of bilateral contracting alternatives, such as licensing or joint venture agreements between independent firms under conditions of asset specificity and recurrent trading.

It is important that we look critically at transaction cost theory, not only because of its influence in the academy, but also because of its policy implications. Transaction cost theory is not a neutral explanation of corporate development. By equating what exists with what is efficient, transaction cost theory favors those structures that have evolved through the "natural" processes of market competition over those that might exist through politico-regulatory mandates. Thus it legitimizes the modern corporate form and existing business strategies (such as the internationalization of production and distribution, mergers and acquisitions, joint ventures, union-busting, plant closures, leveraged buyouts, greenmailing, pension plan terminations, and even insider-trading), and justifies opposition to most forms of corporate regulation.

Transaction Cost Theory: A Critical Look

Efficiency is a central concept in transaction cost theory. Williamson is concerned with explaining the internal organization of the firm. He argues that economizing on transaction costs is central to this explanation. Unlike neoclassical economics, which attributes differences in efficiency to differences in technology, Williamson attributes efficiency differences to relative transaction costs. (The higher the transaction costs, the less efficient the mode of organization.)

Transaction cost theory presents efficiency as the sole performance criteria for governance structures and as a non-problematic social ideal. It is implicit in the transaction cost literature that efficient production at the firm level will translate into efficiency at the economy-wide level and that there is no incompatibility between the corporate quest for efficiency and the interests of employees, consumers, and other social constituencies.

Efficiency is not usually defined in the transaction cost literature, beyond the equation of efficiency with minimizing transaction costs. But in his article on work organization, Williamson identifies a variety of efficiency criteria (which he uses in the article to evaluate alternative modes of organizing the labor process).[14] Efficient modes of organization expedite product flows. Specifically, they economize on transportation expense (as in the movement of work-in-process inventories between work stations) and on inventory levels. They also reduce the loss of product in manufacturing from embezzlement and/or quality defects. Efficient modes of organization also facilitate the assignment of workers to tasks so that workers are assigned to jobs for which they are relatively well-suited; less, rather than more, coordination is required; and contracting with specialists to service the needs of many work stations is easily accomplished. And finally, efficient modes of organization have superior incentive attributes. They discourage malingering by workers and the abuse and neglect of equipment; they promote the innovation of process improvements at individual work stations; they facilitate quick recovery from shocks at individual work stations (such as when machinery breaks down or workers are ill); and they increase the capacity of the system to both respond to systemic shocks (such as changes in the marketplace) and improve the system without extensive contract renegotiations.

In reorganizing work and introducing new technology, the automobile manufacturers are trying to obtain many of these efficiency economies. They claim that workers as well as the company will benefit from these changes. While some jobs will be lost to the new technology, they will be the boring or dangerous jobs no one wanted anyway and new, highly-skilled jobs will be created. Moreover, workers will now have control over their work, and their jobs will be more challenging.

But, as the automobile industry illustrates, it is difficult, indeed impossible, to separate the quest for efficiency from distributional conflicts between capital and labor. Many of the efficiency objectives listed above clearly refer to conflicts over property rights (for example, the concerns with averting embezzlement, malingering, misuse and neglect of equipment, product quality) and over the nature and intensity of work effort. For the automobile manufacturers, and many of the leaders of the UAW, the team production methods and new technology being introduced in the automobile industry will increase efficiency and will benefit both corporations and labor. For many workers (including the members of the dissident movement within the UAW, New Directions), these methods are intended to increase management's control over the intensity and nature of labor and thereby to increase the value of product produced and appropriated. For such critics, these innovations make workers feel even less secure in their jobs and more vulnerable to corporate whipsawing. They provide fewer jobs where workers can at least partially set their own pace, reduce the skill levels for many jobs, increase boredom and, as the pace of work is intensified, increase stress.[15]

In arguing for efficiency as the primary motivator for organizational innovation, Williamson presents as a competing explanation the quest for market power. He concludes that the search for efficiency is historically more important than the quest for market power because a market control strategy is unlikely to succeed for long if efficiency norms are seriously violated. Richard Du Boff and Edward Herman, in their critique of Chandler's strategy and structure hypothesis and hence indirectly of Williamson's transaction cost theory as well, reveal the flaws in this market power versus efficiency dichotomy.[16] They argue that neither market power nor efficiency is the fundamental objective of businesses in a capitalist system. Rather, it is capital accumulation, profitability and growth, which is inseparable from and compatible with both strategies. Vertical integration, for example, may reduce contracting costs (and hence achieve increased efficiency), but it also imposes barriers to entry (and hence increases market power). Horizontal mergers may permit gains from scale economies (an efficiency gain), but they also increase market power. Furthermore, market power alone has been an effective strategy for ensuring profitability and growth for some enterprises for extended periods of time. Despite inefficient administration and technological stagnation, Western Union, U.S. Steel, and General Motors managed to dominate their respective markets for many years. And even today, despite massive losses, GM (if not all of its employees) has been able to ride out the challenges of international competition, and to secure the resources to launch a response, by virtue of its previously accumulated capital. Framing the question in terms of management's motivations (efficiency versus market control) directs attention away from the social-structural conditions in which management behavior originates and operates.

Transaction cost theory presents efficiency as the sole performance criterion for governance structures and as a value-free, technical ideal. It equates efficiency with cost minimization by using market prices. Thus, in the article on work organization, Williamson offers, as evidence for his criticism of worker participation programs, Gunzberg's finding that although such programs may yield social and psychological gains, they "do not add to the value of goods and services, and can add to their cost."[17] Transaction cost theory's social priorities, allegiances and measurement biases are made clear here. It prefers innovations that add to the value of goods and services (as measured by market prices) over gains that are not mediated by the market. The basis for this preference is implicit; it is the assumption, from neoclassical economics, that market prices are determined by the impersonal workings of economic laws that ensure that the prices of factors of production equal the values of their marginal products. Piero Sraffa has shown, however, that contrary to this neoclassical assumption, prices reflect a socially and historically determined distribution of income that depends on the relative strength and configuration of social classes. Efficiency, when measured by market prices, is a social and not merely a technical relationship.[18]

Transaction cost theory's emphasis on the technical and its neglect of the social also appears in the focus on the contract as the elemental social relationship and on the transaction as the basic unit of analysis. Implicit in the term contract is the notion of a reciprocity in exchange that is satisfactory to both parties, and is not a victory, whether total or partial, of one party over another. Yet the history of employer-employee relations is one of ongoing conflict. These conflicts have frequently been overt and violent as in the Homestead case. Using the term contract to describe these relations mystifies and obscures their nature. In his study on the organization of work, Williamson acknowledges that the parties to the contract may have unequal bargaining strength. But his examples focus only on those resources that empower employees and not on the sources of the almost invariably greater bargaining strength of employers (who own the means of production, have greater access to support from the state and the legal system, have successfully commodified, deskilled, and replaced by technology increasing numbers of workers).

The use of the term transaction similarly mystifies the social character of corporate development. According to transaction cost theory, a transaction occurs whenever a good or service is transferred across a technologically separate interface. The theory takes the origins of these interfaces as given. In his paper on the organization of work, Williamson attempts to illustrate, by an "abstract assessment" of the transactional properties of alternative work modes, that hierarchical modes (specifically, capitalist authority relations) are the most efficient. He assumes in his analysis that technology is constant and that tasks are divided in the same way for each mode of work organization under consideration. (The modes differ in whether tasks are centrally located or geographically dispersed and in who owns the means of production and the output of the intermediate and final work stations.) Williamson doesn't seem to recognize that the technology and the interfaces that he takes as given depend upon prior design decisions concerning the mode of work organization, and hence, that what constitutes a transaction depends, in part, upon the governance structure that it is supposed to explain. For example, once production was organized within the factory, only the factory owners had the money to invest in new machinery, and so technology was developed for factory production. Williamson acknowledges that the choice of technology and internal organization are not independent — technology, he writes, may render some forms of organization inoperable. But he does not mention the alternative possibility, that organization forms may restrict one's choice of technology and may be designed to do so. Managers may selectively adapt technologies and workplace arrangements, and corporations may intercept and shape scientific knowledge, to erect barriers to entry and to foreclose on technological options less compatible with capital accumulation.

The theoretical categories of transaction cost theory are ideological because they exclude from consideration the historical and social-structural context of corporations. These categories reify and naturalize socially-created phenomenon (such as the state, capitalist production relations, the various manifestations of the corporate form) by reducing relations between human beings to relations between things: contracts, transactions, governance structures, markets, hierarchies, corporations, technological interfaces, and so on. On one level, this reduction reflects the truth of social ideology and the commodification of social relations within capitalism.

But on another level, by affirming and preserving the appearance of capitalist society, it prevents us from comprehending its formative processes and historical mediations.

Coase, Chandler and Williamson express some reservations concerning the modern corporation. Coase acknowledges that there may be situations where the gains from government regulation exceed their costs. Although in general the checks of competition prevent the corporation from falling prey to the abuses and political pressures to which government is subject. For Chandler, concentrated economic power violates basic democratic values and corporate managers need to be made more responsible for their actions. Williamson acknowledges that conglomerates and multinationals may pose some troublesome public policy issues. But his theoretical framework provides no way for him to incorporate their negative social costs in any systematic fashion. Williamson seems to approve of government intervention that reinforces "natural" developmental processes and to object to efforts that attempt to obstruct them. Thus, on the one hand, he approves of state and federal government intervention to help Carnegie and Frick prevail over labor when they decided to de-unionize the Homestead mill. On the other hand, Williamson appears to object to anti-trust regulation. He notes that anti-trust efforts to block vertical integration mergers ironically served to accelerate the natural growth of conglomerates, a growth that was inevitable as techniques for managing diverse assets were refined.[19]

The developmental logic implicit in transaction cost theory's history of the corporation reflects a social Darwinist perspective. It takes for granted that competitive markets are directly analogous to evolutionary mechanisms that allow only the fittest (i.e., the most efficient) governance structures to survive. Williamson and Ouchi assert that the main test of a theory is its implications, and that these implications should be refutable. But the free hand that such an epistemology gives to social science researchers becomes apparent when we look for the application of this standard in their work. The authors define transaction costs so broadly (for example, as "the costs of running the economic system," and elsewhere as all costs except the costs of production) that, as Perrow points out: "Any competing analysis can be reinterpreted by saying X or Y is really a transaction cost."[20] Moreover any refuting instances are dismissed by Williamson and Ouchi as either a mistake — as in, "Not all business executives, Andrew Carnegie included, accurately perceive their business opportunities and faultlessly respond" — or as an instance in which the "organization sacrifices efficiency to serve special interests."[21] Williamson and Ouchi also claim that transaction cost theory is supported by ecological survival tests. They offer a hypothesis to explain the dominance of large multi-divisional, multinational enterprises, that proposes that over time only those governance structures that minimize transaction costs will survive. They then offer as evidence of this hypothesis the persistence of the very organizational forms that it was designed to explain. Moreover, since the theory makes no claims for the speed of adjustment, the period of correction may be very long indeed, and the penalties for inefficiency need not be imposed on those reponsible for them, but on employees and communities. Regardless of the debatable effect of the greenmailing, leveraged buyouts and junk bond financed acquisitions of the 1980s on the economy's long run efficiency, in the short run thousands of workers have lost their jobs, hundreds of communities have lost key employers, taxpayers, and customers for local businesses, and millions of dollars in income and wealth have been wrenchingly redistributed.

To sum up, transaction cost theory treats efficiency as a socially neutral, technological/ engineering relationship, when it is instead a sociological and ideological one. The theory reduces social relations to relations between "things" through the use of categories that reify and naturalize socially-created phenomenon. And finally, it makes epistemological claims that equate what is (the modern corporate form and existing relations of production), with what ought to be. In the next chapter I will further develop this critique of transaction cost theory by suggesting an alternative, more socially grounded and contextually aware, approach to the study of corporate change.

CHAPTER III

THE DIALECTICAL APPROACH TO ORGANIZATIONAL CHANGE

In the previous chapter we looked critically at the transaction cost explanation of the origins and development of the modern corporation. Transaction cost theory assumes that corporate management is driven by a quest for efficiency, especially the reduction of transaction costs, and that competitive forces ensure that only the most efficient strategies and structures will survive in the long run. In this chapter I suggest an alternative to this explanation. I argue that corporations are motivated by a drive for capital accumulation, for ever greater quantities of capital in the form of money, plant, equipment, and inventories of materials and commodities, and that capital accumulation is achieved through profitability, growth, and social control. This is not to say that efficiency, the economy with which inputs are transformed into outputs, doesn't matter. It does, but only to the extent that it contributes to these over-arching objectives. Contrary to transaction cost theory's assumption, efficiency is not a neutral goal but is attached to the sectional interests of capital; and these interests are not necessarily harmonious with those of labor or the community-at-large.

This way of looking at corporate history draws on the work of Karl Marx. In a world in which neoclassical economics is the international orthodoxy, Communist governments topple, and former socialists embrace free markets, many argue that Marx has been thoroughly discredited. Certainly Marxism, as politicized and implemented in the former Soviet Union and its satellite and client states, seems to be thankfully moribund. Marx's strength, however, lay, not in his sparse writings about socialism or communism — but in his understanding and analysis of capitalism. Despite the enormous changes that have taken place since Marx's day — Marx never anticipated capitalism's resiliency and flexibility nor the ways government would expand and intrude into business and public life — many of his insights into the way the capitalist system works remain valid. For seventy years, Marxist-inspired scholarship has carried with it the baggage of the Cold War. Now that the Cold War is over, perhaps Marx too can be liberated.

The Vehicles of Capital Accumulation:
Profitability and Growth

To survive in a capitalist economy, a firm must prosper and grow. The problem of ensuring continuing profitability and growth can be decomposed into two interrelated parts. The first is the problem of productivity — how to produce as large a profit as possible for the inputs consumed. The second is the problem of realization — how to realize in the market place the market value of the output that has been produced. These dual aspects of the problem of enterprise survival, and their underlying social dimensions, will become clearer if we examine them in connection with the rate of profit.

The rate of profit, as it is commonly understood, is the money rate of profit: $r = p/c$, where p is net income, and c is the average capital investment during the period. But for our purposes another formulation will be more useful. This formulation is called the value rate of profit: $r' = s/(c' + v)$, where s is surplus value, c' is constant capital (means of production such as materials, plant, and equipment), and v is variable capital (labor).

The value rate of profit differs from the money rate of profit. The expression is presented in terms of value, and value is measured not in money terms, but in terms of socially necessary labor hours. Socially necessary labor is the time required to produce a commodity under normal production conditions with labor of average skill and intensity. Thus the output of a less skilled or lazy worker is not more valuable just because it requires more labor time — the excess time this worker requires above the social average is useless and wasted. Socially necessary labor provides a measure of value because a society's most valuable resource is its collective labor power, and how this labor power is allocated among alternative uses reflects the value society places on each of these alternatives. The advantage of using labor hours is that they provide us with a conceptual unit of measure that is common to all of the variables and also allow us to focus directly on the variables' social dimensions.[1]

In the value rate of profit formulation, the value of both constant capital (means of production) and variable capital (labor) are measured by the number of socially necessary labor hours required for their reproduction. In the case of constant capital this simply refers to the labor hours that went into producing the plant, equipment and materials consumed in the period's production. In the case of variable capital it refers, not to the total labor hours worked, but to the labor hours required to reproduce the worker. (That is, the labor hours necessary to produce a basket of commodities that will sustain the worker at a level of subsistence that society regards as appropriate). Plant, equipment and materials are called constant capital because their embodied labor hours are preserved and become part of the value of the new commodities that are produced. Labor is considered variable capital because the number of hours worked is greater than the number of hours required to reproduce the worker. Hence, labor not only reproduces its own value, it creates new (that is, surplus) value. Surplus value (s), then, is measured by the difference between the length of the working day and the hours necessary to reproduce the laborer. s is a social metric in that it measures the relative power of capital and labor. The value rate of profit is the return to capital on the amounts of variable and constant capital consumed in the period.

Surplus value is not the labor hour equivalent of profits in the conventional income statement. Many of the expenditures incurred by the organization (and treated as expenses in computing profit) are treated as distributions of surplus value in the value rate of profit formulation. These include, for example, many of the costs incurred to realize the market value of the firm's output, to provide management perquisites, or to pay taxes, rent, or interest. The relationship between the money rate of profit and the value rate of profit depends upon the significance of these costs as well as on the relationship between the labor hours embodied in commodities and their actual market prices. In addition to embodied labor hours, many contingent factors enter into the determination of market prices, such as relative scarcity, the availability of substitute products, monopoly power, government policy, and so on.[2] The social dimensions of the profit relationship become apparent if we divide both the numerator and the denominator on the right side of the value rate of profit formulation by v:

$$r' = \frac{s/v}{c'/v + 1}$$

The ratios in the numerator and denominator express social relationships: s/v, which measures the rate of surplus value is also known as the rate of exploitation of labor; and c'/v, known as the organic composition of capital, reflects the relative capital intensity of the production technology.

Why is the rate of surplus value, s/v, also called the rate of exploitation? Say that a worker produces a single unit of a commodity in 12 hours and is paid an hourly wage. It appears that she is being compensated for each hour of her time. But the wage, in total, is just enough to enable the worker to purchase a basket of commodities sufficient for a day's subsistence at the socially acceptable level. If it requires less than 12 hours of labor to produce this basket of goods, 7 perhaps, then the worker is working for 12 hours but is in reality being compensated with only 7 hours. The difference, 5 hours, is embodied in the resulting product and belongs to the employer by virtue of the employment relationship and her ownership and control of the means of production. The higher the ratio, s/v (which in the above example is 5/12), the greater the rate of exploitation and the rate of profit. If the employer is able to get the worker to work longer hours for the same wage, reduce the hourly wage, or work more intensely (thereby reducing the socially necessary hours required to produce one unit of the product), the rate of exploitation will increase. If workers organize and are able to collectively reduce the length of the working day, the intensity of work, or increase the hourly wage, then the rate of exploitation and the rate of profit will fall.

To maintain or increase the rate of profit, the individual firm seeks to increase the rate of surplus value (s/v). In the absence of technological innovations, however, the potential for increasing the rate of surplus value is limited. There are physical, social and competitive constraints beyond which the working day cannot be increased; nor wages reduced (either directly, or by fragmenting and simplifying work tasks so that they require less skilled and hence less costly labor). And there are also limits on the extent to which the intensity of work can be increased, for example, by increasing the speed of the assembly line or the amount of supervision.

While there is little that can be done about physical limitations, beyond ensuring that the labor force is healthy and physically fit, there is some flexibility with regard to what is socially acceptable. Production can be relocated to regions or countries where lower wages, longer hours, and more intense labor are both more socially acceptable and necessary for survival. In addition, efforts can be made to channel the social and personal needs of workers into the production of surplus value through various behavior modification strategies intended to create the appearance of an identity between the worker's perceived self-interest and the needs of the company. And if labor becomes too costly, it can be replaced with technology.

The level of technology is selected by the employer based on the relative costs of using variable and constant capital in production. The more costly labor is, relative to capital, the more capital intensive the production technology will tend to be. But an increase in capital intensity will also increase the organic composition of capital (c'/v). If the net output per worker increases, fewer workers will be required for a given output (that is, v will decrease). Not only will the rate of surplus value (s/v) increase, but so will the organic composition of capital (c'/v). If the former increase is greater than the latter, the rate of profit will increase. But if it is not, the rate of profit will decrease. Underlying the problem of productivity is what Marx posed as the central dilemma of capitalism: the race between the increasing organic composition of capital, which reduces the rate of profit, and the increasing rate of surplus value, which increases the rate of profit.

The problem of productivity — the production of surplus value — does not reduce to a neutral, value-free matter of efficiency. Rather it involves a struggle between employers and labor over such issues as the length of the working day, what constitutes a socially acceptable level of subsistence, the intensity (and quality) of labor, the level of wages and benefits, the size and nature of the labor force (that is, to questions of immigration, the age and sexual composition of the work force, retirement age and benefits), the power and composition of labor unions, the role and allegiances of the state, even the extent to which living labor will be replaced by machines, and so on. In treating efficiency as a technical datum whose benefits will accrue to society-as-a-whole, transaction cost theory assumes that what is good for the capitalist is good for the worker, the local community, and the nation. This assumption masks the social conflict that is inherent in the system of property relations and wage labor that characterizes capitalism. It also ignores the social costs imposed on individual workers and society in general by efficient innovations that result in unemployment, make skills, equipment and entire communities obsolete, endanger the health and safety of workers, consumers, and the public, and degrade the environment. As Charles Perrow suggests, we must always ask, "Efficiency for whom?"[3]

However these conflicts are resolved, and they are never resolved once and for all, the surplus value that is produced and embodied in the commodity must be realized in the market place. Unless the business is able to transform its commodity capital into money capital by selling its products, it will not be able to begin a new cycle of production. Realization is as central as productivity to the firm's reproduction and expansion. For much of this century, capitalists have been at least as concerned with the problem of realization as they have been with productivity. There is wide agreement among economists that the economic crisis of the 1930s was one of underconsumption, of inadequate effective demand for the level of productive capacity.[4] Many subsequent social innovations — the Keynesian welfare state, the military-industrial complex, the development of a mass consumer market through advertising, marketing, consumer credit, and expanded commodification, for example — can be traced to capitalism's need to increase consumption levels to realize its increasing pool of surplus value. Some analysts suggest that the recent trends toward speculative financial assets reflect the inability of these consumption-enhancing strategies to continue absorbing the huge quantities of surplus value that the world economy is capable of producing; and hence the diminishing attractiveness and increasing uncertainty of investments in productive assets.[5]

The struggle between capitalists and labor over the terms and conditions of work and the social innovations needed to realize the increasing pool of surplus value constitute the social dimensions that underlie the rate of profit. It is through these social dimensions that social control — the ability of capitalists to obtain patterns of work and consumption that will solve the dual problems of productivity and realization — becomes inseparable from the quest for profitability and growth.

The Vehicles of Capital Accumulation: Social Control

The history of capitalist-labor relations is not the neutral quest for efficiency lauded by the transaction cost theorists. It is a struggle for control of the production process and its fruits (surplus value). The capitalists' weapons in this struggle have taken many forms, ranging from physical coercion to ideology, from the application of science and technology to politics. But, however it is waged, for capitalists the objective of the struggle is to increase their control over labor.

The creation of a class of wage laborers — individuals who must sell their labor in order to survive — is itself an act of coercion. The habits of work and the culture of millions of people, accustomed to the rhythms of agricultural life and independent commodity production, have to be shattered to transform them into wage laborers, obedient to the routine of the factory, its machines, and its hierarchy, and to the discipline of monetary incentives.[6] It takes the threat of starvation, made tangible by the appropriation of land and the absence of community-based social services, to transform subsistence farmers into wage laborers. Whether we are talking of Great Britain in the 17th-19th centuries, or most of the third world in the 20th, workers did not enter factories willingly, they came to them only when other alternatives had been exhausted. And once they were gathered into factories, workers continued to resist their mastery. The history of capitalist-labor relations in the U.S. is punctuated by episodes of labor militancy that were crushed, often violently, by corporate, government and judicial power.

Coercion continues to be an important factor in disciplining the work force in both developed and developing countries — directly, through the use of para-military, military and police power to smash "illegal" strikes; and indirectly, through labor legislation that restricts the range of acceptable conflict, and through the consequences of unemployment, particularly in the absence of a guaranteed wage, national health care and other social services. But it was clear by the end of the 19th century, at least in the industrialized states of Europe and North America, that relying on periodic police violence and the threat of starvation are not the best ways to motivate workers to produce surplus value in increasing quantities and to willingly accede to its appropriation by the owners of the enterprise.

One of the major obstacles to the production of surplus value was the fact that labor initially retained control over the technology of production, which was largely handicraft-based. Hence one of the capitalists' earliest strategies was to commandeer the services of science and engineering to undercut the power of skilled labor. Technological innovations — such as the introduction of power-driven machinery — played an important role in these efforts by capitalists to impose control over the work process. They were supplemented by the introduction of scientific management techniques which reorganized and fragmented production tasks into easily learned, performed and supervised units.[7]

The introduction of continuous-flow production in Boston textile mills in the middle of the 19th century provides an early illustration of the use of technology to impose social control. By attaching the spindles and looms to a water-driven central power shaft, the Boston manufacturers were able to establish the pace of work, impose a uniform rhythm, and fix the worker to a physical location (thereby sharply reducing the opportunities for contact and conversation among workers). Moreover, machinery, by simplifying the tasks performed by many workers, reduced their wage levels and made workers easier to replace. Continuous-flow production introduced a form of social control in the factory which was embedded in the physical and technological aspects of production.[8]

The assembly line had a similar revolutionary effect on the automobile production, when it was introduced in 1913. The assembly line dramatically altered the character of work and the social relations of the workplace. Work became more specialized, repetitive, and automatic. It required little thought, judgment, or skill. The pace, intensity and quality of production were all controlled through the design of machines, by their arrangement on the shop floor, by new forms of recordkeeping and inspection, and by the mechanical process itself. The number of foremen, sub-foremen, straw-bosses, clerks and inspectors increased in order to provide more direct and closer supervision over a less skilled workforce.[9]

More recent technological innovations have raised the potential for social control at the workplace to where it rivals Jeremy Bentham's panoptic vision. Bentham designed his Panopticon so that its inhabitants never knew whether or not they were being observed at any given moment, but were convinced of the possibility, indeed probability, that they were. The psychological effects of this unknown but certain visibility ensures that its object "assumes responsibility for the constraints of power . . . he inscribes in himself the power relation in which he simultaneously plays both roles; he becomes the principle of his own subjection."[10] The Panopticon achieved individualized social control through its architectural design; information technology achieves a similar capacity for control through its ability to "automatically and continously record almost anything its designers want to capture."[11] Through its capacity for monitoring and capturing every step of a worker's behavior on the job, information technology "can transmit the presence of the omniscient observer and so induce compliance without the messy conflict-prone exertions of reciprocal relations."[12]

Whether achieved by coercion or by technology, social control imposed on unwilling, resistant workers cannot ensure that they will put all of their efforts and intelligence into performing their jobs. The workplace is a contested terrain on which management constantly seeks new ways to impose control and employees, individually and collectively, discover ways to evade or sabotage their efforts. Hence, the ultimate aim of social control within the organization is to convince workers that the real opposition of interests that underlies the production of surplus value by labor and its appropriation by capitalists does not exist. By convincing labor that their interests and those of "the corporation," actually its owners and managers, are harmonious, that in producing more for the boss they are also producing for themselves, social control will be willingly imposed on the worker from within rather from the outside by coercion or technology. I am not suggesting that workers have no stake in their employers' profitability. It is obvious that without profits a business will no longer be viable and its workers will be unemployed. But, by focusing exclusively on the mutual dependency created by the employment relationship, proponents of labor-management cooperation, or "jointness," as it is called in the automobile industry, avoid discussing the more fundamental questions of where surplus value originates and who owns it.

One way that corporations have tried to achieve self-imposed control is by developing company programs to increase employees' allegiance to the organization. Beginning with welfare capitalism at the turn of the century many corporations have attempted to win employees' loyalty by providing benefits, such as health care, housing, life insurance, recreation, and pensions, contingent on continued employment. Although Welfare Capitalism, as a formal corporate project, disappeared in the depression in the 1930s, many corporations continue to provide a variety of social services that either are not provided by the government or are provided at sharply reduced levels. In the absence of comparable public services, these programs are double-edged, since they can be easily withdrawn by the employer when competitive conditions change or simply by terminating employment. Many workers today remain at jobs they would prefer to leave, but don't for fear of losing their health insurance.

In the years since Welfare Capitalism faded away, corporations have developed many other programs to persuade workers that their interests lie in cooperation. These programs have been called by various names — human relations, job enrichment, quality of life, and most recently, the team concept and jointness. The periodic reappearance of such programs on the corporate agenda, albeit in refurbished garb, suggests both how attractive the idea of worker self-regulation is to capitalists and the enduring and pervasive character of capitalist-labor conflict.

The need for social control is not limited to the workplace, where it emerges out of the struggle between capitalists and labor over the production and appropriation of surplus value. Social control also becomes a factor in solving the problem of realization. Indeed, the management of consumption is as essential to realization as the management of the work process is to productivity.[13]

As recently as the early part of this century, in the world of many of our grandparents and great-grandparents, much of what one consumed was produced and provided in the home or community. Aglietta estimates that in the 1920s from 40–45% of households in the U.S. remained outside the market for all but the most basic consumer goods.[14] Today most of what we need, we buy, and most of what we buy is produced by large national and multi-national corporations. This is still more true of goods than of services, but even this is changing with the growth of legal and medical corporations, entertainment and sports conglomerates, nationally marketed child-care services and so on. Building a mass consumer market required a change in peoples' traditional, home- and community-centered patterns of consumption, and in their attitudes towards debt, obsolescence, leisure time, and the determinants of social status. This new social consumption norm — along with an increase in the size of the wage-earning population and in wage levels, a massive expansion of government spending, and the internationalization of distribution — contributed to the great post-WWII economic expansion in the U.S. The following quotation from John Galbraith captures the essence of this new social consumption norm:[15]

> The individual serves the industrial system . . . by consuming its products. On no other matter, religious, political or moral, is he so elaborately and skillfully and expensively instructed.
>
> Specifically, along with the production of goods go energetic and no less important efforts to ensure their use. These emphasize the health, beauty, social acceptability and sexual success — in sum, the happiness — that will result from the possession and use of a particular product. This communication combined each day with the effort on behalf of countless other products becomes, in the aggregate, an unremitting argument for the advantage of consumption. In turn, inevitably, this affects social values. A family's standard of living becomes an index of its achievement. It helps insure that the production, and *pari passu,* the consumption of goods will be the prime measure of social accomplishment.

But business does not depend entirely on its own efforts to create both a disciplined work force that identifies with the corporation and a mass consumer market for its products. No discussion of organizational change is complete without considering the symbiotic relationship between private enterprise and the state. On the one hand, state policies both support private capital accumulation and mediate businesses' relations with consumers, labor and other business and social interests. On the other hand, the state depends upon economic growth through private accumulation for the revenues it needs to fund its various activities and for insuring its continuing legitimacy.

The Role of the State

Beginning in the 1930s, the U.S. federal government assumed increasing reponsibility for promoting economic stability and growth — a policy that it carried out by means of a massive expansion of public spending to counter stagnating capital accumulation.[16] This policy, known as Keynesianism, along with the massive destruction of capital and the military outlays associated with WWII, provided the foundation for the post-WWII economic recovery in North America and Western Europe.

State involvement in business was not new to the U.S. The growth in the size and power of the business sector throughout the 19th and 20th centuries was accompanied by an increase in the size and role of government. According to Herman, even before the Civil War the government was involved in constructing public works, providing subsidies, engaging in joint ventures, and even in direct production.[17] In the comparatively laissez-faire period between the Civil War and the end of the 19th century, the government aggressively used tariff policies to protect U.S. industry and made huge contributions to the transcontinental railroads. Around the turn of the century "the public" (usually smaller, threatened businesses) demanded that the state intervene to protect them from increasingly powerful, monopolistic competitors. The resulting anti-trust laws, railroad regulation, retail price maintenance laws, and anti-chain store and branch bank legislation greatly increased the scope of government. In the early part of this century, public schools, charities and health agencies helped fashion disciplined workers out of new immigrants and rural migrants to city factories by indoctrinating them with the principles of "right living."[18]

The expansion of state intervention that began in the 1930s dwarfed these earlier programs in both magnitude and scope. James O'Connor classifies this new state spending into two forms.[19] First, there are those state expenditures that directly, and indirectly, promote profitable private accumulation by increasing the productivity, or lowering the reproduction costs of labor. Businesses, for example, rely on the public education system to produce a workforce with technical skills and personal characteristics that are compatible with the work-world's values, technologies, methods of production and hierarchical relationships. Recent incursions by the business community into the realm of public education to increase its "effectiveness" illustrates its importance to them. The failure of most educators and the public to resist these intrusions suggests how natural we take this interest to be. In addition to education, government spending on physical and human capital infrastructures (such as transportation, communication, R&D, industrial development, and so on), collectively consumed goods (such as roads, schools and home mortgage subsidies, public housing, mass transit and parking, hospital and medical care facilities), and various forms of social insurance (against sickness, old-age, economic insecurity, etc.), all reduce the cost of doing business.

The second form of state spending involves expenditures that deal with the consequences of capitalism's tendency to generate surplus industrial capacity, surplus labor (technological unemployment), environmental damage, and the threats to social harmony and political stability these consequences pose. For example, foreign aid is used to expand and support world markets for U.S. capitalists; the welfare system deals with the adverse consequences of surplus labor; various programs support small businessmen, farmers and investors who have been adversely affected by the growth of the monopoly sector; and labor legislation mediates and limits the conflict between capitalists and labor. Some of these latter activities may actually constrain the autonomy and reduce the profits of individual organizations (such as laws that restrict pollution or require the hiring of minorities). According to O'Connor, such regulatory activities perform a legitimation function that is both essential and contradictory to the state's role in promoting capital accumulation.

The anti-social spending and de-regulation policies of Reagan in the U.S. and Thatcher in the U.K. were directed explicitly at resolving the impediments this second category of spending imposed on continued capital accumulation. Their massive assault on social programs took place at the same time as a corporate restructuring program was cutting the cost of labor and benefits. Under attack from both the government and private sectors, a beleagured work force seemed to feel it had no choice but to accede to give-backs to both their employers and the state.

As the preceding discussions suggest, the theory of organizational change that I am developing in this chapter is based on the argument that the corporate quest for capital accumulation (and hence for profitability and growth) takes place within a context of social conflict which shapes, and is shaped by, both the corporate sector and the state. Before discussing how the elements of this quest are related, I want to distinguish the kind of social conflict introduced above from the notions of conflict that are implicit in transaction cost theory and in other social science literature.

Social Conflict

Conflict enters transaction cost theory through a behavioral model in which individual behavior is characterized by opportunism, that is, self-interest seeking with guile.[20] Such behavior on the part of capitalists is considered socially beneficial because it is motivated by the drive for efficiency and regulated by competition. Opportunistic behavior by workers, on the other hand, is not considered beneficial because it resists progressive, efficient innovations by capital. The transaction cost theory model of conflict then is atomistic, unstructured and, under the guise of scientific neutrality, biased toward the interests of capital. It shares these qualities with the pluralistic view of social conflict that prevails throughout the social sciences.

Although pluralist-based theories are a heterogenous lot, they share a number of common characteristics in the way they describe contemporary society and organizations. Pluralist theories recognize that conflict is a permanent feature of capitalist society, but see it as a constructive equilibrating process that, when controlled and channelled through a system of normative regulation, plays an adaptive, safety-valve role for maintaining societal or organizational stability. Although change can occur as the result of conflict, it is of a limited kind and does not threaten the nature of the system as a whole, since conflict is assumed to be confined to relatively narrow issues and details. Conflict is a vehicle for stability, and not, as I will argue in the next section, a means of structural transformation. Pluralist theories also generally assume that there are no undue concentrations of power that will systematically bias the outcomes of conflict in favor of a particular protagonist or group. Power is assumed to be either widely diffused or offset by countervailing concentrations (for example, the power of large firms is assumed to be balanced by that of labor unions). The state (and within organizations, management) is assumed to pursue a neutral, mediating role in social conflict. Finally, pluralist theories assume that underlying these conflicts is a widespread consensus about the nature of the polity, the economy or the organization, and the system of rules and regulation.[21]

Within organization theory, pluralistic models view organizations as coalitions of interdependent, yet self-interested individuals, marketplaces, loosely coupled systems, or organized anarchies.[22] Consider, for example, James March and Herbert Simon's inducement-contribution model of the firm.[23] The inducement-contribution approach views the firm as a coalition of participants whose contributions are individually necessary and collectively sufficient to reproduce the firm over time. A firm remains viable only so long as the sum of the resources and services provided by the participants to the firm's transformation process (a broadly defined production function) are sufficient in quantity, quality and kind to generate the necessary quantity, quality and kind of inducements to elicit their continued participation and hence future contributions. March and Simon recognize that participants and potential participants have differing values, goals, and perceptions and must be persuaded both to join the coalition and, once in it, to stay and to produce. This is achieved by using the organization's control system (supervisory practices and rewards) to change the perceptions of the participants so that their goals, values and perceptions are brought into congruence with the needs of the organization. Conflict is assumed to be a disequilibrium state for the organization which all participants are motivated to resolve. Because individuals and groups in pluralist studies are defined atomistically, they are not viewed as belonging to a structure of social relations that is part of the wider society. March and Simon, for example, have no way of explaining the sources of the individual's assumed reluctance to produce or the sources of conflict within the firm. Nor do they recognize that there may be structural inequalities that privilege the inducements and contributions of some participants over others.

Jeffrey Pfeffer and Gerald Salancik introduce into the organization theory literature both inequalities in the distribution of power and resources and the capacity of power holders to impose their definitions of social reality on other participants.[24] They are aware that the definition of what resources are critical and scarce (and hence form the locus of power within the firm) is not fixed but is open to change and definition; and that efficiency (which, they argue, is a relatively value-free standard of performance) may be used as an argument to achieve objectives that are being sought for other reasons. But they do not examine the origins of differential control over resources, nor do they ask how and why particular resources come to be regarded as critical, or how such control is used to provide and/or withhold inducements or contributions. Like other pluralist theorists, they neglect the possibility that beneath seemingly fair exchanges there may be a structure of social relations that systematically favors the interests of some above those of others; that systematically excludes from the marketplace some kinds of exchanges, individuals, and/or groups; and that effectively controls the way decisions are made.

This pluralist view of social conflict differs from the Marxist perspective I have adopted here. Pluralism focuses on variegated and apparently unstructured clashes between self-interested individuals and overlapping collectivities. A Marxist approach situates social conflict in the very structure of capitalism's unequal social relations and the accumulation process itself. Because these conflicts are structural, reforms that mitigate the system's harshest aspects and remove its most rapacious practitioners (such as the Ivan Boeskys and Michael Milkens, or the owners of sweatshops), desirable though they may be, will have little effect on its inherent contradictions and fundamental operations (more about these below). The enormous changes that have taken place in the mode of ownership and control over the past 150 years — from the owner-manager of the early textile factories to the diffusely-held multinational enterprises of today — have changed the form and scale of capitalism but have not eliminated the dual problems of productivity and realization and the social conflict inherent within them. It may no longer be possible to point to an individual and unambiguously classify him or her as "labor" or "capital" — most workers in the U.S. are part of pension or insurance plans that own corporate stock and most managers are as dependent on wage labor for their survival as the employees they supervise — but the existence of such ambiguities, and of what Wright refers to as "contradictory class locations," do not mean that capital and labor no longer exist as analytically distinct social categories.[25]

When I use the term capital in this and subsequent chapters, I am refering to those who, through ownership or managerial authority, collectively control one or more of the elements essential to capital accumulation: making investment decisions, deciding how the physical means of production are to be used, directing the authority structure within the labor process. When I use the term labor, I am referring to those whose survival depends on the sale of their labor power and who are largely excluded from control over authority relations, the physical means of production and the investment process.

In this chapter I have emphasized the struggle between capitalists and labor over the production and appropriation of surplus value and I have also referred to the existence of conflicts between the capitalists' pursuits of capital accumulation and the general social welfare. But these are not the only conflicts that occur.

Intraclass conflict is as permanent and pervasive in capitalist societies as the conflicts between capitalists and labor. Individual firms and factions of the business community compete for the resources required for production and over the distribution of the total surplus value that is produced. Domestic capitalists vie with multinational capitalists, financial capitalists vie with those in industry, small and regional businesses compete with national and multinational enterprises for access to and control over natural resources, labor, manufactured parts and components, capital equipment, government subsidies, and favorable legislation and regulation. It is the pervasiveness of this intraclass conflict that forces capitalists to constantly seek ways to increase their production of surplus value and to grow — for no firm can rest secure with its existing market position and level of profits.

Nor is conflict between capitalists the only other source of conflict. One of the most effective strategies for capitalists in their on-going struggle with labor has been to encourage intraclass conflicts that divide workers. The division of the working class — between American-born and immigrant workers, Protestants and Catholics, whites and blacks, skilled and unskilled — has fragmented and undermined attempts to organize U.S. workers into unions and to forge a labor-based political party throughout the 19th and 20th centuries. In Mike Davis' view, these divisions led to labor's present assimilation into an unequal partnership with capital.[26] Nor are these divisions an anachronism of the past — as the British miners found during their last strike, when they split into two competing bodies, the original, militant National Union of Mineworkers and the new, more pliant, Union of Democratic Mineworkers; or as strikers in the U.S., from mines to pulp and paper plants to airlines, have discovered when neighbors, colleagues, and strangers cross their picket lines to take their jobs. The internationalization of production introduces another dimension to this intraclass conflict. Just as capitalists in industrialized countries are increasingly competing with those from less developed ones, so too do workers in countries such as the U.S. compete against both capitalists and labor in these other countries.

The mutual dependence between capitalism and the state has become another source of conflict in contemporary society. On the one hand, the private decisions of corporate executives affect jobs, economic growth, prices, the balance of payments and so on. And the health of these variables, in turn, affects state revenues, social order, political stability, and ultimately, government tenure. On the other hand, businesses depend on the state to create a domestic and international environment that favors profitability and growth.[27] This situation of mutual dependence between nation states and their resident capitalists generates conflict (sometimes violent) between states over jobs for their citizens and for access to natural resources and markets for their domestic producers.

The transaction cost history of the corporation, in which increasingly efficient, transaction cost-economising entities, supplant older and less efficient ones, legitimates the modern corporate form and its oligopolistic market structures. It presents a biased, incomplete, and inaccurate story of corporate development, one which ignores its exploitative and conflictual dimensions and the symbiotic relationship between private capital and the state. The efficiency explanation is inadequate because it ignores the conflicts that underlie corporate decisions about technology, the organization of work, the location of production, vertical or horizontal integration, relations with suppliers, product marketing, and so on. The history of the corporation is a history of social conflict over the production and distribution of income and wealth. This conflict is not between atomistic, opportunistic individuals but between, and within, distinct social classes, who are differentiated from each other on the basis of their relationship to the means of production and their roles and rights in the process of accumulation. Social conflict is structured both because it originates in capitalism's basic structure of accumulation and also because of its role in forging the trajectory of economic, social and political development in capitalist societies.[28] It is to this role to which we turn in the next and final section of this chapter.

The Dialectical Model of Social and Organizational Change

The framework I have developed in this chapter is dialectical.[29] By dialectical I mean that it embodies a way of looking at the world that consists of three major elements. The first of these elements is the pervasiveness of social change. A dialectical perspective regards all social systems and institutions as being in a continuous process of transformation. A primary objective of social analysis is to identify and explain the sources of change and the processes through which they occur. In this book, I am concerned with explaining the current restructuring of GM (and through it, that of the automobile and U.S. industry, more generally) by showing how the roots of change lie in the cyclical downturn and labor struggles of the 1930s and 1940s and the processes set in place by the efforts to resolve them — socially and institutionally — in the ensuing decades.

The second element within a dialectically informed social analysis is the importance of contradictions as sources of social change. Contradictions refer to conditions that are necessary for, but are also destructive of, particular social processes or entities. In this sense, contradictions are neither "good" nor "bad," but are part of the dynamics of the process through which change occurs — they are the motor of social change.

The contradictions within capitalism are inherent in its very structure as an economic and social system. We have already seen several examples of this in this chapter. Consider the value rate of profit. The introduction of labor-saving technology to increase the rate of exploitation (s/v) may have the contradictory effect of increasing the organic composition of capital (c'/v). For an increase in capital investment to increase the rate of profit it must also increase productivity by at least as much as it increases the organic composition of capital. But the race for technological advance may make this difficult to achieve as competitors bid up the cost of technology while at the same time make its introduction a necessity. If businesses are unable to raise the rate of exploitation to keep pace with increases in the organic composition of capital, the rate of profit will fall. Contradictory, too, is the incompatibility between the capacity to produce surplus value (the development of the forces of production) and the capacity to realize surplus value (through the development of effective demand). If surplus value cannot be realized, and unsold commodities pile up, a realization crisis will occur.

Perhaps the fundamental contradiction within capitalism is the incompatibility between private appropriation and socialized production. By private appropriation, I am referring to the system of private ownership through which possession of the means of production entitles the capitalist (whether an individual entrepreneur or a corporation) to ownership of the final product. Socialized production refers to the dependency of these same capitalists on the decisions of others for their capacity to produce, their ability to realize the value of their products, and the availability of means of subsistence (for themselves and their employees). The decisions that individual capitalists make in the pursuit of their own interests (that is, in the pursuit of capital accumulation) are often collectively destructive of the larger system of socialized production upon which that pursuit depends. For example, while it is in individual capitalists' interests to pay workers as little as possible, it is also in their interests that other capitalists pay their workers well, so that their products can be purchased. One possible outcome of this dilemma is a realization crisis triggered by ineffective demand; another is a profit crisis triggered by a wage squeeze which, in turn, pushes some capitalists to seek alternatives to the current labor force. In either case, the outcome is destabilizing to the status quo.

The international debt crisis provides another example of the contradictory character of capitalism. On the one hand, banks, in order to secure repayment of their loans to third world countries, are pressuring these countries to increase their exports to developed countries and decrease their imports from them. On the other hand, increased competition from third world exports on domestic and international markets is contributing to the crisis in the manufacturing and farm sectors of the U.S. The international debt crisis thus pits the interests of bankers against those of farmers, industrialists, and their employees in the developed countries, and in the long run is destabilizing to the system overall.

Capitalism's contradictions arise from its very structure and from the result of the unequal and antagonistic nature of its social relations. The ongoing conflicts between capitalists and labor and among capitalists are experienced by individual organizations as impediments to accumulation. They seek to overcome or displace these impediments by introducing ideological, social, technological and organizational innovations to attenuate labor conflict, reduce their costs of production relative to their competitors, and/or increase their share of the total surplus value that is produced. They may, for example, install new machines or implement new methods of organizing and carrying out work; they may devise new ways of marketing existing products, create markets for new products, or discover new markets entirely; or they may draw new workers into the labor force (such as women, immigrants, peasant farmers). These innovations will change the conditions for accumulation and the terrain of conflict and they may temporarily yield super-profits for their developers. But as these strategies become known, they will be adopted by others. An innovation that conferred an advantage over a business's competitors no longer does so when it becomes a necessary cost of doing business for everyone. Moreover, in the absence of a central planning mechanism, businesses will collectively tend to over-invest in the new machines, methods, or products. Overproduction and over-capacity will result unless markets grow apace. But for effective demand to grow, workers' incomes will also have to increase, and this will reduce the rate of profit, and/or new markets will have to be developed. Reagan's about-face toward the Soviet Union, the West's embrace of glasnost and perestroika, and its temporarily abandoned romance with China, reflect the dual strategy of both expanding the supply of labor and increasing the demand for products. Since the underlying contradictions remain untouched, however, such resolutions are always unstable, partial and contingent in their effects. It is the dynamic interplay of impediments to accumulation and the consequent resolutions that generate further impediments, that create the cycles of booms and slumps and the changing face of social relations.

The third element within the dialectical approach concerns the relationship between organizations and their environments. Rather than regarding the organization and its environment as logically independent entities that are externally related to one another, the dialectical perspective views them as forming an internally related totality within which they are each the product and determinant of the other's conditions of existence. Organizational change is best understood by examining the changes that take place in society — both historically and contemporaneously — and the ways organizations simultaneously respond to and initiate them.

From the perspective of transaction cost theory, the restructuring of labor-management relations that I described in the opening chapter of this book, simply represent further innovations in the series of transaction-cost economizing efficiencies that have characterized the development of the modern corporate form. From the perspective of a dialectical analysis, however, the restructuring is the interaction, continuation, and consequence of several ongoing conflicts: between labor and capital over the production of surplus value (not only the quantity to be produced but the conditions of production) and its distribution; between capitalists themselves, whose competition is taking place on an increasingly global scale; and between nation states (and their populations) who are vying with each other for jobs for their workers, markets for their products, and revenues to ensure their own regimes' legitimacy and survival.

The search for more efficient ways to produce is not absent from this dialectical perspective: indeed it is understood to be a central element in the capitalists' quest for continuing profitability and growth. But efficiency is not a neutral goal in a world in which the distribution of its benefits are contested at best, and where the ownership of the means of production (and therefore the ability to control access to livelihoods) confers a disproportionate advantage in the struggle. A dialectical perspective is concerned with the nature of these contests and with the consequences and equities of their outcomes. Nor is efficiency a purely technical or quantitative datum in a dialectical analysis. How inputs are consumed (that is, the quality of worklife, the availability and quality of leisure time) is at least as important as the economy with which they are consumed; and what is produced (its nature and quality) and how it is distributed is at least as important as the quantity produced.

In the next chapters I will use the key elements of this dialectical model — the focus on social conflict and contradictions as sources of social change and the understanding of organizations as part of a social context which they both shape and are shaped by — to examine the restructuring that is taking place in the automobile industry.

CHAPTER *IV*

YEARS OF CRISIS AND CONFLICT

The last time the U.S. automobile industry experienced a structural up-heaval as significant as the one taking place today was during the economic crisis, labor-management conflicts and state interventions of the 1930s and 1940s. Over the course of those two decades business, labor and the state managed to hammer out the institutional and ideological framework that would govern their relations for the next fifty years. Although this frame-work helped to resolve the immediate crisis it was rent with contradictions. By the 1970s these contradictions began to threaten the framework's stabil-ity and continuity and ultimately led to a new crisis, which the current restructuring both reflects and attempts to resolve. In order to understand this linkage — between past and present crises, between prior resolutions and current impediments — we need to begin at the beginning, not of today's crisis but of yesterday's.

To facilitate this examination I have divided the years from 1933 to 1950 into four periods. The initial period, from 1933 to mid-1937, begins with the first major uprising of labor militancy in the U.S. since 1921. It includes the passage of the major New Deal labor legislation, recognizing labor's right to organize, and the formation of the Congress of Industrial Organizations (CIO), and it culminates with the end of the great wave of sit-down strikes that began in the winter of 1936/1937. The second period, mid-1937–1941, begins with the onset of the "Roosevelt Depression" that reinforced an already-emerging corporate backlash and, in 1938, an elec-toral one as well, against New Deal policies. This was also the era of internecine struggles within the labor movement between the AFL and the CIO, and within the latter, the victory of the faction allied with the Presi-dential wing of the Democratic Party over the faction seeking to build an independent political base for labor. It is also a period in which foreign policy issues gain increasing predominance over domestic policy on the Roosevelt agenda. In the third period, 1941–1950, we will see the final triumph of the trade union bureaucracy over rank and file militancy and autonomy, and a reconciliation between the Roosevelt administration and its corporate opponents, in the wartime effort. Finally, we will look at the postwar consolidation of the alliance between capitalists, the state, and the trade union bureaucracy. Before beginning, however, we need to look briefly at the origins of the depression and the nature of labor-management relations in the preceding decade.[1]

The Origins of the Economic Crisis of the 1930s

Although few of us alive today actually lived through the depression of the 1930s, its images remain with us in film, photography, literature and music, and every economic slump and stockmarket hiccup is examined in comparison to "the" depression and its stockmarket crash. But contrary to the popular scenario, in which the depression struck suddenly and unexpectedly when the stockmarket crashed, the roots of the depression reached back to World War I and were readily apparent to all who would see: the technological forces that were revolutionizing the processes of production after the war were not being matched by concomitant increases in effective demand. Throughout the U.S. economy, productive capacity was rapidly outstripping society's ability to consume. The output of producer goods (those products which are themselves used to manufacture other products) exceeded the growth in the production of consumer goods, which meant more producer goods were being produced than were needed. Between 1923 and 1929, for example, producer goods output increased by 50% while industrial production as a whole increased by 25%. At the same time, income inequality was sharply increasing. For example, from 1920 to 1929 the share of disposable income appropriated by the top 1% of income recipients rose from 12% to 18%; and the share of the top 5% climbed from 24% to 33.5%. Industrial profits, rent and interest increased 45%, while real earned income rose by 13% and hourly real wages of manufacturing workers rose by a mere 2%.[2]

By 1926 it was clear that the expansion of consumer durables had reached its limit. For example, housing construction increased 215% from 1920 to 1926, and decreased 37% from 1926 to 1929; consumption of consumer durables increased 66% from 1920 to 1926, and decreased 5% thereafter. Nor was the automobile industry immune to these developments. In contrast with the period from 1908 to 1920, when the supply of automobiles could not keep up with the demand for them, the 1920s was a period of "competition rather than growth".[3] By the middle of the 1920s the motor vehicle industry had the capacity to produce 6 million cars but was selling less than 4 million a year.[4] Replacements, which represented one-fifth of sales in 1921, accounted for 60% by 1929; and although new car registrations increased between 1921 and 1929, the percentage increase fell in every year but 1929. In its 1924 annual report GM acknowledged that future growth would have to come from replacement sales, population growth, increases in income, and exports. Existing markets, the report states, will be "well exploited and intensely cultivated by all manufacturers." Thus, in the 1920s GM shifted from a preoccupation with the continued growth of the U.S. market to competing for market share within it and to a search for alternative sources of revenue. This search led to several different strategies.

The most obvious strategy, following from the approach suggested by the above quotation, was to develop the existing market for automobiles. Indeed, many of GM's marketing decisions in the 1920s and 1930s initiated practices that would become essential to building post-WWII social consumption norms. In 1919, for example, GM created its credit arm, GMAC (General Motors Acceptance Corporation) "to assist dealers in financing their purchases of General Motors products, and also to finance to some extent retail sales".[5] The installment sales concept was so successful that by 1925, 65% of retail sales of new cars were being made on the installment basis.[6] GM also introduced the policy of establishing "a complete line of motor cars from the lowest to the highest price that would justify quantity production,"[7] "A Car for Every Purse and Purpose,"[8] and the annual model change. Although the company did not formalize the annual model change as a concept until the 1930s, when the company first began to speak of such changes in a positive way in its annual reports, GM began making annual model changes in 1923. By the time the annual model change became an industry norm in the mid-1930s, GM was no longer apologizing for changing models, as they had in their 1923 annual report. But the company apparently still felt it necessary to justify the changes to its annual report readers. Thus the annual reports in the 1930s explain the annual model change not in the language of the marketing hype so familiar to the post-WWII consumptionist period but in terms of safety, economy of operation and maintenance, the contribution of obsolescence in making up-to-date transportation available to those who cannot afford new cars, and the reduction in costs obtained from introducing the ever-new production technologies the new cars required. The acceptance of used cars as trade-ins for the purchase of replacements also facilitated the sale of additional numbers of new cars in the 1920s. So too did the introduction of the closed-body automobile by Fisher Body, in which GM acquired a controlling interest in 1919. The sale of closed-body cars increased from 10% of industry sales in 1919 to 85% by 1927.[9]

In his reminiscences of his years at the head of GM, Alfred Sloan Jr. writes that the combination of installment sales, used car trade-ins, the closed body, and the annual model change, transformed the automobile market in the 1920s. Sloan acknowledges that U.S. car sales were also helped by the development of improved roads and this recognition motivated GM to play a major role in U.S. transportation policy. Throughout the 1930s, GM's annual reports advocated increased public expenditure for the construction of highways, the ear-marking of all revenues from highway users (such as registration fees, fuel taxes, excise takes, personal property taxes and municipal taxes) solely for the development, maintenance, and protection of the highway system, and reduced expenditures on mass transportation (that is, on railroads). In 1932 Sloan organized the National Highway User's Conference to establish and capture highway 'trust funds' and regularly used its "influence to deflect any reallocation of resources to public transportation."[10]

But the development of the domestic market for passenger cars was not sufficient to accommodate the imbalance between production capacity and effective demand. Additional strategies were needed. One of them was to internationalize distribution. In its 1928 annual report the company wrote that: "It is recognized that the curve of development within the U.S. must necessarily flatten out — as a matter of fact it already has — as the years progress. The opportunity for further progress in all overseas countries, however, is and will continue to be great for many years to come." In the years after WWI, GM aggressively established international assembly facilities (in London, Copenhagen, Berlin, Antwerp, Buenos Aires, Sao Paolo, Wellington, Bombay, Port Elizabeth, Montevideo, Osaka, Bavaria, Stockholm and in five Australian cities), and acquired foreign subsidiaries (McLaughlin in Canada, Vauxhall in England, Opel in Germany, and Holden's Body Builders in Australia). Although the company would have preferred to reach these new markets by exporting U.S.-built vehicles, the form of internationalization it adopted (local assembly of U.S.-produced kits and the acquisition of foreign auto-makers) was shaped by protectionist tariff and internal taxation policies that discouraged foreign imports throughout the 1920s, and even more so with the deepening depression in the 1930s.[11] Indeed, internationalization was so important to GM that discussions of its growth consumed some 23% of the company's annual reports from 1925 through 1939 (second only to discussions of GM's relations with labor). This strategy yielded some success.

According to GM's annual reports, U.S. and Canadian sources accounted for virtually all of the company's sales through 1928; by 1935 less than half (47.5%) of GM's sales were from North America. But internationalization was not without its problems as the depression deepened worldwide. Throughout the 1930s, GM's annual reports recounted a litany of depreciating currencies, retaliatory tariffs, limitations on the international transfer of funds, and the impact of falling commodity prices on purchasing power in many countries. In 1937 the company praised itself for anticipating the trend toward local manufacture which helped cushion the effects of these conditions. But as the depression worsened in the U.S. and labor-management relations deteriorated further, many of GM's employees did not share this view.

Presumably in response to employee and union criticism, the 1937 annual report explains to the reader that the company's international operations are not competitive with but are complementary to their U.S. facilities:[12]

> ... there is a marked difference between the engineering conceptions of automotive products manufactured in the United States and those produced in other manufacturing countries. This is because of the necessity of adapting the engineering design to the economic standards of the market. . . . Therefore, the Corporation in developing manufacturing plants overseas is supplementing and expanding its activities rather than competing with domestic factories.

A further strategy for resolving the structural impediments to continued capital accumulation presented by the imbalance between productive capacity and effective demand (which limited investment opportunities in corporations' original lines of business) was to invest in other corporations in the same or other lines of business. The wave of mergers and acquisitions that took place during the 1920s in the U.S. was the largest since the turn of the century. The number of firms absorbed was not reached again until the even greater merger wave that occurred in the late 1960s.[13] Between 1916 and 1930, GM engaged in various horizontal, vertical and diagonal (diversifying) domestic combinations. Indeed, discussions of these activities represented the largest single topic in the company's annual reports between 1916 and 1925.[14] For the automobile industry as a whole vertical integration increased substantially in the decade after WWI. The value of purchased components compared to the value of the finished vehicle fell from 55% in 1922 to 26% in 1926.[15] According to GM's annual report in 1927, the company saw vertical mergers as an opportunity to invest accumulated capital and to capture suppliers' profits: "In addition to the satisfactory return on the increased capital thus employed there has resulted, in general, a lower cost and a better product."

But none of these strategies to maintain the company's rate of capital accumulation were sufficient to insulate it from the ensuing global depression. Between 1929 and 1933, U.S. industrial output was more than halved; gross national product, in constant dollars, fell by 29%; consumption expenditures fell by 18%; and gross investment virtually stopped.[16] Car production in the U.S. and Canada between 1929 and 1932 fell 75% (from 5.6 million units to 1.4 million), and dollar sales fell 78%. In 1932 GM was operating at 30% of capacity. By quickly and sharply reducing inventories, costs, and capital investment expenditures, and by retiring surplus plant and equipment, however, GM managed to continue earning profits ($248 million over the three year period), pay dividends of $343 million, and actually increase the company's holdings of cash and short-term securities by 36%.[17]

But GM's workers did not weather the storm so gently. The relative tranquillity of labor-capital relations in the 1920s was shattered; and the resulting period of labor militancy has been described as "arguably the high water market of the class struggle in modern American industry."[18] It initiated a restructuring of the relations between labor, capital (the corporations that dominated the mass production sector) and the state that would take two decades to complete. This restructuring will be the focus of the balance of this chapter, but first, some background into labor-management relations in the automobile industry is necessary.

The Early Decades of Labor-Management Relations

In 1891 a union of carriage and wagon workers that had been affiliated with the Knights of Labor entered the American Federation of Labor (AFL) as the International Union of Carriage and Wagon Workers. With the growth of automobile production, around the turn of the century, many carriage and wagon workers transferred their skills to the new industry. In 1912 the union changed its name to the Union of Carriage, Wagon and Automobile Workers. But the union's expansion into the automobile industry angered the AFL craft unions, which also claimed jurisdiction over certain auto workers. At their annual conventions in 1915 and 1916, the AFL demanded that the union drop the word "Automobile" from its name. The union refused, and in 1918 they were suspended from the AFL and became the independent Auto Workers Union (AWU). The AWU benefited from the general upsurge in union activity in the years immediately following WWI, and between 1918 and 1919 their membership doubled to 45,000 in 35 locals. (Automobile employment at the time was 343,000.) The union struck plants in Detroit, Flint, Milwaukee, Grand Rapids and New York City.[19]

Employer response to the rise in labor militancy after WWI was swift, and took place in a climate of anti-radical and anti-foreign hysteria, which the employers' campaign took advantage of by linking strikes and unions with foreigners and radicals. In 1920 the Department of Justice ordered the arrest and deportation of individuals who "believed in communist and anarchist doctrines." In Detroit, the heart of AWU membership, these "Palmer raids" resulted in the arrest of 827 persons, of whom 234 were subsequently deported.[20] The harsh climate for union activity, combined with an active employer-led open shop drive and the willingness of conservative trade union leaders, such as those in the AFL, to make bargains with employers to ensure their own survival soon made Detroit the "paradigm open shop city." By 1922 the AWU's membership was down to 800.

Throughout the 1920s the AFL's efforts to organize in the automobile industry were desultory, half-hearted, and plagued by rivalries among the eighteen international unions that claimed jurisdiction in the industry. According to *Fortune* magazine, by 1933 the AFL was suffering from "pernicious anaemia, sociological myopia, and hardening of the arteries."[21] The little organizing that did take place was carried out by the remnants of the AWU with the help of organizers who were either members of, or closely affiliated with, the Communist party.

There were many spontaneous walkouts in the auto industry between 1926 and 1930 (the AWU recorded over fifty). Although these actions obtained some concessions from employers, they usually also resulted in the dismissal of the labor leaders.[22] Despite these sporadic signs of a nascent militancy, neither the AWU nor the AFL made much progress in signing up new members during the decade. According to AFL head, William Green: "The appalling indifference of the [auto] workers themselves is a difficulty that seems to be insurmountable."[23] While clearly the failure of the AFL organizers can be attributed to the half-heartedness of their attempts, the AWU, despite intense effort, was not much more successful. Keeran attributes the indifference described by Green to a variety of factors: "the relative prosperity and easy credit of the 1920s; the militant anti-unionism of the employers and the government; the inexperience, diversity and transiency of the auto workers themselves."[24]

An important aspect of employers' efforts to undermine worker opposition in the post-WWI period was the adoption of "welfare capitalism." Edwards describes the welfare capitalism movement:[25]

> The plan was simple: corporations would provide (selected) workers with recreational services, clinics and health care, pensions, stock-sharing and other savings plans, housing and educational and other benefits and services. The welfare benefits, it was hoped would persuade workers

of the corporation's genuine concerns for their well-being and by actually improving their existence, undermine worker militance. In a somewhat more heavy handed vein, the participating corporations also sought to bind their workers to them by creating stronger dependence — a dependence based not only on the workers' income but also on essential service. For example, workers who joined strikes found that their leases required them to vacate company owned housing immediately. Finally, the corporations perceived the usefulness of welfare programs as a public relations device, to convince the public that they were responsible and caring employers.

By 1919 GM was an enthusiastic participant in welfare capitalism. In fact the greater part of the discussions about labor in the company's annual reports in the 1920s involved discussions of what GM was doing to provide housing, health and life insurance, bonuses, stock purchase and savings plans, and about the company's concern with providing for the health and safety of employees on the job.

With the benefit of hindsight, the company's concerns for health and safety may have been somewhat disingenuous. The 1925 annual report, for example, includes a discussion about "several much-to-be-regretted accidents" at a plant that processed the Tetra-ethyl lead used in manufacturing ethylised gasoline. The company's Ethyl subsidiary temporarily suspended the sale of the gasoline, and asked the U.S. Surgeon General to study the product's possible health hazards — although the accident "had nothing to do with ethylised gasoline, the commercial product." The Surgeon General found that the gasoline was "entirely safe for public use," GM reported in its 1925 annual report. What they failed to reveal, however, was the full extent of the controversy over the introduction of tetra-ethyl lead into gasoline that was taking place both before and after the accident. In their study of the incident, Rosner and Markowitz point out that one of the defenders of the use of tetra-ethyl lead, Emery Hayhurst, a noted industrial hygienist and advisor on the subject to organizations such as the Worker's Health Bureau, was at the same time working secretly as a consultant to the Ethyl Corporation and was supplying the advocates of the additive with information regarding the tactics of their opponents.[26] Although today we are well aware of the health hazards of leaded gasoline in the U.S., where cars that use it are no longer being produced, leaded gasoline is still widely used elsewhere in the world.

The auto industry during this period was also known for its relatively high wages — a strategy initiated by Henry Ford's famous five dollars a day, in 1914. But hidden behind its welfare capitalism and relatively high wages were difficult and dangerous working conditions, characterized by long shifts, monotonous work, enormous pressure to work quickly, layoffs and rehiring that often depended upon the whims of the foremen, and a system of company espionage and reprisal that discouraged open union activity.[27]

The economic breakdown of the 1930s precipitated a revival of labor militancy throughout the U.S. It is important for understanding subsequent developments to recognize that the leadership for the new labor militancy of the 1930s did not come from the trade unions themselves, but from the rank and file. Indeed there were three sets of struggles occurring simultaneously within the labor movement during the 1930s. The first was taking place between workers and employers in the plants and in the streets of America's industrial cities. The second was taking place between local plant committees and labor councils, and the trade union bureaucracies, for control over the renewed movement. And the third struggle was for leadership and power within and between the revitalized trade unions themselves. Needless to say these struggles overlapped and influenced each other to a considerable extent and there are no clear boundaries to delineate one from the other. It is also important to recognize that these struggles did not take place in a political vacuum. As we will see below, the state played an important mediating role in these struggles as President Roosevelt sought simultaneously to defuse social unrest and maintain his political hegemony by alternately allying himself with various labor, corporate, and political factions.

The Initial Rebellion: 1933–1937

By 1933, corporate America felt very much under siege. Business, especially big business, was coming under increasing attack for its failure to provide work (unemployment reached 25% in 1932 and 1933 and was still a high 17% in 1939), for layoffs and wage cuts, and for its apparent lack of concern for its depleted workforce's well-being on the job.

In June 1933 Congress passed the National Industrial Recovery Act (NIRA). This legislation, an American version of corporatism, exempted businesses from anti-trust laws to allow them to reach industry-wide agreements to fix prices and allocate markets, if they also agreed to codes establishing minimum wages, maximum hours, and prohibiting child labor. Its most controversial provision, however, was passed over the objections of corporate America. Section 7A guaranteed the right of workers to "organize unions of their own choosing" and the right to collective bargaining. Although the NIRA contained no enforcement powers, section 7A was of great symbolic significance, and its passage was followed by the greatest strike wave since 1921.

In contrast with the years from 1925 to 1932, when an average of 300,000 workers annually engaged in work stoppages; some 1,168,000 workers did so in 1933, and 1,500,000 in 1934.[28] The momentum for these job actions came from the rank and file, and was largely independent of any official union apparatus, the latter having been weakened by the capital-state offensives of the 1920s. In August 1933, Roosevelt established a National Labor Board (NLB) to mediate the growing number of labor disputes. Like the NIRA, the NLB had no enforcement authority.

Between 1933 and 1935 a coalition of progressive business executives, the AFL, and the executive branch of government sought to defuse the growing labor militancy. They agreed to an interpretation of the labor representation section of the NIRA which buttressed the formation of company unions in the mass production industries, while accepting a more pro-union interpretation for companies in lighter industries.[29] In addition, the AFL, which opposed the idea of industry-wide labor organizations, responded to requests for AFL charters from the new labor insurgents by agreeing to form "federal locals." These federal locals were to be temporary, with their members eventually to be redistributed among the AFL's craft internationals. In the meantime the locals' organizing drives were placed under the control of AFL operatives, whose prime concern was to reach accommodations with management through the mechanisms of the NRA (the National Recovery Administration, responsible for drawing up and administering the NIRA codes) and the NLB.

In the auto industry the NRA and the National Automobile Chamber of Commerce drew up a "code of fair competition" in the summer of 1933 that was approved by President Roosevelt. The code included a "special merit clause" that qualified the right to organize provisions of section 7A of the NIRA by reaffirming traditional open shop practices in the auto industry. The code provided that "employers in this industry may exercise the right to select, retain, or advance employees on the basis of individual merit, without regard to their membership or nonmembership in any organization."[30] According to the industry publication, *Automotive Industries,* the code represented "the first victory of industry over organized labor under the Industrial Recovery Acts." Although AFL President Green testified at the code hearings against any qualification of section 7A, he refrained from criticizing it once it was promulgated.

Other large corporations, with GM prominent among them, adopted a more militant stand. By October 1933, companies were refusing to appear at NLB hearings; and the National Association of Manufacturers (NAM) (which was taken over by the large corporations as the vehicle for their counteroffensive) launched a massive open attack against the NLB. GM strongly opposed the labor provisions of the NIRA. In its 1933 annual report GM warned that unless these were clarified, "there is the certainty of industrial strife, the equal of which this country has not yet seen."[31] Implicit in these provisions, the report continued, looms "the spectre of the greatest monopoly that ever existed in any country in the world — the closed shop." The report then posed the question: "Does not the record of American industry with its freedom and independence, as developed through the mutual confidence of management and labor in the automobile industry — providing the American workman the highest standard of living in the world — justify a decision in favor of the open shop?" The conservative, anti-New Deal, American Liberty League, founded in 1934, drew most of its important support from major financial and industrial interests clustered around GM and its largest shareholder, Du Pont.[32]

The "showdown" came in March 1934, when GM's Fisher Body Plant in Detroit discharged a number of union members for union activities (they had formed a skeleton organization affiliated with the AFL's craft-based auto union). Rank and file leaders threatened a strike unless the corporation agreed to recognize the union, re-hire the dismissed workers, and agree to a 20% wage increase. Such actions in a city like Flint took courage. Like many industrial towns in the U.S. in the 1930s, Flint was virtually owned by its dominant corporations (in this case, GM).[33] Six of the nine city commissioners in Flint were GM executives. The mayor was a former GM comptroller. GM directly supervised the police force and it did not hesitate to use espionage to identify union sympathizers. Later in the decade the Senate's La Follette Committee estimated that between 1934 and 1936 GM had paid over $836,000 to detective agencies and maintained "the most colossal supersystem of spies yet devised in any American Corporation," a "far-flung industrial Chekka" that included fifty-two Pinkerton detectives to report on union activity in GM plants. The estimate was based on partial information, since when the committee subpoenaed GM's labor relations director, Henry Anderson, he destroyed GM executives William Knudsen's and Charles Wilson's files.[34]

President Roosevelt turned the case over to the NLB. William Knudsen, of GM, appeared before the committee and stated that GM would not deal with any labor organization or recognize the NLB's authority to conduct elections in any GM plant. Bending to rank and file pressure the craft leaders of the AFL auto union announced that the union would strike on March 21st. Roosevelt responded by essentially repudiating the labor clauses of the NIRA. He interpreted section 7A as not requiring majority rule and exclusive representation; and substituted, instead, a system of plural unionism and proportionate representation that gave equal rights to company and rank and file unions.[35] According to GM executive, Donaldson Brown, the company was "tremendously happy" with the settlement.[36]

In the meantime, pressure continued to grow among the AFL's federal locals for the formation of a central governing body to coordinate their organizing efforts with national employers. The combination of this pressure and general worker dissatisfaction with the NIRA auto code and the March 1934 settlement finally forced the AFL to respond. In June 1934, they called a National Conference of United Auto Workers Federal Labor Unions. The AFL proposed the formation of an elected national council to serve the AFL's chief auto industry organizer in an advisory and data collection capacity, meeting only at his request. The federal labor unions, AFL President Green argued, were too small and immature to support an international union, but one would be formed "just as soon as the workers have demonstrated their ability to sustain themselves as an integral part of the trade union movement." Green also reaffirmed the AFL's determination "to develop a 'cooperative relationship' with the employers and to direct industrial disputes away 'from the field of conflict to the council chamber where the law and rule of reason can settle labor's problems.'"[37] By September the dissension among the federal locals was so great that Green renounced the March auto settlement and in October the AFL convention authorized the Executive Council to issue an international charter to the auto unions. The charter was officially presented to the auto workers at the AFL's convention in the summer of 1935, almost one year later. It contained two controversial limitations: it limited the union's jurisdiction to those workers "directly" involved in the manufacturing and assembly of automobiles; and it provided for the AFL's President to appoint the union's officers.[38]

In January 1935 the Henderson Report, written for the NIRA, was issued. Its discussion of the auto industry revealed that earnings were so low, and employment so sporadic, that most workers depended upon relief for four to five months of the year. The report concluded that: "Labor unrest exists to a degree higher than warranted by the Depression. The unrest flows from insecurity, low annual earnings, inequitable hiring and rehiring methods, espionage, speedups and displacement of workers at an extremely early age. Unless something is done soon, they [the workers] intend to take things into their own hands."[39]

These remarks stand in stark contrast to GM's defense against "any arbitrary increases in real costs" (meaning wage increases) in their 1934 annual report. Pointing out that "total wages paid to factory workers in 1934 were higher than in any year since 1929," and that the cost of materials and supplies had also increased, "reflecting wage increases on the part of the Corporation's suppliers," GM warned that: "There is only one possible economic result of any arbitrary raising of real costs, i.e., an increased disparity between selling prices and purchasing power, hence (a) a reduction in profits to the extent that such increased costs cannot be passed on to the consumer and/or (b) a shrinkage in the volume of business, with increased unemployment."[40] The notion that there is a natural relationship between wages and profits, and that any further wage increases will upset this relationship to the detriment of both business and labor, is a persistent theme in GM's annual reports in the 1930s. But the company was also prepared to take some steps to try to make production more regular, and hence reduce fluctuations in employment. In 1935, in conjunction with the rest of the automobile industry, GM changed the introduction date for new models to the fall. The company also announced the creation of a Labor Stabilization Fund "to maintain the manufacture of component parts in excess of completed cars during the winter months and hence to provide employment when outside work is unavailable; also to reduce the influx of temporary workers during the season of high consumer demand by still further minimizing the peaks of production."[41]

Throughout the discussions of labor relations in GM's annual reports in the 1930s the company firmly maintained its position of authority and control over the relationship. The tone of these reports makes it clear that it is GM, and GM alone, who can be relied upon to recognize when wages and profits are at their natural levels, and that it is GM alone who is capable of maintaining the "proper balance between the equities of all parties concerned, including not only those of employer and employes [sic] but also those of the public, upon whose continued demand for its products depends the welfare of the Corporation and of its employes themselves."[42] This top-down perspective is apparent, for example, in GM's announcement in its 1934 annual report that the company has developed "A Statement of General Motors Corporation's Basic Policies Governing Its Relations with Factory Employes." The statement, the report says, "was issued first to the executive and supervisory personnel, down to and including the plant foremen, and shortly afterwards was placed in the hands of all workers in General Motors factories throughout the United States. Copies of this statement have recently been mailed to stockholders." In a letter to all factory employees from the GM President "at the time of placing copies of the above mentioned statement in their hands," GM warned that "how much can be accomplished will depend upon the cooperation of all concerned." It seems evident just whose cooperation will really be required in any forthcoming collective bargaining which GM says it accepts as a principle, so long as it can formulate the basic policies and principles to be followed.

But when neither the efforts to stabilize production, the acceptance of the principle of collective bargaining, the NIRA codes, nor the NLB succeeded in stemming the tide of labor unrest, both Congress and organized labor acted to dam the torrent of mass militancy. In the summer of 1935, Congress passed the National Labor Relations Act (the NLRA, also known as the Wagner Act), to replace the NIRA (which the U.S. Supreme Court had declared unconstitutional earlier that year). This legislation outlawed company unions, declared traditional anti-union practices by employers illegal, legalized union organizing efforts, and established the National Labor Relations Board (NLRB) to administer all provisions of the act. Until the Supreme Court upheld the Wagner Act in 1937, however, organized business presented virtually a united front against New Deal labor policy. For many students of the period,the Wagner Act represented a great victory for labor: it "was the first serious attempt to bring the class struggle under the aegis of government supervision."[43] "For the first time," Milton writes, "the traditional united front against labor by business, the government, and the judiciary was broken."[44] For others, the emphasis on juridical procedure and reasoning processes that gave primacy to the contract and "responsible" collective bargaining, combined with a critical judicial opinion in 1939 that placed sit-down strikes beyond the protection of the NLRB, served to deradicalize the potential of the legislation.[45]

Two significant shifts in alignment took place in 1936. The first was the formal split between the industrial and craft unions within the labor movement when the Committee for Industrial Organization (CIO) left the craft-based AFL. Within the AFL, John L. Lewis, head of the United Mine Workers (UMW), and other industrial unionists, were urging the AFL leadership to grant industrial charters to workers in the mass production industries. They were rebuffed by the AFL's Executive Council, who were concerned with protecting the jurisdictional claims of the existing craft unions. In November 1935 Lewis, and ten other union leaders, formed the Committee for Industrial Organization, as a splinter group within the AFL. By the beginning of 1936 industrial locals that had been denied charters by the AFL were requesting affiliation with the CIO. The AFL Executive Council demanded that the CIO be dissolved. The UMW responded to this demand at their January 1936 convention by voting to support the CIO and to authorize the UMW Executive Council to withhold payment of per capita taxes to the AFL. A committee was set up to mediate the split between the two groups, but it was clear to all that it was irrevocable. From then on, until they were rejoined in the AFL-CIO in 1955, the two groups remained bitter antagonists. At their spring 1936 convention, the UAW broke with the AFL, and in July they affiliated with the CIO. The following

September, UAW delegates approved a program for an international industrial union, controlled by the rank and file, and committed to an aggressive organizing drive. The delegates also declared themselves in favor of a general strike in 1937, if employers failed to negotiate.[46]

The second shift was the formation of an alliance between President Roosevelt and the CIO in the 1936 Presidential elections. According to Thomas Corcoran, a close adviser, Roosevelt had initially viewed both Section 7A of the NIRA, and the Wagner Act, as economic moves to "pump up workers' purchasing power." Labor's significance as political and financial supporters "dawned on Mr. Roosevelt's brain trust slowly."[47] Facing increasing hostility from even his progressive business supporters, President Roosevelt needed to expand his political base if he hoped to be re-elected in 1936. In 1936 Roosevelt forged a coalition with the CIO, which provided both money and rank and file organizing support, to win reelection in 1936. His campaign was built around an attack on the large corporations and the call for a "people's government" in Washington. Roosevelt's victory marked, for the first time in U.S. politics, a clear polarization of workers and capitalists between the Democratic and Republican parties, in place of traditional ethno-religious loyalties. In return for the CIO's support, Roosevelt appointed labor supporters to key positions in New Deal agencies, particularly those involving labor, such as the NLRB.

The first test of the new alliance between the President and the CIO came with the General Motors sit-down strikes. The result of spontaneous rank and file actions, the first strike occurred at the company's Fisher Body plant in Cleveland, on December 28, 1936. Two days later, workers at a Fisher Body plant in Flint, Michigan, occupied the plant. Although sit-downs and walk-outs occurred at GM plants in Detroit, Anderson, Indiana, Norwood and Toledo, Ohio, Janesville, Wisconsin, St. Louis, Kansas City, and Atlanta, the Flint occupation became the focus of attention and the key to the strike, which shut-down GM's operations. The UAW immediately supported the strikers and announced that the strike would not end until GM signed a national collective bargaining agreement that recognized the UAW as the sole bargaining agency for GM workers. (The AFL sent a telegram to GM to protest giving exclusive bargaining rights to the UAW.) This was the key demand from the union's point of view; the workers, on the other hand, were more concerned with the pressures of line speed-ups, wage cuts, unsafe and unsanitary working conditions, the lack of steady work, the capricious power of foremen, and the absence of any control over workplace conditions.[48]

GM refused to negotiate with the workers' representatives until the plants were vacated and the sanctity of corporate property restored; and then negotiations would be on a plant-by-plant basis only. From GM's perspective, the unions were attempting to invade management's fundamental prerogatives over the establishment of work schedules, the setting of standards, the disciplining of workers, and the setting of pricing policy. Although a court injunction was obtained by GM, Michigan Governor Murphy refused to use the state's police power to enforce it. Instead, he entered directly into negotiations and the combination of pressure from him, along with the direct intervention of Labor Secretary Frances Perkins and President Roosevelt, finally compelled GM's management to negotiate with the UAW-CIO.

An agreement was reached on February 11th, 1937. It provided for a six-month contract. GM agreed to recognize the UAW-CIO as the collective bargaining agent at Flint and the other striking plants. In the remaining GM plants the UAW would represent only its own members. GM also agreed not to interfere with the rights of employees to join the union; not to discriminate against employees who belonged to the union; to rehire all strikers; and to begin negotiations for a full collective bargaining agreement. GM also unilaterally granted workers a 5% wage increase. The UAW, in turn, agreed to end the strike, vacate the plants, refrain from coercing employees, and also to refrain from work stoppages during the negotiations and during the life of any resulting agreement until all grievance procedures were exhausted.[49]

None of these conflicts were explicitly mentioned in GM's annual reports, but they did have an impact. In 1936's annual report, the company introduced a new section called "Labor Economics." The very title of this section is significant, for it transforms the conflictual nature of management-labor relations into relations that are neutrally governed by the natural laws of economic science. In this section (which continued into the 1940s but was renamed Organizational Relationships in 1943), GM depersonalizes the setting of wages and profits, developing a theme noted in the 1934 report. Wages "should be as high as practicably possible," but not so high as to put costs, prices, and purchasing power out of balance. (The latter refers to GM's unstated assumption that any cost increases must be passed along to consumers thereby "forcing the prices of automotive products to a point where many consumers will be unable to continue buying.")[50] Working hours, GM continues, "should be reasonable," meaning, "not so long as to preclude the opportunity for a reasonable amount of leisure; but, on the other hand, not so short as to unduly burden costs, and hence unreasonably raise prices, and thereby reduce the amount of employment." The relationship between wages, prices and profits are governed by an economic equilibrium that is independent of management's discretion: "too many are of the [mistaken] belief that the wage level is at the discretion of management, that there is no ceiling other than that which management seeks to establish arbitrarily."[51]

According to GM, the deepening of the depression in 1937 was entirely due to an abnormal increase in labor costs that "led to the unbalancing of the economic equilbrium, as purchasing power was not evenly distributed in relation to wages."[52] The only source of increased wages and reduced prices, GM argued, are improvements in productivity from technological progress and improved operating techniques. Both GM and the UAW quietly dropped reduced prices as a goal after WWII, when the success of the postwar accords depended in large part on the company's ability to pass along labor's economic gains to the public through higher prices.

Despite subsequent difficulties in negotiating an agreement with GM — "Every meaningful demand put forward by the union was regarded as a challenge to the corporation's authority, to their property rights, which they regarded as sacred"[53] — the UAW's victory over GM was regarded as a great triumph. It stimulated a massive wave of sit-down strikes that spread well beyond the auto industry. The UAW's membership increased from 88,000 in early 1937 to 400,000 by the fall. In 1937 a total of 4.7million workers went on strike, in contrast with 2.1 million in 1936.[54] According to Thomas Lamont, of the House of Morgan and U.S.Steel, Myron Taylor, U.S. Steel's President, was so frightened by the prospect of a similar strike against his company — he believed that a strike "might prove such a major crisis as to constitute almost a social revolution" — that the company settled with the CIO before a strike occurred.[55] By 1938 CIO unions succeeded in organizing the bulk of the workers in the mass production industries, including mining, automobiles, rubber, the electrical workers, oil, meat-packing, aluminum, shipping and shipbuilding.

Backlash and Internal Strife: 1938–1941

By the middle of 1937 the CIO's organizing drive began to falter as the U.S. economy entered a new downturn and the political climate for labor struggle had also begun to change. Within nine months, production was down 30% and employment 25%. By January 1938, over 25% of GM's production workers were on layoffs. Employment for the auto industry fell from 517,000 in 1937 to 305,000 in 1938, and the UAW's membership was cut by three fourths.[56]

Within the UAW, divisions intensified between the left and union President Homer Martin. The latter formed a Progressive caucus in 1937 that excluded the left. The caucus "advocated moderation in the calling of strikes, strict adherence to contracts, tight administrative control of locals, and severe penalties for those engaged in unauthorized strikes."[57] In response, the Communists, Socialists, and other dissidents formed a Unity caucus which, while calling for union discipline and an end to wildcat strikes, stressed the need for local autonomy and democracy and called for an organizing campaign at Ford Motor Company.[58] Although the delegates to the UAW's August 1937 convention adopted the Unity program, Martin retained the Presidency and control of the Executive Board. Martin and the Board then proceeded to consolidate their position and undermine the influence of the left. They prohibited the locals from communicating with each other; prevented rank and file conferences from ratifying agreements; disallowed public discussion of Executive Board affairs; established an intelligence system to inform on Communist activity; abolished local union papers (mostly controlled by the left); granted Martin power to suspend union members without trial; and denied Unity caucus members important assignments, or reassigned them to peripheral areas. Martin then responded to the economic crisis by adopting a conciliatory attitude in the negotiations then going on between GM and Chrysler.

In September 1937, the UAW's Executive Board approved a public letter to GM, in which they agreed that GM would have total authority to discipline unauthorized strikers and that the "union would take effective disciplinary action against those involved in wildcats."[59] In November a conference of union delegates from GM plants voted unanimously to repudiate the letter.[60] The test came that month during the sit-down strike in Pontiac's Fisher Body Plant. GM President Knudson demanded that the UAW end the strike. Such unauthorized strikes, he said, "will eventually make agreements valueless and collective bargaining impossible."[61] Governor Murphy, who a few months earlier had refused to call out the state militia to end the Flint strike, threatened to do so here. The CIO's John L. Lewis also called for an end to wildcat strikes. UAW President Martin, after leaking a story to the *New York Times,* that the strike had been fomented by the left to discredit the union, secured Executive Board condemnation of the strike, went to the plant, and ordered the strikers to leave. He was supported by the Communist Party leadership. "The defeat was total, the four local leaders stayed fired, and the local union was soon placed under trusteeship."[62]

Internal dissension was not the only problem confronting the UAW and the CIO by late 1936. A conservative and corporate backlash was fragmenting the New Deal's Congressional coalition. The AFL joined the conservatives in attacking the La Follette Committee, which had been investigating, with some success, corporate-sponsored illegal anti-labor practices, and the National Labor Relations Board. They claimed that the Committee and the NLRB were staffed by Communist Party supporters, and were pro-CIO. With the coalition's support the House Committee on Un-American Activities (HUAC) was formed, headed by Martin Dies. Not surprisingly, HUAC's first investigations were of the La Follette Committee and the CIO. The anti-CIO, anti-radical backlash was fueled by the press and broadcast media, and provided the AFL with a broad patriotic sanction for its actions. In the 1938 elections, the New Deal liberals lost control of Congress. President Roosevelt found his desire to pursue an interventionist foreign policy increasingly hostage to conservative Southern Democrats; and the price they extracted was his New Deal reforms, concessions to labor, and the purging of "pro-CIO leftists" from the NLRB.

The retrenchment of the New Deal program was reinforced by the courts. In 1939, the U.S. Supreme Court outlawed the sit-down strike in the Fansteel decision. In other decisions the courts upheld the rights of employers to hire and fire workers; and to unilaterally impose terms if they had bargained to an impasse. While upholding workers' rights to collective bargaining, the courts decided that workers could not strike while under contract; that the right to strike did not include the right to seize employers' plants; and that unions were institutions apart from their members and that union leaders were obligated to police their unions and ensure "responsible behavior."[63] Both the courts and the NLRB were moving the entire structure of collective bargaining in the direction of "a more routinized, businesslike relationship between top leaders of labor and management, with the government as referee," a transition that would be completed during WWII.[64] One of the consequences of this trajectory was that the issue that had triggered the initial labor revolts, the extent of labor's control over the production process, was relegated to the arena of "guerilla warfare on the shop floor" and wildcat strikes, and excluded from collective bargaining at the national level. Emboldened by the corporate-congressional attack on the CIO, the AFL acted to preempt the CIO's organizing drive with an aggressive effort of its own to form industrial unions. In a "veritable civil war" between the two unions, the AFL pitted its own form of "respectable" industrial unionism against the "un-American" industrial unionism of the CIO.[65] The AFL signed "sweetheart" contracts, and even chartered company unions in its battle against the CIO in this period.

The factional struggles within the UAW continued into 1939, when the CIO intervened, appointing Sidney Hillman, of the Amalgamated Clothing Workers union, and Phillip Murray, of the Steelworkers union, to virtually take over the UAW. At a special convention in September 1939 the delegates expelled Martin from the UAW and elected as President R.J. Thomas, "a steady apolitical union leader who had recently defected from the Martin camp."[66] Although the struggles over control of the UAW and the role of the left within it were by no means over, the removal of Martin renewed the UAW's energies. The UAW-CIO easily defeated Martin's newly-formed AFL rival in a series of NLRB elections, and launched organizing drives at Ford and in the California aircraft industry.[67]

The events within the UAW signified a major shift in the political balance within the CIO itself, a shift that would be formally completed, after Roosevelt's reelection in 1940, with John L. Lewis's resignation as President and the election of Phillip Murray to replace him. The shift reflected the ascendancy of those factions of the CIO, led by Hillman and Murray, who were seeking to reach an accomodation with employers through the mediation of the state (the Presidential wing of the Democratic Party), a strategy that seemed to require a lessening of rank and file autonomy and the imposition of a strong central bureaucracy. With foreign policy gaining increasing amounts of Roosevelt's attention after 1938, this faction also adopted a strong anti-fascist, interventionist stance. The alternative strategy — the formation of an independent labor party to oppose Roosevelt and the dismantling of his New Deal Reforms (which themselves promised only limited change) and to develop and support a pro-labor agenda for more aggressive social transformation — became increasingly less likely with the rising prominence and authority of the Rooseveltian wing of the CIO, the new organizing successes of the AFL, and the nationalistic, anti-communistic climate. The last possibility for this strategy in the pre-war period ended when John L. Lewis, convinced that "workers never gained anything from wars," decided to support the isolationist Republican candidate, Wendell Willkie in the 1940 Presidential election.[68]

By 1941, the struggle for control of the labor movement had been roughly resolved in favor of a trade union bureaucracy that had aligned and subordinated itself to the Presidential wing of the Democratic Party. The trade-off was clear: an independent political base for labor was traded off to the state in return for collective bargaining rights. The CIO's left was increasingly isolated (and would be entirely purged in the immediate postwar period), and its influence within the executive agencies of the government that administered labor affairs was significantly diminished. What remained was for these tendencies to be consolidated and formally institutionalized. This was to take place in the 1940s.

The War Years: 1941–1946

The war years were a watershed period in the development of labor-capital-state relations in the U.S. It was during this period that the basis for the postwar accord that established the parameters for the current crisis were laid. Labor militancy during WWII reinforced for both capital and state the importance of a strong collaborative union bureaucracy for ensuring both high productivity and industrial peace in the future; and wartime integration of the labor bureaucracy into the state apparatus provided the model for doing so.

Four significant developments occurred in the area of labor relations during WWII. The first was a major recomposition of the workforce, as millions of women, rural immigrants, and blacks entered the industrial labor force. The second was the absorption of previously-estranged elements of the business community into the war effort, such as GM's Knudsen, who went to Washington D.C., to head the key War Production Board. The permanent collusion between the military and war contractors and their political agents, with which we have become so familiar, was forged during WWII. GM became the number one military contractor during WWII, a position it maintained until the early 1950s and the end of the Korean War. Thus it is not surprising that GM moved from opposition to military spending in 1940 ("production for national defense is unproductive wealth in the sense that it does not add to the standard of living, it is added overhead on the economy") to being an enthusiastic supporter of continued military-industrial cooperation in 1944 ("after the war, if we are to win the peace we must continue to move forward by maintaining for preparedness equally close liaison between the armed services and industry").[69] The third wartime development was a further enlarging of the federal government's role in mediating relations between business and labor. The government participated directly in the collective bargaining process through the National Defense Mediation Board and the National War Labor Board. In addition, the collaboration of the labor union bureaucracy in securing the required level of labor productivity and industrial peace was secured by the unions' agreement to a no-strike pledge and to a ceiling on wage increases. In return, the unions received a minor role on the War Production Board, and more importantly, the inclusion of a maintenance of membership clause in virtually all wartime collective bargaining agreements, along with automatic dues check-off. The postwar union shop agreements generally grew from the quasi-union shops established by maintenance of membership during the war.[70] The final major developments of the war years were the continuation of labor militancy at the rank and file level and its opposition to the union bureaucracies.

During WWII the number of strikes, mainly wildcat, increased from 2,968 in 1943, to 4,956 in 1944, surpassing comparable figures during the 1937 strikes.[71] In the automobile industry 50.5 percent of the workers were on strike at some time during 1944.[72] There were so many violations of the no-strike pledge that George Romney, managing director of the Automobile Council for War Production, told a Congressional committee that: "There have been more strikes and work stoppages and employees directly involved during the first eleven months of 1944 than in any other period of the industry's history."[73] UAW President Thomas described the job actions as "one of the greatest crises in [the UAW-CIO's] history." The strikes, he said, "are destroying the UAW." The wartime strikes had a different tone from those of the 1930s. According to Post, in the 1930s "elected strike committees and stewards councils decided tactics and controlled negotiators in struggles that often centered around questions of the nature and pace of the labor process."[74] In contrast, Lichtenstein writes that the strikes during the war years had "an inherently parochial and localistic focus"; were mostly limited to strategically placed work groups, not on assembly line work; were called over grievances specific to those groups; and occurred with little regard for the interests of other workers.[75] Many of the strikes were the result of racial tensions in the automobile plants. Between March and June, 1943, over 100,000 man-days were lost in a wave of hate strikes over the hiring or upgrading of black workers in these plants.[76]

The wartime strikes were a battleground for control between the rank and file and an increasingly centralized and bureaucratic CIO leadership. The struggles and the outcomes varied among the unions. For example, among the steel workers, whose union had long been centralized, the leadership was easily able to isolate the dissidents. The UAW, in contrast, had a tradition of local autonomy and factional division, and there the conflicts were more intense. But in the end the bureaucracy triumphed. In 1944, the UAW convention accepted a leadership-sponsored membership referendum supporting a no-strike pledge.[77]

To reduce the industrial conflict, the Federal Government established a tri-partite agency — the National Labor Mediation Board, in November 1941, which was replaced by the National War Labor Board in early 1942 — to participate in and administer the collective bargaining process. The boards included representatives from labor, industry and government, who were able to set industry-wide wage patterns, fix a system of "industrial jurisprudence" on the shop floor, and influence the internal structure of the new unions.[78] The National Defense Mediation Board (NDMB) promoted centralized and routinized negotiation and arbitration; it punished local, direct worker actions; and it reinforced the CIO bureaucracy's authority over the ranks of labor.

Throughout the wildcat strikes in 1942 and 1943 the CIO leaders continued to call on workers to rely upon the NWLB and other state agencies to resolve disputes over wages, hours and shop floor conditions and to condemn wildcat strikes as "communist-inspired." In response to stepped-up strike actions in defense industries, the NWLB imposed a highly bureaucratized grievance procedure which shifted disputes from the shop floor (and the direct influence of stewards and work groups) "to the realm of contractual interpretation, where the authority of management and the value of orderly procedure weighted more heavily. In the meantime — possibly several weeks — the discipline and authority of management remained intact."[79] The procedures also held local union officials responsible for their enforcement and included provisions for compulsory arbitration. If local officials failed to enforce the grievance procedures, they would lose the maintenance of membership agreements. In 1944, the UAW's Executive Board adopted a policy that required local officials to assist NWLB and UAW leadership in ending local wildcats. The collective bargaining agreements signed in the 1946–1950 period incorporated many of the practices that were established by the federal agencies during WWII. The experiences of WWII provided the final demonstration to business executives and government officials of the benefits of formalized worker relations through the mechanism of strong trade union bureaucracies.

When WWII ended in late 1945, a wave of strikes, numerically the most massive in U.S. history, erupted throughout the mass production industries. In contrast with the previous wildcat strikes, however, these were carefully orchestrated and controlled by the CIO's central leadership. By January 1946, auto, steel, electrical and packinghouse workers were simultaneously on strike. In the post-war strike wave, "the top labor officials quashed all local autonomy, dictated tactics and negotiated contracts that dealt *solely* with questions of wages and hours, all with the merest pretense of involving the rank and file."[80]

The UAW strike against GM lasted 113 days. It served as a "safety-valve" for the pent-up anger of the automobile workers, who were tired of four years under the no-strike pledge and the wage freeze. It also consolidated the hegemony of the UAW's central organization and helped to dismantle the rank and file caucus movement that had provided the leadership for the wartime walkouts.[81] The strike elevated Walter Reuther to national prominence; he appeared on the cover of *Time,* and was featured in major articles in *Fortune* and *Life.*[82] Reuther demanded a 30% wage increase, without an increase in automobile prices, and he offered to continue working if GM would let an arbitration board inspect its books and decide the size of wage increase the company could afford without raising prices. GM officials were horrified at the suggestion that the ability to pay should be an index of what a company ought to pay. According to one GM representative, these demands were "an opening wedge whereby the unions hope to pry their way into the whole field of management."[83] The company took out an advertisement in *The New York Times* in which it warned: "America is at the crossroads! It must preserve the freedom of each economic unit of American business to determine its own destiny. . . . The idea of ability to pay, whatever its validity may be, is not applicable to an individual business within an industry as a basis for raising its wages beyond the going rate."[84] GM refused to discuss prices, open its books, or submit anything to arbitration. Although any settlement required government approval — wartime wage and price controls were in place — and Truman sent a wire to the company supporting a study of the relation between wages and prices, GM boycotted hearings before a presidential fact-finding panel.[85]

In the end, according to Brody: "It was the government that gave way. To settle the nationwide steel strike, the Truman administration scuttled its price-stabilization program. In exchange for an 18.5 cent an hour increase, the industry was permitted five dollars more a ton for steel."[86] GM refused to settle for a penny more — the fact-finding board had recommended 19.5 cents — and the strike ran on for another month before Reuther backed down. "To preserve what it considered to be its management prerogatives, GM had taken a 113-day strike, accepted losses of nearly $89 million (of which $52.9 million was recovered through tax credits), and most important, conceded its headstart to competitors in the race for postwar markets."[87] The strike was settled with a two-year contract and an increase in wages substantially below that initially demanded; an increase that was largely wiped out by postwar inflation increases that occurred when Truman acted to continue wage controls but eliminate price controls. By August 1946, the government approved three price increases for GM and at year's end, Congress abolished controls entirely. Despite the shortfall between what was realized and what had been demanded, the visibility Reuther received through the strike helped him defeat Thomas to become President of the UAW in March 1946.

Post-war Consolidation

By 1950 the institutional components of the social accord that would govern relations between labor, capital and the state for close to a generation, were basically in place. They consisted of three key elements: the collective bargaining framework agreed upon by the mass production industries and the industrial unions; a legislative/judicial framework consisting of the National Labor Relations and Taft-Hartley Acts and related judicial and NLRB decisions; and the political alliance between both the CIO and AFL and the Democratic Party.

The Collective Bargaining Framework

The collective bargaining framework that was carved out between the UAW and GM in the negotiations that followed the end of WWII (in 1946, 1948, and 1950) established a model that was adopted not only in the automobile industry but, with some variations, in other mass production industries as well (such as steel, rubber, trucking). In the collective bargaining agreements, the unions agreed not to strike except under specific conditions or at the termination of the contract; to accept quasi-judicial grievance procedures that removed disputes from the shop floor; to the Taylorist fragmentation of work in the form of elaborate job classifications; and in their most important concession, to accept the sanctity of "managerial prerogatives" over the organization of the work process. In return, the unions received wage formulas tied to increases in productivity and the cost of living, and acceptance by management of the union shop.

The cost of living increase was given to the union by GM in 1948, not won by them, in an attempt to bring stability and predictability to its dealings with the UAW. It was initially conceived in 1940, by Charles E. Wilson, GM President and later Secretary of Defense under Eisenhower, in 1940. Because of the war and the difficult 1945/6 strike, GM hadn't found an opportunity to propose it. In 1948, convinced of the need to institutionalize labor relations to avoid any repetition of the previous hostilities and uncertainties regarding their outcomes, Wilson proposed the cost-of-living formula (COLA) and a plan for an annual wage increase — the annual improvement factor (AIF) — based upon increases in productivity. The union, after some hesitation, accepted the proposal.[88] Although national contract negotiations over the ensuing thirty years modified these wage rules, occasionally partially diverting the programmed wage increases to cover the costs of improvements in fringe benefits (such as insurance, holiday, and vacation costs) and provided for additional increases for craft workers, their basic structure was preserved until 1979.

Throughout this period, neither wages nor fringe benefits were explicitly linked to firm profitability or employment conditions in the industry. The formula-based wage structure reduced the potential for disagreement between the union and management over compensation by explicitly accepting what GM had been asserting in its annual reports in the 1930s — that the only source of increased real wages was productivity improvements. The 1950 contract, for example, stated that "the annual improvement factor . . . recognizes that a continuing improvement in the standard of living of employees depends upon technological progress, better tools, methods, processes, and equipment, and a cooperative attitude on the part of all parties in such progress."[89] The formulas also provided a structure for negotiations, a regularity and predictability to wage settlements, and a benchmark by which both union and corporate negotiators could be evaluated by their respective constituencies. Indeed, at no time after 1950 did the automobile industry experience a strike as long or as bitter as those before and immediately after WWII.

Throughout the post-war contract negotiations, GM's management fought to narrowly circumscribe the areas open to collective bargaining negotiations. For example, the 1945 contract included the following:[90]

> The right to hire, promote, discharge or discipline for cause, and to maintain discipline and efficiency for employees, is the sole responsibility of the corporation except that union members shall not be discriminated against as such. In addition, the products to be manufactured, the location of plants, the schedules of production, the methods, processes and means of manufacturing are solely and exclusively the responsibility of the corporation.

Former GM Chairman Alfred Sloan wrote that the challenge to managerial prerogatives was the most threatening aspect of unionism:[91]

> What made the prospect seem especially grim in those early years was the persistent union attempt to invade basic management prerogatives. Our rights to determine production schedules, to set work standards, and to discipline workers were all suddenly called into question. Add to this the recurrent tendency of the union to inject itself into pricing policy, and it is easy to understand why it seemed, to some corporate officials, as though the union might one day be virtually in control of our operations.

> In the end, we were fairly successful in combating these invasions of management rights. There is no longer any real doubt that pricing is a management, not a union function. So far as our operations are concerned, we have moved to codify certain practices, to discuss workers' grievances with union representatives, and to submit for arbitration the few grievances that remain unsettled. But on the whole, we have retained all the basic powers to manage.

It required a Supreme Court decision, Inland Steel vs. NLRB, in 1949, to expand the scope of collective bargaining to embrace such fringe benefits as pension plans, life insurance, and sickness and accident benefits.[92] GM had unilaterally instituted such programs and the company did not consider them appropriate areas for bargaining with the union. According to GM's President, and later Secretary of Defense, Charles Wilson in 1948:[93]

> If we consider the ultimate result of this tendency to stretch collective bargaining to comprehend any subject that a union leader may desire to bargain over, we come out with the union leaders really running the economy of the country; but with no legal or public responsibility and with no private employment except as they may permit. . . .
>
> Only by defining and restricting collective bargaining to its proper sphere can we hope to save what we have come to know as our American system and keep it from evolving into an alien form, imported from East of the Rhine. Until this is done, the border area of collective bargaining will be a constant battleground between employers and unions, as the unions continuously attempt to press the boundary farther and farther into the areas of managerial functions.

In the conclusion to his study of the CIO in WWII, Lichtenstein points out that the inclusion of fringe benefits in collective bargaining agreements had a significant effect for the development of welfare state policies in the U.S. in subsequent decades.[94] By winning such benefits as health insurance, pensions, and supplemental unemployment benefits for precisely those workers most capable of effective political action (the 23% or so who belonged to labor unions), the unions and large corporations diffused pressure for increased social benefits for all workers. The welfare state became far more privatized and exclusionary in the U.S. than in Western Europe.

Within the collective bargaining framework, wages (and to a large extent work rules as well) were standardized across firms within the industry and across plants within firms. From the time of the first labor agreement between the UAW and GM in 1938, pay and fringe benefits were set exclusively in national negotiations between the UAW and the company. These national agreements also set certain work rules (such as seniority, overtime, and transfers), although the details of these rules (for example, the exact form of the seniority ladder, the specific job tasks for each job classification, job bidding and transfer rights) were negotiated by the union locals in supplementary bargaining agreements, subject to approval by the national UAW. The locals were also responsible for administering the national contract.

Wage standardization, by limiting intercompany differences in wages and working conditions, reduced intercompany competition and the possibility that plants within a firm would be whipsawed against each other by either the union or management. It also assured workers that they were maintaining their social position vis-à-vis their critical reference group, other workers in the same industry. The standardization of wages also strengthened the hands of the dominant firms in an industry, who benefited most from economies of scale and the availability of the newest, most efficient production technology, against the remaining smaller firms. Although the Big Three in the automobile industry accounted for over 90% of industry sales, in 1940 six smaller firms remained, all of whom disappeared within the next two decades.[95]

The collective bargaining framework also established a multi-level grievance procedure for ajudicating employer-employee disputes. This procedure solved a problem shared by both the company and the union leaderships, that of shop floor militancy. As Brody put it:[96]

> For the union, hardly less than the company, active work groups posed a troubling challenge. They disrupted the contract. They invaded the union's representative function. And they gave the shop stewards an independent base. While he might exploit rank and file militancy on the road to power — ultimately the test of any union leader consisted of his ability at managing the pressure from below. In this endeavor he needed the help of management. And it, in turn, needed him.

The grievance procedure removed conflicts from the shop floor and provided a set of formal bureaucratic procedures to resolve them. Under the grievance system, the disputed management action remains in effect until resolved by the grievance procedure, which may take many months. Continuity of production is assured while the dispute is being resolved. The worker, however, is subject to immediate disciplinary action. By shifting disputes from the shop floor — where stewards and work groups have their greatest leverage — to the realm of contractual interpretation where management authority, technical expertise, and the value of orderly procedure count more, the grievance system defuses union power and legitimates managerial authority. The process rapidly became one of interpreting written contracts and following an increasingly complex set of case law. Since one of the most important functions of locals is the processing of grievances, the procedure effectively co-opts union officials into enforcing the collective bargaining agreement and to some degree acting as instruments of management. Most importantly, because grievances are handled individually, the process undermines collective action.[97] Union leadership and company management further attenuated the potential threat to stability posed by shop-floor activists, especially shop stewards, by sharply reducing the number of shop stewards. For example, the 1946 UAW-GM contract included an agreement to replace working shop stewards, each representing twenty-four workers, with fulltime committeemen, each representing hundreds of workers.[98]

With the negotiation of 1950's five-year contract, the basic terms of the collective bargaining framework were in place between GM and the twenty-six unions that had been certified by the NLRB to represent GM workers. Also in place were the other two legs of the postwar consolidation: the legislative/judicial framework and the alliance between the AFL and the CIO and the Democratic party.

The Legislative/Judicial Framework

By 1950, the accord between labor, capital and the state consisted of two major legislative components: the National Labor Relations Act (1935) and the Taft-Hartley Act (1947).[99] Almost immediately after its passage the National Labor Relations Act (NLRA) was challenged in the courts. In fact many employers refused to obey it until it was declared constitutional by the U.S. Supreme Court in a series of decisions in 1937 and 1938. The National Association of Manufacturers, the American Liberty League, and the Chamber of Commerce organized campaigns to discredit the legislation and the NLRB.[100] In this they were sometimes helped by the AFL which accused the NLRB of favoritism toward the CIO. Conservative Congressmen and the U.S. Attorney General launched three full-scale investigations of the NLRB, claiming it was biased toward labor and the CIO. Roosevelt, responding to these campaigns, began appointing members to the NLRB who rejected its earlier, more radical, thrust. Between 1940 and 1947 a number of bills were introduced in Congress to amend or abolish the NLRA. And at the local level, state legislatures enacted a variety of anti-union laws including right-to-work laws which prohibit making union membership a condition of employment under any circumstances. The Taft-Hartley Act, passed over Truman's veto in 1947, represented the successful culmination of these attacks on the NLRA.

The Taft-Hartley Act both amends and adds to the NLRA.[101] Among its most important provisions, the Taft-Hartley Act makes the closed shop (in which an employer can hire only union members) illegal, and makes the union shop (in which all workers must join the union but need not be members when hired) illegal in states that have right-to-work laws. This latter provision weakened the CIO's efforts to organize textile, furniture, food processing, and chemical plants in the right-to-work states in the South. The Act also outlaws and restricts a number of labor's basic organizing weapons by declaring them unfair labor practices. These include strikes in support of other unions (so-called sympathy strikes); almost all secondary boycotts (efforts to get third parties to stop dealing with the employer the union is striking and/or trying to organize); jurisdictional strikes; and picketing to support any of these activities. Before striking, unions must give employers 60 day's notice; if workers strike within the 60 day period they lose their protection under the Act. The Act contains a broad freedom-of-speech provision for employers, which allows them to wage aggressive anti-union campaigns during representation elections; for example, the company can require workers to attend anti-union meetings during work hours. Among its other anti-union provisions the Taft-Hartley Act prohibits unions from making political contributions; it requires unions to file voluminous amounts of financial and other data with the Department of Labor and the NLRB; and it classifies as managers many supervisory workers (such as foremen in the automobile and other mass production industries who had been attracted to unionism in the 1940s) and prohibits them from using NLRB procedures to seek union recognition.[102] Taft-Hartley also grants the U.S. President broad authority to declare a major strike a national emergency, and then seek an injunction to stop the strike for an 80 day "cooling-off" period during which the government tries to mediate the strike. To some critics this last provision is a legal device for the federal government to use in trying to break the strike. And finally, the Act required all union officers to sign statements that they were not members of the Communist Party. By the time the Supreme Court struck down this provision in 1965, the labor movement had been thoroughly purged of its radical (and most active) members and unions.[103]

U.S. labor law is made not only by specific legislation, of course, but by how the legislation is interpreted by its administering agency (NLRB) and the courts. Although labor benefited from a number of legal victories following the passage of the NLRA, there also were several decisions that narrowed and limited legally-protected union activity.[104] For example, in NLRB v. Fansteel Metallurgical Corporation (1939), the U.S. Supreme Court effectively eliminated the sit-down strike as a legitimate labor weapon; in NLRB v. Sands Manufacturing Co.(1939), the Court withdrew protection from certain strike activity in the context of an existing collective bargaining agreement; and in NLRB v. Mackay Radio & Telegraph (1938), the Court allowed companies to permanently replace economic strikers. According to this last decision, although an employer has the right to protect and continue his business, no concomitant right to a job is given to an employee. This decision facilitates union-busting, since the strikebreakers can then vote out the union. (Under the Landrum Griffin Act, economic strikers retain voting rights for only 12 months after they have been replaced.)

A detailed examination of the ways the courts and the NLRB have interpreted labor legislation to create a climate that makes it difficult for workers to organize and carry out strategies to advance their class interests is well beyond the scope of this book and has been ably done by others.[104] One of these scholars, Katherine Van Wezel Stone, concludes that despite the broad provisions of the NLRA, "a procedural interpretation has emerged that treats the Act as a 'bare legal framework'" that has been interpreted to negate many of the substantive rights that it initially explicitly conferred on labor. By assuming an equality between management and labor, these judicial and administrative interpretations effectively make the NLRA incapable of realizing the very equality of standing that it was designed to create.[106] Another scholar, James B. Attleson, concludes that:[107]

> Thus, just as the nineteenth-century notion of contract was infused with older master-servant doctrines, a similar conclusion can be reached concerning modern American labor law. Although I do not mean to disparage the accomplishments and value of collective bargaining as a device for limiting otherwise arbitrary or at least exclusive exercise of managerial power, the institution does not seem to have altered basic legal assumptions about the workers' place in the employment relationship.

One measure of the success of the legislative/judicial climate in stifling the U.S. labor movement is the fact that union membership reached its peak (at 36% of the nonagricultural labor force) right after WWII and by 1988 had fallen to 12% of private-sector workers.

The political alliance between the Democratic Party and the labor unions constituted the third and final leg of the postwar consolidation.

Alliance with the Democratic Party

As WWII came to a close, the question of what direction U.S. labor would take in American politics still seemed open—there were proponents of non-partisanship, of an alliance with the Democratic Party, and of the formation of an independent labor party. Non-partisanship had a long tradition in the U.S. labor movement.[108] Indeed, the AFL did not endorse a Presidential candidate until Stevenson in 1952; and the CIO called the organization it formed to support FDR's candidacy in 1936 the Labor Non-Partisan League (LNPL). Even the LNPL's successor in the 1944 Presidential elections, the CIO-Political Action Committee (CIO-PAC), formally espoused non-partisanship, although it too aggressively worked to re-elect Roosevelt. But almost all viable Democratic Party candidates could count on PAC support, regardless of their opponents. Even the progressive Wisconsin Senator, Robert La Follette, couldn't get PAC support in his 1946 reelection bid, and lost as a result. Moreover, by 1936 it was clear that labor was increasingly voting for Democrats and that the Democratic Party agenda was more sympathetic to labor interests than the Republican.

Liberal union leaders, such as Murray and Hillman, rejected both non-partisanship and the formation of a third party in favor of an an alliance with the Democrats. (The PAC's treasurer, David J. McDonald, suggests in his autobiography that the CIO-PAC was started to head-off third-party activity.) During the 1944 campaign, PAC chairman Sidney Hillman worked vigorously to defeat any moves in the direction of a third party. New York's American Labor Party, for example, was transformed into an adjunct of the Democratic Party, and the once radical Farmer-Labor party in Minnesota was merged with the Democrats. The formation of an independent labor party had long been considered by many union leaders. Interest in a third party revived during the war in the face of both growing conservative sentiment in Congress and rank and file militancy. In 1944 the CIO in Michigan came out for a third party, the Detroit autoworkers formed a Michigan Commonwealth Federation, and the insurgency spread to several other states. So long as FDR was alive, however, the possibilities for third parties were limited to local campaigns. But Harry Truman was no FDR, and labor quickly became disenchanted with his domestic policies.

Although Truman spoke out for Roosevelt's 1944 Economic Bill of Rights, which expanded the scope of human rights to include health, education and housing, he was unable to manage the conservatives in his Congressional party — his economic conversion program failed, as did tax reform, national unemployment insurance, a higher minimum wage, effective price control, and a full employment bill — and his heavy-handed response to the postwar strike wave dismayed labor. In the spring of 1946 Walter Reuther, along with Norman Thomas and John Dewey, issued a call for a National Education Committee for a New Party.

The final straw came when Truman sacked the New Deal symbol, Henry Wallace, from his cabinet. In response, over 300 CIO delegates and allies formed the Progressive Citizens of America (PCA). In 1947 the PCA evolved into the Progressive Party, whose standard bearer in the 1948 Presidential election was Henry Wallace. But the Wallace candidacy did not get the support of organized labor. "On the contrary, it wedded trade-unionism to the two-party system" — specifically to the Democratic Party. The CIO leadership, and the major CIO unions, including the UAW, supported the Truman candidacy. Perhaps they were grateful for Truman's veto of the Taft-Hartley Act (even though it was overridden) — the threat of which may have moderated the legislation's terms. Perhaps they were hopeful that with a friend in the White House they might be able to have it repealed. But the marriage between the unions and the Democratic Party cannot be fully understood without also considering the role of Cold War foreign policy and the anti-communist hysteria that accompanied it. The Wallace candidacy became a Cold War loyalty litmus test. In January 1948, the CIO executive council passed a resolution rejecting the Wallace candidacy and endorsing the Marshall Plan; and any departure from the CIO position on the election was tantamount to organizational treason.

At the end of WWII the U.S. was poised to become the major economic power in the world. At the same time, many economic and political leaders were fearful that a demobilized economy could slip back into depression, and believed that access to international markets by U.S. corporations was essential if this was to be avoided. "So far as I know," Assistant Secretary of State Acheson told Congress, "no group which has studied this problem [conversion to a peacetime economy], and there have been many, as you know, has ever believed that our domestic markets could absorb our entire production under our present system."[109] There were, however, several obstacles to realizing the vision of open international markets for U.S. products. The existence of monopolies and protectionist tariffs, import quotas, and imperial preferences restricted access to the markets of the European powers and their colonial empires.[110] Some of these obstacles fell rapidly with the dismantling of the old colonial framework, but others took years to come apart, and many remain in place to this day. The General Agreement on Trade and Tariffs (GATT) has been only partially successful from the U.S. perspective; the International Monetary Fund (IMF) is still trying to impose free market principles in developing countries; and it was not until Thatcherism and Reaganism that the privatization of state monopolies began in earnest in Western Europe and North America.

Soviet expansion and the threat of Communism in countries such as France and Italy posed a further obstacle to realizing an international trade solution to the problem of how the U.S. could convert to a peacetime economy without falling back into depression. "Every time the Soviet Union extends its power over another area or state," wrote William C. Bullitt, the U.S.'s first Ambassador to Moscow, in 1946, "the United States and Great Britain lose another normal market."[111] According to David Eakins, many U.S. businessmen and politicans were not opposed to communist victories—electoral or otherwise—on political grounds primarily but by the threat such victories would pose to U.S. investment abroad.[112] The slowdown in what initially had been a vigorous European Recovery in the winter of 1946/7, accompanied by an upsurge of popular support for

Communist parties in France and Italy, made the possibility of Communist victories even more palpable. In appealing for approval of the Marshall Plan in December 1947, for example, Will Clayton warned that if the U.S. did not provide this aid, "the Iron Curtain would then move westward at least to the English Channel. Consider what this would mean to us in economic terms alone. A blackout of the European market could compel radical readjustments in our entire economic structure."[113]

For Truman, the combination of anti-communism and economic self-interest provided the key to obtaining approval for the institutions of the new economic order from a diverse constituency of Eastern financiers, domestically-oriented Midwest businessmen, liberals and conservatives in Congress, and the trade union bureaucracy. In exchange for Southern support for the Marshall Plan — "whose millions of dollars for rebuilding Europe's factories, roads, and cities would return as purchases of American goods" — and his anti-communist crusades abroad, he traded off what was left of the New Deal agenda and purged the remaining members of the New Deal inner circle.[114] For the union bureaucracy, the anti-communism crusade served as a vehicle for further solidifying their own power. The UAW serves as a case in point.

Reuther narrowly won the Presidency of the UAW in March 1946, and he did not finally consolidate his power against the Thomas-Addes-Communist faction (which had retained control of the Executive board and continued to dominate the life of the union) until the November 1947 convention.[115] Although Reuther and Thomas agreed on many issues, they differed in their identification of labor's main enemy. For Reuther, it was Communism and the Soviet Union. He supported the Cold War and the Marshall Plan, believed no communists should hold union office, and favored compliance with Taft-Hartley's non-communist affidavit. Indeed he became the first CIO opponent of the law to advocate compliance. Thomas and his supporters believed that the main enemy continued to be the large corporations. They argued, albeit weakly, against discrimination because of political beliefs and for formal procedures before removing anyone from office; and they opposed compliance with the Taft-Hartley law's non-communist affidavit. After a bitter campaign, characterized by slander and red-baiting, Reuther emerged triumphant, and within weeks the UAW was purged of all Communists, Communist sympathizers, and other leftists.

The purge in the UAW echoed similar steps throughout the CIO as the union, once and for all, repudiated the alliance with the left that, in the opinion of many, had made it possible in the first place. In 1949 the CIO expelled eleven allegedly communist-controlled unions. The UAW was among the CIO unions that used the anti-communist provisions of the Taft-Hartley Act to launch piratical raids against supposedly left-led unions, such as the Farm Equipment Union and the United Electrical Workers (UE). By 1953, for example, after five years of raids and the chartering of a rival international union, the UE, once the third-largest CIO union, had been parcelled out among eighty different unions and had lost half its membership.[116] Davis blames the anti-communist purges and the interne-cine battles they triggered, along with overt racism, for the failure of the CIO's "Operation Dixie" (its drive, launched in 1946, to organize the industrial workers of the South). The civil war among the unions spelled the end, he writes, of any substantive organizing in the South. Reflecting on the decision of the trade union bureaucracy to ally themselves with the Presidential wing of the Democratic Party, and thereby its foreign policy priorities, Davis concludes that: "By accepting the discipline of the Cold War mobilization, the unions and their liberal allies surrendered indepen-dence of action and ratified the subordination of social welfare to global anti-communism."[117] In the case of the AFL these loyalties included giving money, advice and direction to conservative European unions in their struggle with progressive unions for the hearts and minds of European workers. Although both the CIO and the AFL established European offices and staffs, the latter's were larger and more closely tied to the U.S. government both politically and financially. Since their merger in 1955, the AFL-CIO, through their Department of International Affairs and their AIFLD (American Institute for Free Labor Development) project in Cen-tral and South America and the Caribbean, the combined union continues to support, indeed some would say act as an arm of, U.S. foreign policy.[118]

Conclusion

The U.S. emerged out of WWII with the resolution of the crisis of the 1930s in hand: a combination of Keynesian-inspired, state spending (largely military) and increased consumption (domestic and international) to boost effective demand; and a new regime of labor-capital relations to dampen and control labor militancy. I have sketched out the institutional framework of this structure above and will next develop its ideological foundations. Before doing so, however, let us look at what this framework promised each of its participants.

For the corporations that dominated the mass production sector and for the state, the post-war framework purchased labor peace and a new level of social consumption to help absorb a productive capacity that had doubled during the war. The combination of legislation, administrative regulation, and collective bargaining contracts redirected labor militancy into predictable channels. Moreover, the peace was largely enforced by the trade unions themselves as the result of the legal liability provisions of Taft-Hartley, contractual constraints on the right to strike, the juridical procedures of the NLRB and contractual grievance mechanisms, and the acknowledgement of both managerial prerogatives and the linkage of wage increases to cost of living and productivity.

Bureaucratic control was built into the post-war collective bargaining settlements as management sought to use it to limit the impact of the unions, and to incorporate them into the joint disciplining of workers. Unions accepted the bureaucratization of the workplace as one of the quid pro quos for wages and other benefits, to codify and defend their negotiated gains, and perhaps more importantly, to strengthen the hand of their own leadership against the rank and file who had proved so contentious during the past decade. There is a difference of opinion regarding the culpability of union leadership for the bureaucratic structures that evolved in the 1930s and 1940s. To some, such structures resulted, at best, from the social democratic ideologies and corporatist visions of union leaders such as Reuther; and, at worst, from their self-interested pursuit of power and privilege. To others, the roots of bureaucratization were endemic to the U.S. system. For Gartman, for example, it was the strength of capital and its demands, and neither union perfidy nor ideology that were mainly responsible for the UAW's course. "All union leaders, regardless of their ideologies, were forced to operate within the structural constraints of the extant American political economy," in which the only role for unions was as a "partner to capital in disciplining and stabilizing the work force."[119] The state played a role in this process throughout the formative war years. To ensure stable, high level war production, it enforced a labor policy that gave the industrial unions security and benefits, such as maintenance of membership guarantees, in return for centralized control of rank and file militancy.

Domestically, the collective bargaining agreements' association of rising productivity, profits, and wages, combined with a "super-liquid domestic credit system," helped to bring about what has been described as the "intensive regime of accumulation."[120] The only legitimate area for labor-capital negotiations under the post-war contracts were economic issues. And, as we will see further in the following chapter, this emphasis on economism was reinforced by a social ideology that the consumption of goods was the prime measure of social achievement. Internationally, the post-war prosperity:[121]

. . . also fed on the desperate needs of the rest of the world for food, materials, and manufactures. Farms, factories, and homes in war-torn Europe and Asia had been ruined at the same time that the United States had been able greatly to boost its agricultural and industrial capacity. The only limitation on the foreign market for U.S. goods was the lack of gold or dollars in the customers' till. This was soon remedied to an important extent by the means of payment furnished by the Marshall Plan and similar types of aid to allies and client states. Financial obstacles to this generosity had been removed by the Bretton Woods agreement under which the United States had in effect been granted a license to print money for use in international trade and finance.

Labor's support for the postwar regime of labor-capital relations and U.S. foreign policy was thus instrumental in helping to realize almost a quarter century of U.S. capital's predominance over world production, trade, and finance. For those largely white, semi-skilled workers and their families who were covered by collective bargaining (some 25% of the population), the post-war agreements provided increasing wages and benefits that elevated them to previously middle-class or skilled worker thresholds of home ownership and credit purchases.[122] Although Davis estimates that another one-third to one-quarter of the population (most blacks and all agricultural workers) remained outside the post-war consumption boom, this still represents a substantial gain over the pre-war decades. Moreover, the new contracts incorporated a seniority system and an internal promotion system that mitigated the impact of seasonal production and business cycles on the core employees. And the contracts' welfare benefits, protection against inflation, and built-in progressive wage, provided a level of family security that was otherwise unavailable to U.S. workers in the absence of a welfare state of the form adopted in many Western European countries after the war.

The grievance procedures and system of job classifications in the new contracts also protected workers from being replaced by lower-waged competition, from having their job duties expanded, and from the previously arbitrary powers of foremen and line management. The importance of the latter should not be underestimated. In a majority of cases one of the fundamental grievances motivating the industrial uprisings of the 1930s, was "the petty despotism of the workplace, incarnated in the capricious power of the foremen and the inhuman pressures of mechanized production lines."[123] The pace of the line remained in the area of managerial prerogatives, however, and continued to be a source of conflict in the ensuing decades.

But the main advantage of the new agreements, in addition to "a lot of money," according to *Fortune,* in 1950, was that it provided the union bureaucracy with "a good rest" from the "constant merry-go-round" of short-term agreements and the pressures to continually deliver "more," in the face of ever-present challenges to their leadership. Moreover, for management, the new contracts meant that they have "regained control over one of the crucial management functions in any line of manufacturing — long range scheduling of production model changes, and tool and plant investment," by giving them the capacity to "plan with complete confidence in its labor relations."[124]

The achievement of these benefits did not take place without a change in the consciousness of American workers and consumers. In the next chapter we will look more closely at the development of the ideologies that supported the post-war regime and the ways they were being mirrored, interpreted and formulated in GM's annual reports.

CHAPTER V

ACCOUNTING REPORTS AND SOCIAL ENACTMENT

The 1950 contract between GM and the UAW was neither the first agreement between GM and the union (that was in 1937), nor the first of the post-war collective bargaining pacts (there were contracts in 1946 and 1948), but it was the most important, for its provisions "cast American labor relations in their post-war mold."[1] *Fortune* magazine applauded the agreement as a basic "affirmation . . . of the free enterprise system," and noted with approval that it accepted the existing distribution of wages and profits as "normal." Moreover, *Fortune* continued, by accepting cost of living changes and productivity as "basic economic facts" determining wages, the agreement both threw "overboard all theories of wages as determined by political power, and of profit as 'surplus value,'" and accepted the "macroeconomic principle of the progressive wage." And, by agreeing to limit negotiations to economic issues, and to cede such questions as the organization and control of the labor process and product pricing to the corporation as managerial prerogatives, the contract "expressly recognize[d] both the importance of the management function and the fact that management operates directly in the interest of labor." Finally, the contract acknowledged the principle of private supplementation of pensions and health insurance, thereby making it clear that they were not a responsibility of the government.[2]

As *Fortune* recognized, the agreement between the UAW and GM was based upon a number of overlapping and mutually reinforcing assumptions — about the nature of the relationships between the corporation and its workers and between wages and profits, about the role of the state, and about the limits to income redistribution. Continued acceptance of these assumptions and others, as we will soon see, was an essential ingredient for the success of the post-war social accord.

95

The social accord among the UAW, GM, and the state, depended for its continuation on three elements: the maintenance of the automobile industry's oligopolistic structure (dominated by GM); state policies to promote economic growth; and the depoliticization of the labor force. The first two conditions ensured GM's ability to pass on the price increases necessary to fund the contract's progressive wage structure, without impinging on profits and capital accumulation. The third condition ensured that labor would continue to accept the assumptions and limitations on which the 1950 contract was based. Although most apparent in the third case, all three conditions depended upon the creation and maintenance of a set of beliefs about the way the world works and about the individual's part in it; that is, upon ideologies. These three mutually reinforcing conditions, and the ideologies on which they in part relied, illustrate the interdependence of capital's quests for profitability, growth and social control.

In this chapter I will discuss the ideologies that reinforced these conditions in the decades following WWII and will show how GM, through its annual reports, helped to form and reproduce them. Before doing so, however, let us make a brief detour in our narrative to look more closely at the concept of ideology.

Ideology and Social Enactment

Social scientists interpret the concept of ideology in various ways. For some, ideology refers to a system of beliefs that is in opposition either to what is "real" or to what is scientifically correct. This interpretation spans the political spectrum and can be found, in somewhat different forms, in authors as diverse as Talcott Parsons, Alvin Gouldner, Clifford Geertz, Karl Popper, Louis Althusser, and even in the early Marx. When politicians in the U.S. refer to Communism as an ideology – in contrast with their own *non-ideological* beliefs in free enterprise and market competition – they are using ideology in this sense. This is *not* the way I will be using the concept here, for several reasons. Opposing ideology to science ignores the extent to which science and technology function as ideologies in contemporary society. Opposing ideology to reality assumes that there exists "out there" a material reality that is accessible to the "objective" observer who can more or less accurately represent it in terms of a neutral language. This assumption has been challenged in recent years by philosophers who argue that there are no absolute grounds for words such as reality and knowledge; that the object of knowledge, the so-called reality, is always already preinterpreted; that the observer belongs to the very world s/he wishes to interpret and that language is not a neutral vehicle for representation[3].

Ideology, as I am using the term here, does not refer to a set of illusions that can be contrasted with what is "really true." Instead, by ideology, I am referring to the vehicle through which people make sense of the social reality that they live and create day to day. It is "the interpretation in thought of the social relations through which they constantly create and re-create their collective being."[4] As such, ideologies are not illusions. They are real, "as real as the social relations for which they stand."[5] Ideologies help the members of society make sense of the things they do and say on a daily basis. As Goran Therborn puts it, ideologies tell individuals what exists, what is possible for them, and "*what is right* and wrong, good and bad, thereby determining not only conceptions of legitimacy of power, but also work ethics, notions of leisure, and views of interpersonal relationships, from comradeship to sexual love."[6] They are embodied in kinship organizations, in educational systems, in work situations, in social relationships in general, and in the legal contexts for kinship, education, work and social activity.[7]

Although, when understood this way ideology is not a uni-directional form of mind-control, imposed by a dominant class on everyone else, it still is linked with both power and domination. As Giddens argues, the ideologies that prevail in a given social system are those that have been incorporated within systems of domination so as to sanction their continuance.[8] But the ideologies that prevail do so, not simply by the handing down of appropriate attitudes from one generation to the next, but through their recreation in the rituals, institutions, practices, and language of day-to-day life — behaviors that enable human beings to negotiate a certain social terrain. As Barbara Fields puts it, "exercising rule means being able to shape the terrain."[9] And one way the ruling class shapes the terrain, she says, is through its access to resources through which it shapes the linguistic categories that constitute the parameters of our consciousness, and generates and disseminates ideas that in the name of common sense, self-evident truth, and/or natural behavior, legitimate and rationalize its domination.

Terry Eagleton illustrates the interpenetration of language, power and domination with the example of women. The oppression of women is a material reality (involving domestic labor, job discrimination, unequal wages, domestic violence, and so on); but it cannot be reduced to these factors alone. It is also a matter of sexual ideology, "of the ways men and women image themselves and each other in male-dominated society, of perceptions and behaviour which range from the brutally explicit to the deeply unconscious."[10]

The work of the French philosopher, Michel Foucault, provides another example of this linkage. In what Edward Said terms his greatest intellectual contribution, Foucault explains "how the will to exercise dominant control in society and history has also discovered a way to clothe, disguise, rarify and wrap itself systematically in the language of truth, discipline, rationality, utilitarian value and knowledge" — that is, in practices that are themselves ideological.[11]

Anthony Giddens identifies three ways that ideologies sanction and sustain the existing system of domination (whatever its form).[12] The first is by representing sectional interests as universal. For example, bourgeois ideologies present the egoistic pursuit of profits through market competition and the inviolability of property and freedom of contract as universal rights. These ideologies, which initially served to dislodge the aristocracy, were then used to reinforce the capitalists class's own social domination. Well into the 20th century, businessmen based their opposition to the passage of legislation to improve working conditions and wage levels, and to promote unionization on the right of individual laborers to privately and freely contract for their services with their employers. (In 1991, George Bush used the same argument to oppose legislation that would provide unpaid parental leave.) According to V. L. Allen, by universalizing sectional interests in this fashion, the dominant ideologies of capitalist society have influenced the mass of the population:[13]

> ... to see virtue in necessity. Individualism has been presented as a prime virtue. Private property has been sanctified; the accumulation of capital has been projected as an ideal objective; the receipt of profit has been given superiority over the manner of its making. The dominant ideology has other facets which also satisfy the needs of the system of capital. Virtue is attributed to inequality; only allocation by the market mechanism is described as free while only free enterprise activities are regarded as independent; success is synonymous with the ability to accumulate while poverty is failure.

A second way ideologies ally themselves with the dominant class (and/or race or sex) is by denying or obscuring the existence of contradictions and tensions that would otherwise translate into social conflict. One way this is done is by circumscribing the political agenda to exclude certain issues from the realm of political discourse, and to confine political activities to those regulated by the franchise. For example, the entire edifice of U.S. labor law removes class conflict from the political agenda by separating economic issues, subject to collective bargaining, from political issues, regulated by the two-party system and the vote. The boundaries of acceptable subjects in labor-management conflicts are carefully delineated and exclude, as "political issues" not subject to collective bargaining, so-called managerial prerogatives, such as decisions about what, where and how to produce and sell. Modes of conflict resolution are also narrowly defined (for example, the right to strike is limited, and industrial disputes are resolved through a time-consuming process of arbitration that defuses their impact). The role of the state in industrial disputes is limited to discrete interventions to facilitate their resolution, often in the interests of employers, although always in the putative interests of the public. This separation of the social and political from the economic is also illustrated in neoclassical economic theory, where the distribution of income, along with other political and sociological questions, are expunged and treated as either exogenously determined variables or accepted as given parameters.

Finally, ideology may take the form of naturalizing the present (that is, the status quo). In this case, existing patterns of social and institutional relations that have been socially constructed to reflect and reinforce sectional interests are presented as having resulted from the fixed and immutable workings of natural laws. Classical and neoclassical economics' reification of the self-regulating market economy inhabited by "economic man," with his inherent "propensity to barter, truck and exchange one thing for another," is an example of this ideological form.[14] Rather than seeing markets and the market economy as historically specific social constructs that represent only one alternative for regulating the production and distribution of social goods and services, markets are treated as natural and universal social phenomena. Transaction cost theory's paen to the modern corporate form represents another illustration of the ideological tendency to reify the status quo.

The *Fortune* magazine article about the post-war agreement between GM and the UAW, to which I referred in the introduction to this chapter, is ideological in all three senses. When it claims that management operates directly in the interests of labor, it represents management's sectional interests as universal ones. When it normalizes the existing distribution of wages and profits it naturalizes the present. And when it limits negotiations to "economic issues" that exclude managerial prerogatives and claims that the only source for wage changes are the basic economic facts of cost of living and productivity, and not political power, *Fortune* obscures the conflict between capital and labor over the fruits of social production.

Ideology assumes a special importance under capitalism. As Gouldner points out:[15]

> Never before in a class society did the security of a ruling class depend so much on the presence of belief systems appropriate to its rule. The new dependence on ideology by the ruling economic class under capital-

ism makes it a special ruling class, a class which must win over the minds of men [sic.], and especially over those of the other dominant classes; it is a class exceptionally dependent on ideologies in whose terms its dominance is defined as *legitimate*. The importance of an ideologically sustained legitimacy makes the ruling class under capitalism a new kind of ruling class — a hegemonic class (to use Gramsci's term).

In the balance of this chapter we will look at the various ways GM used its annual reports to create, reflect and sustain the ideological structures associated with the post-war social accord.

Ideology and Annual Reports

In using GM's annual reports as a major data source for the following discussion of post-WWII ideological constructions, I am rejecting two commonly-held views of these documents. The first is that they are neutral reflections of reality, a passive recounting of the year's events. The second is that they are outright fabrications intended to manipulate a somnolent audience: at best harmless public relations fluff, at worst, powerful propaganda that brainwashes a susceptible public. Contrary to each of these perspectives, I see annual reports as forming part of the symbolic universe of language, signs, meanings, norms, beliefs, perceptions, and values, through which individuals and institutions define themselves and are defined by others. These definitions do not exist once and for all, rather, as the recent histories of women and minorities have shown, they are contested terrains. Annual reports are among the many arenas in which such contests are played out.

Companies use their annual reports to construct themselves and their relationships with others as they they strive to create and maintain the conditions necessary for their continued profitability and growth. Obviously, annual reports are not the only weapons available to companies in these struggles over meaning, nor are they the most important ones; advertising, sales promotion, public relations campaigns, political lobbying, charitable contributions and sponsorships, support for scientific research, and so on, are all used. The ultimate source of corporate influence is through its ability to control, through property ownership, both access to the means of production (and hence one's ability to survive materially in the world) and the conditions of work. But there are several advantages in using annual reports, in this study, as a surrogate for these other vehicles.

Each year, in preparing the annual report, a company's management makes choices about the issues and social relationships that they consider sufficiently important or problematic to address publically. The annual report presents the world of corporate concerns in microcosm; it is a repository that is both comprehensive and compact. Moreover, because annual reports are regularly produced, they offer a snapshot of the management's mindset in each period; before they have had too much time to reflect on or fully digest the events they are describing and/or trying to influence. I do not intend to imply that annual reports are not prepared with care and forethought. They are; but the preparers of the annual report do not have the benefit of hindsight nor an extended period of reflection, and thus are caught up in the moods and passions of their time. Nor do I intend to convey the notion that the architects of annual reports have a privileged consciousness, an awareness that the world "really" isn't like the world they are presenting. The preparers of annual reports are part of the world they are describing. They are enmeshed in the very ideological constructions that they are simultaneously creating and perpetuating. So while, on the one hand, they may be very conscious of the partisan nature of what they are presenting, on the other hand, they may genuinely understand the world in exactly the terms they are conveying.

In this chapter we will be looking at a number of ideologies that in the post-WWII period reinforced the structure of the accord between labor, capital and the state. These ideologies, as we will see, did not emerge, full-blown, for the first time in 1950. Rather, they frequently appeared in earlier annual reports; sometimes, as in the case of the post-war social consumption norm, they are evident in foetal form; at other times, as in the cases of GM's relations with the state and with labor, the shape of the discourse changed with the changing terrain of struggle. Each of the ideologies served to reinforce the conditions necessary for the maintenance and reproduction of the post-war labor-capital-state accord: by rationalizing the basis for the oligopolistic structure of the automobile industry, by reinforcing the depoliticization of the labor force, by legitimating the military-industrial complex, or by fueling economic growth. I am not suggesting that GM invented these ideologies; all of them have had wide currency in American business thought. But by discussing them in their annual reports, GM contributed to their integration into social consciousness.

The Ideological Basis for Oligopoly

Drawing on the theories of Mill, Locke and Rousseau, the democratic ideal that prevailed in the United States through most of the 19th century assumed that a viable middle class, composed of small businessmen and landowners, would ensure the optimal functioning of political democracy. This ideal was exemplified by Abraham Lincoln when he said:[16]

> There is no permanent class of hired laborers among us. The prudent, penniless beginner in the world labors for wages a while, saves a surplus with which to buy tools or land for himself, then labors on his own account another while, and at length hires another new beginner to help him. . . . If any continues through life in the condition of the hired laborer, it is not the fault of the system, but because of either a dependent nature which prefers it, or improvidence, folly, or singular misfortune.

Whether Lincoln was accurately describing the experiences of most Americans in his day, is arguable. But accurate or not, the beliefs in individual opportunity and market competition, on which the ideal depended for its realization, were powerful elements in America's self-image in the 19th century, as they are today. The emergence, at the end of the century, of large corporations, trusts and cartels, and the economic power they represented, threatened this self-image and led to the first serious attempts at corporate regulation (for example, the Sherman and Clayton anti-trust acts, the establishment of the Department of Commerce, the hearings of the Industrial Commission between 1898 and 1902) and to the idea that through widespread stock ownership, all Americans, even if no longer self-employed, could still enjoy the benefits of property. Economists, politicians, stock exchange leaders, and investment bankers all encouraged widespread stock ownership as a way of giving people a vested interest in the existing economic order, and thereby promoting democracy and improving industrial and social relations.[17] The stock market crash of 1929, which was popularly attributed to a pattern of manipulative behavior by some of the hitherto most respected names on Wall Street and in the corporate community, challenged this vision of economic democracy. In 1932, the same year that the highly publicized hearings of the Senate Banking and Currency committee confirmed for many their belief that the securities industry was riven with fraudulent practices, Berle and Means published *The Modern Corporation and Private Property*. By arguing that some corporations had become so large and their ownership so diffuse that their managers could no longer be assumed to act in the interest of their owners, this seminal work provided advocates of regulation with further evidence of the dangers of the corporate form. And just as concerns about growing corporate power in the late 19th and early 20th centuries resulted in anti-trust legislation, they now led to the creation of the Securities and Exchange Commission to regulate both the securities markets and the disclosure of information by corporations.[18]

It was in this period of renewed public concern about the existence and uses of corporate power that GM began its rapid climb to the top of the

U.S. and world corporate hierarchy. GM eclipsed Ford as the number one auto-maker by the early 1930s, became the largest defense contractor during WWII, and when *Fortune* magazine began its *Fortune 500* listing in 1955, the company made its debut in the number one position. During this period, two ideologies emerge in GM's annual reports, that seem intended to counter public concerns about the corporation's dominant position and the power of its managers — the stakeholder model of the firm and managerialism.

In their influential work, Berle and Means argued that by surrendering control and responsibility, the passive owners of the widely-held modern corporation had surrendered their right that the corporation be managed in their sole interest. Berle and Means suggested further that by their self-interested behavior, the control groups (meaning top management) have cleared the way for the claims of a far wider group: "They have placed the community in a position to demand that the modern corporation serve not alone the owners or the control but all society."[19] Berle and Means are quite explicit that what they have in mind here is the diversion of a portion of corporate profits to these broader interests and a new role for management. The control of the great corporations, they argue, "should develop into a purely neutral technocracy balancing a variety of claims by various groups in the community and assigning to each a portion of the income stream on the basis of public policy rather than private cupidity."[20] As if anticipating the modern multinational corporate form Berle and Means concluded their work by warning that "the modern corporation has brought a concentration of economic power which can compete on equal terms with the modern state."[21] Indeed, "The future may see the economic organism, now typified by the corporation, not only on an equal plane with the state, but possibly even superseding it as the dominant form of social organization."

Berle and Means' prescription provided a potent formula for two ideologies which would serve to defuse the potentially explosive consequences of such a concentration of economic power in the absence of any democratic accountability.

The Stakeholder Model

Although GM never used the term "stakeholder," the picture of the corporation the company presented in its annual reports in the 1930s and 1940s, looks much like the later stakeholder model. This model of the corporation, which had its heyday in the 1960s, embeds the corporation within a network of interdependent stakeholders (employees, shareholders, suppliers, customers, and the general public), all of whom have a stake in the functioning and consequences of corporate activities. Throughout the conflicts of the 1930s and 1940s GM's annual reports stress the pluralistic basis of the corporation, and also management's responsibility for harmonizing the interests of, and maintaining the balance among, the various participants in the corporation's network of relationships.

In 1934, for example, GM asserts that "the maximum of progress is possible only by maintaining proper balance between the equities of all parties concerned, including not only those of employer and employee but also those of the public, upon whose continued demand for its products depends the welfare of the Corporation and of its employes themselves." (AR 1934, p.56) This view is expanded in GM's 1937 annual report:

> One of the prime responsibilities placed upon the modern industrial organization is that of encouraging and preserving satisfactory relationships throughout all the various phases of its business. . . . Dealers, suppliers, employes, stockholders, customers and the general public, as well as governments – all play essential parts in the industrial scheme of things. It is also true that in the case of large scale enterprises encompassing a wide scope and diversity of operations, this need for sound mutual relationships assumes greater importance and becomes at the same time more difficult.

> General Motors has long recognized that good and equitable relationships in their broadest sense begin with constructive and mutually satisfying policies as affecting those with whom the Corporation has direct and immediate dealings. Previous reports have emphasized the desirability of a fair and just distribution of the productivity of industry between their component parts – the supplier, the dealer, the employes, the stockholder and the customer. This is an extremely difficult task and one to which, in General Motors, a great deal of study and attention is constantly being given, for upon the continued maintenance of such an economic balance depends, to an important degree, the future development and progress of the Corporation.

> More recently a further responsibility has claimed an increasing amount of attention from management, and that is the relationship of industry to the community as a whole. (AR 1937, p.56)

In 1939 the annual report introduces the notion of responsibility beyond "the supplier, the dealer, the employee, the stockholder and the customer" to embrace "the community as a whole. . . . Today there is greater necessity than ever before for improving the relationships of industry as affecting human progress and for new interpretations of the fundamental place of industry in our social and economic structure." (AR 1939, p.33) This interest in the well-being of the community in general was used in earlier annual reports to justify the company's policy of decentralizing plant locations (which in the eyes of some was a strategy for diluting the impact of collective labor action by locating plants in areas with less militant labor forces). In both 1935 and 1937 GM presents and justifies its policy of decentralizing production in community interest terms:

> Such a policy is predicated upon the belief that the concentration of production in the great urban centers of population must necessarily lead to a higher cost of living as well as less desirable living conditions socially speaking. The Corporation believes that on every count its policy should be to operate in the smaller communities and in as many such communities as is economically sound and desirable. And in harmony with this policy it will be conducting in 1938 manufacturing operations in ten additional communities. . . . (AR 1937, p.40)

During WWII, tensions erupted between the large, technically-advanced businesses, to whom the bulk of the war contracts were going, and the smaller, generally less technically-advanced firms. The conflicts between these factions of capital were played out in Washington in the various agencies that were established to administer the different facets of wartime production in 1942 and 1943. These factional conflicts helped to further increase the relative autonomy of the Roosevelt government during the period. GM emerged during WWII as the number one military contractor in the U.S., a position they held until the end of the Korean war. Its representatives were central figures in the war management effort; most notably, its President, Knudson, who left the company to head the important War Production Board in 1941. These tensions, and the central place of GM in military production, explain the company's concern in 1942 and 1943 to expand the stakeholder model to emphasize both the interdependencies of its relations with its subcontractors, and the fact that GM itself was often a subcontractor as well. In 1942's annual report, for example, GM wrote that the company:

> went into the production of war materials with a valuable background of experience in working with thousands of other manufacturing concerns skilled in the supply of production of specialized items. It is working with nearly 19,000 outside suppliers and subcontractors throughout the country in its war production program.

> A special study of the 4,713 suppliers of fabricated parts included among these firms shows that 43% of them employ less than 100 people; 31% employed between 100 and 500 people; and 26% employ more than 500 people. . . .

> These facts serve to illustrate the pattern of American industry. In this pattern each one of a great variety of individual businesses of all types and sizes has its own background of experience and its own accumula-

tion of technical skills. But no one of them can be completely independent of the others. Each company, large or small, in the conduct of its business buys from and sells to other companies large and small.

As we stated in a recent stockholders message: "If the promise for accomplishment and progress in the postwar world is to be fulfilled, the broadest possible field of opportunity must be kept open for the launching of new businesses and the further development of existing businesses. The industrial methods and processes which have contributed, through lowered prices and increased efficiency, to the highest peacetime standard of living in the world must be still more intensively employed. There must be developed a still better understanding of the mutual benefits of a close relationship between small and large enterprises." (AR 1943, pp.15–16).

GM's management plays a key role in its stakeholder model of the firm, since it is management that must anticipate and orchestrate the interests of all of the parties.

Managerialism

As in the stakeholder model of the firm, the development of managerialism as a corporate ideology appears in GM's annual reports in the 1930s as the company began developing a response to the alleged dangers of the separation of ownership and control in the modern corporation. Throughout the 1930s GM's annual reports emphasized that, because GM's managers were also stockholders, they and the other stockholders had a common set of interests. The 1938 annual report, for example, acknowledges "that the old concept of individual ownership of mass production industries is no longer applicable" and that the "position is being approached, even if it has not already been reached when management, speaking in the broad sense, has become largely divorced from ownership." This creates a new role for management, that of trustee, and raises the question of whether "the responsibility of management . . . [is] likely to be as adequately discharged in the public interest and in the interest of the business itself . . . as when management and ownership are synonymous." (AR 1938, p.29). The report concludes that the solution is for managers to be stockholders in the Corporation: "While such managerial ownership may not bulk very large on a percentage basis, due to the large aggregation of capital involved, yet if it is to be assumed that the responsibility of any management to any business cause has any relationship whatsoever to the personal stake involved in that cause, then that relationship is important to the instance of the General Motors Corporation." As stockholders, GM's 1943 annual report explains, GM management's "interests are identical with those of other stockholders. Thus in General Motors there has been retained to an important degree the basic concept of owner-management under which in earlier days, when business were smaller, management and ownership were synonymous." (AR 1943, p.37).

In 1945, when a post-war strike wave shook public confidence, GM began to broaden the scope of management's responsibilities. By this time GM had established the view that management does not operate the corporation in the narrow interests of the owners alone. Rather, management harmonizes these interests with those of the firm's other constituencies. We can see this theme reflected in the following:

> It is not enough for industrial management to engineer and manufacture more and better products at ever lower cost. Industry has the additional responsibility of demonstrating sound social as well as sound economic objectives. The way a company produces is often as important as what a company produces. The successful business must adopt wise, constructive policies in the mutual interest of all concerned. It must apply these policies effectively. But more than that it must interpret them to employees, stockholders, suppliers, local communities, and the public at large, so that all will have a clear understanding of the company's actions and aims.
>
> Naturally, business must assume leadership for defining policy, not solely in its own interests but with recognition also of the prime importance of coordinating its interests with those of the public at large. Should any policy appear to be out of harmony with the public thinking at the moment, it becomes the responsibility of industry to present the facts to the forum of public discussion, fearlessly and aggressively.
>
> The policy of GM management is actuated by the principle that *"What is good for the country is good for General Motors."* This broad concept provides a basic pattern for building good relationships with the public and guides the organization in all its plans and activities. (AR 1945, p.26, emphasis added).

Towards the end of and immediately after the war years GM began to use its annual reports to lay the groundwork for the forthcoming negotiations with the trade unions by emphasizing labor's dependence upon management and the importance of management's organizing and planning activities for both corporate and overall economic growth. The elevation of managerial skills reaches its apotheosis in 1946 with the inclusion of a special section, signed by Chairman Alfred Sloan, on "The Importance of Management," which was accompanied for the first time by photographs of GM's officers. In this tribute to management Sloan spoke of GM's need for individuals with "talent of the highest order" to determine policy and provide effective administration. There are only a limited number of such individuals available, he cautions, and the demand for them "is always far in excess of the supply." Moreover, "the standards demanded of the future will be higher than ever before." The cost of attracting and retaining such talent is "relatively inconsequential" because: "What such talent may create in terms of more job opportunities, better product values, and additional profits is more important."

American mangement also had a key role to play in the Cold War, for Sloan. We are entering, Sloan wrote, an era of decision and opportunity:

> The decision to be made is whether or not the American economy over the long-term is to continue free and competitive or is to be regimented and directed by some form of governmental bureaucracy, following socialistic trends in the balance of the world.

> Here is a real challenge to the managers of American enterprise. They must display economic statesmanship of the highest order and demonstrate to the world at large and to our own people in particular that a free competitive economy, stimulating as it does technological progress based on increasing scientific knowledge, insures always an expanding volume of goods and services at progressively lower prices, thus promoting higher living standards and a more abundant life.

> The management of General Motors long ago accepted this broader responsibility. Likewise, in addition to applying itself to the day-to-day problems of business administration, it has recognized the importance of preparing for the future in the management phase of its own responsibility.

The immediate post-war annual reports also point out to employees that they have direct access to management and input into the labor process (implying, of course, that they need not rely upon the union as a means of communicating concerns). For example, the 1945 annual report discusses GM's "officially-encouraged two-way flow of ideas between management and employes" which is "symbolized by the 'open door' policy, by management's endeavor to understand and to anticipate the problems of employes on the one hand and on the other by the opportunity offered to employes, both to voice their viewpoints and to submit constructive suggestions for more effective operations and for the improvement of products to meet customers' needs." To further the "continuing objective of informed and understanding cooperation among all the people of the organization, the Employe Cooperation Staff was established under the supervision of a vice-president, in June, 1945." (AR 1945, p.16)

The 1945 and 1946 annual reports also try to demonstrate that the company can be relied upon to unilaterally "help make General Motors plants even better places in which to work." (AR 1945, p.15) The reports point out that as part of the company's modernization program there will be improved lighting and ventilation, cafeterias, restaurants, and parking lots; that the company provides vacation pay and a group insurance plan; and that General Motors is committed to providing employees with a "safe and healthy place to work." (AR 1946, p.21)

The notion of interdependency developed in the context of the stakeholder model is also used at this time to describe the internal relationships within the enterprise. Thus GM's 1947 annual report develops the importance of teamwork and the centrality of management to its working effectively:

> General Motors is made up of more than a third of a million men and women with a wide variety of abilities and viewpoints. For such a group to work together effectively takes good teamwork. Such desirable teamwork is furthered to the degree that each individual in the group understands that the interests of all are in a broad sense related. Progress of the group is dependent on every member doing his own particular job well. Such progress for the group as a whole provides opportunities for the individuals who compose the group. Management endeavors at all times to make sure that the business operates under conditions that encourage such teamwork and understanding.

These words were followed by a report on the company's "My Job Contest":

> A letter-writing contest was held for GM men and women in non-supervisory classifications and prizes were awarded for the best letters submitted on the subject, "My Job, and Why I Like It." In this way employes were encouraged to think seriously and constructively about their jobs. A board of independent judges determined the winning letters on the basis of sincerity, originality and subject matter. (AR 1947, p.24)

But lest employees forget that interdependency is a two-way street, the 1946 annual report points out that while the greatest asset GM possesses may be its people, "perhaps too little emphasis has been placed on the fact — and an important one — that this works both ways. Employe relationships are a two-way street, and it is equally true that the greatest economic asset of an employe is his job in a strong and successful company." (AR 1946, p.21)

The stakeholder model implies that there is a natural balance that must be maintained between the interests of employees, stockholders, suppliers, dealers, customers, and the general public. Managerialism suggests that only corporate management is capable of identifying, establishing, and maintaining this balance. Together, these ideologies helped displace public concerns regarding industrial concentration and reinforced public acceptance of America's oligopolies.

In the previous chapter, I traced the transformation of the labor struggles of the 1930s into an institutional framework dominated by corporations, the trade union bureaucracies, and juridical bodies (such as the NLRB) and that clearly defined the permissible terrains for both negotiation and labor activism. The framework placed certain items — for example the nature of the work process, investment decisions, pricing, and product design — outside the realm of collective bargaining, because they were managerial prerogatives. It defined certain labor actions — such as sit-down strikes, wildcats, and secondary boycotts — to be beyond the boundaries of legitimate behavior. To some extent, it even kept wages off the negotiating table, since the periodic increases gained by labor were, at least at the level of rhetoric, attributed to cost of living adjustments and productivity increases rather than to a redistribution of the relative shares of labor and capital. The maintenance of this social accord, particularly its built-in presumption of long-run increases in wages and benefits, only partly depended on the continuation of the industry's oligopolistic structure and on the ability to pass increased labor costs on to consumers. It also depended upon continuing economic growth; since the metaphorical pie was not being re-divided it had to grow larger.[22] Thus the post-war accord was not only designed to facilitate growth, it was dependent upon growth happening for its own success.

In addition to growth, the post-war accord developed from, and depended for its reproduction on, a social consciousness among workers regarding the nature of their interests and the limits of their capacities. This social consciousness contributed to the depoliticization of the America's labor force by elevating the norms of individualism and materialism, by normalizing the absence of choice and autonomy on the job, and by affirming the inevitability of scientific progress, technological change and their social consequences.

In the next sections of this chapter I will use GM's annual reports to examine the ways this social consciousness was shaped through a heightening of two quintessentially American ideologies: the social consumption norm and the ideology of science and technology.

Social Consumption Norm

The post-war period introduced a new norm of social consumption that redirected workers' energies into the pursuit of individualistic and familial consumption, and increased aggregate demand (and thus the realization of surplus value). The emphasis on economic issues (wages and benefits) as the only legitimate subjects for labor-capital negotiations under the collective bargaining agreements was reinforced by a social ideology that made the consumption of goods the prime measure of social achievement, and consumer choice a central element of democracy.

American business helped carry out the post-war consumption ideology by inducing changes in fashion, creating new wants, setting new standards of status, and enforcing new norms of consumptive behavior. The impact of this norm on post-war labor consciousness was to rechannel social energies away from social conflict and political participation into privatized consumption. Its lesson was that class struggle was not necessary in a liberal capitalist society where everyone was (or soon would be) middle class.

The building of the new social consumption norm takes a priority place in GM's annual reports in the 1950s and 1960s. Indeed, an average of 23% of the reports' text between 1950 and 1966 is devoted to creating and reinforcing the norm and its accompanying patterns of suburbanization, the idealization of the nuclear family, and the drive to possess the latest in styling and technology. (This contrasts with 6.5% of the reports' text between 1926 and 1939.) In GM's case, the norm was built by suggesting to consumers that the ownership of GM products (automobiles and appliances) was essential to living the "American way of life;" by linking GM products with the individual's leisure activities, social standing, and upward mobility; and by emphasizing "dynamic obsolescence," and the necessity of trading in and trading up to the latest features in design, styling, and "performance."

In Chapter IV I identified several marketing innovations that GM introduced in the 1920s and 1930s. These innovations, which helped shape consumer tastes and practices in the post-war period, included the extension of credit, initially to dealers but then, through installment sales, to customers; the introduction of the annual model change; the acceptance of trade-ins; and the creation of a complete line of motor cars from the lowest to the highest price. Lawrence White credits these early marketing decisions with setting into place the practice of upgrading consumer preferences by convincing the customer to trade-in more frequently and to a more expensive model or make, for example, from a Chevrolet to a Pontiac.[23]

Many of the characteristic "improvements" of the automobile in the post-WWII period also made their initial appearances in the 1930s. In addition to annual model changes, these included "the Sculptured Design, The Brightly Colored Body, The Large Engine, The Low Lean Look."[24] In discussing the latter feature, known as "Streamlining," in its annual reports in the mid-1930s, GM showed a reticence that is surprising to those familiar with the enthusiasm displayed for such features in the post-WWII period. The company cautions readers that while streamlining reflects a trend in design that is "quite in vogue," in the case of motor cars, "it does not offer any important economies in either fuel cost or operating cost." (AR 1933, p.14). "Except for a negligible portion of motor car travel, the contribution of streamlining is definitely limited to the question of styling. There are no other advantages that can be obtained otherwise." (AR 1934, p.17). Throughout the 1920s and 1930s the emphasis in GM's annual reports was on riding comfort, safety, engineering innovations and value. There is a hint of the coming social consumption norm in the following excerpt from GM's 1937 annual report (which is also clearly related to the high level of labor militancy in GM's plants at the time):[25]

> The Corporation recognizes the importance of improving the economic position of its workers from the standpoint of both their progress and stability, hence advancing their status in a fundamental way. Such a policy is not only socially desirable but economically necessary, because of the vital necessity of developing every worker into the broadest possible consumer. (AR 1937, p.43).

But the job of expanding consumption on a broad scale, "the relentless war against saving and in favor of consumption,"[26] awaited the end of WWII. It began in earnest with GM's 1948 annual report (the first to include a picture on its cover as well as color photographs inside). In the immediate post-war years the automobile companies were able to sell any car they could produce, and it was not until 1949 that a combination of expanded production and a slight recession brought demand and supply into balance. During the Korean war, the government controlled both prices and production, so it was actually not until 1953 that the U.S. auto industry entered the period of "active styling competition, rapid model changes, and a proliferation of models" that characterized the automobile industry for the next generation.[27]

The new social consumption norm involved a great deal more than multiple makes and models and rapid styling changes. It meant a new way of life and pattern of beliefs. Wage earners were stratified on the basis of their consumption patterns and oriented their lives around career, leisure and consumption. In this nation in which everyone was (or soon would be) middle class, upward mobility was taken for granted. The norm also invested a deep and distinct emotional meaning in the nuclear family. Political life revolved around a formal rather than a substantive democracy, with consumer sovereignty subtly supplanting the latter as the vehicle for exercising free-choice. The development of a social ideology around the role of women was an integral part of the new pattern of beliefs.

Women became an important part of the labor force during World War II. In the automobile industry, the number of women employees increased from 6% of the production work force in 1940 to a wartime peak of 26%. (By 1943, women comprised 30.7% of GM's hourly rate force; up from 9.5% at the end of 1941.) Women even appeared in GM's annual reports during the war. In 1943 the annual report included a series of photographs of women wearing over-alls, peering around six-blade aircraft propellers and assembling and inspecting carburetors: "That women have displayed a fine attitude towards their work and have made an exceptional record in the tasks assigned is the unanimous testimony of plant managers." (AR 1943, p.27) In 1942 the War Labor Board, in a case brought against GM by the UAW and the United Electrical Workers (UE), actually established the principal of equal pay for equal work as national policy.[29]

At the end of the war the UAW and automobile industry management cooperated in purging women from the labor force; a pattern that was repeated throughout the U.S. economy. The UAW and GM, for example, agreed that women who did "men's" work during the war had earned only temporary seniority, selectively applied seniority rules only to women who had worked for GM before the war, and attributed wartime seniority only to these pre-war positions. The UAW did little to challenge the local seniority lists and agreements that provided that no female could replace a male without the union's agreement. By July 1945, women comprised only 19% of the automotive workforce; by the end of August, the proportion was 10%. As production recovered and workers who had been laid off during the immediate post-war recession were re-hired, companies and unions simply ignored the women on the seniority lists. State governments rapidly reinstated the "protective" legislation they had relaxed during the war years and reclassified large numbers of jobs as restricted to men.

The interest of male workers in reasserting their prerogatives in the labor market combined with the staying power of patriarchal ideology and the concern of industry to accelerate the level of consumption. The result was a social consumption norm in which women played a central but restricted role. The photographs in GM's annual reports in the 1950s and 1960s present numerous examples of both the ways this new social consumption norm was reflected in these reports, as well as how it reinforced patterns of belief concerning women's place.

Throughout the 1950s women appear in the annual reports as adornments and symbols of (presumably) male achievement. In 1954, 1955 and 1956, for example, the annual reports included a series of photographs of women alongside automobiles. In each case, the female model's appearance, how she is dressed, her hairstyle and make-up, her posture, combine to communicate a "style" that is appropriate for the social level of the automobile with which she is presented: for example, from the elegantly coiffed, gowned, and bejewelled society woman standing by the top-of-the-line Cadillac, down through the Buick, the Oldsmobile, the Pontiac, and finally to the Chevrolet, whose "neat" but not glamorous model is dressed in a simple two-piece suit. The cover of 1954's annual report provides another example. This cover depicts the "climactic moment" at the conclusion of GM's annual "Motorama," where the company introduced their new cars to the public. At the front of the stage, appearing as a frame for the events going on behind them, are seven women, three in evening gowns and four ballerinas. As they stand there, "a car busts through a mist cloud high in the air before whirling gracefully downward on a flying turntable over stage and lagoon" (AR 1954). Male dominance is a constant message throughout GM's annual reports in this period. For example, whenever a woman and a man are in a car, it is the man who is doing the driving.

Consumption patterns oriented around the possession of a house in the suburbs, the ownership of new automobiles and appliances, and nuclear-family-centered leisure activities are developed and reinforced through annual report photographs and covers. In a series of photographs that appeared in the 1962 annual report, GM cars are shown in front of houses. In each case the house and the people (their attire, appearance, activities) convey a social status that is appropriate to the automobile with which they are shown.

In another series of photographs, from 1961's annual report, showing "GM Products in Use" — going to dancing lessons, a day at the hunt club, driving the children to school, at a picnic, attending a club meeting, on a campus, at the florist, or going dining — the families that are depicted are all young, attractive, Anglo-saxon and prosperous. They are all involved in family-centered leisure activities that require the automobile. The small town lifestyle, to which all Americans are assumed (and are learning) to aspire, is depicted on GM's annual report covers in this period as well. For example, in 1949 the annual report cover is titled "Saturday Scene." According to the accompanying text the cover:

has pictured the familiar bustle of a Saturday in the Town Square – the sidewalk groups of neighbors paused for casual talk, the market doors a-swing with laden housewives, the tireless youngsters, the dogs, the bikes, and – of course – the cars.

We are sure you will notice many other familiar details – the cool white church spire, the farmers in town for the week's supplies, the television aerial atop a building of obviously venerable age, the spreading town elm and, sheltering all, the enduring hills, cradling liberty and human dignity in their protective folds.

The social ideology of the nuclear family, and the woman's (that is, mother's) place within it (specifically at home, and in the kitchen and/or the laundry), appears in a series of photographs promoting the Frigidaire line of appliances. As was the case in the prior photographs, the "middle class" home that is illustrated as typical is well beyond the financial resources of most workers but serves to increase their consumption hunger pangs.

"Changing Shifts," the title of the cover of 1951's annual report, illustrates the interplay of a number of the themes characteristic of the post-war social consumption norm. The text accompanying this cover states:

> In no other country could an artist find a scene like the typically American plant John Falter has painted for our cover this year. At first glance – it's as American as the lollipop of the little boy snuggling against his dad's jacket. Or the smiles on the faces of the day shift hurrying to meet their families – the brisk cheerfulness of the evening shift going back to work – even the friendly wag of the little dog's tail.

> Looking a bit closer – it's as American as the cars closepacked in rows around the plant parking lot – and the plant itself. For what clearer expression of our vast productivity than these – the worker's cars which so well define the standard of living our people share. And the busy modern plant which builds – perhaps cars, perhaps any one of the wealth of products which are the common benefits of our way of life. Yes, we think you'll agree this picture describes better than any words or figures that combination of a free industry and a free people which gives this country the ability to produce "more and better things for more people" – and the strength to defend this fruitful heritage against the challenge of any alien creed or power.

We see in this text the extent to which the social consumption norm and a social ideology concerning women's place in the home were intermingled in the 1950s and 1960s. Indeed, the position of women in this period, especially in contrast to the part they played in the labor force during the war years, only makes sense when it is considered within the broader context of the period's social consumption norm.

The post-war social consumption norm depended upon consumers who were motivated to possess the latest in styling and technology and who were dissatisfied with their existing possessions, regardless of their functionality, if they were perceived as being out-of-date. This attitude, along with a fatalism towards the inevitability of machines replacing labor, was reinforced and reproduced by another of the major post-war ideologies, the belief in the omnipotence of science and technology.

Omnipotence of Science and Technology

For many social observers the specific form of ideology that characterizes the capitalism of the late 20th century is the belief in the omnipotence of science and technology, combined with an idealization of progress and expertise. The intellectual roots of this ideology lie in the Enlightenment critique of traditional religious and metaphysical thought and its elevation of the scientific method and rational thought. But for this ideology's fullest expression we must look to what Jurgen Habermas has described as advanced capitalism's "technocratic consciousness."

Technocratic consciousness meets all of Gidden's criteria for an ideology. First, it represents sectional interests as universal. It does this by understanding science, not as one form of possible knowledge, but *as* knowledge. (Habermas refers to this belief of science in itself as "scientism.") Technocratic consciousness represents scientists and technicians as an autonomous class that is devoted to the neutral pursuit of knowledge and technical efficiency and effectiveness, "and whose work can be judged by its fruits, superior consumerism, comfort and health."[30] In addition, behind a facade of objective necessity, technocratic consciousness conceals the interests of the classes and groups that actually determine the function, direction and pace of technological and social development.[31] Technocratic consciousness effaces existing contradictions and tensions by transforming all questions into technical ones, and depoliticizing and defusing them. Allen describes it this way:[32]

> For the vast majority of individuals who play no part in economic or social decision-making because individually they possess no power, technology is a given factor, it is something they live with and accommodate to. Its consequences are forced on them and, even thought it may harm many of them individually by putting them out of work or destroying them in war, it is generally perceived as being beneficial.

Finally, technocratic consciousness naturalizes the status quo by presenting it as having been objectively determined by technical requirements. Technology is elevated into a mechanism that is completely independent of all human objectives and decisions and that proceedes independently of social structures in the automatic manner of a natural law.

The idealization of progress (a perspective which, in the U.S., goes back to the 19th century and the mystique of the frontier) is an integral part of technocratic consciousness. By combining the belief in the omnipotence of science and technology with the idealization of progress, corporations such as GM have been able to get the entire nation to accept as natural and inevitable the technological transformation of the labor process (with all of its social consequences), to willingly spend billions of dollars on more "advanced" weapons systems, and to "demand" more and more product "improvements." For to oppose technology is to oppose progress, an act as outrageous as suggesting that the earth is flat.

The romance between science, technology and progress and U.S. industry blossomed during World War II. And GM, as America's largest defense contractor, had the most to gain from its continuation after the war. Such potential was not immediately apparent, however. For example, in its 1940 annual report, GM warns that spending on national defense provides an economic stimulus that is, at best, temporary:

> Such a prosperity, however, is essentially artificial and because production for national defense is unproductive wealth in the sense that it does not add to the standard of living, it is added to overhead on the economy. As a matter of fact, over the long pull position, it means a reduction in the standard of living, unless off-set. (AR 1940, p.15)

But by 1944, GM was using its annual reports to advocate continuing military-industrial cooperation, as the following excerpt indicates:

> If we are to face the realities and not take another chance on being caught too late with too little, we must learn from present experience and reverse our pre-war concept as to the importance of military preparedness . . .

> After the war, if we are to win the peace, we must continue to move forward by maintaining for preparedness equally close liaison between the armed services and industry. This calls for unceasing application of the day-to-day developments of science and industry to the improvement of war materials and methods of manufacturer, so that American industry shall ever be ready to set in motion quickly, if needed, its vast powers of mass production for war with minimum changes in plant and equipment. (AR 1944,p.19)

In the same annual report, GM connects military programs with consumer product improvements, and science with both unimpeded business enterprise and progress:

> The Corporation at the right time will expand its peacetime research, engineering and development staffs and aggressively pursue its past policy of continual product improvement. This will include the development of new products and the utilization of new inventions, and the application to the art of metal fabrication of scientific knowledge, use of materials and technological processes discovered and developed during the war.
>
> Modern science is the real source of economic progress. It has brought within reach of more and more people comforts and conveniences, more leisure, more and better job opportunities. There can be no real ceiling on opportunity if science continues to move forward. It is of course of prime importance that national economic policies be progressive, removing obstacles that limit business opportunity and encouraging the spirit of business venture. The objective is to utilize properly all existing knowledge and techniques in engineering, production and distribution which will lead to a consistently advancing standard of living. General Motors in its postwar program is dedicated to that objective. (AR 1944, p.28)

Throughout the 1950s, GM's annual reports emphasize progress and change as universal virtues that are characteristic of the American people and American industry. For example, the cover of the 1950 annual report, titled "3PM — Anytown U.S.A.," shows children leaving a handsome brick schoolhouse at the end of the school day. The accompanying text explains that "Youth and the vigor that goes with it are peculiarly the characteristics of America . . . reflected in our attitude towards new things, new ideas; in our willingness to experiment and to risk in the hope of doing still better the things we have been doing well." A similar message is communicated in the 1953 report cover, depicting the traveling show called the "General Motors Parade of Progress," "a traveling educational show designed to make clear the processes by which American industry contributes to our national well-being and progress. The basis of that contribution is the efforts and initiative of individuals perfecting new methods and processes, making new discoveries and inventions." (AR 1953, p.17) Another traveling show, "Previews of Progress," is described as "a two-man science and engineering show designed primarily for appearances at school assemblies. Since 1946, when the present Previews activity began, 12¾ million people have attended showings by the seven Preview units traveling in the United States . . . and countless others saw the shows at the Motorama or on television." (AR 1955, p.15).

GM uses its annual reports to explicitly link science and progress, as universal values, with its own activities. For example, 1949's annual report associates GM's "leading role in the 'revolution on wheels'" with the "equally miraculous" past fifty years of progress "in the mechanical arts, in medicine, in physics, in chemistry. Three motivating forces have made possible this amazing performance: expansion of fundamental knowledge through scientific research; provision of adequate economic rewards for great accomplishment; and exercise of individual responsibility and self-reliance." (AR 1949, p.5)

GM uses the rhetoric of science and technology in its annual reports to mystify the true nature of the superfluous product variation and differentiation that are essential to the implementation of the social consumption norm. For example:

> The traditional quality and value that GM offers its customers stem from a never-ending search for new and improved products and better ways of making them. In highly competitive modern industry, technological progress is a "must."
>
> General Motors owes its long-time leadership in large part to its continued advancement in research, engineering, process development and styling. A great many of the features the consumer takes for granted in today's products are the results of years of study, experimentation and testing in the research laboratories of the Corporation and the divisions. (AR 1953, p.13)

The Motorama, which is featured in GM's annual reports between 1953 and 1955, not only introduced each year's new cars to the public but was "also a means of lifting the curtain on some of the forward developments being created in General Motors studios and laboratories. The reaction of the public to GM experimental or 'dream' cars and the Frigidaire 'Kitchen of Tommorrow' displayed at the Motorama have played an important part in future design planning." (AR 1955, p.15) But "The benefits of GM research and engineering are not confined to General Motors alone. GM engineers and scientists often carry information about their work to the technical community and to education where all may share its benefits. In these and other ways the information gained through technical advancement in GM adds to the general progress of the nation." (AR 1956)

The word progress is used repeatedly in the 1950s by GM in its annual reports: "GM Employes Benefit Through Serving Progress" (AR 1955); "From the Progress of the Past . . . The Promise of the Future," (AR 1957); "Fifty Years of Progress"(AR 1957); "Review of Operations and Product Progress," (AR 1957); "Shareholder Growth Reflects Fifty Years of Progress" (AR1957); "Product Progress" (AR1958); and "The Fifties – A Decade of Progress" (AR 1959). And progress, GM takes care to point out, depends upon technology, which in turn enlarges the comforts of life: "Technology has become a major force for opening the frontiers of economic progress and for further improving the standard of living of the American people" (AR 1956, p.7). The following item from the 1957 annual report sums up very well the attitude GM wishes to convey:

> If the progress of the past 50 years seems remarkable, the promise of the next 50 years is even more so. To bring that promise to reality General Motors will continue to place emphasis on the "inquiring mind" approach to problems. This attitude of the inquiring mind, which holds that everything and anything can be improved, is cultivated in all fields at GM, from technical research to human relations and financial planning. While to some it may sound old fashioned, it holds the key to progress. It is the only attitude that will make it possible to continue to provide MORE AND BETTER THINGS FOR MORE AND MORE PEOPLE. (AR 1957, p.9)

White's conclusion — "Perhaps the most striking thing about automotive technology in the postwar period has been the lack of fundamental change or advance" — stands in marked contrast to GM's post-war claims about its advances in product engineering. "Cars built in 1968," White argues, "are not fundamentally different from cars built in 1946." And, he continues:

> Even in the areas in which modern cars do differ from their early postwar predecessors, such as the widespread application of automatic transmissions and power-assisted equipment, the basic technology had been developed before the war, and postwar developments represented achievements in refining this technology rather than in any fundamental change.[33]

Conclusion

The social consumption norm reinforced the terms of the collective bargaining accord by focusing the worker's attention away from the job and fellow workers toward the pursuit of "more and more things." The job was not an end in itself but rather a means to an end, the acquisition of consumer goods. Moreover, the productive apparatus itself, and the goods and services which it produces help to impose the social system as a whole upon all of us. In his seminal study of contemporary society and ideology, Herbert Marcuse emphasized how:[34]

> The means of mass transportation and communication, the commodities of lodging, food, and clothing, the irresistible output of the entertainment

and information industry carry with them prescribed attitudes, habits, certain intellectual and emotional reactions which bend the consumers more or less pleasantly to the producers and, through the latter to the whole. The products indoctrinate and manipulate; they promote a false consciousness which is immune against its falsehood.

The endless pursuit of happiness through the acquisition of things reinforced the post-war labor agreements' emphasis on economic issues. The social consumption norm offers consumption and consumer choice as substitutes for social conflict and political participation. If we do not participate as citizens and workers, Marcuse suggests, "we do participate as consumers, exercising our freedom to choose our satisfactions whenever we wish — as if by magic when new products suddenly materialize on the store shelves, we feel that the economy is responding to our every impulse and desire — which is more than we can say about our elected representatives and nonelected public administrators," or about our bosses or trade union officials.[35] The availability of "choice" in the marketplace, Marcuse argues, substitutes for the lack of the availability of choice in the rest of life — especially on the job, where the rationality of technocratic consciousness "demonstrates the 'technical' impossibility of being autonomous, of determining one's own life."[36]

The ideologies of social consumption and science and technology were reinforced by state policies and spending practices. The Federal government came out of WWII committed to pursuing anti-depression policies. The 1946 American Employment Act, for example, committed the state "to use all practical means . . . to promote maximum employment, production and purchasing power."[37] In practice, this meant the massive use of Keynesian-inspired state spending to stimulate economic growth. In the case of the automobile industry, much of the post-war state spending was for programs that promoted the use of the automobile, indeed favored it over mass transit (for example, by building roads, schools, hospitals and water and sewer systems in the suburbs).[38] Government programs offered low-interest loans and tax advantages to homeowners and families with children, and encouraged consumer borrowing. GM is among the many U.S. corporations whose research and development activities have been heavily subsidized by the state through tax policies, research and development grants to industry and universities, and by massive spending for weapons development and production.

The institutional and ideological structures described in this and the preceding chapter were in large part the result of decades of social conflict. And while they by no means represented an unabashed victory for the working class — indeed they included significant compromises and innovations that strengthened employers' hands in future conflicts and promoted capital accumulation — they also were not called into being simply *because* they were functional for business interests. But once in place these structures became part of the conditions under which business was required to operate. What was at one point a consequence of social conflict, becomes at a later time the premise upon which capitalist accumulation takes place. In the next chapter we will see how these conditions also became the source of future constraints to continued capital accumulation and the basis for a new round of conflict.

CHAPTER VI

THE UNRAVELLING OF THE SOCIAL ACCORD

In Chapter III I decomposed the problem of capital accumulation into two components: the problem of productivity, that is, of producing as large a profit as possible for the inputs consumed; and the problem of realizing that profit in the market place. For almost two decades after WWII ended, it appeared that U.S. mass production industries had solved both problems. On the one hand, the linking of wages, price levels and productivity seemed to ensure that increased wages would not reduce the rate of profit. On the other hand, the combination of higher wage levels and an expanded level of consumption seemed to ensure that ever increasing quantities of goods would be produced and sold.

The institutional and ideological framework of labor, capital and state relations that was crafted in the years surrounding WWII seemed to offer something for everyone. For capital, and the state, the post-war framework promised labor peace and a new level of social consumption to help absorb a productive capacity that had doubled during the war. For those workers who were covered by them, the post-war agreements represented a trade-off that provided increasing wages and benefits in exchange for the right to power and decision making, both on the job and in the public policy arena. But the continued viability of the post-war framework had several preconditions. For capital (the mass production corporations), it depended upon maintaining oligopolistic control over domestic markets, an expanding economy, and the continuation of the U.S. industry's worldwide productivity advantages. For labor unions, it depended upon their maintaining the capacity to organize and mobilize the working class, while at the same time limiting their demands. These preconditions began to unravel in the late 1960s–early 1970s, and the sources of this disintegration can at least partly be found within the terms of the post-war accord itself and the ideologies that both reinforced and destabilized it. In this chapter we will look at this process of disintegration, and will again draw on GM's annual reports.

Perhaps the best place to begin is with a quote from *The Future of the Automobile,* a report from MIT's International Automobile Program:[1]

> Over a period of some 15 years, beginning around 1960, the Japanese auto producers evolved a production system based on a new approach to the social organization of the factory and the production chain. Different producers have taken somewhat different approaches, and it is an error to overlook these variations; however, it is clear that on average the Japanese auto industry requires fewer hours of labor by factory workers, designers, technicians, and managers at all levels of the production chain to make a vehicle of any given description than any other nation's auto industry. In addition, the Japanese auto industry on average has a very high level (perhaps the highest level) of manufacturing accuracy, a wage level nearly the lowest among the Auto Program countries, a lower level of inprocess inventories, and greater versatility in shifting model mix and in developing new products. This contributes to lower production costs, high product quality, and flexibility in meeting changing market conditions.[2]

In terms of our theoretical framework, the MIT Report is saying that Japanese automakers were more effective than U.S. manufacturers in both generating and realizing surplus value. But the accord that had been so carefully constructed was ill equipped for meeting this competitive challenge. Indeed, by the time the Japanese became significant factors in the U.S. market, beginning after the first oil shock in 1973, the contradictions inherent in the accord's institutional and ideological components were already having an impact on the U.S. domination of the world motor vehicle market. This impact is apparent from world motor vehicle production statistics in the two decades immediately preceding and following WWII:

Average & peak year motor vehicle production
(Cars & trucks in millions of units)

	World Production		U.S. Production		
	Peak Year	Annual Average	Peak Year	Annual Average	U.S. as % of World
1920–1929	6.3 (1929)	4.1	5.3 (1929)	3.6	86.6%
1930–1939	6.4 (1939)	4.1	4.8 (1937)	3.1	75.5%
1946–1955	13.7 (1955)	8.6	9.2 (1955)	6.3	71.9%
1956–1965	24.1 (1965)	16.7	11.1 (1965)	7.8	46.9%

(Source: World Motor Vehicle Data, Motor Vehicle Manufacturers Association, various years.)

Annual average motor vehicle production doubled in the decade following WWII, with the U.S. maintaining its dominance over the industry. But notice what begins to happen after 1955: annual average world production doubles again, but U.S. production doesn't and the U.S. share of world production falls to below 50%.[3] The North American share of production continued to fall in the ensuing decades – to 32.6% from 1966–1975 and to 27.8% from 1976–1981. This shift in the locus of production had two interrelated sources. First, competitors, initially from Europe but later and more significantly from Japan, entered the world market. And second, U.S. manufacturers increasingly internationalized production (for example, GM's total factory sales produced outside the U.S. and Canada increased from 5.7% in 1946–1955 to 16.0% in 1956–1965; to 19.6% in 1966–1975.)[4]

The change in the locus of production also affected the distribution of market shares in the U.S.[5] The first wave of imported cars arrived in the U.S. from Europe in 1956. By 1959 they had captured 10.2% of the U.S. market (from under 1% prior to 1956). The imports, typified by the Volkswagen Beetle, were small and intermediate models, a segment that had been completely ignored by the U.S. manufacturers. The U.S. automakers responded with compact models, and the imported car market share fell back to 5% in 1962 and then gradually increased throughout the 1960s to a new peak of 10.5% in 1970. This led to the introduction of a new round of small American cars that – aided by rising European wages and the devaluation of the dollar in 1971, which made European cars relatively more expensive – once again pushed down the imports market share. Early Japanese imports had relatively little success in the U.S., but the introduction of high quality, low-priced models in the 1970s succeeded in further eroding the market share of the small European imports. The dual energy shocks of the 1970s (in 1973 and 1979) further benefited the Japanese – in 1979, with Japanese imports approaching 20% of the U.S. market, the U.S. and Japan began negotiations to restrict imports of Japanese automobiles to the U.S.

By the mid-to late 1960s these shifts in the profile of the international motor vehicle industry were taking place against the backdrop of what would prove to be a longterm slowdown in economic growth. For the western industrialized nations the two post-war decades were ones of economic expansion and increasing standards of living. In the U.S., the standard of living of the average American rose steadily: average family income, wages and salaries (adjusted for inflation) all climbed, the share of the workforce with wages below the poverty level fell, and an increasing part of the workforce was entitled to such basic benefits as unemployment insurance, health insurance, vacation pay and sick leave.[6] In his book on the automobile industry, *The Reckoning,* David Halberstram describes 1964 as "the highwater mark of the American century, when the country was rich, the dollar strong and inflation low." WWII and the Korean War were in the past, the Vietnam war still largely in the future.[7] But by the end of the decade the U.S. motor vehicle industry once again had to confront problems of market saturation and intensified competition — this time from the motor vehicle multinationals that emerged, with the help of government policies, as part of the post-war expansion in Europe and Japan.

As early as 1972 there were clear signs of market saturation in the developed countries. In that year there were five motor vehicles for every ten persons in the U.S.[8] Although the number was far lower in Japan (1.2) and Germany (2.1), for example, this picture of relatively less saturation changes somewhat if one examines the ratio of motor vehicles per kilometer of paved road (29 for the U.S., 96 for Japan and 44 for Germany); or per kilometer of national land (11, 34 and 52, respectively).[9] North American and European car markets, which had been growing at an annual rate of 12–13% in the 1960, were growing at 2–3%, virtually the replacement rate, by the 1980s.[10]

In this chapter we will look at the elements of the postwar accord — the collective bargaining framework, the reliance on Keynesian state spending, and the ideologies of managerialism, science and technology and the social consumption norm — and examine the ways they contributed to conditions that constrained and shaped the response of the U.S. motor vehicle industry's changing profile.

The Trade-off of Meaningful Work for Economic Benefits

As part of their agreement not to interfere in areas deemed management prerogatives, the UAW, along with other unions in the mass production industries, accepted the continuation of a production system in which jobs were fragmented into discrete, repeatable tasks. This Taylorist job design, when combined with a complex job classification system and a bureaucratic control structure, resulted in a relatively rigid internal plant organization that impeded adjustments that might increase productivity. The cost-cutting measures the automakers did adopt often reduced the quality of the cars being manufactured and intensified rising levels of labor-management conflict.

On the job many automobile industry workers were alienated from the fruits of their labor, bored by the repetitive and limited nature of the assembly line tasks they performed, and frustrated with the fact that on-the-job life do not provide the happiness promised by the pervasive social consumption norm. By the mid-1960s, workers were expressing "a vast discontent, dissatisfaction, resentment, frustration and boredom with their work" by high rates of absenteeism and turnover, declining productivity, work-to-rules actions, local strikes, poor quality and sometimes even sabotage.[11] In some GM assembly plants in 1972, for example, absenteeism ran as high as 13% compared with 3% only a few years earlier.[12]

These problems did not surface overnight. The relative harmony that accompanied the five-year collective bargaining agreement signed in 1950 had eroded by 1955 when, minutes before the strike deadline expired, GM and the UAW signed an agreement that provided for Supplementary Unemployment Benefits for laid-off workers. Negotiations for the 1958 contract were accompanied by numerous plant-level strikes during a four-month period without a contract, and by a one-week national strike. In 1961, 90 plants struck over local issues, although GM and the UAW were not far apart on national contract questions. In 1963, local elections at auto plants swept more than one-third of the UAW's representatives out of office. Local negotiations at the plant level became even more difficult in 1964, when 24,000 local demands were submitted (compared to 11,600 in 1958). A national strike lasted 10 days, but local strikes continued into November. The hottest issue dividing labor and management was work standards, accompanied by accusations of "'filthy plants,' 'speedups on the assembly line' and coercion and terror tactics by foremen at GM plants." The next big strike at GM came in 1970 and lasted 107 days. According to an article by Norman Pearlstine in *The Wall Street Journal,* one of the principal causes of this strike was the need for unity and solidarity in the UAW, which was concerned about its ability to control the demands of its members. Pearlstine identified four specific UAW strike objectives:

> To teach young members who had not known hard times that struggle and unity are necessary.
>
> To help make expectations more realistic.
>
> To foster loyalty and pull together warring factions within the union.
>
> To create an escape valve for workers who are frustrated by the boredom of the assembly line routine.

In his exposé of the 1970 contract negotiations, William Serrin describes GM's collusion in a kind of "stage-managed charade of class struggle," which was intended to help the UAW to maintain its militant image and hence its credibility with an increasingly restive rank and file.[13]

The U.S. motor vehicle industry responded to worker dissatisfaction and its negative consequences for productivity and profitability in ways that ultimately intensified rather than mitigated the problem. First of all, they tried to purchase labor harmony by agreeing to union demands for increased wages and benefits.

Compared to other U.S. workers, autoworkers were very well paid; at the beginning of the 1960s they made 30% more than other industrial workers, and by the end of the 1970s the gap had increased to 70%.[14] The motor vehicle manufacturers were able to follow this high-wage/benefit strategy because of the industry's oligopolistic structure. As a "shared monopoly," automobile industry leaders thought they could both ignore increasing problems with the quality of their products and pass increased labor costs on to consumers.[15] Buyers had little choice since the automobile was so essential to modern life and mass transit alternatives were generally unavailable. According to one advertising industry executive the industry saw itself as "one big company with three divisions [dominated by GM whose domestic market share increased from 42% in 1952 to 50.9% in 1955] in which every division played it safe and no division tried something new unless it was reasonably sure that the other two were going to try it as well."[16] But, as Halberstram points out, the Big Three hadn't yet noticed that there were potential problems in being a monopoly that was open to other countries.

The high wage/benefit strategy broke the link between the cost of labor, price levels and productivity that had been built into the post-war collective bargaining structure. This break contributed to rising rates of inflation in the 1970s and to growing consumer resistance to increased domestic car prices and thus eased the way for Japanese imports.[17] Productivity and profits fell. In the 1960s, for example, GM's profit margin dropped from 10% to 7%. And according to Ford's President, Lee Iacocca, during the 1960s "Japan's productivity gain was 188.5%. Our's [the U.S. auto industry's] was 34.7%."[18]

The industry decided to tackle the productivity problem head-on by demanding greater effort from the workers on the line. At GM this meant the creation, in the mid-1960s, of the General Motors Assembly Division (GMAD), a management team that its critics accused of practicing a rigid sweatshop style of management reminiscent of the 1930s. When GMAD took over a plant it claimed the right to abrogate existing local agreements governing working conditions and production standards and then did what industrial engineers have done for decades: cut back the number of workers on the line and increased the number of separate operations for which each worker was responsible. Not surprisingly, these strategies intensified conflict between labor and management. At GM they resulted in several years of strikes that were costly to both the company and the union. In

1972, for example, a 174-day strike at GMAD's Norwood Ohio plant cost GM production worth at least $125 million, it cost the union $3.5 million in strike benefits, and it cost the workers tens of millions in lost wages.[19]

GM expressed the company's concern with the changing relationship between wages and productivity in their 1969 annual report:

> The continued progress of the Corporation — and indeed the well-being of the entire economy — rests on the industry's ability to bring wages and national productivity into balance. The excess of wage increases over increases in productivity in the past several years have been a major contributor to inflation. Absenteeism and frequent work stoppages have cut into the efficiency of plant operations with predictable effects on manufacturing costs. (AR 1969, p.7)

According to GM, when the company negotiated their 1970 labor contract they maintained the company's "right to sub-contract work, to introduce new technology, to schedule overtime, and to maintain efficiency and discipline. GM insisted that an organized effort be made to improve job attitudes and reduce absenteeism." (AR 1970, p.23) The emphasis on productivity continued in the 1971 annual report:

> Recognizing the decisive importance of greater productivity to the economic future of both our Corporation and the United States, we are continuing our intensive efforts to increase the efficiency of all our operations. Our efforts recognize the principle that to produce more with the same amount of human effort is a sound economic and social objective. (AR 1971, p.6)

In the fall of 1971, GM established a new personnel administration and development staff headed by Stephen Fuller, previously an associate dean of the Harvard Business School. The group had a staff of 144, including 5 psychologists. According to *Business Week*[20]: "Productivity is the key word for Fuller. Decreased productivity caused by absenteeism, high job turnover, poor quality and the rising number of strikes and local grievances alerted GM, and the auto industry generally, to worker unrest." The company's strategy, according to Fuller, is to signal "as actively and as frequently as we can the commitment of top management, that it is interested in improving job satisfaction. We are trying to open the doors and give people an opportunity to share in improving the quality of what they do."

GM's experience at their Lordstown factory in the early 1970s became the symbol of the period's labor discontent. The Lordstown factory began operations in 1970 (after extensive renovations were made to the plant which was originally built in 1966). In October 1971 GM shifted control of the plant to the GM Assembly Division (GMAD), who instituted strict disciplinary rules and tightened plant procedures. Emma Rothschild, in her prescient look at the U.S. motor vehicle industry, *Paradise Lost*, describes Lordstown as "the most expensive and technologically most ambitious factory in modern auto history."[21] But, despite GM's claims for the plant, Rothschild writes that its production technology was virtually unchanged from Henry Ford's original assembly line. Its objective continued to be to increase the number of times each job can be performed in an hour, with the effect that the monotony and intensity of the job and the degree of concentration required all increased. Months of labor conflict in the plant involving "a change in plant management, layoffs, a disciplinary crackdown, an increase in car defects, complaints by workers about the speeding up of monotonous assembly-line tasks, slowdowns, high absenteeism, repeated allegations by GM of worker sabotage" ended in a three-week strike in March, 1972.[22]

In reporting on the strike in *The New York Times,* reporter Agis Salpukas created the Lordstown legend.[23] Overnight the plant became the symbol of idealistic youth, unwilling to tolerate the working conditions of their fathers, standing up to dehumanizing technology and unable to be bought with money alone. The problem for management was to "humanize" the job, and legions of social scientists found employment in the forthcoming industry job enrichment programs.

An alternative picture of auto-workers, shared by automakers and union bureaucrats alike, portrayed them as an undisciplined, disrespectful and recalcitrant lot, who drank too much, used drugs, and did not appreciate what their forefathers had won for them in earlier labor struggles. And it was, of course, an easy step from this perspective to blaming the workers for GM's productivity and profitability problems: problems which, on the contrary, writers like Halberstram lay directly at the feet of automotive management. In an article that looks back at the Lordstown strike from 3 years later, James O'Toole writes:[24]

> The problem of low productivity lies more with management than with workers. The simple fact is that companies like G.M. have become bureaucracies, and management becomes an end in itself in such environments. In many of the large publicly held corporate giants of America, the chief concerns of managers are not profits or productivity but their own statuses, benefits and perquisites ... With such a culture, it is not surprising that the American auto industry has never admitted to itself that the reason it is besieged by competitors, consumers, conservationists, and the Congress is that it is producing unsafe, polluting, gas-guzzling, poorly designed vehicles.

But you wouldn't know about Lordstown (or other instances of worker dissent) from GM's annual reports. Although the 1970 report cover features the entrance to the Lordstown assembly plant and includes photographs of the assembly line and a computerized electrical system test station, neither this nor subsequent reports make any other direct references to the facility or to the wide-spread worsening of labor-management relations there and elsewhere.

The only suggestion of disharmony in the annual reports is indirect: in 1972 GM suddenly includes a lengthy discussion of all the things the company is doing to ensure their employees' health, safety, dietary satisfaction, entertainment, and job participation. In a section titled "Business Goals and Human Needs," GM writes that: "Recognizing the inevitability of changes in the backgrounds, attitudes, motivations and life styles of people — including its own — GM has initiated many people-oriented programs" whose "goal has been to combine people and the job to more effectively achieve GM's business goals, while at the same time recognizing the relationships between people and the importance of their changing needs and aspirations." To this end the company announced it was introducing a management concept called "organizational development, which seeks improvements through changes in such areas as job content, supervisory relationships, organizational structures and the overall working environment." (AR 1972, p.18) Throughout the 1972 annual report there are photographs of GM employees enjoying a variety of GM-sponsored activities and facilities. These include the annual GM Employee Hobby Show (which "also features special displays on safety, pollution control, research, engineering and manufacturing technology"); the Electro-Motive Division's Model Railroad Club; the Oldsmobile Division's Outdoor Club's professional rodeo; the annual meeting of the Delco-Moraine Division's Quarter Century Club; Guide Lamps Division's annual Junior Firemen's Day; and the dining rooms for hourly employees (which "provide for an attractive display of well-prepared food, comfortable surroundings and efficient traffic flow. All General Motors' manufacturing facilities provide such eating areas for the convenience of employees"); a modern medical department ("staffed by doctors, nurses and medical technicians who, in addition to providing medical services, cooperate with other plant personnel to ensure that manufacturing areas provide a healthy environment"); and vending machine and rest areas that are located throughout the manufacturing area "for the relief period comfort and convenience of employees." (AR 1972, pp.17–22)

Beginning in 1973 the UAW and GM began jointly developing programs — variously labeled quality of worklife (QWL), work improvement, and worker participation — to try to deal with worsening shopfloor relations and to improve productivity by "democratizing" the workplace and giving workers more voice in decisions affecting their jobs.[25] In September, 1975, the joint labor-management *GM-UAW National Committee to Improve the Quality of Work Life* held a one-day Quality of Work Life Seminar (QWL) for 15 union representatives and 12 high-level GM line managers.[26] The seminar was billed by GM as "not only the first of its kind in the automobile industry but in all probability the first of its kind in American industry." According to GM's Director of Organizational Research and Development, among the conclusions reached at the seminars was agreement that:

- the QWL movement is moving "toward more active participation of workers in decisions and matters which directly affect the quality of their working lives;"
- not only is experience showing that union and management can work cooperatively but that by doing so they can contribute more to enhancing the quality of working life than either can accomplish independently;
- "to avoid mandatory legislation in the future," union and management groups must work in harmony with the Federal Government's National Center for Productivity and Quality of Working Life.

QWL really began to take off, however, in the 1979–1982 recession. According to a September 17, 1979 article in *Business Week*, the UAW has done far more than any other union in developing such programs; GM and the union have jointly set up QWL programs in from 18 to 24 plants. But while the UAW was clearly cooperating with GM in many cases, the union was also accusing GM of using QWL programs as a mechanism to keep the union out of the non-union plants that the company was opening in "right-to-work" states, as part of its "Southern Strategy."[27]

While the initial QWL programs were simply extensions of earlier efforts to improve productivity by improving morale through "job enrichment" (efforts whose results proved to be mixed at best), by the 1980s they had become transformed into the "team concept" and infused with a variety of Japanese management techniques. As we saw in Chapter I, the team concept is now a central element of a wholesale restructuring of labor-management relations, along with concessionary contracts (almost 60% of the unions bargaining with employers in the first half of 1982, for example, accepted real wage freezes or reductions in their new contracts); outsourcing (buying a component or part that the company could or has produced itself); outside contracting (hiring another firm to perform work on company property or on company materials that is usually or potentially done by union members); whipsawing (using threats of plant closings to pit workers in one plant against those in another plant); and "management-by-stress" (a set of techniques, called by management "synchronous production," which uses stress as the force that drives and regulates the production system.)[28] Davis saw this trend as the portent of a new shift in the pattern of labor-capital relations in the U.S.:[29]

> The ultimate trajectory of such a restructuring of collective bargaining might be a new industrial relations system based on highly individuated single-plant contracts and increased wage differentiation within the monopoly sector of the economy. With the concession of employment guarantees to certain strata of workers and some cosmetic attention to the 'quality of work life,' such a system would not be unlike the Japanese model of decentralized company unionism which inspires cult devotion in many U.S. business schools.

Nor would it be very different from the form of labor-capital relations desired by GM and other large corporations in the first three decades of this century.

In his introduction to *Choosing Sides,* a critical account of the team concept, Victor Reuther reminds his readers of the team concept's historical antecedents in John D. Rockefeller Jr.'s call for "employee representation," U.S. Steel's Charles Schwab's call for "constructive cooperation" in the 1920s, and in GM's proposal of "enterprise" unionism (a separate contract for each plant) in 1937.[30] The team concept, says Reuther, "plays upon the worker's desire to use his or her creativity and intellect." But what begins as cooperation with management turns "ever so subtly" into competition among workers in the struggle for productivity and quality. Most insidiously, Reuther concludes, the union is undermined and the contract undercut.

Reuther argues that today's unions are ill-prepared to defend themselves from this management strategy. They are too centralized and bureaucratic, and they cannot involve and mobilize their members to take on the new challenge. Instead, the UAW and other unions have embraced the team concept. What Reuther doesn't say, however, is that the centralization, bureaucracy and lack of democracy, that he complains lie at the root of the UAW's failure to combat this restructuring of labor management relations, have their origins in the post-war collective bargaining framework.

The role of the mass production industry unions within the post-war collective bargaining accord was as "a partner to capital in disciplining and stabilizing the workforce."[31] The complex system of collective bargaining agreements, labor law and quasi-juridical grievance procedures combined with the liability provision of the Taft-Hartley Act to provide an institutional framework for this role that encouraged the development of centralized union bureaucracies and the distancing of union leadership from shopfloor activism. By 1962, for example, U.S. unions had 60,000 full-time salaried officials — one for every 300 workers, compared to one for every 2,000 workers in Britain and one for every 700 workers in Sweden.[32] Centralized bureaucratic structures are not known for their militancy, but in this case several other factors contributed to the inertia of unions like the UAW: the cold war purges of the most progressive elements of the union leadership deprived them of a potentially radicalizing impulse; labor's alliance with the Democratic Party, itself constrained by its own right wing and the demands of Cold War bi-partisanship, was a further conservative influence;[33] and having agreed not to impinge on so-called management prerogatives (an agreement reinforced by court interpretations), union leaders were reluctant to incorporate local workplace issues into their agenda.

The unions' power lies in their potential to organize, mobilize and control the working class. The factors noted above, along with a series of decisions in the post-war decades, gradually eroded this power. There was little support within the trade union movement for organizing workers outside of the mass production industries; that is, workers in low-wage, competitively-structured, often service industries, who were often predominantly people of color and/or women. Nor was there much support for either the women's or the civil rights movements, or for inter-industry or international labor movement cooperation. The slide in trade union membership that is so bemoaned today actually began in the late 1950s. For example, between 1957 and 1962, the percentage of non-agricultural workers in trade unions fell from 31.7% to 26.7%.[34] The AFL-CIO recruited only 2 million of the 35 million new workers added to the labor force between 1960 and 1970; and if public sector workers organized during the 1960s are excluded, there was a net loss in union membership in the decade.[35] The failure to address local workplace issues or to support the various work actions of the 1960s meant that these actions, while disruptive, were never transformed into a united effort. Instead they convinced employers of the need to act unilaterally by introducing various human relations programs that further marginalized the unions in the eyes of workers. By 1968, for example, nearly 30% of national settlements were voted down by union memberships.[36] So while the collective bargaining framework counted on the capacity of the unions to maintain discipline among workers, the same framework gradually eroded the capacity of the unions to do so.

The social consumption norm itself also contributed to the weakening of U.S. trade unions vis-à-vis management in the late 1970s and 1980s. The norm's inducements, along with easy credit and the emphasis both unions and management placed on narrowly-defined economic issues, helped to create a shared consciousness among workers that was individualistic and materialistic and that rechanneled workers' energies away from social conflict and political participation into privatized consumption.

Despite the decline in union membership over the years—and the obstacles to union organizing and collective labor action presented by the collective bargaining agreements, labor law and the courts—corporations, politicians and union bureaucracies all had an interest in presenting unions as a formidable force in U.S. economic and political life. The public, most of whom did not belong to unions, readily accepted the widely promoted view that unions had become too powerful and blamed them for rising prices and declining product quality. Not surprisingly, for the majority of workers who toiled in relatively low-wage, largely unorganized sectors, the existence of a labor elite stirred resentment. Hence, the management offensive of the last decade or so had widespread support from the general public, and members of an atomized workforce were all too willing to compete with each other in the scramble to join team programs, agree to concessionary contracts, and participate in corporate whipsawing.

When compared to these later assaults on the post-war collective bargaining accord, the QWL programs of the 1970s were, in their scope and effectiveness, but feeble efforts to resolve the capital accumulation dilemma that began to surface in the late 1960s. Nor were these programs the only alternatives pursued by corporations such as GM. Perhaps even more important, because of their role in eroding the bargaining authority of U.S. labor unions, were the moves to internationalize the locus of production by moving production sites throughout the world in a search for lower production costs and more compliant workers.

The Internationalization of Production

In Chapter IV I noted that when the growth of the U.S. automobile market began to slow down in the 1920s, GM began looking to overseas markets and, in response to tariffs and taxes that discouraged foreign imports, began exporting kits that could be assembled at plants abroad and investing in foreign manufacturing facilities. But whereas the primary motivation for producing abroad in the pre-WWII period was to secure access to markets that were otherwise blocked by foreign government policies, an additional motivation for the internationalization of production after the mid-1960s has been to reduce production costs, particularly labor costs. Moreover, international production is no longer largely limited to the production or assembly of finished products intended for export or for local markets. It increasingly includes the production of parts and components for use in firm plants in other countries.[37]

This form of internationalized production offers a number of benefits to manufacturers. Certain major components can be designed and engineered once — for use in a number of different products and facilities — and their costs can be spread over huge volumes in a few manufacturing centers. Companies can select production locations not only on the basis of their proximity to desired markets but also on the relative cost and militancy of their labor force. Previously inefficient production sites that primarily serviced local markets — sites that may have been opened because of government-imposed local content or other restrictions — can be transformed into important regional suppliers. And by producing key components at more than one location, companies can reduce their vulnerability to strikes and other labor actions. They can also use the availability of alternative production sites to whipsaw on an international scale, playing off nation states and whole unions against each other. For example, one analyst explains Ford's decision to concentrate final assembly operations for its Fiesta in Saarlouis, Germany, as follows:[38]

> Assembly is labor intensive, heavily dependent on workers on the line. The weakest point in any auto company production line is the assembly plant. It obviously made sense for Ford to concentrate assembly in a location where it was strongest vis-a-vis the workforce. In Saarlouis, for example, there was high unemployment and migrant workers constituted a large percentage of the workforce. They were dependent on Ford for permission to stay and that depended on good behavior. In addition, wildcat strikes were illegal there. . . .

And finally, the internationalized production of components and parties is a step toward achieving the still distant goal of producing a "world car."

Although one hears little talk about a world car today, the underlying concept still informs current production strategies. The idea of the world car is to produce a car that can be built from standardized parts and sold with few changes in any major market. Ford began manufacturing a "European car" some time in the late 1960s/early 1970s. The car, which came in five sizes, was based on a single uniform design and was built at locations throughout Europe. A truly world car, of course, requires a worldwide homogenization of design preferences, and to some extent this seems to be taking place (for example, the success of Japanese imports in both the U.S. and European markets despite import limitations, "voluntary" in the case of the U.S., obligatory in the case of Europe; and the adoption of similar vehicle profiles by U.S., Japanese and European manufacturers).[39] But while complete standardization is still a far-off and likely unattainable dream, interchangeability of major parts and the multi-sourcing of major components has been an integral element of corporate production strategy since the mid-1970s.

GM first mentions such programs in their annual reports in 1971, when they contemplate introducing "interchangeable programs for vehicle components on a regional basis to achieve economies in volume production, which contribute to the industrial growth of each country." (AR 1971, p.16) The company expressed similar sentiments in 1972 and 1973 when they announced establishment of a new automotive components organization to plan and coordinate engineering, manufacturing and sales. One of the organization's responsibilities will be "coordinating participation in international complementation programs. Complementation provides for components manufacture and vehicle assembly in several countries of a region, with each country having specialized components production responsibility for the entire region." (AR 1973, p.7). By the late 1970s, complementation was a keystone of GM's internationalization strategy. GM's capital spending outside the U.S. doubled, from 11% in 1978, to 22% in 1979, and then increased to 28% in 1980 and 33% in 1981. In these years, according to the annual reports, GM constructed new facilities to manufacture components in France (1978); manufacture seat belts in Ireland (1978); manufacture radios and assemble components in Singapore (1978); manufacture and assemble components and vehicles in Spain (1979); manufacture components in Ireland and Portugal (1980); and assemble vehicles in Greece (1981). In addition, the company acquired Chrysler's assembly facilities in Venezuela and Colombia (1979).

Not surprisingly, as I noted in Chapter I, *where* GM decides to locate its international production facilities depends on both the inducements offered, and constraints imposed, by various governments. Low wages and a compliant labor force may be assured by government cooperation with industry; for example, independent labor unions may be prohibited, strikes outlawed, and wage levels controlled. Governments also offer subsidies, tax benefits, credits, infrastructural investments and exemptions from restrictive legislation. But governments may also seek to protect local industries and/or improve employment opportunities for its own workforce by imposing tariff barriers that discourage imports of completed vehicles and/or parts and components, and by passing legislation that requires that a certain proportion of vehicles consist of domestically produced parts (known as local sourcing) or be locally manufactured or assembled. The passage of such legislation in Latin America (as in Argentina in 1956, Brazil in 1959, and Mexico in 1962), for example, induced manufacturers such as GM to locate production facilities there and then, through the complementation strategy, to expand them. By 1973 U.S.-domiciled companies accounted for 46% of the output produced in Latin America, and Western European companies accounted for 53%.[40] These constraints were, however, spiced by some incentives, such as tax relief, local credit at favorable rates, permission to import and capitalize used equipment, preferential tariffs on imported parts, and of course rules that outlaw strikes, eliminate collective bargaining, and place ceilings on wages. In the case of GM's $20 million investment to expand its facilities in Argentina, for example, "the parent firm made no cash contributions at all, relying entirely on the reinvestment of locally earned profits ($6 million) and used equipment from Detroit (capitalized at $14 million)."[41] GM's decision, in 1967, to build a $100 million assembly plant in Antwerp may have been influenced by the Belgian government's willingness to provide tax waivers and a long-term loan with an interest rate subsidy of 2–2½% payable out of earnings and secured by the assets of GM's European subsidiaries. Similarly, GM's decision to locate a car plant and two components factories in Spain in the early 1980s, was very likely influenced by the $280 million subsidy, various tax benefits, long-term credits, 95% tariff reduction on imported machinery, and the provision of such infrastructural benefits as access roads, water, lighting and so on, provided by the Spanish government.[42] Third world countries, sensitive to the degree of foreign ownership of their domestic industries, have often insisted that nationals or the government itself have an equity stake (often a majority) in foreign companies that operate on their soil. Hence, many of the assembly plants established by GM in the 1970s and 1980s were in the form of joint venures: for example in the Phillipines (60% GM ownership); Korea (50% GM ownership); Iran (45% GM ownership); Japan (34.2% GM ownership); Uruguay (49% GM ownership); and Egypt (31% GM ownership).

The internationalization of production creates problems for multinations in both their domestic economies, where the work force fears the loss of jobs, and overseas, where governments fear the loss of autonomy. In contrast to GM's annual reports in the 1930s, when the company tried to assure a domestic audience that internationalization would not affect domestic employment, GM's reports in the mid-1960s and 1970s focus primarily on legitimation issues that arise in the host nations and among the socially concerned in the U.S. (who were becoming increasingly important, as we will see below). In these reports GM speaks about the multinational company's roles in providing capital, technical and managerial skills, jobs, and products that otherwise may not be locally available. It emphasizes the responsibilities that come with global production. For example:

GM actively seeks to participate in supplying the world's growing transportation requirements in all areas where such participation is consistent with the interest of the countries concerned and the Corporation. GM's good industrial citizenship, technological resources, and employee training programs contribute significantly to the development of the nations in which it operates. (AR 1971, p.15)

This trend to industrialization has brought new opportunities to citizens of developing countries and provided a means for these countries to develop and employ local resources in accordance with advanced technology. Additional employment opportunities are generated by the infusion of capital and knowledge and the latest marketing, manufacturing, and management methods. Overseas investments also serve to stimulate the development of local manufacturing industries which supply large quantities of specialized services, materials, parts and components to motor vehicle producers. In addition, the expansion of dealer organizations for the marketing and servicing of motor vehicles provides a further contribution to the economic development of the country. (AR 1982, p.23)

But GM is also clearly aware that the internationalization of production threatens the security of its employees in the U.S. In 1972, it was still able to reassure these workers, but such reassurances do not appear in future annual reports:

GM's growth overseas has not been at the expense of expanded investment and employment in the United States. Between 1962 and 1972, General Motors domestic employment rose 19% compared with only 12% for U.S. manufacturers as a whole. Although GM overseas employment during the same period rose at a higher rate, this was because automobile production overseas was at a much lower level of development in 1962. (AR 1972, p.25)

In a previous chapter we saw the state playing a contradictory role: on the one hand encouraging the formation of labor unions with collective bargaining rights, and on the other hand limiting their effectiveness through legislation and judicial decisions constraining their organizing options. Similarly, by confronting corporations looking to gain access to foreign markets and reduce production costs by relocating, the governments can either encourage and/or constrain capital accumulation. This "on the one hand"/ "on the other hand" role of the state was virtually built-in to the post-WWII apparatus of governance and reflects what O'Connor describes as the capitalist states' "two basic and often mutually contradictory functions — *accumulation* and *legitimization.* This means that the state must try to maintain or create the conditions in which profitable capital accumulation is possible. However, the state must try to maintain or create the conditions for social harmony."[43] We turn next to this contradictory role of the state and its part in the break-down of the post-war accord.

Activist Government, Corporate Social Responsibility and Capital Accumulation

As we have already seen, the state played a major role in mediating labor-management relations during World War II and, through the National Defense Mediation Board and the National War Labor Board, participated directly in the collective bargaining process. Both mass production companies such as GM and the government emerged from the war convinced that not only was a strong collaborative union bureaucracy essential to ensuring high productivity and industrial peace in the future but that the state itself needed to play an important role in economic pump-priming. By 1972, Federal expenditures on goods and services, transfer payments to persons, grants-in-aid to state and local governments, interest payments and net subsidies were 21% of the GNP in the U.S., eight times the corresponding figure for 1929.[44]

Capitalist enterprises, particularly in the oligopolistic sectors (such as the automobile industry), became increasingly dependent upon state spending to maintain profitable capital accumulation after WWII. Through what O'Connor calls *social capital* expenditures, the state provides projects and services that are collectively consumed by business and/or workers and thereby either increase the productivity of a given amount of labor power and/or lower the reproduction costs of labor. When the state spends money on constructing the physical economic infrastructure (for example, on transportation facilities, utilities required for industrial development, plant and equipment for education and research and development, and urban renewal projects) or on developing the human capital infrastructure (by spending on educational, scientific and research and development services), it is helping business by socializing the costs of developing the infrastructures needed to carry out advanced business activity. The importance of such collectively consumed goods and services in promoting capital accumulation is apparent today in Eastern Europe and the former Soviet Union, where the absence of modern transportation and communications systems and a shortage of employees trained in capitalist financial and management techniques, are impeding the transformation to a capitalist form of economy. The state subsidizes capital by socializing the costs of reproducing labor, thereby reducing the level of money wages, when it provides projects and services that are consumed collectively by the working class (such as roads, schools, recreation facilities, home mortgage subsidies, mass transit and other commuter facilities, hospitals and child care facilities) and social insurance against economic insecurity. These categories of state spending were both the consequences of, and the basis for, the expansion of capital accumulation in the post-WWII decades.

But economic growth in the post-WWII decades and the expansion of the oligopolistic sectors that accompanied it included concomitant demands for outlays to deal with the negative consequences of capital's growth (such as unemployment, poverty, and environmental damage) and to smooth capital's access to foreign resources and foreign markets. O'Connor classifies as *social expenses* those outlays that support the "Warfare-Welfare State." Domestic producers need foreign markets and investment outlets in order to keep aggregate demand in step with their ever-growing productive capacity, and they are constantly on the look-out for opportunities to reduce their costs of production by exploiting global material and labor resources. The warfare state (through military and other state outlays, such as foreign aid) supports the global reach of its domestically domiciled capital and defends it from both foreign rivals and, during the Cold War, from the destabilizing impact of Soviet supported political interests. Domestically the warfare state, through the police and criminal justice system, provides the coercive power needed when ideology, the threat of unemployment, or the mitigating benefits of social welfare programs are insufficient to maintain social order and control.

Like the warfare state, the welfare state has expanded substantially in the post-WWII decades as "the gains from technical progress and economic growth have not been distributed equitably, but rather have been concentrated in the hands of the large corporations dominating the monopoly sector, together with the professional, technical, white-collar and blue-collar strata in the monopoly and state sectors."[45] While the pie was getting bigger, thanks to a combination of technological progress and the success of capital accumulation, neither the workers nor the small businessmen and farmers in the competitive sector were getting their "fair share." Not only did the benefits of social capital spending tend to flow largely to monopoly capital and organized labor for at least two decades after the end of WWII, but the costs associated with expanded production were imposed on competitive sector labor and capital, who became, in various ways, increasingly dependent upon state welfare programs as the price of their continued participation in the broad political consensus. Beginning in the 1950s, but more forcefully in the 1960s, people began to turn to the state to address the adverse social consequences of a system in which the social surplus (including profits) continues to be privately appropriated while more and more of its costs are socialized. Women, minorities and other disadvantaged persons began to demand from the state that they be integrated into the system so they too could enjoy the benefits promised by the post-war social consumption norm. The belief in the power of science and technology and the expanded role of the state combined to create expectations regarding the quality and safety of the products produced by modern technology, its ability to prevent or at least correct such social costs of production as environmental pollution and job-induced health hazards, and its capacity to deal with the OPEC-induced energy crisis.

The dual character of ideologies — on the one hand they legitimate already-existing social institutions, on the other hand they can lead to pressures to change these institutions — became increasingly evident in the mid-1960s, at around the same time that the post-war expansion was beginning to slow down. The public began to demand that many heretofore socialized costs — auto emissions, industrial air, water and noise pollution, abandoned cars, energy shortages, unsafe products and working conditions — be absorbed by industry itself. Their concerns fell on fertile soil in Washington, where a more activist government readily expanded its brief beyond economic pump priming to include social engineering. The National Traffic and Motor Vehicle Safety Act, the Consumer Product Safety Act, the Energy Policy and Conservation Act, the Clean Air Act, and so on, were all products of this period. And whether the results of these demands were legislation, regulation, lawsuits, or the effects of adverse publicity on corporate "image," their impact was to increase the impediments to capital accumulation. GM found itself increasingly having to respond to charges of social irresponsibility for failing to seek and develop alternative energy sources, or vehicles that are more fuel efficient, safer, more serviceable and do not pollute the air.

The Demand for the Socially Responsible Corporation

By 1956 over 1,125,000 Americans had died, and millions more had been injured, in motor vehicle accidents.

> On July 16, 1956, Congressman Kenneth A. Roberts (D-Ala.) . . . opened public hearings — the first of their kind — on the role in the slaughter played by automobile design. Expert witnesses testified that the auto industry had the capability to design cars so that occupants could survive crashes that were routinely fatal, and to lessen the severity or eliminate injuries.[46]

Some nine years and 450,000 highway deaths later, Senator Abraham A. Ribicoff (D-Conn.) opened new hearings into automobile safety, hearings that included the highly publicized revelation that GM had hired detectives to investigate the private life of Ralph Nader, the consumer activist whose book, *Unsafe At Any Speed,* showed that GM's Chevrolet Corvair was unsafe. In 1966 Congress passed the National Motor Vehicle Safety Act. The legislation established what became the National Highway and Traffic Safety Administration, under the Department of Transportation, charged it with establishing safety standards for new cars, and required that manufacturers publically announce motor vehicle recalls. At the hearings surrounding this legislation, automobile company executives – as they had at all prior hearings – professed their interest in safety, but stressed the need for more research and information, consumer education, and better highways and vehicle inspection programs – a position echoed for a decade in GM's annual reports.

At about the same time that Congressman Roberts was calling for hearings into the carnage on the nation's highways, GM began to emphasize its commitment to safety and the rigor of its testing program:

> Safety of driver, passenger and pedestrians has always been of paramount importance to General Motors. All steel bodies, safety plate glass and larger window areas for better vision, improved brakes and steering, more responsive engines and transmissions – these and a host of other developments have contributed to make GM cars safer each year. In the engineering test laboratories at the Technical Center and on the GM Proving Grounds important components of new designs and complete automobiles are subjected to the most rigorous testing, including thousands of miles of test driving, before they are approved for production.

> The 1956 GM cars reflect this tradition of safety consciousness. All have the new crash-proved door locks introduced in 1955 to decrease the possibility of doors springing open in collisions. Especially important to families with children, all rear door have safety locks that cannot be opened from the inside when the lock button is pushed down. Seat belts are offered for all models, and padded instrument panels (when not standard) and multi-position power seats are optional on many. (AR 1955, pp.16–17)

After years of promoting ever-increasing engine power, seemingly for its own sake and for some never specified "improved performance" characteristics, the 1955 report's discussion of "more powerful high-compression engines," points out that: "The improvement in acceleration is an important safety factor when immediate response and reserves of power are required to avoid a hazardous situation." (AR 1955, p.16) In the 1957 annual report, in striking contrast with the implicit messages of its advertising campaigns at the time, the annual report asserts that GM "has emphasized many times that reserve horsepower often improperly connected with high speed, provides a factor of safety to drivers in passing and should mean safer driving." (AR 1957, pp.15–16) This same report also describes GM's support for various highway planning, traffic safety and driver training programs, its commitment to "manufacture the safest and most reliable automobiles its engineers could design" (AR1957, p.15), and announces its "Aim to Live" advertising campaign to "make night driving safer," along with a contest inviting the public to submit "a slogan of ten words or less on night-time driving safety."

The emphasis on automobile and highway safety reappear in 1965's annual report in a two-page section on "GM and Highway Safety," as well as in photographs throughout the report that illustrate the company's vehicle testing program. Once again GM shares the public's concern to achieve "greater safety on our highways with a reduction in accidents." But the company also deflects attention away from the role of the car by emphasizing that a solution to the problem requires "a cooperative effort that includes consideration of the car, the highway and the driver." GM has been doing its bit: "As it has in the past, General Motors will continue, with all the energy and determination that it has, to design and build cars offering the greatest measure of safety possible within the limits of technology and the *economic realities of the marketplace*" (emphasis added), and has been cooperating with "all groups working toward the improvement of highway safety." If some cars are "unsafe at any speed," the fault is not GM's; the company is clearly doing all it can but is constrained by the limits imposed by the exogenous forces of the market (in effect, consumers just don't want and won't pay for safer cars). (AR 1965, pp.405)

Despite their rhetoric about safety, whether in annual reports or in executive appearances before Congress, economist White has concluded that automobile manufacturers, by and large, behaved "as if safety did not enter into the preference functions of consumers and as if the mention of safety considerations might well deter customers."[47]

GM noted the passage of the 1966 legislation in that year's annual report's Letter to Shareholders. Product recalls received particular attention:

> In the past year there has been considerable discussion of product recall campaigns. Recall campaigns are as old as the industry and they provide a practical and responsible method of correcting the infrequent problems which may occur in a highly complex mass produced product after it has been in use. This responsibility is pursued both before and after a car is sold and is in keeping with the stated policy of General Motors. These

procedures reflect the determination of General Motor to assure the integrity of its cars and the safety of all who use them. (AR 1988, p.5)

Not only will the company cooperate fully with the provisions of the National Traffic and Motor Vehicle Safety Act of 1966, "We will continue our long-standing policy of cooperation with all levels of government toward improving traffic safety, reducing traffic congestion and eliminating air and water pollution." This text is noteworthy because it illustrates what becomes GM's standard way of responding to unwelcome (and usually strongly opposed) legislation — whether it involves safety, the environment, equal employment opportunities and so on. In each case, GM assures its readers that the behavior required by the proposed legislation has always been company policy. In a section in 1970's annual report ("Meeting Our Responsibilities: A Progress Report"), approximately 2/3 of which involves "Vehicle Safety," GM asserts that: "Long before the imposition of Federal safety standards, GM was a leader in safety research and the safe design and construction of automotive products." The report notes a number of GM "firsts": the Proving Grounds; the energy-absorbing steering column "adopted in advance of the federal standards," which since its introduction in 1966, "has been credited with reducing injuries and saving many lives;" and side guard beams, now "the basis for a discussion of a proposed Federal standard on door strength."

But the bulk of 1970's discussion on vehicle safety dealt with GM's difficulties in meeting proposed regulations that would require passive restraint systems and improved bumper protection. Neither would be easy to develop, wrote GM, and the major research program to develop passive restraints "would not be necessary if drivers and passengers would use the lap and shoulder belts which are standard equipment on all GM cars." (AR 1970, pp.28–30) There is some truth to this claim; in general, people did not really start wearing seat belts until the mid-1980s, mainly because of state laws requiring their use (laws supported by the manufacturers in their ultimately unsuccessful effort to avoid federal requirements for passive devices such as automated belts or air bags.)[48] Even in 1990, only around 50% of vehicle occupants used front belts and 16% used rear belts. But GM was also being somewhat disingenuous, for the company (along with Ford and Chrysler) opposed mandatory safety requirements every step of the way. Seat and shoulder belts did not become standard equipment in front seats until they were required by regulators in 1968, and they were not provided for rear seat passengers until the National Highway Safety Administration, under pressure from Congress, required them after December 1989. What is shocking about both this twenty-year delay and the industry's resistance, is that automotive safety engineers have known since the early 1960s that "lap-only belts don't prevent injuries as well as the lap and shoulder variety and could actually cause injuries in certain situations." Regulators have, in fact, required that manufacturers install the anchor points for rear shoulder belts since 1972. Many European car makers began installing three point belts in rear seats in the 1970s, and GM's Adam Opel subsidiary has been doing so in Sweden since 1975 and in West Germany since 1979. According to Randall Edwards, Chrysler's Manager of Safety Programs, automakers opposed safety improvements for years because they believed that safety didn't sell: "It comes right out of profit margins," he recently told the *Wall Street Journal*.

A subtle shift in tone becomes evident in GM's discussions of automotive safety (and anti-pollution) during the 1970s. Throughout the preceding decades, GM, through its annual reports, contributed to an uncritical faith in the power of science and technology and an idealization of progress and expertise, as illustrated in the following excerpts:

> Modern science is the real source of economic progress. It has brought within reach of more and more people comforts and conveniences, more leisure, more and better job opportunities. There can be no real ceiling on opportunity if science continues to move forward. (AR 1944, p.28)

> In General Motors the importance of research is recognized and the belief is encouraged that almost everything can and will be done better tomorrow than it is being done today. (AR 1947, p.21)

> The continuing, rapid expansion of scientific knowledge means that research and engineering will become even more important in the future than in the past. Existing products will be improved and new ones will be developed. (AR 1952, p.15)

> The traditional quality and value that GM offers its customers stem from a never-ending search for new and improved products and better ways of making them. In highly competitive modern industry, technological progress is a "must".

> General Motors owes its long-time market leadership in large part to its continued advancement in research, engineering, process development and styling. A great many of the features the consumer takes for granted in today's products are the results of years of study, experimentation and testing in the research and engineering laboratories of the Corporation and the divisions. (AR 1953, p.13)

> The benefits of GM research and engineering are not confined to General Motors alone. GM engineers and scientists often carry information about their work to the technical community and to education where all may share its benefits. In these and other ways the information gained through

technical advancement in GM adds to the general progress of the nation. (AR 1956)

The endless search for new knowledge, for better ways of doing every job, for constant improvements in our products and operations — this has been the basis of General Motors' success. As in the past, our success in the future will depend not on merely accepting the challenge of change, but in aggressively seeking creative change and the opportunities for progress it provides. (AR 1966, p.21)

Beginning in the 1970s, however, at around the same time that pressures to impose higher fuel efficiency, safety and environmental standards were just beginning to mount, GM began to acknowledge that there are limits to what it can technologically achieve. By 1975 these demands were explicit, and GM's suggestion that technology has its limits becomes even clearer:

An even more immediate problem now compounded by the new gasoline-mileage requirements, is to meet the further tightening of the Federal emission standards scheduled for the 1978 models. We have informed Congress, which is now reviewing these standards, that neither General Motors — nor any other manufacturer as far as we know — can comply with them. Certification of 1978 cars must begin this year, but the engine technology does not exist which will enable us to meet the standards on a mass-production basis. This is true not only of the conventional piston engine but of any of the alternatives which we have been exploring, such as the gas turbine, the diesel, or the stratified-charge engine.

These laws demand that we achieve significant breakthroughs in technology — and soon. While we have searched for such breakthroughs daily, and while we have had some success in the past, we have only the hope — and certainly no assurance — that they will be achieved this time, and in time. The consequences, both human and economic, of any substantial curtailment of automobile production in future years would be severe, as recent experience has taught. It would matter little to the laid-off worker or the frustrated car-buyer that the cause lay in the laws of man rather than the laws of economics. (AR 1975, p.5)

The demands for socially responsible behavior by the motor vehicle manufacturers went beyond concerns about automobile safety and fuel efficiency. Engineers were recognizing that automobiles were a major source of air pollution as early as the 1950s; but the manufacturers, believing that pollution devices would add to the cost of a car without contributing anything to its sales, preferred to study the problem rather than to implement concrete solutions or accept government regulation. White's study chronicles the industry's concerted efforts throughout the 1950s and

1960s to delay the development of pollution control devices and the establishment of emission standards.[49] But according to GM's annual reports in this period, the company had been hard at work to reduce exhaust emissions "for many years." (AR 1965, p.5)

In 1959, under what White describes as mounting pressure, the industry discovered that the blowby vent was a major source of polluting emissions. To meet California standards that required the installation of ventilation devices to recycle blowby air by 1963, and probably also to stave off potentially more onerous and precedent-setting federal legislation, the companies *voluntarily* installed positive crankshaft ventilation devices on all new cars sold in the U.S. beginning with the 1963 model year. The California legislature then required that exhaust control devices be installed on all new cars after the State Motor Vehicle Pollution Control Board approved two devices. In 1964 the manufacturers announced that they would have the devices ready for the 1967 models in California, although they opposed installing them nationwide. Under ongoing public pressure the companies retreated from this position and in 1965 announced that they would be able to install the devices if Congress required it. Congress then passed the national Motor Vehicle Air Pollution and Control Act, imposing emission standards on new vehicles that required the installation of pollution control devices. The manufacturers began installing exhaust devices similar to those in California in all 1968 vehicles.

Once again GM's annual reports mirror the pressures being exerted on the industry. In these reports the company simultaneously minimizes the role of automotive emissions in air pollution while praising the company's efforts to reduce them—while in Washington and state capitals GM was actively participating in industry efforts to defeat or delay legislation to mandate improved levels of air quality. In 1961, GM's annual report describes a joint research project conducted with Sloan Kettering Institute for Cancer Research: "Although several known cancer producing substances have been identified in the automotive tars, present indications are that automobiles contribute only a minor fraction of the trace amounts found in city atmosphere." (AR 1961, p.14) A decade later, GM enlists the tool of cost-benefit analysis to deliver essentially the same message.

> Scientists are finding that transportation is responsible for a much smaller percentage of this nation's air-pollution problem than was once suspected. . . . In overall cost-benefit evaluation, it is important that the general public and government officials objectively view the automobile's role in the total air-pollution problem. Although the automobile is blamed for approximately 40% of the nation's air pollution on a tonnage basis, most experts now recognize that a more accurate measure should be based on the relative effects on health and plant life. The most recent

information incorporating health and plant damage — together with tonnage — would show that the auto is more nearly 10% of the nation's problem. (AR 1971, p.20)

This use of cost-benefit to minimize the automobile's role in air pollution is followed up in 1972 with a call for amending the Clean Air Act and for suspending the forthcoming Environmental Protection Agency air quality standards:

> We are urging that the Clean Air Act be amended to bring the standards into line with the nation's air quality needs. Meanwhile we will continue to work with the government so that regulation may be administered with a more balanced regard for the economy and the ecology, and with a more careful consideration of the inevitable cost to the consumer. (AR 1972, p.3)

The battle over clean air continues into the 1990s, with essentially the same script. The manufacturers allege that the costs of the latest air quality standards exceed the benefits: "It's an enormous technical challenge for essentially a small gain in the atmosphere" (GM's Chairman Roger C. Stempel, regarding the 1990 Clean Air Act). And environmental activists charge that the standards give industries: "too much time to do too little" to solve pollution problems (Richard Ayres, Chairman, National Clean Air Coalition.)[50]

GM's responses to the demands for corporate social responsibility in the 1960s and 1970s follow the same pattern, regardless of the issue. First, the annual reports point out that GM's own efforts in the area have predated the current concern and are part of a long-standing corporate policy. For example, GM's 1969 annual report included a special section, "Progress Toward Clean Air and Water." In addition to describing GM's progress in reducing vehicle emissions, the section discusses GM's efforts "in solving industrial air and water pollution problems long before they were a matter of national concern." (AR 1969, p.27) And in 1967, three years after the passage of the Civil Rights Act, the company notes that it has had a non-discriminatory policy for many years. Second, the reports describe the company's most recent efforts in these areas as important, and frequently voluntary, advances. In 1969, for example, GM reports that they:

> have actively researched and developed electric,steam, gas turbine and hybrid engines for use in automobiles. We will not hesitate to substitute any of these for the internal combustion engine if this is what is required to solve the pollution problem insofar as vehicles are concerned and still meet the needs of our customers for economical automotive transportation. (AR 1969, pp.6–7)

In 1971 GM announced the formation of the General Motors Science Advisory Committee to assist "in technological and scientific matters and [to advise] the Corporation on its research activities, with emphasis on meeting environmental and social objectives." (AR 1971, p.7) Finally, the reports argue that the government's regulatory efforts are unreasonable when evaluated in cost-benefit terms (which is to say that the problem isn't so serious and/or the costs of resolving it are excessive and consumers will not be willing to pay them).

Despite GM's protests that their actions with regard to such social issues as auto safety, auto emissions and air pollution were voluntary and pre-dated legislative and regulatory requirements, the timing of these avowals — and the amount of space devoted to discussing corporate social responsibility issues, close to 18% between 1967 and 1976 — suggest that they were defensive responses to actual and potential constraints on the company's ability to continue externalizing these various social costs. Writing about automobile safety questions in his study of corporate control and power, Edward Herman notes, for example, that on safety questions, the major U.S. companies "vigorously resisted pressures toward seat belts, air safety bags, and other safety changes."[51] Speaking specifically about GM, Herman writes that "neither on safety nor other social issues has GM's performance been encouraging as to the promise of managerial social responsibility." Former GM executive, John De Lorean, claims that "At General Motors the concern for the effect of our products on our many publics was never discussed except in terms of cost or sales potential."[52]

The environmental, safety and consumer protection legislation of the 1970s recognized the existence of what economists call externalities — the effects of corporate behavior on the well-being of community members outside the corporation who are unable through legal, contractual or other means to obtain redress — and attempted to require companies such as GM to impound some of these externalities into their cost functions through a combination of performance standards and penalties. As the above examples from GM's annual reports illustrate, however, corporate America strenuously resisted these efforts. And where they had sufficient market power, corporations, in turn, passed the costs on to consumers through price increases, thereby contributing both to rising inflation in the 1970s and to their own vulnerability to foreign competitors.

Conclusion

GM's relations with the state are an important part of the company's history. In various ways the state has mediated GM's relationship with various constituencies including labor, consumers and the general public. State policies have influenced the conditions for capital accumulation by encouraging a way of life that depends on automotive transportation, by providing a physical and human capital infrastructure that reduces corporate costs, and by absorbing, at least temporarily, the costs of many of the more adverse consequences of corporate growth. But the relationship between the state and GM was never one-sided, and has a contradictory facet. State policies which advance the interests of the automobile industry can impede the interests of others (such as competing industries, like railroads, as well as the public, through environmental damage or unsafe vehicles). The state's interest in preserving social order and its own legitimacy can result in policies that reduce corporate autonomy and profits (such as anti-pollution, auto safety or fuel efficiency regulation). Furthermore, by the 1970s the level of state spending to support capital accumulation and to deal with its consequences began to threaten the process of accumulation itself.

GM noted this threat in its 1979 annual report, pointing out that, despite having had the third best year ever in unit sales, company profitability (net income as a percentage of sales) was a dismal 4.4%, well down from its high of 10.3% in 1965. To GM, the remedies were obvious: "disciplining the rise in government spending," "reducing the federal deficit," "curtailing unnecessary and excessively costly regulation" (such as higher fuel economy and auto emission standards, and mandatory air bags and passive restraints), and creating "an industrial environment conducive to restoring and maintaining the health of the industrial base." (AR 1978, AR 1979, AR 1983) This agenda was only partly realized in the ensuing decade. Despite draconian cuts in federal spending on domestic programs in the 1980s, federal deficits rose to record levels, and the nation's industrial base continued to shrink as U.S. corporations, including GM, launched their full-court press against the collective bargaining accord that, for 40 years, had provided the framework for labor-management relations in the mass-production industries.

CHAPTER VII

WHAT IS TO BE DONE?

Today the consequences of the corporate and government assault on labor and the welfare state are only too evident, not only in the automobile industry (as noted in Chapter I), but throughout the U.S. economy. The restructuring that began in the automobile industry in the 1970s, and accelerated in the 1980s, has been echoed throughout U.S. manufacturing (from steel to machine tools, from textiles to tires) for similar reasons and with like results; and is now reverberating throughout sectors of the service economy (including hospitals, stockbrokers, banks, insurance companies and law firms).[1] The labor statistics tell part of the story of its consequences: falling wages, longer working hours, widening gaps in income and wealth between the rich, the working class, and the poor, and a 15-year plunge in the rate of union membership. Government budget deficits — federal, state and local — and the dismantling of social safety nets, the decay in such basic elements of material well-being as housing, health care and education, and increasingly regressive tax policies, tell another part of the story. Clearly, what may be good for GM is not turning out to be very good for most Americans.

The Rich Are Getting Richer

The 1980s was not a good decade for most working Americans. During this period, hourly wages fell 9%, fringe benefits fell almost 14%,[2] and most people were working harder than ever. (Excluding unpaid household labor, it takes an average 750 hours of paid work annually per capita to keep the U.S. economy going, up from 625 in the early 1960s and 700 in the early 1950s.)[3]

Family income has grown more slowly over the past ten years than it did in the 1970s and far more slowly than it did in the period between the

153

end of WWII and 1973.[4] Averages are not the best basis for comparison, of course. As economist Michael Tanzer puts it: "To an economist, if you have one foot in ice water and the other in boiling water, on average, you're just fine." Averages mask distributional differences, and the burden of declining incomes in the 1980s has not been distributed evenly: "After adjusting for inflation, the bottom 40% of families lost income in the 1980s. Families in the middle gained only slightly, mainly thanks to the income of working wives. . . . And as everyone knows by now, the top brackets made out like bandits."[5]

According to the Center on Budget and Policy Priorities: "Census data indicate that the gap between the poor and the rich and the middle class is wider now than at any other time since the end of World War II."[6] Moreover, as the following chart shows, the rich had a little extra help from their friends.

Percent change in household income 1980–1990

	Before Tax Income Change	Tax Burden Change	After Tax Income Change
Poorest 10%	−8.6%	27.7%	N/A
Poorest 20%	−3.8	16.1	−5.2%
Next Poorest 20%	1.4	6.0	0.2
Middle 20%	3.1	1.2	2.7
Next Richest 20%	7.8	−2.2	8.6
Richest 20%	29.8	−5.5	32.5
Richest 5%	44.9	−9.5	50.6
Richest 1%	75.3	−14.4	87.1

Source: Sklar, 1991[7]

At the federal level, as well as in many states, the tax burden has been pushed down the income pyramid through cuts in top personal income taxes and capital gains rates, and through increases in regressive taxes.[8] The cumulative effect is hardly trivial: Robert Reich claims that the U.S. treasury would have received $93 billion more in taxes in 1989, had the top 10% paid their taxes based on the 1977 tax code.[9] Today the richest 1% of Americans (2.5 million individuals) receive nearly as much income after taxes as the bottom 40% (100 million individuals); ten years ago they received only half as much.[10]

Beneath these changes in income distribution are changes in the composition of the work force, as employment growth has moved away from the relatively high-wage unionized, industrial jobs, that formed the elite of American labor in the immediate post-war decades, to lower-wage non-unionized service jobs, disproportionately staffed by women and people of color. According to the U.S. Bureau of Labor Statistics, between 1984 and 1995 the ten occupations that will require the largest number of new workers (in order) are: cashier, registered nurse, janitor, truck driver, waiter and waitress, wholesale trade salesworker, nurses aides and orderlies, retail salespersons, accountants and auditors, and kindergarten and elementary school teachers.[11] The trend, many researchers say, is to a two-tier work force, with a small group of creative, highly skilled people at the top, and a large pool of people needing relatively low job skills, and earning correspondingly lower wages, at the bottom. But low skills in today's labor market does not mean *no* skills; indeed many of the usually manual labor jobs that historically provided entry-level opportunities for workers without training, adequate education or English language skills are rapidly disappearing, lost to technology or even lower-wage workers abroad. According to a *Business Week* report, "Where the Jobs Are Is Where the Skills Aren't," a serious mismatch is developing between the kinds of skills needed for areas of high projected job growth and the skills that will be available in the U.S. labor force between now and the year 2000.[12]

The U.S. Labor Department has developed a scale of one to six for measuring the levels of reading, writing, and vocabulary needed in a wide variety of jobs. The Hudson Institute has matched these skills against the new jobs the economy will be creating. More than three-quarters of new workers will have limited skills (that is, skills at level one, the ability to write only simple sentences, and level two, the ability to write compound sentences) and will be competent for only 40% of the new jobs. Retail sales, one of the major new job-producing areas, for example, requires skills at level three (the ability to "read safety rules and equipment instructions, and write simple reports") in order to write up orders, compute price lists, and read merchandise catalogues. Jobs in nursing and management, two other growth areas, require more than a high school education and level four skills (the ability to "read journals and manuals, write reports, and understand complex terminology"). The Hudson Institute says that just 5% of new employees will be at level four. *Business Week* warns that as new job seekers compete for a dwindling number of low-skill jobs, they will drive down wages for those who can least afford it; and in the U.S. this means primarily blacks and latinos.

This is already happening. Starting in the late 1970s, the so-called "college wage premium," the wage levels for job categories that employ disproportionately more whites, such as professionals, managers, and sales personnel, grew substantially faster than wage levels for those categories that employ disproportionate numbers of blacks, such as machine operatives and clerical, service and household workers.[13] At the same time that real incomes have been falling for many Americans, the social safety net that was the product of the Keynesian economic policies of the post-war decades is being systematically dismantled.

The Unravelling of the Social Safety Net

Under the Reagan and Bush administrations,[14] the federal government has been simultaneously gutting federally financed public housing, jobs and public assistance programs; cutting the budgets (and hence the enforcement effectiveness) of agencies responsible for worker and consumer safety and health; immobilizing antitrust laws (in the midst of the greatest merger wave of the century); and shifting responsibility for many public services to state and local governments, while cutting back on funds to these jurisdictions. In turn, state and local authorities have been paring back their own social programs. In the 1970s, federal aid to local governments represented 3.1% of the Gross National Product (GNP); by 1991, it fell to around 2.4%.[15] Or, to look at it another way, at their peak in the late 1970s, federal grants comprised 26% of state and local government spending; today, they represent some 18%.[16] Unlike the federal government (which, writes the *Wall Street Journal,* "can and often does create money out of thin air through Federal Reserve operations"), state and local governments must keep their books in balance.[17] If their revenues fall short of their expenditures, they must raise taxes and/or cut spending, and do so immediately. They are doing both, in traditional and not so traditional ways.

Responding to cuts in federal support, many states are transferring programs to cities and towns, which are now responsible for over 50% of the costs of water, sewage, roads, parks, welfare, and public schools. Teachers are being laid off; libraries are being closed (or their programs curtailed); programs such as elementary school and athletic activities and day care are being charged for, eliminated, or cut back; desperately needed public housing is not being built; nor are physical infrastructure repairs being made. In 1976, state and local governments were spending $203.25 per $1,000 in personal income on general expenditures; $26.14 on welfare; and $77.32 on education.[18] In 1988, the corresponding expenditures were $186.36 per $1,000 in personal income on general expenditures; $22.95 on welfare; and $64.40 on education.

The impact of these cutbacks varies by class. Indeed, according to Robert Reich, the top fifth of Americans "is quietly seceding from the rest of the nation."[19] The secession takes several forms. The wealthy are privatizing the public services that are decaying for everyone else: sending their children to private schools, spending their leisure time in private health clubs instead of deteriorating public parks and playgrounds, commuting to work by car or via private transportation services instead of mass transit, hiring private police and security services (whose numbers, Reich reports, exceed the number of public police officials) to protect themselves and their property, and even living in residential communities that maintain their own roads.

The wealthy, says Reich, have splintered most urban centers into two separate cities:

> a "revitalized" downtown consisting of "clusters of post-modern office buildings . . . multilevel parking garages, hotels with glass-enclosed atriums, upscale shopping plazas and galleries, theaters, convention centers and luxury condos. . . . The lucky resident is able to shop, work and attend the theater without risking direct contact with the . . . other city. . . .

The other city is the home of service workers, who staff the offices, shops, condos, hotels, and hospitals, and the remaining blue-collar workers, all of whom are disproportionately people of color. The public services on which these other residents of the city rely — their hospitals, schools, transportation system, parks — are not only decaying but are themselves being taken out of the public realm. (This transfer is another form of privatization and we will return to it below.)

A parallel secession is taking place in the suburbs, according to Thomas Byrne Edsall and Mary D. Edsall. The 1992 Presidential election will be the first in which the suburban vote will be an absolute majority of the total electorate.[20] These suburban voters are finding that they can satisfy their desire for public services for themselves, at the local level, while still supporting austerity at the federal, and even the state, level. Since they no longer live in the cities they have less self-interest in making the kinds of investments in public services that the cities need. Public schools illustrate clearly this growing race-based division of interest. In 1986, 96.7 percent of white children were being educated outside of the twenty-five largest central-city school districts, compared with 27.5 percent of all black school children and 30 percent of all latino school children.

Another way to cut spending is to transfer responsibility for public services to the private sector. Increasingly, throughout the U.S., cities and states are hiring private companies to manage prisons, roads, parks, commuter railways, social service agencies, hospitals and ambulance services, trash collection, park maintenance, vehicle towing, cemeteries, and airports.[21] Critics of privatization argue that it may save less public money than expected while generating greater social costs. In order to make a profit, the private companies usually cutback on pay, benefits, and numbers of employees, with predictable results. The city employees who lose their jobs often end up on the rolls of public welfare and health agencies. The low wages and benefits often lead to high turnover and impaired service delivery. Nor is there any guarantee that a private provider will operate more efficiently than a public one. Studies of public utilities, for example, have found that they are no less efficient or competitive than private ones.[22]

A related strategy for dealing with rising state, local, as well as federal deficits is to sell off publicly-owned and -operated services. A number of major Wall Street investment bankers, smelling an opportunity to profit from the financial woes of America's states and cities, are among the boosters of this form of privatization. According to the *Wall Street Journal,* firms such as Goldman Sachs, Lazard Freres, and Shearson Lehman, are gearing up for what they hope will be one of the Street's booming businesses in the 1990s.[23] They are encouraging cities and states to sell anything they own with predictable earnings (such as energy authorities, toll roads, water systems, even prisons, colleges, and liquor stores) and, of course, to hire them to put the deals together.[24]

According to spokespersons for the Reagan and Bush administrations, the trend toward privatization, the cuts in taxes, welfare, and public services, and the dismantling of the federal regulatory apparatus, are all part of the solution and not part of the problem. The problem, as they see it, is that excessive government regulation and taxes have been choking off corporate America's inherent economic vigor. What we need, they say, is a combination of deregulation and tax incentives that will both unleash America's competitive forces and subject them to the old-fashioned discipline of the market. This combination of unfettered competition and market discipline will, their argument continues, generate economic growth whose benefits will trickle down to all Americans. So far, however, the prescription does not seem to be working.

No communities in the U.S. have been more devastated by these policies than those least able to fend for themselves—the poor and their children, disproportionately black and latino. Nearly 20% of children under 18 in the U.S.—13 million boys and girls—live in poverty (up 5 percentage points since 1973).[25] For black and latino children the percentages are 45% and 39%, respectively. Infant mortality, which had been declining dramatically from the 1940s through the 1970s, barely moved in the 1980s. The U.S. now ranks nineteenth in the world in the rate of infant mortality (the rate for blacks is twice that of whites), behind countries such as Singpore, Spain and the former East Germany; it ranks seventeenth in the share of one-year olds who are immunized against polio; and twenty-eigth in children who are born at the proper weight. These childhood statistics translate into equally grim statistics for adults; statistics that are similarly skewed by race. Male or female, if you are an adult in Harlem between the ages of fifteen and sixty-five, your chances of dying in a given year are higher than in parts of Bangladesh. Nationally, between 1973 and 1986, average real earnings for blacks below twenty-five years fell by 50%; and their employment rate fell from 44% to 35%. Nearly 26% of all young black men in the U.S. are in jail, on probation or on parole. Overall, on a per capita basis, the U.S. imprisons more people per 100,000 of population than any other country in the world — more than the former Soviet Union, more than South Africa — and 46% of those prisoners are black. (Blacks constitute 12% of the population.)

As Americans reel from the consequences of the dual business-government assault on labor and the welfare state, they are told that the massive budget deficits at the federal, state, and local levels preclude any efforts to rebuild either the impoverished social welfare system or the nation's crumbling physical and human capital infrastructures.

Budget Deficits: Liberal or Conservative Tool?

Under Reagan and now Bush, two conservative presidents, the federal budget deficit has been on an upward trajectory. Deficit spending, supposedly the economic tool of liberal Keynesians, has become the weapon of two presidents intent on taking apart the legacies of both Roosevelt's New Deal and Johnson's Great Society. Over the long term, *Business Week* warned in the summer of 1990, the level of public debt that will be required to finance the growing deficit will put an intolerable burden on future generations. In the short term, dealing with the deficit has virtually paralyzed the government while the nation's critical needs — "educating new generations, rebuilding a decaying infrastructure, and ensuring the competitiveness of the U.S. — go largely unmet."[26]

Business Week, one of the U.S.'s premier business publications, is clearly worried about the deficit. In the summer of 1991 the Office of Management and Budget's midsession review projected a cumulative deficit for 1991–1995 of $1.087 trillion, double that of nine months earlier.[27] The deficit projected for 1992 is the largest ever, $348 billion, an amount that is no longer being offset by the state and local surpluses that accompanied the record Reagan deficits of the 1980s. Without these offsetting state and local surpluses, warns economist Paul Craig Roberts, the U.S. will have not only the "biggest budget deficit in the world in dollar terms," but also the "second biggest budget deficit in the world as a share of GNP."

Roberts was not always worried about the deficit, and he shared this perspective with *The Wall Street Journal* and a number of more liberal economists, including Robert Eisner and Robert Heilbroner.[28] After all, the size of the deficit depends upon a number of arbitrary decisions about measurement and the timing of receipts and expenditures. Should we include state and local budgets in measuring the public sector deficit? Back in the 1980s, when state budgets were running surpluses, Roberts and others argued that the true public sector deficit was about one-third less than when one looked at the federal budget alone. Moreover, they pointed out, this "general government deficit" and related public debt, as a percentage of GNP, ranked about average when one looked at comparable figures for our major trading partners, such as Japan.[29] A number of other, more controversial measurement decisions were also reducing the reported deficit. The federal government includes the surpluses in the social security and various trust funds in calculating the deficit — money whose use is restricted and therefore not available for operating expenses (although it is invested in Treasury securities that finance the deficit). If these surpluses were not included in calculating the 1991 fiscal year budget, the projected deficit would have been $138 billion higher. And what about the cost of the savings and loan bailout? The Bush administration includes the costs of acquiring and disposing of S&L assets in the operating budget. In the short run this inflates the deficit, but as the newly acquired assets are sold it will reduce deficits in later years (although the amount of the reduction depends on their selling prices). This strategy allowed the administration to claim that 1994's budget deficit would be lower than 1992's. Furthermore, since the U.S. budget is based on cash inflows and outflows, the deficit can be (and is) manipulated by adjusting the timing of receipts and payments and by selling government assets (as in privatization programs). Finally, the deficit numbers politicians argue about are government projections, and these projections require numerous assumptions and estimates about the future. What will be the level of corporate profits and personal income? the rate of growth in GNP? in inflation? in unemployment? in interest rates? In an angry op-ed in the *Wall Street Journal,* Paul Craig Roberts recently accused the Bush administration of "cooking the books" by, among other things, basing their October 1990 budget projections on assumptions and projections they knew were unrealistic assumptions in order to understate the growth of forthcoming deficits.[30]

None of these caveats means that we should not be worried about the current deficit (however measured) and the level of government debt. We should. But whether a specific deficit is a problem or not depends on how the money is spent and how its benefits and the burden of interest payments are apportioned. Businesses make a distinction between spending on capital investments — that is, spending to acquire resources that will provide a future stream of benefits (capital accumulation) in excess of the initial outlays — and spending on current operations whose benefits, if any, will not extend beyond the present. The U.S. government does not make such a distinction in its budgeting, although it should. As *Business Week* recognizes — and as is obvious from our decaying infrastructures, the state of health care, job training and education, and the lack of affordable housing — wherever the money we borrowed has gone, it has not been used to acquire and develop the resources, physical or human, that will provide a better future. That is, it has not been spent on capital investment, or what is in this case more appropriately termed social investment.

Nor have the Reagan-Bush economic strategies — the combination of deregulation, cuts in social spending and taxes and rising deficits — worked. According to Samuel Bowles, David Gordon, and Thomas Weisskopf, in their recent book, *After the Wasteland,* recent economic policies have failed to jumpstart our stalled economy.[31] According to one chart in their book, the U.S. ranked last in productivity growth and real (inflation adjusted) investment in the 1980s. From 1959 to 1969 real GNP growth averaged 4 percent a year; from 1969 to 1979, 2.8 percent and in the 1980s, 2.6 percent. Last year's figure was an anemic 0.3 percent and for 1991 the Federal Reserve Bank is predicting 1.1 percent. As Doug Henwood puts it: "This is not a happy prospect."

Reagonomics unleashed a boom. But it was a boom in military spending and financial speculation that included junk bonds, risky commercial real estate development, greenmail, leveraged buyouts, and an imaginative variety of financial instruments and strategies. It was fueled by the largest tax reduction act in U.S. history. Its fruits were the invasions of Granada and Panama, the Gulf War, and massive federal, state, and local government budget deficits, the savings and loan debacle, and mounting failures among commercial banks, insurance companies and, increasingly likely, in publicly guaranteed pension plans. Hundreds of billions of taxpayer dollars will be required in forthcoming decades to undo the damage done by these speculative excesses and by the environmental abuses wrought by corporations and the U.S. military.

The new prosperity of the rich and the very rich reported above comes not from their share of an increasing pie but from a massive redistribution of an existing, at best slowly growing one, in their favor. While restructuring taxes and reordering our spending priorities will improve the quality of working peoples' lives (assuming such goals can even be achieved in the political climate of the U.S. in the 1990s), social investment spending will be constrained for years by the policies of Reagan and Bush. There is not much we can do now about the explosive and wasteful burden of debt, the S&L bailout, the broadening crises in commercial banking, insurance, pensions, the environment, and the years of interest payments we will be making on them all. This legacy of fixed costs will make it all the harder to restore and improve the social programs that have been gutted. There are some who say that this was just what the conservatives had in mind all along.

But if things are so bad, why haven't we "voted the bastards out?" After all, the very rich are also very few in number. To answer this question we have to return to the legacy of the post-war ideological framework and some important modifications that have taken place in the last decade or so.

Race and Changing Ideology: Conservative Populism

There is no question that many Americans are unhappy about the state of America: today's generation of under thirty-year olds may be the first U.S. generation ever — since the Great Depression did not affect an entire generation — that will not match their parents' living standards.[32] Millions of Americans have lost their jobs and are finding that they cannot replace them at comparable levels of earnings. There is hardly a community in the U.S. that is not affected by crime, drug use, AIDS, homelessness, deteriorating public services, rising medical costs — the list goes on and on. But these concerns have not been translated into progressive politics.

There are many reasons for this, but it is beyond the scope of this book to identify or examine them in any depth. Clearly the post-war ideological framework examined in Chapter V, particularly the social consumption norm and the omnipotence of science and technology, played a major role in depoliticizing most Americans. For over fifty years the real choices, the ones that mattered most, have been the choices that take place in the realm of consumption. Political choice has meant simply voting yea or nay periodically for pre-chosen candidates. Most U.S. workers accept automation of the workplace, concessionary labor agreements, the movement of jobs overseas, as the unpleasant but inevitable consequences of external forces, of technology, competition, globalization, the Japanese — forces that victimize their employers as much as themselves. The mechanisms required for a democratic, oppositional politics — one that can identify, analyze, and articulate grievances and channel protest — did not develop in post-war America. The workers are the victims of Cold War anti-communist hysteria, a union bureaucracy subservient to Democratic Party politics, and a media and popular culture that became increasingly concentrated in corporate hands. Nor is it likely that such a politics could develop easily from the grass roots.

Most Americans today have had little experience in collective action. The much vaunted American mobility means that many Americans seldom stay in one place long enough to put down roots and build social ties. Suburban sprawl places many Americans in dispersed communities, often located far from their jobs, so that it is difficult for workers to gather together at the end of the day. Americans have also been working longer hours than they did twenty years ago; the equivalent of an additional month of work a year.[33] Today's Americans are often too tired after work to engage in active leisure, let alone in political organizing. And every step in their socialization, from school to work to the apparatuses of consumption, to TV, emphasizes their individuality.

Although the spread of religious fundamentalism in recent years reflects the hunger of many Americans for a more connected, communal life and their deep dissatisfaction with the values of post-war America, the movement's political thrust has not been progressive. Indeed it has played an instrumental role in the development and spread of conservative populism; a movement that began with George Wallace's third-party candidacy in 1968.

By co-opting the conservative populist movement, Ronald Reagan and George Bush completed the disintegration of the political coalition behind Roosevelt's New Deal and Johnson's Great Society, a coalition of Southern conservatives, Northeast liberals, blacks, and working class whites. During the recession of 1980, for example, forty-two percent of unionized autoworkers voted for Ronald Reagan; a similar percentage voted for him in 1984, despite the loss of thousands of auto-industry jobs. In their May 1991 essay in the *Atlantic,* Thomas Byrne Edsall and Mary D. Edsall sketch out the process through which a swing in allegiance by a mere 5% to 10% of the voting electorate, mostly white working class, has shifted the majority in American presidential politics from liberal to conservative.

In a period of two decades, write the Edsalls, the government has been converted from ally to adversary; the enemy, from an establishment ruled by corporate interests and aligned with the Republican Party, to a "hated new liberal establishment, adversarial to the common man: an elite of judges, bureaucrats, newspaper editors, ACLU lawyers, academics, Democratic politicians, civil rights and feminist leaders — determined to enact racially and socially redistributive policies demanding the largest sacrifices from the white working and lower-middle classes."[34] This new majority opposes busing, affirmative action, and much of the rights revolution on behalf of criminal defendants, prisoners, homosexuals, welfare recipients, and other marginalized groups. They blame these policies, their liberal advocates, and the blacks, latinos, poor, feminists, and gays who benefit from them, for the rising rates of crime, welfare dependency, illegitimacy, and educational failure that are absorbing their taxes, making them afraid to go out at night, threatening their jobs, and corrupting their children.

The Republican Party recognized, developed, and exploited these sentiments in advance of the Democrats, and have largely succeeded, at least at the level of Presidential politics, in linking the Democrats with the discredited liberal agenda. But the Democrats are scrambling as fast as they can to disassociate themselves from this label and to jump on the conservative populist bandwagon clad in neo-liberal garb. Governor Bill Clinton of Arkansas exemplifies this "new" Democratic politics.[35] He talks about helping the poor, but also about requiring "that everybody who can go to work do it"; he emphasizes that the Democratic promise of "opportunity for all" includes the middle class; and while he calls for a more active Federal government, he also calls for a new emphasis on values, particularly the value of personal responsibility.

So What Is To Be Done?

We can begin by placing the blame where it really belongs, on corporate America and, yes, on government too. But doing so is more difficult than it sounds, as Jane Slaughter learned during a visit to a town rally in Ypsilanti, Michigan, in January, 1992.[36] Just before Christmas, 1991, GM announced that it would eliminate 74,000 jobs by 1995, and that either the Willow Run plant near Ypsilanti or a plant in Arlington, Texas would close. Slaughter writes:

> At the rally, well attended by politicans and UAW local officials, *not one word* was said in criticsm of GM. Not one word was said about the other 71,000 jobs that will be lost in addition to the ones in the Willow Run-Arlington fray. Not one speaker suggested that Arlington workers and Willow Run workers were in this fight together.
>
> The largest applause of the day went to UAW Region 1A Director Bob King, who brought down the house with his call for 'no more Japanese products coming in here.' The second largest went to Rep. William

Ford, who jokingly urged the crowd to beat up people who like Japanese cars. . . .

There was no questioning of GM's decision to close one of the two plants and the other 20 it has on the chopping block.

The price paid by labor for the post-war accord has finally come home to roost. Without countervailing forces — such as strong trade unions — the dynamics of capitalism will drive employers to extract more surplus value from workers and will promote high levels of unemployment that ensure that those with jobs are appropriately grateful for their good fortune. As Slaughter points out, the real problem is not that high quality automobiles are coming into the U.S. but that there aren't enough jobs in this country for people who need them. And there aren't enough jobs because "the free enterprise system . . . doesn't provide jobs for everyone. It's not intended to. It needs a substantial percentage of unemployment to keep the employed in line. Nervous. Ready to blame anyone but the beneficiaries of the system for their anxiety."

This dynamic works even in Western Europe where, because of their much stronger unions, European workers benefit from shorter work weeks, faster rising weekly earnings, and extensive national health care systems that provide better and cheaper health care than in the U.S.[37] In Germany, "co-determination" gives workers a voice in management, the thirty-five hour work week is becoming the norm, and annual vacation of six weeks are typical. It should therefore come as no surprise that some European employers are moving rapidly to take advantage of Europe's latest underclass: the 500,000 to 1,000,000 migrant laborers flooding in from the East each year.[38] In Germany, where wage and benefit costs average $23.53 an hour (compared with $14.77 in the U.S. and $12.64 in Japan), the lure of cheap labor is irresistible. A Mercedes contractor in Nagold, on the edge of German's Black Forest, for example, hires Polish workers who labor six-day, sixty hour weeks, for $3 a hour (four times the wages in Poland, but barely a quarter of what Germans earn at the same factory.) A spot check among German construction companies found that 90% of them use illegal Eastern European workers.

Even strong national unions are no match for today's free-wheeling global capital with its ties to the state apparatus. American labor needs powerful unions, democratically accountable to broad-based memberships, and able to work in solidarity with unions in places like Japan, Korea, Mexico, and Europe. American labor needs a clear understanding of who is responsible for, and benefits from the past decades' assaults on their jobs and standard of living. What they have instead are weak, authoritarian, hierarchical, nationalist unions, with shrinking memberships (close to 85%

of all workers do not belong to any union). Atomized and isolated, workers' anger at lost jobs and declining living standards provides fertile soil for rightwing appeals to nationalism, racism, sexism, and homophobia.

For several decades after World War II, it seemed as if the system could indeed provide jobs for everyone (and especially for white men). But those decades were an aberration and the conditions that produced them began to disappear by the mid-1960s. According to *The Economist*, "America in the post-war years really was a self-contained economy that could provide its unquestionably American people with virtually everything they wanted."[39] But this America, with its rising rates of productivity, marriage and fertility, and its soaring increases in real disposable personal income was, by historical measures, "an oddity." Or, as economist Alan Blinder puts it: "It couldn't last, and it didn't. Once you realize that much of what is viewed as America's decline is merely a return to normalcy, it doesn't seem so bad."[40] Not so bad for whom? And how long will it take for this "return to normalcy" to include a return to the more self-conscious class-based politics of late nineteenth century and most of the earlier years of the twentieth?

There are schemes aplenty for reversing what many still see as America's decline. Along the liberal-left spectrum, economists, such as Bennet Harrison and Barry Bluestone, call for the formation of a national industrial policy to be administered by a tripartite body of representatives from the corporate, labor, and state sectors; an expanded role for workers and unions in making business decisions (including investment, plant location, product design, quality and prices, etc.); the expansion of trade unionism and a simultaneous commitment by trade unions to increasing productivity; the rebuilding of the public infrastructure (such as highways, bridges, water systems, railroads, education, and training) and of social welfare programs; the replacement of current international trade practices and agreements (GATT) by global trading relationships that are "negotiated and planned, managed in such a way as to smooth economic transitions within and between countries."[41] Economists Samuel Bowles, David Gordon and Thomas Weisskopf recommend building a "democratic economics" built on four basic rights: "economic security and equity (job programs, higher minimum wage, affirmative action); a democratic workplace (honest unions, profit sharing and cooperatives, right-to-know legislation); democratic economic decision making (election of the Fed, a public investment bank, more local influence over development and environmental decisions); and, simply, the right to a better life (lower military spending, national health insurance, expanded public housing, improved education, a more progressive tax system, a non-nuclear, non-fossil-fuel energy program)."[42]

Fair enough, as far as they go; indeed who could argue against their appeals for a more just and cooperative society? But neither set of authors goes far enough. The problem isn't simply that they provide no map for getting from here to there, it is that there is no there, there. In offering their respective solutions, the authors are exhorting America's decision makers to behave voluntaristically in ways that are antithetical to the basic presumptions of the capitalist dynamic: the drive for capital accumulation through profits and growth. Their proposals ignore both the ways that the current balance of power between labor and capital and the absence of a coherent oppositional politics in the U.S. work against such utopian scenarios being realized and the likelihood that, even if realizable (as in post-war Sweden, say), such outcomes will be unstable at best.

The short run may be long enough to begin with, however, and instability is a fact of life. The important question then is how do we create the kind of labor movement and political climate that would make such changes possible? One way is by building mechanisms for corporate accountability, which brings us back to the Introduction to this book: "If one is going to take the issue of accountability seriously one must imagine, not only a radically different role for accountants and a radically different kind of accounting, but a vehicle for communication that differs from today's financial statements and the annual reports in which they appear."

Corporate Accountability for the Twenty-first Century

Corporate annual reports are permeated with conflicts of interest. The certified public accounting firms that audit the financial statements cannot be independent of the firms they audit, despite the profession's claims to the contrary. They are hired and paid by the enterprises they audit and many of them also perform substantial additional consulting work for these same clients. Yes, auditors are formally authorized by shareholders to report to audit committees that consist of outside members of Boards of Directors, and to direct their opinions to the firms' shareholders, not management. And auditors are subject to formal peer review procedures and professional standards of ethics. But "form" is the operative word here. The substance of auditors' relationships with the firms they audit is determined by the economic relationship between them. I have never met an auditor who, when using the term "client," was referring to anyone other than the company's management. CPA firms are private, profit-making enterprises, subject to the same pressures for profitability and growth as all other business in a free-enterprise economy. And the pressures of today's economy—in which the numbers of mergers, acquisitions and business failures are reducing the client pool and intensifying competition among audit firms—make it increasingly difficult for any audit firm to risk losing a client, particularly a large one.

Step one in ensuring corporate accountability is to break the economic links between the audit firm and the corporation. Auditors should be assigned to clients by an independent body and rotated periodically. The practice of auditing financial statements should also be severed from the provision of consulting services. Unless this is done, auditors will remain vulnerable to real or anticipated client pressures, in order to preserve these other sources of income, and will continue to find themselves responsible for evaluating some of the very systems and business decisions they have helped frame and implement.

Step two in ensuring corporate accountability is to take the nonfinancial statement portion of the annual report out of the hands of management. GM's annual reports may have been valuable to me as a scholar, but they were of virtually no value to the company's customers, employees, suppliers, or the communities in which they operate their facilities and sell their products. Even GM's so-called "Public Interest Reports," which they have been producing for the past twenty years, are, like their annual reports, one-sided and self-congratulatory. Neither document provides information that can be used to challenge management and hold GM accountable for their activities.

For there to be genuine corporate accountability there must be an independent system for gathering information from corporations about their activities, for assessing the impact of those activities on the public, and for disseminating the findings to all those to whom the corporation is accountable including employees, customers, suppliers, communities, shareholders, creditors, political bodies. The heart of this system of accountability could be a reconstituted and truly "public" accounting profession compensated by neither shareholders nor corporate management directly, but from taxes levied on corporate income. In addition to financial professionals, these public accounting firms would be staffed by economists, engineers, environmental scientists, sociologists, and would be accountable to boards—perhaps one for each corporation being audited and a single supervisory body—consisting of rotating representatives from unions, customers, minorities' and women's groups, communities, shareholders, legislators. These new public accounting bodies would monitor, evaluate, and report on the impact of corporate activities on the public, much like the Government Accounting Office (GAO) monitors government performance. Corporate management could be invited to respond and their comments published in the reports.

If we had had truly constituency-oriented annual reports the American public would have learned long before the 1992 elections that U.S. CEOs earn 160 times what the average worker does (up from 34 times in the mid-1970s) and that Japanese CEOS earn significantly less (16 times average worker earnings).[43] They would know what many car-buyers have long known, that after years of promising improved quality, U.S. cars still do not match those of their international competitors.[44] They would know that at a time that most Americans, including motorists, want environmental protection along with lower operating and insurance costs, GM has been spending freely for ads, lobbyists, and expensive, glossy Public Interest Reports, that argue for rolling back even the most modest standards in the areas of safety, fuel efficiency, pollution or bumper strength, and that GM lags behind its competitors in installing air bags.[45] They would know that a joint GM-UAW study has found that workers at GM's Lordstown, Ohio, complex are dying from cancer at a substantially faster rate than the general population despite GM's initial claims that the company's "records and test data indicate that there is no problem."[46] It is not that this and other critical information is not out there — it is often in news articles, reports from critics such as Ralph Nader, *Consumer Reports, Labor Notes* and other watchdogs — but it is not always accessible on a timely basis; it certainly is not found in one place; and some of the most important information is simply buried in corporate files. Independent, publicly accountable bodies (such as the reconstituted public accounting firms I envision above) that are authorized to conduct accountability audits and prepare constituency-oriented annual reports, however, would make such information available and accessible on a timely basis and could form a basis for political organizing around corporate accountability issues.

Requiring such reports, developing the constituency-based institutions for producing them, and financing their development and distribution won't be much easier than achieving some of the lofty goals of the economists I criticized above. Making it happen will be the challenge for critical accounting in the coming years.

ENDNOTES

Introduction

1. Chrysler still remains number three when truck sales are included. In 1991 GM's car market share was 35.4% and Ford's was 19.9%. (*Wall Street Journal,* January 7, 1992, p. B1.)
2. Lindblom, Charles, *Politics and Markets: The World's Political-Economic Systems,* New York: Basic Books, Inc., Publishers, 1977, p.171.
3. Lindblom, 1977, p.173.
4. The following draws on examples discussed in editorials in volumes 1 and 3 of *Advances in Public Interest Accounting,* Greenwich, CO: JAI Press, 1986, 1990.
5. Since the 1960s, a number of alternatives to the mainstream accounting perspective have appeared in the accounting literature, among them social accounting, public interest accounting, and radical accounting. Although I am using the term critical accounting to embrace all of these counter-perspectives, I do not intend to imply that they are in any sense homogenous. They are not. For example, not only are radical accountants often critical of social and public interest accounting, there are sharp differences among radical accountants, many of whom would even reject use of the term "radical" to describe their work. (The interested reader may want to examine past issues of *Accounting, Auditing and Accountability, Accounting, Organizations and Society, Advances in Public Interest Accounting,* and *Critical Perspectives on Accounting.*)
6. These questions were intially posed by the editors of *Critical Perspectives on Accounting* in their inaugural issue in March 1991.

Chapter I: That Was Then, This Is Now

1. Lindblom, Charles, *Politics and Markets: The World's Political-Economic Systems,* New York: Basic Books, Inc., Publishers, 1977, p.187.
2. *The Wall Street Journal,* June 15, 1987, p.1.
3. American Honda Motor Corporation finished the 1990 model year a mere 0.7% behind Chrysler in car sales. *Wards Auto World,* November 1990.

GM's world market share: *The Wall Street Journal,* July 20, 1990. In 1991, both Honda's and Toyota's U.S. car sales exceeded Chrysler's. *Wall Street Journal,* January 7, 1992, p.B1.

4. White, Joseph B. and Mitchell, Jacqueline, "Detroit Rolls Out Old Ploy: Quotas," *The Wall Street Journal,* January 14, 1991. In contrast with Iacocca, Ford Chairman Poling would like to see Japan reduce its exports enough to cut its trade surplus with the U.S. by 25% a year for the next four years. GM opposes any such restrictions, arguing that "Market shares are determined by competition."

5. Ferguson, Thomas and Rogers, Joel, "Big Labor Is Hurting Itself," *The Nation,* September 1, 1984, pp.129+.

6. *Business Week,* September 10, 1990, p.26.

7. On December 18, 1991, GM's chairman and chief executive, Robert C. Stempel, announced the closing of 21 plants in North America and the loss of 74,000 jobs (20,000 from its present 91,000 salaried employees and 54,000 from its present 304,000 hourly work force) by the mid-1990s. He declined to say which plants would be closed and he left open the possibility of further cuts should the recession continue. *New York Times,* December 19, 1992; *Economist,* January 3, 1992, p.80, *Wall Street Journal,* December 19,1992.

8. Flax, Steven, "Did GM Give Away The Floor," *Fortune,* October 15, 1984, pp.223+; *The Wall Street Journal,* May 30, 1986, p.6; *Wards Auto World,* October, 1990, p.77; Schlesinger, Jacob M. and White, Joseph B., "Shrinking Giant: The New Model GM Will Be More Compact But More Profitable," *The Wall Street Journal,* June 6, 1988, p.1; Slaughter, Jane, "New Auto Contract Trades Jobs for Income Protection," *Labor Notes,* October, 1990.

9. *The Wall Street Journal,* November 6, 1985; *General Motors Counter Annual Report, 1987,* Transnationals Information Exchange (T.I.E.), Amsterdam, Netherlands.

10. In the five year period from 1961–1965 retail sales of automobiles in the U.S. increased by 30.5%, but then the growth rate began to fall sharply in each of the next five-year periods: to 18.2% in 1966–1970, 11.0% in 1971–1975, and then to 4% in 1976–1980. Sweezy, Paul, "The Deepening Crisis of U.S. Capitalism," *Monthly Review,* October 1981, pp.1–16, using as sources US Dept of Commerce, Business Statistics and Survey of Current Business, various years.

   Retail sales of cars and light trucks averaged 11.1 million in the three years from 1981–1983; 15.2 million in the three years from 1984–1986; and 14.9 million in the three years from 1987–1989. Sales fell sharply in the recession years 1990 and 1991.

   Judge, Paul C., "He Didn't Ask, but Here's Some Advice for GM's Bob Stempel": *The New York Times,* August 5, 1990, p.5, using statistics from the Motor Vehicle Manufacturers Association. Levin, Doron P.,

"Vehicle Sales In Decline But Hope Is Seen," *The New York Times,* June 5, 1991, p.D1.

Americans increasingly depend on their automobiles for transportation. According to the Highway Users Foundation only 6.2% of Americans take mass transit to work, less than one-half the percentage in 1960. From *Wards Auto World,* October, 1990.

11. *Wall Street Journal,* August 4, 1986, p.14.

12. *Economic Notes,* Labor Research Associates, July/August, 1984.

13. *The Wall Street Journal,* October 28, 1985.

14. *How World's Automakers Are Related,* Ward's Automotive International, Detroit, Michigan, 1991.

15. *General Motors Counter Annual Report, 1987,* Transnationals Information Exchange (T.I.E.), Amsterdam, Netherlands. The Zaragosa workforce turned out to be more militant than expected and five years after the plant opened workers conducted a series of one-day work stoppages to demand improved wages, benefits and working conditions.

16. O'Reilly, Brian, "Business Makes A Run For The Border," *Fortune,* August, 1986, pp.70+.

17. *Wards Auto World,* July, 1990, December, 1990, June, 1991.

18. For example, GM's joint venture with the Hungarian owned truck and parts-maker, Hungarian Railway Carriage and Machine Works, RABA, to assemble cars for local sale, and engines for export to Western Europe; and with Czechoslavakia's Bratislava Automobilove Zavody, BAZ, to produce cars for local consumption, and transmissions for export. From *Ward's Automotive International,* 1991.

19. North American Transplants:

Manufacturer	Location	Employment	Capacity
Nissan	Smyrna, TN	3,900	250,000 cars & light trucks; 450,000 by 1992
	Decherd, TN	announced 1/18/91	300,000 engines
Toyota	Georgetown, KY	3,450	218,000 cars; 300,000 engines
		5,000 by 1994	420,000 cars by 1994
	Cambridge, Ont.	1,000	60,800 cars
Subaru-Isuzu	Lafayette, IN	1,900	120,000 cars & trucks. Expanding to 170,000 in mid 1991 and to 240,000 in mid 90s
Honda	Anna, OH Marysville, OH E. Liberty, OH	10,050	360,000 cars in Marysville; 150,000 cars in E. Liberty; 500,000 engines in Anna & 60,000 motorcycles
Honda	Alliston, Ont.	1,200	100,000 cars

Manufacturer	Location	Employment	Capacity
Hyundai	Bromont, Quebec	800	100,000 by 1992
*Nissan/Ford	Avon Lake, OH	1,726 3,000 by 1993	135,000 minivans; 150,000 econoline bodies
*NUMMI***	Fremont, CA	2,500	240,000 cars expanding to 340,000, adding pickups
*Ford/Mazda	Flat Rock, MI	3,500	240,000
*Diamond- Star	Normal, IL	3,000	240,000
**CAMI	Ingersoll, Ont.	2,000	120,000 cars; 80,000 suvs

* UAW plant

** Canadian Auto Workers Union plant

*** The agreement between Toyota and GM expires in 1996. According to Wards, Toyota expects to acquire the plant at that time.

20. *Wards Auto World,* March, 1991.
21. *Business Week,* August 10, 1987, p.76.
22. In the mid-1980s, General Motors had 650–750 suppliers; today they have about 400. Ford is reported to be planning to cut the number of their suppliers by one-third in the next 5 to 10 years. *Wards Auto World,* January, 1991; March, 1991.
23. *Wards Auto World,* January, 1991. According to one recent survey, 67% of the firms reported having significant profit erosion in the past two years; another study found that more than 60% of the Japanese transplants are losing money. *Wards Auto World,* April, 1991; March, 1991.
24. *Labor Notes,* November, 1990.
25. *Wards Auto World,* March, 1991, p.29.
26. *Wards Auto World,* April, 1991, p.33
27. *Wards Auto World,* March, 1991, p.7.
28. Miller, Edward K. and Winter, Drew, "The Other Big 3 Are Becoming All American," *Wards Auto World,* February, 1991, pp.24+. The following discussion draws heavily on this article.
29. Toyota recently announced plans to expand its U.S. design center and make major additions to its Technical Centers in California and Ann Arbor; Nissan is building a North American engineering center in the Detroit suburb of Farmington Hills. Ibid.
30. Under Corporate Average Fuel Economy (CAFE) regulations, when a vehicle reaches 75% domestic content, it becomes a fleet of its own. Hence, for those cars with highest mileage (such as a new car Nissan plans for Smyrna), it is unlikely that the manufacturer will increase content beyond 74.9%, since it would then lose the vehicle's contribution to overall fleet mileage. Ibid.31. *Wards Auto World,* July, 1990.
32. *Business Week,* March 3, 1986.
33. *Wards Auto World,* December, 1990, p.57.

34. Brody, Michael, "Meet Today's Young American Worker," *Fortune,* November ll, 1985, pp.90+.
35. October, 1990 closings: *Wards Auto World,* July, 1990, p.30. The closings are part of GM's plan to increase its plant utilization by reducing capacity to 4.3 million cars, by 1992, from over 6 million in 1986. *New York Times,* November 1, 1990, *Wall Street Journal,* November 1, 1990 and June 15, 1990. NYT and WSJ Nov 1, 1990. The closed plants tend to be the most labor intensive. James P. Womack and Daniel Roos, in *The Machine That Changed the World,* Rawson Associates, 1990, compare 1986 productivity at GM's Framingham, Mass., plant (now closed) with the Toyota plant in Takaoka: Framingham took 40 hours to build a car, Takaoka, 18 hours; Framingham averaged 135 defects per car, Takaoka, 45 defects.

     December, 1991 closings: *New York Times* December 19, 1991, *Wall Street Journal,* December 19, 1991, December 21, 1991, *Economist,* January 3, 1992.
36. *Business Week,* June 16, 1986, pp.100+.
37. Through Hughes, GM became the biggest auto industry player in the Persian Gulf War. Hughes manufactures four missiles, including the Maverick, the TOW, the Phoenix and AMRAAM. The company also makes night vision systems for aircraft and armored vehicles. *Wards Auto World,* February, 1991, p.9.
38. *Wall Street Journal,* December 6, 1985.
39. Bylinsky, Gene, "GM'S Road MAP to Automated Plants," *Fortune,* October 28, 1985, pp.89+; *Wall Street Journal,* October 15, 1985.
40. Quoted in Winter, Drew, "Assembly: Let the Revolution Begin," *Wards Auto World,* June, 1985, pp.42+.
41. Winter, Drew, "Robots Get A New Attitude," *Wards Auto World,* April, 1991, pp.33+.
42. Winter, Drew, "High-Tech's Midlife Crisis: Advanced Plant Technology Loses Some of Its Luster," *Wards Auto World,*June, 1986, pp.22+; *Wall Street Journal,* February 16, 1982.

     The technology problems were enough to panic top executives, according to Winter (writing about robotics, specifically, in *Wards,* 1991). In 1986 GM cancelled 25% of its robot orders from GMF and announced that it was cutting back on planned capital expenditures by about one-third. (Winter, 1986; *Wall Street Journal,* July 14, 1986.) The company began to place more emphasis on systems engineering and training and on reorganizing social relations at the workplace. The purchases of the high-tech subsidiaries, such as EDS and Hughes, have begun to bear fruit in the 1990s. When EDS was acquired, GM's thousands of computers couldn't even talk to each other and plants were unable to coordinate scheduling or purchasing with other facilities. This is said no longer to be the case. (Winter, Drew, "EDS Systems Link GM's Dealers, Plants, Vendors," *Wards Auto World,* November, 1990, p.35.) GMF V.P. Robert Potok claims that automobile manufacturers account for

50% of the 4–5,000 robots ordered and shipped each year and that robots now operate 99.8% of the time and generate real cost savings. (Winter, 1991.)

43. Ohmae, Kenichi, "Steel Collar Workers: The Lessons From Japan," *Wall Street Journal,* February 16, 1982.

44. *Business Week,* April 26, 1982, p.140.

45. The following discussion of Saturn draws on: White, Joseph B. and Greiner Guile, Melinder, "GM's Plan for Saturn, To Beat Small Imports, Trails Original Goals," *Wall Street Journal,* July 9, 1990; *Business Week,* January 28, 1985, April 9, 1990, pp.56+, April 9, 1991, pp.32+; *Wards Auto World,* March, 1991, p.23; Fisher, Anne B., "Behind the Hype At GM's Saturn," *Fortune,* November 11, 1985, pp.44+.

46. Things are not going entirely smoothly at Saturn. First year sales were only 75% of the original target and the company is not making money, partly because the production start up was delayed by quality problems. The car itself has received only lukewarm reviews from the press and this, combined with the recession, has hurt sales. The lack of profits led to unhappiness among workers, many of whom had left higher wages and benefits at other plants. In November, 1991, Saturn's workers approved a new labor contract that scaled back the original accord and moved it closer to the conventional union contract that prevails at other GM plants. The changes reduce the percentage of hourly workers' pay that depends on achieving the goals, gradually increasing it over four years to 20%. They also permit long-time GM and Saturn employees to join GM's more generous pension program, and provide severance payments of up to $50,000 to workers who want to leave.

47. Clutterbuck, David, "General Motors Strives To Motivate Its Workers," *International Management,* January, 1975, pp.13+.

48. Parker, Mike and Slaughter, Jane, *Choosing Sides: Unions and the Team Concept,* A Labor Notes Book, Boston: South End Press, 1988, p.4.

49. *Wall Street Journal,* April 16, 1985.

50. Quoted in *Wall Street Journal,* May 30,1986, p.6.

51. Mann, Eric, "UAW Backs The Wrong Team," *The Nation,* February 14, 1984, pp.171+.

52. Holusha, John, "No Utopia, But To Workers It's A Job," *New York Times,* January 29, 1989.

53. Mann, 1987.

54. Moody, Kim, "How the Winning Team Loses: The New Speedup in Auto," *Against the Current,* 2,5 (new series), Nov-Dec 1987. For a good critique of the Team Concept see: Parker and Slaughter, 1988.

55. *General Motors Counter Annual Report, 1987,* Amsterdam, Netherlands: Transnationals Information Exchange, 1987.

56. *Wall Street Journal,* November 7, 1983.

57. *Wall Street Journal,* October 23, 1984.

58. Brody, Anthony, "GM Comes to Spring Hill," *The Nation*, June 21, 1986, pp.852+.

59. *Wards Auto World*, December, 1990, p.27.

60. *Wards Auto World*, December, 1990, p.39. At the end of June, 1991, GM had paid $850 million out of the $3.5 billion fund for workers laid off over the first 9 months of the contract, which ends in 1993. *Wall Street Journal*, July 22, 1991.

61. Slaughter, Jane, "New Auto Contract Trades Jobs For Income Protection," *Labor Notes*, October, 1990.

62. Slaughter, October, 1990.

63. *Wards Auto World*, December, 1990; January, 1991.Chrysler's new contract with the UAW allows the company to go to three shifts at 35 hours at its St. Louis minivan plant, subject to a worker vote. Last November the workers turned down a three shift plan at 40 hours.

64. *Wards Auto World*, October, 1990.

65. Slaughter, October, 1990.

66. de Jonquieres, Guy, "Car Makers: Faster Gear Change," *Financial Times*, December 3, 1990.

Chapter II: The Transaction Cost Approach to Organizational Change

1. Williamson, O. E., *Markets and Hierarchies: Analysis and Antitrust Implications*, New York: The Free Press, 1975.

2. Coase, R., "The Nature of the Firm," *Economica*, 4, 1937, reprinted in *Readings in Price Theory*, edited by G. J. Stigler and K. E. Boulding, Chicago: Richard D. Irwin for the American Economic Association, 1952; Coase, R., "The Problem of Social Cost," *Journal of Law and Economics*, 3, October, 1960, pp.1–44.

3. Chandler, A. D. Jr., *Strategy and Structure: Chapters in the History of American Industrial Enterprise*, Cambridge, MA: MIT Press, 1962.

4. Williamson, O. E. and Ouchi, W. G., "The Markets and Hierarchies and Visible Hand Perspectives, in *Perspectives on Organization Design and Behavior*, edited by A. Van de Ven and W. Joyce, New York: John Wiley, 1981, pp.347–369,387–390.

5. Williamson, O. E., "The Modern Corporation: Origins, Evolution, Attributes," *Journal of Economic Literature*, XIX, December, 1981, p. 1544,

6. Williamson and Ouchi, p.351.

7. Williamson, O. E., "Transaction-Cost Economics: The Governance of Contractual Relations," *Journal of Law and Economics*, October, 1979, pp.233–261.

8. Williamson, O. E., "The Organization of Work: A Comparative Institutional Assessment," *Journal of Economic Behavior and Organization,* 1, 1980, pp. 30–31; Bowles, S. and Gintis, H., *Schooling in Capitalist America: Educational Reform and the Contradictions of Economic Life,* New York: Basic Books, Inc., Publishers, 1976; Marglin, S. A., "What Do the Bosses Do? The Origins and Functions of Hierarchy in Capitalist Production," *Review of Radical Political Economics,* 6(2), 1974, pp. 60–70,81–86,89–92; Stone, K., "The Origins of Job Structures in the Steel Industry," *Review of Radical Political Economics,* 6, Summer, 1974, pp.61–97.

9. Braverman, H., *Labor and Monopoly Capital: The Degradation of Work in the Twentieth Century,* New York: Monthly Review Press, 1974. For some of the left critiques of Braverman see: Aronowitz, S., "Marx, Braverman and the Logic of Capital," *The Insurgent Sociologist,,* 7, 2/3, Fall, 1978, pp.126–146; Coombs, t., "Labor and Monopoly Capital," *New Left Review,* 107, Jan-Feb, 1978, pp.79–96; Elgar, T., "Valorization and 'Deskilling': A Critique of Braverman, " *Capital and Class,* 7, Spring, 1979, pp.58–99; Wood, S., editor, *The Degradation of Work? Skill, Deskilling, and the Labor Process,* London: Hutchinson, 1982; Burawoy, M., *Manufacturing Consent: Changes in the Labor Process Under Monopoly Capitalism,* Chicago: The University of Chicago Press, 1979.

10. Stone, K., p.66.

11. Williamson, 1981, and Williamson and Ouchi, 1980.

12. Williamson, 1981, p.1556.

13. Ibid, p.1558

14. Williamson, 1980.

15. *Labor Notes,* April, 1987 and May, 1989.

16. DuBoff, R. B. and Herman, E. S., "Alfred Chandler's New Business History: A Review," *Politics and Society,* 10,1, 1980, pp.87–110.

17. Williamson, 1980, p.35; Gunzberg, D., "On-the-Job-Democracy," *Sweden Now,* 12, 4, pp.42–45.

18. Sraffa, P., *The Production of Commodities by Means of Commodities,* Cambridge: Cambridge University Press, 1960. See also Harcourt, G. C., "Some Cambridge Controversies in the Theory of Capital," *Journal of Economic Literature,* 1972, pp.369–405 and Tinker, A. M., "Towards a Political Economy of Accounting: An Empirical Illustration of the Cambridge Controversies," *Accounting, Organizations, and Society,* 5,1, 1980, pp.147–160.

19. Williamson, 1981, p.1557.

20. Perrow, C., "Markets, Hierarchies and Hegemony," in *Perspectives on Organization Design,* edited by A. Van de Ven and W. Joyce, New York: John Wiley, 1981, p.375.

21. Williamson and Ouchi, 1981, pp.364, 389.

Chapter III: The Dialectical Approach to Organizational Change

1. There are two important points to be noted here. First, not everyone has an equal voice in determining the allocation of socially necessary labor in a capitalist society. In the U.S., for example, increasing numbers of people believe that military hardware is overproduced and housing is underproduced.

   And secondly, the problem with using price as a theoretical metric is that we are still left with the theoretical question of what the monetary amount is measuring. The well-known (in economics) Cambridge capital controversy was partly concerned with the question of whether prices can be considered an acceptable metric of physical capital. Wright, E. O., *Class, Crisis and the State,* London: Verson, 1979. (For a discussion of the Cambridge controversy see: Harcourt, G.C., *Some Cambridge Controversies in the Theory of Capital,* Cambridge: Cambridge University Press, 1972; Harcourt G.C. and Laing, N.G., *Capital and Growth,* Harmondsworth: Penguin Modern Economic Reading, Penguin Books, 1971.)

2. Wright, 1979. Wright further explains that "The relationship of values (embodied labor time) to actual exchange ratios among commodities (relative prices) involves two transformations: 1) the transformation of the value of the inputs into the prices of the inputs, or what is usually called the 'prices of production'; and 2) the transformation of the prices of production into the concrete market prices of commodities. The first of these is the object of the debates over what is called the 'transformation problem' [For a discussion of the transformation problem see Meek, R., *Studies in the Labor Theory of Value,* New York: Monthly Review Press, 1956 and Steedman, I., editor, *The Value Controversy,* London: Verso, 1981.] . . . The second transformation, of prices of production into market prices, lies outside of value theory proper." (ibid, pp.115–6n.)

3. Perrow, C., "Markets, Hierarchies and Hegemony," in *Perspectives on Organization Design,* edited by A. Van der Ven and W. Joyce, New York: John Wiley, 1981, p.380.

4. This view is shared by a wide range of economists, including Keynes, Hansen, Gordon, Schumpeter, Galbraith, Klein, Sweezy, and Aglietta. An alternative explanation is proposed by Friedman, who argues that monetary policy propelled a normal business cycle downturn into a crisis by permitting a massive decline in the stock of money. For a critical look at this minority view see Temin, P., *Did Monetary Forces Cause the Great Depression?,* New York: W.W.Norton, Inc., 1976.

5. Gordon, D., "The Global Economy: New Edifice or Crumbling Foundations," *New Left Review,* 168, March/April, 1988, pp.24–64. Also, Magdoff,

H. and Sweezy, P. M., *Stagnation and the Financial Explosion*, New York: Monthly Review Press, 1987.

6. See Fernand Braudel, *The Wheels of Commerce: Civilization and Capitalism 15th-18th Century*, v. 2, New York: Harper & Row, 1982; Stephen Marglin, "What Do Bosses Do? The Origins and Functions of Hierarchy in Capitalist Production," *Review of Radical Political Economics*, 6, 1974, pp.60–112; Karl Polanyi, *The Great Transformation: the political and economic origin of our time*, Boston: Beacon Press, 1957; Sidney Pollard, *The Genesis of Modern Management*, Baltimore: Penguin Books, 1968;

7. Braverman, H., *Labor and Monopoly Capital: The Degradation of Work in the Twentieth Century*, New York: Monthly Review Press, 1974; Clawson, D., *Bureaucracy and the Labor Process: The Transformation of U.S. Industry 1860–1920*, New York: Monthly Review Press, 1980.

8. Edwards, R., *Contested Terrain: The Transformation of the Workplace in the Twentieth Century*, London: Heinemann, 1979.

9. Meyer, S.,III, *The Five Dollar Day: Labor Management and Social Control in the Ford Motor Company, 1908–1921*, Albany, NY: State University of New York Press, 1981.

10. Foucault, M. *Discipline and Punish: The Birth of the Prison*, New York: Vintage Books, 1979, pp.202–3. Quoted in Zuboff, S., *In the Age of the Smart Machine: The Future of Work and Power*, New York: Basic Book, Inc., Publishers, 1988, p.321. Zuboff provides a brief description of Bentham's design.

11. Zuboff, 1988, p.322.

12. Ibid, p.323.

13. Ewen, S., *Captains of Consciousness: Advertising and the Social Roots of Consumer Culture*, New York: McGraw Hill Book Company, 1976; Baran, P. A. and Sweezy, P. M., *Monopoly Capital: An Essay on the American Economic and Social Order*, New York: Monthly Review Press, 1966, ch. 5.

14. Aglietta, M., *A Theory of Capitalist Regulation: The U.S. Experience*, Translated by David Fernbach, London: NLB, 1979.

15. Galbraith, J. K., *The New Industrial State*, Boston: Houghton Mifflin Company, 1967, p.38.

16. Government at all levels accounted for 4% of U.S. GNP in 1900; 8.2% in 1929; and 20.5% in 1978. This trend is true of Western Europe as well. For example, public expenditures in Great Britain were less than 25% of GNP in the 1930s. When the post-war Labour government left office in 1951, the proportion was around 41%. After a period of decline under the Conservatives, the percentage was back to 41% in 1964 and by 1973 it was over 50%. (Gordon, R. A., *Economic Instability and Growth: The American Record*, New York: Harper & Row Publishers, 1974; Herman, E. S., *Corporate Control and Corporate Power: A Twentieth Century Fund Study*, Cambridge: Cambridge University Press, 1981; Wright, E. O., *Class, Crisis and the State*, London: NLB, 1978; London: Verso, 1979; Gamble, A. and

Walton, P., *Capitalism in Crisis: Inflation and the State,* London: The Macmillan Press Ltd., 1976.)

17. Herman, 1981.

18. Bowles, S. and Gintis, H., *Schooling in Capitalist America: Educational Reform and the Contradictions of Economic Life,* New York: Basic Books, 1975; Ehrenreich, B. and English, D., *Complaints and Disorders: The Sexual Politics of Sickness,* Feminist Press, 1973; Ehrenreich, B. and Ehrenreich, J., "The Professional-Managerial Class", in *Between Labor and Capital,* edited by Pat Walker, Boston: South End Press, 1979.

19. O'Connor, J., *The Fiscal Crisis of the State,* New York: St. Martin's Press, 1973.

20. Williamson, O. E., "Transaction-Cost Economics: The Governance of Contractual Relations," *Journal of Law and Economics,* October, 1979, pp.233–261.

21. Hill, S., *Competition and Control at Work: The New Industrial Sociology,* Cambridge, MA: The MIT Press, 1981, p. 125; Allen, V. L., *Social Analysis: A Marxist Critique and Alternative,* London: Longman, 1975.

22. Cyert, R. M. and March, J. G., *A Behavioral Theory of the Firm,* Englewood Cliffs, N.J.: Prentice-Hall, 1963; March, J.G. and Simon, H.A., *Organizations,* New York: John Wiley and Sons, 1958; Pfeffer, J. and Salancik, G., *The External Control of Organizations,* New York: Harper and Row, Publishers, 1978; Weick, K. E., "Educational Organizations as Loosely Coupled Systems," *Administrative Science Quarterly,* 21, 1976, pp.1–19; March, J.G. and Olsen, J., *Ambiguity and Choice in Organizations,* Oslo, Norway: Universitetsforlaget, 1976.

23. March and Simon, 1958

24. Pfeffer and Salancik, 1978

25. Wright, 1979, Chapter 2.

26. Davis, M., *Prisoners of the American Dream: Politics and Economy in the History of the U.S. Working Class,* London: Verso, 1986.

27. Lindblom, C.E., *Politics and Markets: The World's Political-Economic Systems,* New York: Basic Books, Inc., Publishers, 1977.

28. Many of capitalism's social conflicts pre-date the capitalist mode of production and hence have both capitalist and non-capitalist components, for example, those which originate in patriarchy, religion, nationalism, racism. But even the pre-capitalist elements of these conflicts have acquired a capitalist form and function. (Ollman, Bertell, "Letters," *Zeta,* June, 1989). For an example, see Tinker, T. and Neimark, M., "The Role of Annual Reports in Gender and Class Contradictions at GM: 1917–1976," *Accounting, Organizations and Society,* 12, 1, 1987, pp.71–88.

29. The following discussion of dialectics draws upon a number of texts including: Ollman, Bertell. *Alienation: Marx's Conception of Man in Capitalist Society,* 2nd Edition, Cambridge: Cambridge University Press, 1976; Allen, V. L., *Social Analysis: A Marxist Critique and Alternative,* London: Longman, 1975; Giddens, Anthony, *Central Problems in Social Theory: Action,*

Struction and Contradiction in Social Analysis, Berkeley: University of California Press, 1979.

Chapter IV: Years of Crisis and Conflict

1. The decades of the 1930s and 1940s and its conflicts have been extensively examined and documented. I draw on many of these studies in this chapter, including: Green, James R. *The World of the Worker: Labor in Twentieth Century America,* New York: Hill and Wang, 1980; Milton, David, *The Politics of U.S. Labor: From the Great Depression to the New Deal,* New York: Monthly Review Press,1982; Brody, David. *Workers In Industrial America: Essays on the 20th Century Struggle,* New York:Oxford University Press, 1980; Fine, Sidney.*Sitdown,*Ann Arbor: University of Michigan Press, 1969; Keeran, 1980; Bernstein, Irving, *Turbulent Years: A History of the American Labor Movement, 1922–1941,* Boston: Houghton-Mifflin, 1971.

2. Aglietta, Michel. *A Theory of Capitalist Regulation: The U.S. Experience.* Translated by David Fernbach, London: New Left Books, 1979; George, Peter, *The Emergence of Industrial America: Strategic Factors in American Economic Growth Since 1870,* Albany, N.Y.: State University of New York Press, 1982, pp.173–175.

3. Chandler, Alfred D. Jr. *Strategy and Structure,* Cambridge, MA: 1962.

4. Seltzer, Lawrence. *A Financial History of the American Automobile Industry,* Boston: Houghton Mifflin Company, 1928.

5. GM's Annual Report (hereafter AR), 1919, p.13

6. Sloan, Alfred P. Jr., *My Years With General Motors,* edited by John McDonald with Catharine Stevens, Garden City, NY: Doubleday & Company, Inc., 1964.

7. AR, 1923, p.6.

8. AR, 1924, p.8.

9. Sloan, p.151.

10. DuBoff, R. B. and Herman, E. S., "Alfred Chandler's New Business History: A Review," *Politics and Society,* 1980, p.107.

11. In the 1920s, import tariffs alone (excluding additional internal taxes) increased the selling price of a $1,000 car (fob Detroit) by more than $300 in Argentina, Japan, Italy, France and Germany; more than $500 in New Zealand and Czechoslovakia; and more than $850 in Austria. (Epstein, Ralph C., *The Automobile Industry.* New York: A.W.Shaw Company, 1928) In Germany, until 1928, parts could be imported at a lower rate than imported cars (Bloomfield, Gerald. *The World Automotive Industry,* Newton Abbot, England: David and Charles Publishers Ltd., 1978). Great Britain had a 33 1/2% tariff after 1915 plus a horsepower tax on large bore engines; the tariff was extended to parts in the 1920s.

12. AR, 1937, pp.18–19.

13. Aglietta, p.233.
14. Horizontal combinations reported included the acquisition of Chevrolet and Scripps Booth in 1918, and the controlling interest in Yellow Truck and Coach in 1925. The company also made investments in, and acquired, various suppliers of materials, parts and components throughout the period (such as a 60% interest in Fisher Body in 1919). GM's diversifying acquisitions included, in 1919, Guardian Refrigerator (Frigidaire), Domestic Engineering (which became Delco, a manufacturer of farm and home electric light and power plants) and Dayton-Wright (a manufacturer of military aircraft); investments in aviation in 1929 (25% of Bendix and 40% of Fokker); and in 1930 the company purchased Electro-Motive and Winton Engine, manufacturers of power plants and engines for railroads.

    Also during this period, GM reported in its annual reports that it had entered into two joint ventures with DuPont: the formation of Ethyl Gasoline in 1925 and Kinetic Chemicals in 1930. DuPont's involvement with GM began in 1915 when Pierre DuPont became an important shareholder and chairman of the GM Board. With the resignation in 1920 of the company's founder and President, William C. Durant, the DuPont interests, with 21.6% of the outstanding common stock (27% by 1923) secured effective control. (Seltzer, 1928; Chandler, 1962). The federal government began to investigate the relationship between GM, DuPont and U.S. Steel in 1927. (Seltzer, 1928). In 1949 the government filed an anti-trust suit against GM, DuPont and U.S. Rubber, which led eventually to the divestiture by DuPont of its interest in GM and by GM of its interest in Ethyl and other Du Pont subsidiaries.

    Although there were further acquisitions and investments reported in the 1930s — including investments in North American Aviation and General Aviation (Fokker) in 1933 and Engineering Products (airplane propellers) and the entire assets of the controlled subsidiary Yellow Truck and Coach in 1940 — there was almost as much discussion of domestic divestitures. The latter included the 1931 sale of National Plate Glass to Libby-Owens-Ford. (Under the terms of the sale GM agreed to buy an important part of its plate glass requirements from LOF.) In 1934 and 1935, because of restrictions imposed by the 1934 Air Mail Act, GM dissolved General Aviation and sold its holdings in Transcontinental and Western Air.
15. Seltzer, p.59
16. *Wall Street Journal,* October 24, 1984; Temin, Peter, *Did Monetary Forces Cause the Great Depression?* New York: WW Norton and Company, Inc., 1976.
17. Sloan, pp. 176, 177, 199. The three year profit figure of $248 million equalled GM's profits for 1929 alone. Profits in 1932, GM's worst depression year were $165,000.
18. Davis, Mike. *Prisoners of the American Dream: Politics and Economy in the History of the U.S. Working Class,* London: Verson, 1986, p.54.

19. Keeran, Roger. *The Communist Party and the Auto Workers Unions,* Bloomington: Indiana University Press, 1980, p. 32.

20. Keeran, 1980, pp. 33–35.

21. *Fortune,* December, 1933, p.8, quoted in Milton, 1982, op cit, p.27.

22. Keeran, 1980, p.57.

23. Letter from William Green, AFL President, to Paul Smith, AFL Nash organizer, June 17, 1929, in William Green papers, quoted by Bernstein, Irving, *The Lean Years: A History of the American Worker, 1920–1933,* Baltimore: Penguin Books, 1966, p.143, cited in Keeran, 1980, p.57.

24. Keeran, 1980, p.57.

25. Edwards, R., *Contested Terrain: The Transformation of the Workplace in the Twentieth Century,* London: Heinemann, 1979, p. 91.

26. Rosner, D. and Markowitz, G., "A Gift of God? The Public Health Profession and the Controversy Over Tetraethyl Lead During the 1920s," *American Journal of Public Health,* 1983, pp.342–352.

27. Keeran, 1980, p.55. "The authoritarianism of the Ford plant was atypical only in its extremity," writes Keeran.

28. Green, James R. *The World of the Worker: Labor in Twentieth Century America,* New York: Hill and Wang, 1980.

29. Davis, 1986, p.62.

30. Keeran, 1980, p.99

31. 1933 AR, pp.16–17.

32. Skockpol, Theda. "Political Response to Capitalist Crisis: Neo-Marxist Theories of the State and the Case of the New Deal," *Politics and Society,* 10, 1980, pp. 155–201.

33. Milton, 1982, p.31.

34. Klare, K. E., "Judicial Deradicalization of the Wagner Act and the Origins of Modern Legal Consciousness, 1937–1971, *Minnesota Law Review,* 62, 1978, fn.86, p.287; Bernstein, 1971; Keeran, 1980, p. 150; Serrin, William. *The Company and the Union: The 'Civilized Relationship' of the General Motors Corporation and the United Automobile Workers,* New York: Alfred Knopf, 1973, p.116.

35. Milton, 1982, pp.35–36.

36. Keeran, 1980, p.109.

37. Keeran, 1980, p.122.

38. Keeran, 1980, p.135.

39. Serrin, 1973, pp.117–118.

40. 1934 AR, p.10.

41. 1935 AR, p.16.

42. 1934 AR, p.10.

43. Aronowitz, Stanley. *False Promises: The Shaping of American Working Class Consciousness,* New York: McGraw-Hill Book Company, 1973; paperback edition, 1974, p.239.

44. Milton, 1982, p. 73.

45. Klare, Karl E. "Judicial Deradicalization of the Wagner Act and the Origins of the Modern Legal Consciousness, 1937–1941," *Minnesota Law Review,* 62, March, 1978; Gross, James A., *The Reshaping of the National Labor Relations Board,* Albany: State University of New York Press, 1981.

46. Keeran, 1980, pp.142–147.

47. Thomas Corcoran, quoted in Milton, 1982, p.91.

48. Milton, 1982; Green, 1980; Davis, 1986.

49. Keeran, 1980, p.183.

50. 1936 AR, p.27.

51. 1937 AR, p.43.

52. Ibid, p.11.

53. Mortimer, Wyndham, *Organize: My Life As A Union Man,* Boston: Beacon Press, 1971, p.132, quoted in Milton, 1982, p. 102.

54. Green, 1980, p.158; Keeran, 1980, p.184.

55. Lamont quoted by Staughton Lynd, "The United Front in America: A Note," *Radical America,* July-August, 1974, p.32, cited in Keeran, 1980, p.184.

56. *Wards Automotive Year Book,* Detroit, 1943, p.27, cited in Chester E., "The Popular Front and the UAW," *Against The Current,* 3,2, Spring, 1985, p.52.

57. Keeran, 1980, p.194.

58. Keeran, 1980, pp.191–194.

59. *United Automobile Worker,* September 18, 1937, quoted in Chester, 1985, p.50.

60. Keeran, 1980, op cit, p.195.

61. *New York Times,* November 20, 1937, quoted in Chester, 1985, p.51.

62. Chester, 1985, p.52; Keeran, 1980, p.194.

63. Green, 1980, p.166.

64. Green, 1980, p. 172.

65. Davis, 1986, p.69.

66. Keeran, 1980, p.199.

67. Keeran, 1980, p.205. The Ford drive succeeded in 1941 after a 10-day strike.

68. Green, 1980, p.171.

69. 1940 AR p.15; 1944 AR p.19.

70. Brody, David. *Workers in Industrial America: Essays on the Twentieth Century Struggle,* New York: Oxford University Press, 1980.

71. Keeran, Roger R. "Everything for Victory: Communist Influence in the Auto Industry During World War II," *Science and Society,* XLIII, 1, Spring, 1979, p.13.

72. Brody, 1980, p.199 citing *Monthly Labor Review,* 60, May, 1945, pp.959, 961.

73. Keeran, 1980, p.242.

74. Post, Charles, "Review: Nelson Lichtenstein, *Labor's War At Home: The CIO In World War II,* New York: Cambridge University Press, 1982," in *Against The Current,* Winter, 1985, pp.45–49.

75. Lichtenstein, Nelson. "Auto Worker Militancy and the Structure of Factory Life: 1937–1941," *Journal of American History,* 67, September, 1980, p.353,

quoted in Brody, David, "The CIO After 50 Years: A Historical Reckoning," *Dissent,* Fall, 1985, p.469.

76. Davis, 1986, p.81.
77. Post, Charles, 1985. Post (p.49) writes that the vote illustrates Lichtenstein's view that there is a "contradiction in working class consciousness between consciously held cultural values, such as patriotism, and the reality of capitalist work, which often leads to the jettisoning of these values in concrete actions." For the majority of wildcat strikers their actions were a direct response to specific shop floor conditions, and not a conscious act of political opposition. When faced with the more abstract question in the referendum, "many of the workers who rejected the pledge *in practice,* voted for its continuation."
78. Post, 1985, p.46, quoting Lichtenstein, 1983, p.51.
79. Post, 1985, p.48, quoting Lichtenstein, 1983, pp.179–180.
80. Post, 1985, p.49.
81. Davis, 1986, pp.81, 86.
82. Keeran, 1980, op cit, p.252.
83. Brody, 1980, p.176.
84. *The New York Times,* December 30, 1945, quoted in Lichentenstein, Nelson, *Labor's War At Home: The CIO In World War II,* New York: Cambridge University Press, 1982; paperback, 1987, p.226.
85. Lipsit, Seymour Martin. "Trade Unions and Social Structure, II," *Industrial Relations,* 1962, p.5.
86. Brody, 1980, p.183.
87. Brody, 1980, pp.183–184.
88. For a description of the negotiations see El-Messidi, Kathy Groehn. *The Bargain: The Story Behind the Thirty Year Honeymoon of GM and the UAW,* New York: Nellen Publishing Co., Inc., 1980.
89. Gartman, D., *Auto Slavery: The Labor Process in the American Automobile Industry, 1897–1950,* New Brunswick: Rutgers University Press, 1986, p.278.
90. Gartman, 1986, p.278.
91. Sloan, 1964, p.207.
92. Lodge, G. C., "Contract and Consensus at General Motors: 1900–1979," Intercollegiate Case Clearing House, #9–376–170, 1979, Boston, MA., p.5.
93. *New York Times,* March 24, 1948, quoted in Lodge, 1979, p.6.
94. Lichtenstein, 1987, p.240.
95. The automobile industry was concentrated into relatively few hands fairly early in its development. By 1912, although there were at least 57 different companies producing motor vehicles on a commercial scale, more than 50% of the output was produced by 7 companies. By 1923, 90% of the industry's output was produced by 10 of 67 active producers. (Seltzer, p.56) Throughout most of the 1920s, Ford produced about one-half, and GM produced one-quarter of the cars sold in the U.S.; a situation that was reversed in the middle of the 1930s. In 1930 GM, Ford and Chrysler accounted for 90% of

U.S. automobile sales. Further consolidation occurred after WWII. Crossley was acquired by General Tire in 1952 and stopped automobile production; Studebacker and Packard merged in 1954 and stopped producing automobiles in 1966; Nash and Hudson combined to form American Motors in 1955; and Overland combined with the newly-formed Kaiser Motors in 1953 to form Willys, which stopped passenger car production in 1955 and sold its Jeep line to American Motors in 1970. Seltzer, 1928; Rothschild, E., *Paradise Lost: The Decline of the Auto-Industrial Age,* New York: Random House, 1973; Jenkins, Rhys, "Internationalization of Capital in the Motor Industry," *Capital and Class,* October, 1976, pp.RJ1-RJ11.

96. Brody, 1980, p. 207.
97. Stone, K. Van Wezel, "The Post-War Paradigm in American Labor Law," *The Yale Law Journal,* 90, 7, 1981, p.1517.
98. Davis, 1986, p.81, footnote 47.
99. There was also the 1932 Norris-La Guardia Act whose most important section exempted a broadly-defined notion of labor disputes from federal court injunction, thereby protecting such activities as strikes, pickets, union membership, urging workers to strike, picket or join a union, and boycotts. Later legislation (e.g., Taft-Hartley) and court decisions reduced the protective scope of this legislation. The Norris-La Guardia Act was interpreted by the U.S. Supreme Court, in 1941, as exempting unions from prosecution under the Sherman anti-trust legislation. Yates, M., *Labor Law Handbook,* Boston: South End Press, 1987.
100. Yates, 1987; and Klare, 1978.
101. The following discussion of the Taft-Hartley Act draws on Yates, 1987 and Lichtenstein, N., *Labor's War at Home: The CIO in World War II,* Cambridge: Cambridge University Press, paperback edition, 1987.
102. Other classes of employees are not protected by the NLRA, such as the employees of local, state, and federal government agencies (e.g., firefighters, police, school teachers, sanitation workers), domestic workers; railroad and airline workers; employees of companies not involved in interstate commerce; and employees of "small" interstate companies. Some of these employees are covered by state labor laws or other federal laws (such as railroad and airline workers). Yates, 1987.
103. Further restrictions on union activity were included in the Landrum-Griffin Act (1959) which further tightened the Taft-Hartley prohibition of secondary boycotts; limited the voting rights of economic strikers to 12 months; and outlawed certain types of informational picketing. Other provisions of the legislation gave rank and file groups leverage in their struggles against corrupt or autocratic union leaderships. (The provision giving the federal government the right to interfere in the internal affairs of unions is more problematic, however.) These more positive provisions of the legislation have not been enforced. (One exception was when, after the murder of Joseph Yablonski in 1969, the Secretary of Labor

overturned the fraudulent election of Tony Boyle as United Mine Workers President.) But generally the government does little to help progressive members unseat their leaders, regardless of their behavior. Yates, 1987.

104. Atleson, J. B., *Values and Assumptions in American Labor Law,* University of Massachusetts Press, 1983; Klare, 1978; and Stone, 1981.

105. See, for example: Atleson, 1983; Klare, 1978; Stone, 1981; Yates, 1987; and Rogers, J. E., *Divide and Conquer: The Legal Foundations of Postwar U.S. Labor Policy,* Unpublished Ph.D. Dissertation, Princeton University, 1984.

106. Stone, 1981, pp.1513–1514.

107. Atleson, 1983, p.180.

108. The discussion in this and the following three paragraphs draws on Brody, 1980 and Lichtenstein, 1987.

109. Gardner,L. C., "The New Deal, New Frontiers, and the Cold War: A Re-examination of American Expansion: 1933–1945," in *Corporations and the Cold War,* edited by D. Horowitz, New York: Monthly Review Press, 1970, p.124.

110. Cantor, D. and Schor, J., *Tunnel Vision: Labor, the World Economy, and Central America,* Boston: South End Press, 1987, Chapter 2.

111. Gardner, 1970, p.132.

112. Eakins, D. W., "Business Planners and America's Postwar Expansion," in Horowitz, pp.163–164.

113. Ibid, p.162. Clayton was Undersecretary of State for Economic Affairs, Chairman of the U.S. Delegation to the U.S. Conference on Trade and Employment in Havana, and an alternate governor of the World Bank.

114. Cantor and Schor, 1987, p.34.

115. Keeran, 1980, pp.250–286.

116. Davis, 1986, p.92.

117. Ibid., p.96.

118. For an elaboration of this perspective see Cantor and Schor, 1987.

119. Gartman, 1986, p.275.

120. Aglietta, 1979.

121. Sweezy, Paul, "The Deepening Crisis of U.S. Capitalism," *Monthly Review,* 33, 5, October, 1981, p.11.

122. Davis, 1986, p.191.

123. Ibid, p.55.

124. *Fortune,* July, 1950, pp.53–55.

Chapter V: Accounting Reports and Social Enactment

1. Davis, M., *Prisoners of the American Dream: Politics and Economy in the History of the U.S. Working Class,* London: Verso, 1986, p.111.

2. *Fortune,* July, 1950, pp.53–55, quoted in Davis, 1986, pp.111–112.

3. For a good introduction to this line of philosophical thinking, see: Baynes, K., Bohman, J. and McCarthy, T., editors, *After Philosophy: End or Transformation?* Cambridge, MA: The MIT Press, 1987.

4. Fields, Barbara, "Slavery, Race and Ideology in the United States of America," *New Left Review,* 181, May/June, 1990, p.110.

5. Ibid.

6. Therborn, G., *What Does the Ruling Class Do When it Rules?* London: New Left Books, 1978, p.172.

7. Allen, V. L. *Social Analysis: A Marxist Critique and Alternative,* London: Longman, 1975, p.228.

8. Giddens, A., "Four Theses on Ideology," *Canadian Journal of Political and Social Theory,* 7, 1–2, Spring, 1983, p.119.

9. Fields, 1990, p.114.

10. Eagleton, T., *Literary Theory: An Introduction,* Minneapolis: University of Minnesota Press, 1983, p.149.

11. Said, E. W.,*The World, the Text, and the Critic,* Cambridge,MA: Harvard University Press, 1983.

12. Giddens, A.,*Central Problems in Social Theory: Action, Structure and Contradiction in Social Analysis,* Berkeley: University of California Press, 1979, pp.193–195.

13. Allen, V.L., 1975, p.225.

14. Polanyi, K. *The Great Transformation: The Political and Economic Origins of Our Time,* Rinehart & Company, Inc., 1944; paperback edition, Boston: Beacon Press, 1957, p.143.

15. Gouldner, Alvin W. *The Two Marxisms: Contradictions and Anomalies in the Development of Theory,* New York: The Seabury Press, 1980; paperback edition, Oxford: Oxford University Press, 1982b.

16. Rodgers, Daniel T., *The Work Ethic in Industrial America, 1850–1920,* Chicago: The University of Chicago Press, 1978.

17. See, for example: Clark, John Bates, *The Control of Trusts: An Argument in Favor of Curbing the Power of Monopoly by a Natural Method,* New York: Macmillan, 1901; Carver, Thomas Nixon, *The Present Economic Revolution in the United States,* Boston: Little Brown, 1925; Roosevelt, Theodore, *Address and Presidential Messages of Theodore Roosevelt,* New York: Putnam, 1904; Roosevelt, Franklin D., *Looking Forward,* New York: John Day, 1933; Van Antwerp, W. C., *The Stock Exchange From Within,* New York: Doubleday, Page, 1913; Simmons, E. H. H., *Cooperation Against Securities Frauds and Other Addresses,* New York: Committee on Publicity, NYSE. In his discussion of the formation of International Harvester, Kramer cites correspondence in 1902, between Perkins, of J.P.Morgan, and Cyrus McCormick, in which Perkins implied that watered stock would promote the social good, arguing that "if there were more large organizations owned by a great many people in different parts of the country," then "industrial and

social relations would be improved." Kramer, 1964, "Potential Competition and American Anti-trust," *Business History Review,* 38, 1964, pp.283–301.

18. In "Disclosure Regulation and Public Policy," *Journal of Accounting and Public Policy,*1,1,Fall 1982, pp.33–57, Barbara Merino and Marilyn Neimark conclude that "The securities acts were not the acts of political enlightenment that liberal reformers would have us believe. Instead, the legislation may have contributed to the virtual absence of any serious attempts to ensure corporate accountability by broadening the set of transactions for which corporations are to be held accountable." (p.51)

19. Berle, Adolf A. Jr., and Means, Gardiner C., *The Modern Corporation and Private Property,* New York: The Macmillan Company, 1934, p.355

20. Ibid, p.356

21. Ibid, p.357

22. Economists such as James O'Connor and Paul Sweezy have argued that underconsumption is an endemic problem for advanced capitalism. O'Connor argues that, by the terms of the collective bargaining agreements, monopoly sectors tend to increase wages roughly in proportion to productivity; whereas real wages in non-unionized, competitive sectors, remain relatively low. As a result, overall increases in consumer demand tend to lag increases in the productive capacity of the monopoly sector. Sweezy's analysis of the source of capitalism's endemic realization problems differs, but he shares O'Connor's conclusion. Sweezy, P., *The Theory of Capitalist Development,* New York, 1942; O'Connor, J., *The Fiscal Crisis of the State,* New York: St. Martin's Press, 1973.

23. White, L. J., *The Automobile Industry Since 1945,* Cambridge: Harvard University Press, 1971.

24. Rothschild, E.,*Paradise Lost: The Decline of the Auto-Industrial Age,* New York: Random House, 1973, p.39.

25. The connection between wage levels and consumption was recognized earlier by Henry Ford, who observed: "Our own sales depend in a measure on the wages we pay. If we can distribute high wages, then that money is going to be spent and it will serve to make storekeepers and distributors and manufacturers and workers in other lines more prosperous and their prosperity will be reflected in our sales." Quoted by Stavrianos, I.S., "Capitalism's Contradictory History," *Monthly Review,* October, 1984, pp.60–64.

26. Baran, P. A., and Sweezy, P. M., *Monopoly Capital: An Essay on the American Economic and Social Order,* New York: Monthly Review Press, 1966, p.128.

27. White, p.201.

28. For a more extensive discussion of the post-war social consumption norm see: Aglietta, M., *A Theory of Capitalist Regulation: The U.S. Experience,* Fernback, D. (trans.), London: New Left Books, 1979; Busacca, R. and Ryan, M.P., "Beyond the Family Crisis," *Democracy,* Fall, 1972, pp.79–92;

Habermas, J., *Legitimation Crisis,* McCarthy, R. (trans), London: Heinemann, 1976; Baron and Sweezy, 1966.

29. This discussion of women's labor force participation during and just after WWII is based on Milkman, Ruth, "Female Factory Labor and Industrial Structure: Control and Conflict Over 'Women's Place' in Auto and Electrical Manufacturing," *Politics and Society,* 1983, pp.159–203.

Of interest to contemporary feminists is Milkman's discussion of two important War Labor Board cases concerning women. In a 1942 case, brought by the UAW and the United Electrical Workers (UEW) against GM, the WLB established the principal of equal pay for equal work. And in a 1945 case, brought by the UEW against a number of companies including GM's electrical division, General Electric, and Westinghouse, the WLB concluded "that the jobs customarily performed by women are paid less, on a comparative job content basis, than the jobs customarily performed by men" and "that this relative underpayment constitutes sex discrimination." (War Labor Reports 28, p.668, cited in Milkman, p.1982.) The companies decided to ignore the ruling and when the war ended shortly thereafter, the WLB lost its authority.

30. Gouldner, Alvin, *The Dialectic of Ideology and Technology,* New York: The Seabury Press, 1976; Oxford: Oxford University Press, 1982, p.258.

31. Held, David, *Introduction to Critical Theory: Horkheimer to Habermas,* Berkeley: University of California Press, 1980, p.265.

32. Allen, V. L., *Social Analysis: A Marxist Critique and Alternative,* London: Longman, 1975, p.229.

33. White, p.211.

34. Marcuse, H. *One Dimensional Man: Studies in the Ideology of Industrial Society,* Boston: Beacon Press, 1964; Beacon Paperback, 1966, p.12.

35. Wolin, S., "What Revolutionary Action Means Today," *Democracy,* 2, Fall, 1982, pp.17–28, p.24.

36. Marcuse, p.158.

37. Gordon, R. A., *Economic Instability & Growth: The American Record,* New York: Harper & Row Publishers, 1974, p.4.

According to Bertram Gross ("Rethinking Full Employment," *The Nation,* January 17, 1987, pp.44–48), this commitment to maximum employment actually represents a step back from the proposals of the National Resources Planning Board during WWII, which advocated a National Economic Bill of Rights that would include "adequate income, social security, education, housing, medical care, protections against monopolies, civil liberties and equality before the law." Although conservative pressures killed the board in 1943, Roosevelt urged Congress to implement the Economic Bill of Rights in his electoral campaign in 1944. The original draft of the full employment bill that was eventually passed in 1946 included the "right to a useful and remunerative job." Conservatives diluted the bill so that it "expressed not a commitment to full employment but to avoiding depression through the growth of a warfare-welfare state."

38. GM has had a long-time interest in influencing U.S. transportation policy. During the 1930s, for example, the company opposed the use of highway user taxes for any purpose other than the development, maintenance and protection of the highway system, and opposed establishing a National Transportation Commission to regulate and coordinate all transportation. When the 1935 Federal Motor Carrier Act placed highway transportation under the aegis of the Interstate Commerce Commission (a step GM opposed), the National Highway User's Conference (organized in 1932 by GM's Alfred Sloan "to establish and capture highway 'trust funds'") regularly used its "influence to deflect any reallocation of resources to public transportation." (From Du Boff, R. and Herman, E., "Alfred Chandler's New Business History: A Review," *Politics and Society*, 10, 1, 1980, pp.87–110, p.107.) In 1949, GM was convicted of having conspired, mainly with Standard Oil of California and the Firestone Tire and Rubber Company, to replace electric transit systems in various municipalities with bus operations which contracted never to buy new equipment that used any fuel other than petroleum. GM was fined only $5,000 for the offense, and the activities continued until the end of 1955, by which time motorization of most of the country's electric transit systems was virtually complete. In 1974 the U.S. Senate investigated the activities of the three companies and the holding company they formed, National City Lines. According to Bradford Snell, assistant counsel of the Senate Antitrust and Monopoly subcommittee, GM played a dominant role in destroying over 100 electric surface rail transit systems in 56 cities, including New York, Los Angeles, Philadelphia and Boston. GM presented a 67 page reply to the charges presented at the Senate hearings. The company said that it "did not generate the winds of change which doomed the streetcar systems," but did "through its buses, help to alleviate the disruption left in their wake." In the case of their activities in the 1930s GM said that in a period when public transportation systems were collapsing, the company provided technology, enterprise and sometimes capital to "give mass transportation a new lease on life which lasted into the post-war years." At these hearings the company also denied the allegations that it had coerced railroads into buying its diesel locomotives, which were far less efficient than electric motors. (Mintz, M. and Cohen, J. S., *Power, Inc.*, New York: Bantam Books, 1977.)

Chapter VI: The Unravelling of the Social Accord

1. Altshuler, Alan, Anderson, Martin, Jone, Daniel, Roos, Daniel, Womack, James et. al., *The Future of the Automobile: The Report of MIT's International Automobile Program,* Cambridge, MA: The MIT Press, 1984, p.146.

2. Auto Program countries refers to the seven countries studied by MIT. They are France, Italy, Japan, Sweden, the United Kingdom, the United States and West Germany.

3. Over the four decades shown in the table, GM's share of world motor vehicle production fell from 44.1% in the 1930s to 35.2% in the immediate post-war decade, to 29.1% in 1956–1965.

4. General Motors annual reports and 10K reports, various years.

5. White, L., J., *The Automobile Industry Since 1945,* Cambridge, MA: Harvard University Press, 1971; Altshuler et. al., 1984, pp.24–34.

6. Harrison, Bennett and Bluestone, Barry, *The Great U-Turn: Corporate Restructuring and the Polarizing of America,* New York: Basic Books, Inc., Publishers, 1988.

7. Halberstram, David, *The Reckoning,* New York: Avon Books, 1986, pp.366–367.

8. Bloomfield, Gerald, *The World Automotive Industry,* Newton Abbot, England, David and Charles Publishers Ltd., 1978.

9. Rothschild, Emma, *Paradise Lost: The Decline of the Auto-Industrial Age,* New York: Random House, Inc., 1973, p.229.

10. Davis, Mike, "The Political Economy of Late-Imperial America," *New Left Review,* Jan/Feb, 1984, pp.6–38, citing Robert Cohen, "Brave New World of the Global Car," *Challenge,* May/June, 1981.

11. Edwards, Richard, *Contested Terrain: The Transformation of the Workplace in the Twentieth Century,* New York: Basic Books, Inc.,1979, pp.154–155.

12. Lodge, George C., "Contract And Consensus At General Motors," Intercollegiate Case Clearing House, Harvard Business School, 9–376–170, 1979, p.11. The following paragraph draws heavily on Lodge. The Pearlstine article appeared in *The Wall Street Journal* on October 29, 1970, p.1.

13. Serrin, William, *The Company and the Union,* New York, 1973, noted in Davis, Mike, *Prisoners of the American Dream: Politics and Economy in the History of the US Working Class,* London: Verso, 1986.

14. *Business Week,* March 25, 1972, p.46; *New York Times,* September 11, 1971, from Lodge, 1979.

15. Halberstram, 1979, p.22. According to Halberstram the phrase "shared monopoly" was coined for the motor vehicle industry by J. Patrick Wright, *On A Clear Day You Can See General Motors,* Grosse Pointe, MI: Wright, 1979.

16. Ibid. Said by David E. Davis, Jr., of Campbell-Ewald Advertising.

17. Comparative prices of similar U.S. and Japanese cars, from a study by the Boston Consulting Group in Halberstram, 1986, p.308.

	U.S.	Japan
1952	$1500	$2950
1959	1900	2100
1961	1850	1750
1964	1900	1400
1970	2215	1210

18. Ibid, p.55.

19. *Business Week,* October 28, 1972, p.39.

20. *Business Week,* March 4, 1972.

21. Rothschild, Emma, 1973, p.97.

22. Ibid, p.101.

23. O'Toole, J. "Lordstown: Three Years Later," *Business and Society,* 13, Spring, 1975, pp.64–71.

24. Ibid, p.66.

25. *Business Week,* September, 17, 1979, "Hot UAW Issue: Quality of Work Life," from Lodge, 1979, pp.18–19.

26. Memo from Federal Government's National Center for Productivity and Quality of Working Life, November, 1975, quoted in Lodge, 1979, p.17.

27. GM's Southern Strategy was an effort to open non-union plants in "right to work" law states in which the union shop has been outlawed. In these states no one has to join the union after it has been certified although the union must bargain for and represent all of the workers. These states are largely in the South. The union's objections to such programs weakened after they won agreement in the 1979 contract that all new plants would fall under the GM-UAW contract.

28. For an in-depth discussion of the use of QWL and team programs in the current restructuring from a progressive labor perspective, see Parker, Mike and Slaughter, Jane, *Choosing Sides: Unions and the Team Concept,* Boston: A Labor Notes Book, South End Press, 1988.

29. Davis, Mike, "The AFL-CIO's Second Century," *New Left Review,* 136, Nov/Dec, 1982, pp.43–54.

30. Parker and Slaughter, 1988, Foreword.

31. Gartman, D., *Auto-Slavery: The Labor Process in the American Automobile Industry, 1897–1950,* New Brunswick: Rutgers University Press, 1986, p.278.

32. Davis, Mike, *Prisoners of the American Dream: Politics and Economy in the History of the U.S. Working Class,* London: Verso, 1986.

33. Davis, 1986, p.99.

34. Galbraith, John Kenneth, *The New Industrial State,* Boston: Houghton Mifflin Company, 1967, p.275.

35. Davis, 1986, p.128.

36. Aronowitz, Stanley, *False Promises: The Shaping of American Working Class Consciousness,* New York: Mc Graw-Hill Book Company, 1973, paperback edition, 1974, p.220.

37. In 1950, for example, parts constituted 34% of Great Britain's motor vehicle exports; by 1974 it was 64.2%. Bloomfield, 1978, p.317.

38. Hainer, M. and Koslofsky, J., "Car Wars," *NACLA Report on the Americas,* July-August, 1979, pp.3–37.

39. One author suggests that U.S. manufacturers have been forced to adopt the look of foreign models because this was the only way they could meet the

U.S. government fuel consumption standards that became effective in 1980. Maxcy, G., *The Multinational Motor Industry,* London: Croom Helm, 1981.

40. Bloomfield, 1978, p.146.
41. Hainer and Koslofsky, 1979, p.14.
42. Feast, Richard, "GM Spells Spain With a Capital $," *Automotive News,* January 25, 1982.
43. O'Connor, James, *The Fiscal Crisis of the State,* New York: St. Martin's Press, 1973, p.6. This notion of the contractory functions of the state and the classification of state spending that follows is based on O'Connor's work.
44. Gordon, Robert Aaron, *Economic Instability & Growth: The American Record,* New York: Harper & Row Publishers, 1974, p.198.
45. O'Connor, 1973, pp.160–161.
46. Mintz, Morton and Cohen, Jerry S., *Power, Inc.,* New York: Bantam, 1977, p.425.
47. White, Lawrence J., *The Automobile Industry Since 1945,* Cambridge, MA: Harvard University Press, 1971, p.241.
48. The following discussion of seat belts is based on an article in *The Wall Street Journal,* "Reducing the Risk: Auto Shoulder Belts Come Too Late for Many," by Neal Templin, August 24, 1990.
49. White, 1971, pp.230–233.
50. Maynard, Micheline and Spinello, Art, "The Clean Air Battle is Over, But the War is Just Beginning," *Wards Auto World,* December 1990, pp.63–65.
51. Herman, Edward, *Corporate Control, Corporate Power: A Twentieth Century Fund Study,* Cambridge University Press, 1981, p.263.
52. Herman, 1981, p.263. The De Lorean quote is from Wright, J. Patrick, *On a Clear Day One Can See General Motors,* Grosse Point Michigan: Wright Enterprises, 1979, p.5.

Chapter VII: What Is To Be Done?

1. For a comprehensive discussion of corporate restructuring and the complicit role of the Federal government, see Harrison, Bennet and Bluestone, Barry, *The Great U-Turn: Corporate Restructuring and the Polarizing of America,* New York: Basic Books, Inc., 1988.
2. Henwood, Doug, *The Left Business Observer,* 40, September 14, 1990. Starting in 1973 real hourly wages for the two-thirds of the working population classified as nonsupervisory workers began to fall and are now 12% below the 1973 peak and 4 % below the 1984 level. (From Bowles, Samuel, Gordon, David M., and Weisskopf, Thomas E., *After the Wasteland: A Democratic Economics for the Year 2000,* M. E. Sharpe, 1991, cited in a review by Doug Henwood, *Voice Literary Supplement,* April, 1991.)

3. Ibid.

4. Henwood, Doug, "Compendium of Woe," *The Left Business Observer,* 40, September 14, 1990, from Mishel, Lawrence and Frankel, David, *The State of Working America, 1990–1991,* Economic Policy Institute, 1990. What growth has occurred in family income since 1973 results from the massive entry of women into the work force. In a study of families headed by someone under thirty, for example, Northeastern University's Center for Labor Market Studies finds that the best-off segment of this group, the 14% of families headed by a college grad, would show a slight loss in real income since 1973, not a 16% gain, were it not for working wives. ("What Happened to the American Dream: The Under-30 Generation May Be Losing The Race For Prosperity," *Business Week,* August, 19, 1991, p.80.)

5. Defenders of the Reagan tax cuts, such as conservative economist Paul Craig Roberts, argue that "low-skilled jobs are not growing as fast as those that require a lot of training," and that family income statistics are "biased by rising divorce rates and the growth in single family households." What the critics have discovered, Roberts says, "was the effect of the decline of the institution of marriage on family income." In the first case, Roberts ignores the vast difference in absolute numbers, millions in low-skill versus hundreds of thousands in high-skill jobs created. In the second case, Roberts ignores the fact that even "traditional" households cannot maintain their purchasing power today unless both partners work. It is the absence of second wage earners in single parent families (and persistent sexism and racism, since a disproportionate number of these families are headed by women, particularly black women) and not the decline of the institution of marriage itself, that is eroding their purchasing power.

6. Sklar, Holly, "The Truly Greedy," *Z Magazine,* June, 1991, pp. 10–12.

7. Sklar, 1991, from Greenstein, Robert and Barancik, Scott, *Drifting Apart,* Center on Budget and Policy Priorities, July, 1990, citing Congressional Budget Office.

8. Regressive taxes burden those in lower income brackets disproportionately — examples include social security, sales, property, gasoline, tobacco and liquor taxes — because poorer tax payers pay a greater share of their total income in these taxes.

9. Sklar, 1991 from Reich, Robert in *The Atlantic Monthly,* February 1991.

10. Sklar, 1991, from the Center on Budget and Policy Priorities.

11. Harrison and Bluestone, 1988, p.71.

12. "Where the Jobs Are Is Where the Skills Aren't," *Business Week,* September 19, 1988, pp.104–108. The data in the next paragraph is drawn from this article.

13. Edsall, Thomas Byrne with Edsall, Mary D., "Race," *The Atlantic Monthly,* May 1991, pp.53–86.

14. Deregulation actually began before the Reagan administration. According to Harrison and Bluestone, 1988, p.95: "Between 1968 and 1978, steps were

taken toward the gradual deregulation of communications, banking, stock market transactions, and airline transportation." It was Carter who deregulated the airline industry when he eliminated the Civil Aeronautics Board in 1978; and the steps to deregulate banking, codified in the Depository Institutions Deregulation and Monetary Control Act, in 1980, also began under his watch.

Reagan, however, increased the ante manyfold, by cutting federal appropriations for low income housing by 82% and the funding of discretionary low income programs by 55%, after inflation. Changes in the leadership and policies of OSHA (Occupational Safety and Health Administration) and the NLRB made it increasingly difficult for workers to pursue health and safety violations and to carry out successful organizing campaigns. At OSHA, enforcement levels dropped dramatically in terms of inspections and penalties and the NLRB issued a slew of pro-employer decisions. See Harrison and Bluestone, 1988, for details.

15. Henwood, Doug, "The Uses of Crisis," *Left Business Observer,* 46, June 3, 1991.
16. "The Outlook: States and Localities May Slow Recovery," *The Wall Street Journal,* August 5, 1991. Between 1980 and 1990, federal grants to state and local governments fell from $105.6 billion to $100.96 billion (in 1982 dollars). In the same period, national defense spending rose from $164 billion to $247 billion (in 1982 dollars).
17. *The Wall Street Journal,* August 5, 1991.
18. Henwood, Doug, June 3, 1991, from the Tax Foundation.
19. Reich, Robert, *The New York Times Magazine,* January 20, 1991, quoted in Sklar, 1991. The quote from Reich in the following paragraph also draws on this source.
20. The data in this paragraph is drawn from Edsall and Edsall, May 1991, pp.84–85.
21. Hinds, Michael de Courcy, "Cash Strapped Cities Turn To Companies To Do What Government Once Did," *New York Times,* May 14, 1991.
22. Harrison and Bluestone, 1988, cite several studies that reach this conclusion, including: Starr, Paul, *The Limits of Privatization,* Washington DC: Economic Policy Institute, 1987; Rare, Robert, Grosskopf, Samuel and Logan, James, "The Relative Performance of Publicly-Owned and Privately-Owned Electric Utilities," *Journal of Public Economics,* 26, 1985. pp.89–106.
23. Power, William, "Wall Street's Latest: Main Street Is Paved With Gold," *Wall Street Journal,* May 9, 1991. The details in this paragraph are drawn from this article.
24. Lazard Freres, for example, is working with a company negotiating to build and run a state prison in Florida; and Goldman Sachs is putting together a $400 million financing deal for a fifteen-mile extension of the state toll road connecting Washington's Dulles Airport with suburban Leesburg, Virginia.

A private company will own the road for forty years before turning it back to the state.

25. The statistics in this paragraph are from the following: "What Happened to the American Dream: The Under-30 Generation May Be Losing The Race For Prosperity," *Business Week,* August, 19, 1991, p. 83; The National Commission on Children, reported in *The Guardian Weekly,* May 13, 1990, and *The New York Times,* April 26, 1990; Mc Cord, Colin, M.D. and Freeman, Harold P., M.D., "Excess Mortality in Harlem," *New England Journal of Medicine,* 322,3, January 1990, pp.173–177; Marable, Manning, *The Guardian* (U.S.), February 13, 1990; *The Guardian* (U.S.), March 7, 1990, from the report "Young Black Men and the Criminal Justice System: A Growing National Problem," The Sentencing Project, Washington DC; and Wicker, Tom, "The Iron Medal," *New York Times,* based on the report from The Sentencing Project, 1990.

26. "We Must Cut the Deficit Now: Here's How To Do It," *Business Week,* August 6, 1990, pp.60–61.

27. Roberts, Paul Craig, "How and Why Bush's Men Cooked the Books," *Wall Street Journal,* August 5, 1991.

28. Roberts, Paul Craig, "Who's Doing Voodoo Economics Now," *Business Week,* July 30, 1990, p.10; Editorial, *The Wall Street Journal,* August 15, 1990.

29. According to the *Economist,* July 20, 1991, "America's government has the biggest budget deficit in the world in dollar terms, but its general-government deficit (the total of central, state and local government budgets plus social security balances) is a modest 2.8% of GNP." Greece, Italy, Belgium, Germany, Canada, and Holland are all projected to have bigger budget deficits in 1991. Four countries will have a budget surplus: Japan (the biggest, at 2.7% of GNP), Australia, Sweden and Norway. Germany's deficit has grown from 1.5% to 5.2% because of the costs of unification. The *Wall Street Journal,* August 16, 1990, makes a similar case for the level of gross public debt as a percentage of nominal GNP/GDP.

30. Roberts, Paul Craig, August 5, 1991.

31. Bowles, Samuel, Gordon, David M., and Weisskopf, Thomas E., *After the Wasteland: A Democratic Economics for the Year 2000,* M. E. Sharpe, 1991, reviewed by Doug Henwood, *Voice Literary Supplement,* April 1991.

    Harrison and Bluestone, 1988, p. 7, write that: "From a peak of nearly 10 percent in 1965, the average net after tax profit rate of domestic nonfinancial corporations plunged to less than 6 percent during the second half of the 1970s – a decline of more than a third."

32. "What Happened to the American Dream: The Under-30 Generation May Be Losing The Race For Prosperity," *Business Week,* August, 19, 1991, pp. 80–81.

33. Schor, Juliet, *The Overworked American: The Unexpected Decline of Leisure,* New York: Basic Books, 1992, from a review, "No Time to Smell the

Roses Anymore," by Robert Kuttner, *The New York Times Book Review,* February 2, 1992.

34. Edsall and Edsall, 1991, p. 54.

35. Toner, Robin, "Arkansas Chief Seeks to Lead Democrats to Middle Ground," *The New York Times,* August 14, 1991.

36. Slaughter, Jane, "Japan-bashing all the Rage for Capitalists Who Can't Compete," *Guardian,* January 29, 1992, pp. 10–11.

37. Schor, 1992. Moody, Kim, "Competitiveness Through Poverty in Three Easy Steps," *Labor Notes,* December, 1991, pp. 8–9.

38. *Business Week,* "Long Days, Low Pay, And A Moldy Cot," January 27, 1992, pp. 44–45.

39. Elliot, Michael, "America: A Better Yesterday," *The Economist,* October 26, 1991, p. 7.

40. Blinder, Alan S., "The Days of Ozzie and Harriet are Gone for Good," *Business Week,* February 10, 1992, p. 16.

41. Harrison, Bennet and Bluestone, Barry, 1988.

42. From Bowles, Samuel, Gordon, David M., and Weisskopf, Thomas E., *After the Wasteland: A Democratic Economics for the Year 2000,* M. E. Sharpe, 1991, in a review by Doug Henwood, *Voice Literary Supplement,* April 1991.

43. Gigot, Paul A., "Executive Pay — An Embarrassment To Free Marketeers," *Wall Street Journal,* January 10, 1992.

44. Bovard, James, "Don't Brake for Detroit," *The New York Times,* January 7, 1992. According to Bovard, in *Consumer Reports* 1991 survey, nearly all of the cars gaining CR's highest reliability rating were Japanese; nearly all the cars with a poor reliability rating were made by GM, Ford, and Chrysler. When *Road and Track* magazine announced its ten best cars of 1991, nine were Japanese and one was German.

45. Nader, Ralph, "Bloat at the top in GM," *Manchester Guardian Weekly,* January 5, 1992 (originally from the *Los Angeles Times.*)

46. Slaughter, Jane, "Union-Management Study Confirms High Cancer Death Rate at GM-Lordstown," *Labor Notes,* November 1989, p. 16.

SELECTED BIBLIOGRAPHY

The Endnotes to each chapter provide extensive bibliographic references to the books, newspaper articles, journal essays, and General Motors' annual reports referenced in the text. As a reader, however, I have usually found it helpful for books to include a separate, alphabetized bibliography. To that end, I have listed below most of the items referred to in the text, with the exception of those found in GM's annual reports and in the business press.

Aglietta, M., *A Theory of Capitalist Regulation: The U.S. Experience,* Translated by David Fernbach, London: NLB, 1979.

Allen, V. L., *Social Analysis: A Marxist Critique and Alternative,* London: Longman, 1975.

Altshuler, Alan, Anderson, Martin, Jones, Daniel, Roos, Daniel, Womack, James et. al., *The Future of the Automobile: The Report of MIT's International Automobile Program,* Cambridge, MA: The MIT Press, 1984.

Aronowitz, Stanley. *False Promises: The Shaping of American Working Class Consciousness,* New York: McGraw-Hill Book Company, 1973; paperback edition, 1974.

Atleson, J. B., *Values and Assumptions in American Labor Law,* University of Massachusetts Press, 1983.

Baran, P. A. and Sweezy, P. M., *Monopoly Capital: An Essay on the American Economic and Social Order,* New York: Monthly Review Press, 1966.

Baynes, K., Bohman, J. and McCarthy, T., editors, *After Philosophy: End or Transformation?* Cambridge, MA: The MIT Press, 1987.

Berle, Adolf A. Jr., and Means, Gardiner C., *The Modern Corporation and Private Property,* New York: The Macmillan Company, 1934.

Bernstein, Irving, *Turbulent Years: A History of the American Labor Movement, 1922–1941,* Boston: Houghton-Mifflin, 1971.

Bloomfield, Gerald. *The World Automotive Industry,* Newton Abbot, England: David and Charles Publishers Ltd., 1978.

Bowles, S. and Gintis, H., *Schooling in Capitalist America: Educational Reform and the Contradictions of Economic Life,* New York: Basic Books, Inc., Publishers, 1976.

Fernand Braudel, *The Wheels of Commerce: Civilization and Capitalism 15th-18th Century,* v. 2, New York: Harper & Row, 1982.

Braverman, H., *Labor and Monopoly Capital: The Degradation of Work in the Twentieth Century,* New York: Monthly Review Press, 1974.

Brody, David.*Workers In Industrial America: Essays on the 20th Century Struggle,* New York:Oxford University Press, 1980.

Burawoy, M., *Manufacturing Consent: Changes in the Labor Process Under Monopoly Capitalism,* Chicago: The University of Chicago Press, 1979.

Busacca, R. and Ryan, M.P., "Beyond the Family Crisis,*Democracy,* Fall, 1972, pp.79–92.

Cantor, D. and Schor, J., *Tunnel Vision: Labor, the World Economy, and Central America,* Boston: South End Press, 1987.

Carver, Thomas Nixon, *The Present Economic Revolution in the United States,* Boston: Little Brown, 1925.

Chandler, A. D. Jr., *Strategy and Structure: Chapters in the History of American Industrial Enterprise,* Cambridge, MA: MIT Press, 1962.

Clark, John Bates, *The Control of Trusts: An Argument in Favor of Curbing the Power of Monopoly by a Natural Method,* New York: Macmillan, 1901.

Clawson, D., *Bureaucracy and the Labor Process: The Transformation of U.S. Industry 1860–1920,* New York: Monthly Review Press, 1980.

Coase, R., "The Problem of Social Cost," *Journal of Law and Economics,* 3, October, 1960, pp.1–44.

Coase, R., "The Nature of the Firm," *Economica,* 4, 1937, reprinted in *Readings in Price Theory,* edited by G. J. Stigler and K. E. Boulding, Chicago: Richard D. Irwin for the American Economic Association, 1952.

Cyert, R. M. and March, J. G., *A Behavioral Theory of the Firm,* Englewood Cliffs, N.J.: Prentice-Hall, 1963.

Davis, M., *Prisoners of the American Dream: Politics and Economy in the History of the U.S. Working Class,* London: Verso, 1986.

Davis, Mike, "The Political Economy of Late-Imperial America," *New Left Review,* Jan/Feb, 1984, pp.6–38.

Davis, Mike, "The AFL-CIO's Second Century," *New Left Review,* 136, Nov/Dec, 1982, pp.43–54.

DuBoff, R. B. and Herman, E. S., "Alfred Chandler's New Business History: A Review," *Politics and Society,* 1980.

Eagleton, T., *Literary Theory: An Introduction,* Minneapolis: University of Minnesota Press, 1983.

Edsall, Thomas Byrne with Edsall, Mary D., "Race," *The Atlantic Monthly,* May 1991, pp.53–86.

Edwards, R., *Contested Terrain: The Transformation of the Workplace in the Twentieth Century,* London: Heinemann, 1979.

Ehrenreich, B. and English, D., *Complaints and Disorders: The Sexual Politics of Sickness,* Feminist Press, 1973.

Ehrenreich, B. and Ehrenreich, J., "The Professional-Managerial Class", in *Between Labor and Capital,* edited by Pat Walker, Boston: South End Press, 1979.

El-Messidi, Kathy Groehn. *The Bargain: The Story Behind the Thirty Year Honeymoon of GM and the UAW,* New York: Nellen Publishing Co., Inc., 1980.

Epstein, Ralph C., *The Automobile Industry.* New York: A.W.Shaw Company, 1928.

Ewen, S., *Captains of Consciousness: Advertising and the Social Roots of Consumer Culture,* New York: McGraw Hill Book Company, 1976.

Ferguson, Thomas and Rogers, Joel, "Big Labor Is Hurting Itself," *The Nation,* September 1, 1984.

Fields, Barbara, "Slavery, Race and Ideology in the United States of America," *New Left Review,* 181, May/June, 1990.

Fine, Sidney.*Sitdown,*Ann Arbor: University of Michigan Press, 1969.

Foucault, M. *Discipline and Punish: The Birth of the Prison,* New York: Vintage Books, 1979, pp.202–3.

Galbraith, J. K., *The New Industrial State,* Boston: Houghton
Mifflin Company, 1967, p.38.

Gamble, A. and Walton, P., *Capitalism in Crisis: Inflation and the State,* London: The Macmillan Press Ltd., 1976.)

Gardner,L. C., "The New Deal, New Frontiers, and the Cold War: A Re-examination of American Expansion: 1933–1945," in *Corporations and the Cold War,* edited by D. Horowitz, New York: Monthly Review Press, 1970, p.124.

Gartman, D., *Auto-Slavery: The Labor Process in the American Automobile Industry, 1897–1950,* New Brunswick: Rutgers University
Press, 1986.

Galbraith, John Kenneth, *The New Industrial State,* Boston: Houghton Mifflin Company, 1967.

George, Peter, *The Emergence of Industrial America: Strategic Factors in American Economic Growth Since 1870,* Albany, N.Y.: State University of New York Press, 1982.

Giddens, A., "Four Theses on Ideology," *Canadian Journal of Political and Social Theory,* 7, 1–2, Spring, 1983.

Giddens, Anthony, *Central Problems in Social Theory: Action, Struction and Contradiction in Social Analysis,* Berkeley: University of California Press, 1979.

Gordon, D., "The Global Economy: New Edifice or Crumbling Foundations," *New Left Review,* 168, March/April, 1988, pp.24–64.

Gordon, R. A., *Economic Instability and Growth: The American Record,* New York: Harper & Row Publishers, 1974.

Gouldner, Alvin W. *The Two Marxisms: Contradictions and Anomalies in the Development of Theory,* New York: The Seabury Press, 1980; paperback edition, Oxford: Oxford University Press, 1982.

Gouldner, Alvin, *The Dialectic of Ideology and Technology,* New York: The Seabury Press, 1976; Oxford: Oxford University Press, 1982.

Green, James R. *The World of the Worker: Labor in Twentieth Century America,* New York: Hill and Wang, 1980.

Gross, Bertram, "Rethinking Full Employment," *The Nation,* January 17, 1987, pp.44–48.

Gross, James A., *The Reshaping of the National Labor Relations Board,* Albany: State University of New York Press, 1981.

Gunzberg, D., "On-the-Job-Democracy," *Sweden Now,* 12, 4, pp.42–45.

Habermas, J., *Legitimation Crisis,* McCarthy, R. (trans), London: Heinemann, 1976.

Hainer, M. and Koslofsky, J., "Car Wars," *NACLA Report on the Americas,* July-August, 1979, pp.3–37.

Halberstram, David, *The Reckoning,* New York: Avon Books, 1986, pp.366–367.

Harcourt, G. C., "Some Cambridge Controversies in the Theory of Capital," *Journal of Economic Literature,* 1972, pp.369–405.

Harrison, Bennett and Bluestone, Barry, *The Great U-Turn: Corporate Restructuring and the Polarizing of America,* New York: Basic Books, Inc., Publishers, 1988.

Held, David, *Introduction to Critical Theory: Horkheimer to Habermas,* Berkeley: University of California Press, 1980.

Herman, E. S., *Corporate Control and Corporate Power: A Twentieth Century Fund Study,* Cambridge: Cambridge University Press, 1981.

Hill, S.,*Competition and Control at Work: The New Industrial Sociology,* Cambridge,MA: The MIT Press, 1981.

Jenkins, Rhys, "Internationalization of Capital in the Motor Industry," *Capital and Class,* October, 1976, pp.RJ1-RJ11.

Keeran, Roger. *The Communist Party and the Auto Workers Unions,* Bloomington: Indiana University Press, 1980, p. 32.

Keeran, Roger R. "Everything for Victory: Communist Influence in the Auto Industry During World War II," *Science and Society,* XLIII, 1, Spring, 1979.

Klare, K. E., "Judicial Deradicalization of the Wagner Act and the Origins of Modern Legal Consciousness, 1937–1971, *Minnesota Law Review,* 62, 1978.

Kramer, 1964, "Potential Competition and American Anti-trust," *Business History Review,* 38, 1964, pp.283–301.

Lichtenstein, N., *Labor's War at Home: The CIO in World War II,* Cambridge: Cambridge University Press, paperback edition, 1987.

Lindblom, Charles, *Politics and Markets: The World's Political-Economic Systems,* New York: Basic Books, Inc., Publishers, 1977.

Lipsit, Seymour Martin. "Trade Unions and Social Structure, II," *Industrial Relations,* 1962.

Lodge, G. C., "Contract and Consensus at General Motors: 1900–1979," Intercollegiate Case Clearing House, #9–376–170, 1979, Boston, MA.

Magdoff, H. and Sweezy, P. M., *Stagnation and the Financial Explosion,* New York: Monthly Review Press, 1987.

Mann, Eric, "UAW Backs The Wrong Team," *The Nation,* February 14, 1984, pp.171+.

March, J.G. and Olsen, J.,*Ambiguity and Choice in Organizations,* Oslo, Norway: Universitetsforlaget, 1976.

March,J.G. and Simon, H.A., *Organizations,* New York: John Wiley and Sons, 1958.

Marcuse, H. *One Dimensional Man: Studies in the Ideology of Industrial Society,* Boston: Beacon Press, 1964; Beacon Paperback, 1966.

Marglin, S. A., "What Do the Bosses Do? The Origins and Functions of Hierarchy in Capitalist Production," *Review of Radical Political Economics,* 6(2), 1974, pp. 60–70,81–86,89–92.

Maxcy, G., *The Multinational Motor Industry,* London: Croom Helm, 1981.

Merino, Barbara and Neimark, Marilyn, "Disclosure Regulation and Public Policy," *Journal of Accounting and Public Policy,*1,1,Fall 1982, pp.33–57.

Meyer, S.,III, *The Five Dollar Day: Labor Management and Social Control in the Ford Motor Company, 1908–1921,* Albany, NY: State University of New York Press, 1981.

Milkman, Ruth, "Female Factory Labor and Industrial Structure: Control and Conflict Over 'Women's Place' in Auto and Electrical Manufacturing," *Politics and Society,* 1983, pp.159–203.

Miller, Edward K. and Winter, Drew, "The Other Big 3 Are Becoming All American," *Wards Auto World,* February, 1991.

Milton, David, *The Politics of U.S. Labor: From the Great Depression to the New Deal,* New York: Monthly Review Press,1982.

Mintz, Morton and Cohen, Jerry S., *Power, Inc.,* New York: Bantam, 1977.

O'Connor, James, *The Fiscal Crisis of the State,* New York: St. Martin's Press, 1973.

O'Toole, J. "Lordstown: Three Years Later," *Business and Society,* 13, Spring, 1975, pp.64–71.

Ollman, Bertell. *Alienation: Marx's Conception of Man in Capitalist Society,* 2nd Edition, Cambridge: Cambridge University Press, 1976.

Parker, Mike and Slaughter, Jane, *Choosing Sides: Unions and the Team Concept,* A Labor Notes Book, Boston: South End Press, 1988.

Perrow, C., "Markets, Hierarchies and Hegemony," in *Perspectives on Organization Design,* edited by A. Van de Ven and W. Joyce, New York: John Wiley, 1981.

Pfeffer, J. and Salancik, G., *The External Control of Organizations,* New York: Harper and Row, Publishers, 1978.

Karl Polanyi, *The Great Transformation: the political and economic origin of our time,* Boston: Beacon Press, 1957.

Sidney Pollard, *The Genesis of Modern Management,* Baltimore: Penguin Books, 1968.

Rodgers, Daniel T., *The Work Ethic in Industrial America,*

1850–1920, Chicago: The University of Chicago Press, 1978.

Roosevelt, Franklin D., *Looking Forward,* New York: John Day, 1933; Van Antwerp, W. C., *The Stock Exchange From Within,* New York: Doubleday, Page, 1913.

Roosevelt, Theodore, *Address and Presidential Messages of Theodore Roosevelt,* New York: Putnam, 1904.

Rosner, D. and Markowitz, G., "A Gift of God? The Public Health Profession and the Controversy Over Tetraethyl Lead During the 1920s," *American Journal of Public Health,* 1983, pp.342–352.

Rothschild, E.,*Paradise Lost: The Decline of the Auto-Industrial Age,* New York: Random House, 1973.

Said, E. W.,*The World, the Text, and the Critic,* Cambridge,MA: Harvard University Press, 1983.

Seltzer, Lawrence. *A Financial History of the American Automobile Industry,* Boston: Houghton Mifflin Company, 1928.

Serrin, William. *The Company and the Union: The 'Civilized Relationship' of the General Motors Corporation and the United Automobile Workers,* New York: Alfred Knopf, 1973.

Sklar, Holly, "The Truly Greedy," *Z Magazine,* June, 1991, pp. 10–12.

Skockpol, Theda. "Political Response to Capitalist Crisis: Neo-Marxist Theories of the State and the Case of the New Deal," *Politics and Society,* 10, 1980, pp. 155–201.

Sloan, Alfred P. Jr., *My Years With General Motors,* edited by John McDonald with Catharine Stevens, Garden City, NY: Doubleday & Company, Inc., 1964.

Sraffa, P., *The Production of Commodities by Means of Commodities,* Cambridge: Cambridge University Press, 1960.

Stavrianos, I.S., "Capitalism's Contradictory History," *Monthly Review,* October, 1984, pp.60–64.

Stone, K. Van Wezel, "The Post-War Paradigm in American Labor Law," *The Yale Law Journal,* 90, 7, 1981, p.1517.

Stone, K., "The Origins of Job Structures in the Steel Industry," *Review of Radical Political Economics,* 6, Summer, 1974, pp.61–97.

Sweezy, Paul, "The Deepening Crisis of U.S. Capitalism," *Monthly Review,* October 1981, pp.1–16.

Sweezy, P., *The Theory of Capitalist Development,* New York, 1942; O'Connor, J., *The Fiscal Crisis of the State,* New York: St. Martin's Press, 1973.

Temin, P., *Did Monetary Forces Cause the Great Depression?,* New York: W.W.Norton, Inc., 1976.

Therborn, G., *What Does the Ruling Class Do When it Rules?* London: New Left Books, 1978.

Tinker, A. M., "Towards a Political Economy of Accounting: An Empirical Illustration of the Cambridge Controversies," *Accounting, Organizations, and Society,* 5,1,1980,pp.147–160.

Tinker, T. and Neimark, M., "The Role of Annual Reports in Gender and Class Contradictions at GM: 1917–1976," *Accounting, Organizations and Society,* 12, 1, 1987, pp.71–88.

Weick, K. E., "Educational Organizations as Loosely Coupled Systems," *Administrative Science Quarterly,* 21, 1976, pp.1–19.

White, L. J., *The Automobile Industry Since 1945,* Cambridge: Harvard University Press, 1971.

Williamson, O. E., "The Modern Corporation: Origins, Evolution, Attributes," *Journal of Economic Literature,* XIX, December, 1981.

Williamson, O. E., "The Organization of Work: A Comparative Institutional Assessment," *Journal of Economic Behavior and Organization,* 1, 1980.

Williamson, O. E., "Transaction-Cost Economics: The Governance of Contractual Relations," *Journal of Law and Economics,* October, 1979, pp.233–261.

Williamson, O. E., *Markets and Hierarchies: Analysis and Antitrust Implications,* New York: The Free Press, 1975.

Williamson, O. E. and Ouchi, W. G., "The Markets and Hierarchies and Visible Hand Perspectives, in *Perspectives on Organization Design and Behavior,* edited by A. Van de Ven and W. Joyce, New York: John Wiley, 1981.

Wolin, S., "What Revolutionary Action Means Today," *Democracy,* 2, Fall, 1982, pp.17–28.

Wright, E. O., *Class, Crisis and the State,* London: NLB, 1978; London: Verso, 1979.

Yates, M., *Labor Law Handbook,* Boston: South End Press, 1987.

Zuboff, S., *In the Age of the Smart Machine: The Future of Work and Power,* New York: Basic Book, Inc., Publishers, 1988.

MARILYN KLEINBERG NEIMARK

Marilyn Kleinberg Neimark is an Associate Professor of Accounting at Baruch College — The City University of New York. She received a B.A. in Government from Cornell University, and M.B.A. and Ph.D. degrees in Business Administration from New York University.

Professor Neimark writes extensively about the socio-historical origins and consequences of accounting theory and practice. Her work has been published in *Accounting, Auditing and Accountability, Accounting, Organizations and Society,* the *Journal of Accounting and Public Policy,* and the *Journal of Management,* as well as in several edited volumes. She is currently on the editorial boards of *Critical Perspectives in Accounting* and *Advances in Public Interest Accounting* and is a regular commentator on business and economic issues for WBAI Radio in New York City.